D1196658

Voices and Visions of Aging:
Toward a Critical Gerontology

Thomas R. Cole, Ph.D., is Professor and Graduate Program Director at the Institute for the Medical Humanities, University of Texas Medical Branch, Galveston. He is a past Chair of the Humanities and Arts Committee of the Gerontological Society and serves on various editorial boards. Senior editor of *What Does It Mean to Grow Old? Reflections from the Humanities* (1986) and of *Handbook of the Humanities and Aging* (Springer Publishing Company, 1992), he is also author of *The Journey of Life: A Cultural History of Aging in America* (Cambridge, 1992). He is now completing *No Color is My Kind: The Life Story of Eldrewey Stearns, Texas Integration Leader* (University of Texas Press), and *The Oxford Book of Aging*, to be published in 1994.

W. Andrew Achenbaum, Ph.D., is Deputy Director of the Institute for Gerontology and Professor in the Department of History at the University of Michigan. His books include *Old Age in the New Land* (Johns Hopkins, 1978), *Shades of Gray* (Little Brown, 1983), and *Social Security: Visions and Revisions* (Cambridge, 1986). He is completing a book on the history of gerontology.

Patricia L. Jakobi, Ph.D., is Administrative Director of the Center on Aging at the University of Texas Medical Branch, Galveston, and Assistant Editor, *Journal of Aging and Health*. A recent graduate from UTMB's Institute for Medical Humanities, her major research interests focus on federal-care policies and programs for poor and dependent populations.

Robert Kastenbaum, Ph.D., left a promising career as a skating messenger to enter University of Southern California on a fellowship in philosophy. He emerged as a clinical psychologist, and later served as director of a geriatric hospital before taking up his current responsibilities as professor of communication at Arizona State University. Along the way, he founded *International Journal of Aging and Human Development*, and *Omega, Journal of Death and Dying*. He is a past president of American Association of Suicidology and past chair of the Section on Behavioral and Social Sciences of the Gerontological Society of America. Kastenbaum scripted the National Public Radio series: "Essays for the Ear: Youth's the Tune, Age the Song." He was a co-editor of *Handbook of the Humanities and Aging* (Springer Publishing Company, 1992), companion volume to the present book.

Voices and Visions of Aging:
Toward a Critical Gerontology

Thomas R. Cole
W. Andrew Achenbaum
Patricia L. Jakobi
Robert Kastenbaum
Editors

Springer Publishing Company
New York

Springer Publishing Company, Inc.
536 Broadway
New York, NY 10012-3955

For acknowledgments and other copyright information please see the back of the book; acknowledgments there are to be considered an extension of the copyright page.

cover design and illustration by Holly Block

93 94 95 96 97 / 5 4 3 2 1

Library of Congress Cataloging-in-Publication Data

Voices and visions of aging : toward a critical gerontology / Thomas
   R. Cole . . . [et al.], editors.
      p.   cm.
   Includes bibliographical references and index.
   ISBN 0-8261-8020-5
   1. Gerontology. 2. Gerontology—Methodology. 3. Aging—Social
aspects.   I. Cole, Thomas R., 1949–   .
HQ1061.V59   1993
305.26—dc20   92-10680
                                                                    CIP

Printed in the United States of America

Contents

Part II   Humanistic Gerontology

Part III   Political Gerontology/Ideology Critique

Preface

This volume is a sequel to the *Handbook of the Humanities and Aging* (Cole, Van Tassel, and Kastenbaum, 1992). Whereas the *Handbook* is a reference volume for humanistic gerontology, *Voices and Visions* attempts to integrate perspectives from the humanities into gerontology—a long-term goal at least as important as generating new knowledge about aging within the humanities disciplines themselves.

There is a widespread unease in gerontology today, an inchoate sense that old paradigms, conventional styles of research and practice are inadequate. As Harry R. Moody (Moody, 1988) has argued, contemporary gerontology is beset with fundamental epistemological problems. On the one hand, various biological, psychological, sociological, and political theories of aging multiply in different conceptual worlds that bear no clear relationship to one another. On the other hand, gerontology's vast and rapidly growing accumulation of empirical data cannot be assimilated to existing theories or to any single, unified theory of aging. These problems, Moody rightly claimed, cannot be resolved by methodological fiat, by improved positivistic "rigor," or by some form of physical, social, or psychological reductionism. They are inherent in contemporary gerontological theory and practice, where technical rationality generally ignores what cannot be reduced to quantitative methodology even as it conceals value commitments and forms of domination.

Obviously, the humanities are not going to "solve" such problems. They are part of the broad cultural uncertainty and instability that characterizes contemporary social life. But stock-in-trade of the humanities—self-knowledge, historical understanding, imaginative communication, and critical appraisal of assumptions and values—can promote a more intellectually rigorous gerontology in several ways: *heuristically*, by offering new hypotheses for empirical inquiry; *critically*, by revealing values and power relations often concealed in existing methods and findings of empirical research; and *practically*, by offering reflection on the intentions and values realized by human actors in particular cultural settings.

Cultural studies, for example, bring to light the social relations and ideological assumptions embedded in gerontological knowledge. Philosophy and literature provide principles of interpretation that link empirical findings to social practices. History—the most developed discipline in gerontology—tests social scientific assumptions about aging in the past, contextualizes gerontological knowledge, and creates broader perspectives for understanding our aging society. By constructing self-conscious, critical frameworks to appraise theory and practice, the humanities can help shape a style of gerontological reasoning distinct from instrumental, technical rationality. These goals cannot be accomplished by isolated scholars pursuing their own research agendas (however well funded) but rather through genuine dialogue between humanistic, scientific, and professional colleagues.

With these ambitions in mind, we held a conference at the Institute for the Medical Humanities on January 18 and 19, 1991. This "Critical Gerontology" conference was the first of a new series of collaborative research conferences at Galveston, made possible by the Institute's Jesse Jones Memorial Research Endowment and a Challenge Grant from the National Endowment for the Humanities. The Gulf War had just broken out, and the first Iraqi bombs fell on Tel Aviv as the participants travelled to Galveston. CNN news was broadcasting mass killing as if it were a Nintendo game, which led Bob Kastenbaum to compare television coverage of the war to a Greek tragedy, where most of the action takes place off stage. The war was rarely referred to in the formal proceedings of the conference, but it provoked strong undercurrents of anxiety and outrage.

Eight years earlier, Sally Gadow and I had organized a conference at the Institute on the theme of "Aging and Meaning." The resulting volume, *What Does It Mean To Grow Old? Reflections from the Humanities* (Cole & Gadow, 1986) shifted attention from the "human values" approach that informed earlier work in humanistic gerontology toward issues of personal, textual, historical, and cultural meaning. Since then, the central scholarly trend in the humanities has been an acceleration of the "postmodern" turn, primarily associated with thinkers like Nietzsche, Heidegger, Foucault, Deleuze and Guattari, Derrida, Baudrillard, Lyotard, and Rorty (Best & Kellner, 1991; Turner, 1990). Mainstream gerontology has not yet seriously engaged postmodern thought, though some work on aging (including several chapters in this volume) does bear its imprint (Cole, 1992; Featherstone & Hepworth, 1989; Kaminsky, 1992; Woodward, 1991). Such engagement remains a central task for a socially responsible and intellectually vibrant, "critical" gerontology.

"Postmodernism" is a notoriously vague and slippery term, whose descriptive and theoretical meanings vary widely (Best & Kellner, 1991; Featherstone, 1988; Turner, 1990). Despite its various overlapping and contradictory uses, the term reflects a growing sense that contemporary life is marked by a break from "modernity." Although it too is a contested term, "modernity" generally refers to the historical period that followed the Middle Ages or feudal society. Characterized by the emergence of mercantile and (later) industrial capitalism, the development of modern society brought with it a host of processes that roll easily off the tongues of sociologists: individualization, secularization, industrialization, cultural differentiation, commodification, urbanization, bureaucratization, and rationalization.

According to postmodern theorists, we are living amidst the development of a qualitatively new sociocultural formation—the postmodern era—generated by the vast powers of computers and high-tech media to process information as well as multiply images. There are, of course, serious differences regarding both the normative evaluation of and the degree of rupture between modernity and postmodernity (Jameson, 1987). Despite these unresolved (and probably unresolvable) differences, the term postmodernism reflects a powerful cultural sense that many of the goals and assumptions of modern culture are mistaken, obsolete, or morally problematic. Just as the God of Christian Theism died at the end of the nineteenth century, Science as God (term) is dying at the end of the twentieth century—along with demi-gods like Progress, Socialism, Economic Growth, Family, and Morality. The implications for our aging society and for gerontology have yet to be deeply probed.

Postmodern theorists generally reject the view underlying much modern philosophy and science—that theory mirrors reality. Instead, postmodernists view all theories as partial perspectives on their objects. They claim that all intellectual representations of the social and natural worlds are influenced by history and language. In the "discourses" of postmodernism, modern assumptions of causation and social coherence give way to multiplicity, plurality, fragmentation, and indeterminacy. Certain postmodern literary and social thinkers speak of a decentered and fragmented subject rather than a rational and unified self (Rosenau, 1992). At times, thinkers like Lyotard and Foucault have gone so far as to undermine notions of rationality or the individual altogether.

The most forceful opponent of extreme postmodernism is Jurgen Habermas—a leading figure in the Frankfurt School of Critical Social

Theory. Habermas acknowledges the "dark side" of modern society, emphasized by his predecessors in the Frankfurt School and by post-modern theorists. But he claims that both overlook the positive legacy of the Enlightenment—the creation of democratic public spaces in which to pursue communicative, dialogical rationality. Along with other critics (Wolfe, 1989), Habermas believes that the bureaucratized state, the institutionalization of expertise, and the commodification of social life have seriously eroded public spaces that sustain the free exchange of ideas in a democratic society. The "unfinished project" of the Enlightenment, according to Habermas, requires recreating demo-cratic institutions capable of cultivating a rationality oriented toward mutual understanding and consensual action rather than efficiency and success (Best & Kellner, 1991; Bernstein, 1992).

The implications of a Habermasian perspective for gerontological research, practice, and policy have prompted Harry R. Moody's call for a critical gerontology. Moody's introduction to this volume both pre-sents his vision of critical gerontology and provides an overview of the volume as a whole. I hasten to add that Moody's theoretical vision of critical gerontology is not shared by all authors or editors. Rather, we have used it as a useful framework for initiating interdisciplinary cri-tiques and for linking the volume's three main sections: (1) Theory, Epistemology, Method; (2) Humanistic Gerontology; and (3) Political Gerontology, Ideology Critique.

We are grateful to several people: Mrs. Sheila Keating, who handled arrangements for the Critical Gerontology Conference; Kathleen Modd, who typed correspondence and coordinated successive versions of chapters; and Eleanor Porter, who tracked down bibliographic sources, proofread several versions of the volume, and handled innumerable details for authors and editors. Pam Lankas of Springer Publishing did a superb job of copyediting and shepherding the book through produc-tion.

THOMAS R. COLE

REFERENCES

Bernstein, R. (1992). *The new constellation: The ethical-political horizons of modernity/postmodernity.* Cambridge: MIT Press.

Best, S., & Kellner, D. (1991). *Postmodern theory: Critical interrogations.* New York: The Guilford Press.

Cole, Thomas R. (1992). *The journey of life: A cultural history of aging.* New York: Cambridge University Press.

Cole, T., & Gadow, S. (1986). *What does it mean to grow old? Reflections from the humanities.* Durham: Duke University Press.

Cole, T., Van Tassel, D., & Kastenbaum, R. (Eds.) (1992). *Handbook of the humanities and aging.* New York: Springer Publishing Co.

Featherstone, M. (1988). In pursuit of the postmodern. *Theory, Culture, and Society, 5*(2–3), 195–216.

Featherstone, M., & Hepworth, M. (1989). Aging and old age: Reflections on the postmodern life course. In B. Bytheway et al. (Eds.), *Becoming and being old: Sociological approaches to later life* (pp. 143–157). London: Sage.

Jameson, F. (1987). The politics of theory: Ideological positions in the postmodernism debate. In P. Rabinow & W. M. Sullivan (Eds.), *Interpretive social science: A second look* (pp. 351–364). Berkeley: University of California Press.

Kaminsky, M. (Ed.) (1992). Introduction to Barbara Myerhoff, *Remembered lives: The work of ritual, storytelling, and growing older.* Ann Arbor: University of Michigan Press.

Moody, H. R. (1988). In J. E. Birren & V. L. Bengston, (Eds.), *Emergent theories of aging.* New York: Springer Publishing Co.

Moody, H. R. (1992). Introduction. In T. Cole, W. A. Achenbaum, P. L. Jakobi, & R. Kastenbaum, (Eds.), *Voices and visions in aging: Toward a critical gerontology.* New York: Springer Publishing Co.

Rosenau, P. M. (1992). *Post-modernism and the social sciences: Insights, inroads, and instrusions.* Princeton, NJ: Princeton University Press.

Turner, B. (1990). Periodization and politics in the postmodern. In B. Turner, *Theories of modernity and postmodernity* (pp. 1–13). London: Sage.

Wolfe, A. (1989). *Whose keeper? Social science and moral obligation.* Berkeley: University of California Press.

Woodward, K. (1991). *Aging and its discontents: Freud and other fictions.* Bloomington: Indiana University Press.

Contributors

Robert C. Atchley, Ph.D.
Professor and Director,
Scripps Gerontology Center,
Miami University,
Oxford, Ohio

Fred L. Bookstein, Ph.D.
Center for Human Growth and
    Development,
and Institute for Gerontology,
University of Michigan,
Ann Arbor, Michigan

Ronald A. Carson, Ph.D.
Director,
Institute for the Medical Humanities,
University of Texas Medical Branch,
Galveston, Texas

Bertram J. Cohler, Ph.D.
The Committee on Human
    Development,
Department of Behavioral Sciences,
University of Chicago,
Chicago, Illinois

Msgr. Charles J. Fahey
Director, Third Age Center,
Fordham University,
New York, New York

Brian Gratton, Ph.D.
Associate Professor,
Department of History,
Arizona State University,
Tempe, Arizona

Jaber Gubrium, Ph.D.
Professor,
Department of Sociology,
University of Florida,
Gainesville, Florida

Carole Haber, Ph.D.
Associate Professor of History,
and Coordinator of American
    Studies,
University of North Carolina,
Charlotte, North Carolina

Martha Holstein, M.A.
Graduate Program, Institute for the
    Medical Humanities,
University of Texas Medical Branch,
Galveston, Texas

Nancy S. Jecker, Ph.D.
Department of Medical History and
    Ethics,
School of Medicine,
University of Washington,
Seattle, Washington

Marc Kaminsky, M.A., M.S.W.
Founding Co-director,
Myerhoff Center at the YIVO
    Institute for Jewish Research,
Brooklyn, New York

Laurence B. McCullough, Ph.D.
Professor of Medicine and Medical
    Ethics, Center for Ethics, Medicine,
    and Public Issues,
Baylor College of Medicine,
Houston, Texas

Meredith Minkler, Ph.D.
Professor and Head, Program in
   Health Education,
Department of Social and
   Administrative Health Sciences,
School of Public Health,
University of California,
Berkeley, California

William F. Monroe, Ph.D.
Associate Professor,
University Honors Program,
University of Houston,
Houston, Texas

Harry R. Moody, Ph.D.
Associate Director,
Brookdale Center on Aging,
Hunter College,
New York, New York

Beverly Ovrebo, Ph.D.
Health Education Department,
San Francisco State University,
San Francisco, California

Michael R. Rose, Ph.D.
Department of Ecology and
   Evolutionary Biology,
School of Biological Sciences,
University of California/Irvine,
Irvine, California

Steven Weiland, Ph.D.
College of Education,
Michigan State University,
East Lansing, Michigan

Overview: What Is Critical Gerontology and Why Is It Important?

Harry R. Moody

Critical gerontology is an approach to the study of aging inspired by the tradition of critical theory associated with such figures as Adorno, Horkheimer, Marcuse, and more recently, Jurgen Habermas. (For an up-to-date bibliography and treatment of Habermas, see Braaten, 1991). Critical theory in the tradition of the Frankfurt School has been preoccupied with problems of social justice, with interpreting the meaning of human experience, and with understanding cultural tendencies that underlie disparate spheres such as politics, science, and everyday life. Above all critical gerontology is concerned with the problem of emancipation of older people from all forms of domination. Hence, in its mode, critical gerontology is concerned with identifying possibilities for emancipatory social change, including positive ideals for the last stage of life.

Critical theory stands in opposition to the conventional positivism and empiricism so prevalent in social gerontology. It equally stands in opposition to domination by bureaucracy and marketplace, whose characteristic modes of thought inspire the positivist regime of thought. On the political plane, critical theory is suspicious of the pragmatic liberalism so congenial to mainstream gerontology; suspicious, that is, of the idea that interest-group politics and value-free science promote well-being and progress for all. In fact, both interest-group politics and the market serve to reinforce a version of American pluralism that conceals systematic structures of domination and oppression.

The mainstream liberal ideology of the "aging enterprise" holds that research, practice, and policy all work together for the benefit of "the elderly" (Estes, 1979). Those who subscribe to this view celebrate gerontology as, in Robert Butler's phrase, the "union of science and advocacy." In opposition to this optimistic view, critical gerontology offers a critique of ideology and hidden interests, seeking to unmask conflicts and contradictions that lie behind this superficial harmony of ideas.

In its most far-reaching intent, critical theory offers a sustained critique of instrumental reason itself, that is, a critique of the effort to explain the natural and social world in order to predict or control it. This critique of instrumental reason seeks to expose the connection between knowledge and domination, to show how our interest in explaining a phenomenon (e.g., old age) is linked to a covert strategy of social control. Instrumental reason alone serves only to reify or mystify structures of social domination. Instrumental reason by itself can never provide a rational foundation for purpose, value, or meaning in life. Reason cannot ground normative standards by which we can criticize existing institutions.

The result of knowledge-building without a critical spirit serves to perpetuate structures of domination. For example, in an analysis of aging policy, instrumental reason can compare alternative policy options by a standard of cost-effectiveness. But what reason or policy analysis cannot do is promote emancipation—human freedom—from structures of domination that perpetuate the status quo of old age in society. The triumph of instrumental rationality is linked to broader processes of modernization and the rationalization of society (Horkheimer & Adorno, 1975). This modernization and rationalization is everywhere visible in mainstream gerontology, in policy, practice, research, and education.

But at this moment of triumph there is a ghost at the banquet: the specter of old age and an aging society. Among both young and old there is at large a vague feeling that "something is missing." Indeed, what is missing is precisely what a substantive critical social science might offer to make intelligible the experience of aging as part of the whole course of life. What is also missing is a positive vision of how things might be different or what a rationally defensible vision of a "good old age" might be. This positive vision corresponds to the emancipatory intent of critical theory.

Critical theory distinguishes itself from "traditional" social theory by its intention of locating actual "openings" or spaces for potential emancipation within the social order. This intention amounts to more than imagining utopian alternatives to domination; it demands a detailed empirical account of why structures of domination persist and what can be done to change those structures. Now, it can be argued that an emancipatory interest is intrinsic to human reason itself insofar as reason has an intrinsic interest in furthering the conditions for its own development.[1] But to flesh out this abstract claim means confronting specific conditions for human development at a distinctive point in history, and it is to this task that I turn now.

CRITICAL GERONTOLOGY AND THE HISTORICAL MOMENT

The demand for a critical approach to gerontology does not arise in a historical vacuum but at a precise historical moment: the last decade of the 20th century, when gerontology has flourished in America for nearly a half century (Achenbaum, in press). In order to assess the prospects for critical gerontology, it is useful to review recent trends that underscore the need for alternative theoretical perspectives.

Prominent among these trends has been what Carroll Estes (Estes & Binney, 1991) has called the "biomedicalization of gerontology." This trend has meant a shift in interest and funding in favor of biological and medical approaches to the study of aging. The medicalization of gerontology has served to obscure positive images of old age in favor of disease models and biological reductionism.

Another trend has been a debate over generational equity for different age groups, a development that has challenged the legitimacy of the aged as a worthy beneficiary group (Kingson, Hirshorn, & Cornman, 1986). That debate surfaced during the decade of 1980s, a time when we witnessed a shift away from policy innovation because of fiscal constraint. While cutbacks fell more heavily on the non-aged poor, the elderly did not escape cuts, beginning with the advent of DRGs in Medicare and the Social Security crisis, both in 1983.

The mood of cost-containment has had an influence on knowledge building in gerontology. Funding agencies have shifted away from knowledge for its own sake and toward results-oriented research. In service delivery, the watchwords of the day have become privatization, means testing, and rationing. Interest in the humanities, or "life enrichment" programs, has waned as service groups for the aging have become concerned with sheer survival.

At the same time, among the wider public there is a clear nostalgia for positive images of old age. This is most evident in media and in advertising and is demonstrated by the appearance of new publications such as *Lear's* and *Longevity* magazine. The nostalgia for positive options in late life is also evident in the continued growth of Elderhostel and other programs for lifelong learning in old age. On the ideological plane, discourse about the "third age," "productive aging," or "successful aging" responds to a latent recognition that the disease model of aging is not the whole story.

The new vogue for productive aging reflects two new realities in the economy: (1) emergence of the aging as a powerful consumer force with discretionary income (for investment, travel, leisure, culture, and health care) and (2) emergence of the aging as a reserve pool of unused labor power or human capital in society. This structural change in demography and political economy marks the coming of population aging, the historically unprecedented transition to an "aging society" (Moody, 1988; Pifer & Bronte, 1986). Yet the structural transformation is taking place at a historical moment, when ideological images of old age have remained caught in contradictions. This "culture lag" in our present circumstance explains why positive images of aging remain marginal or nostalgic rather than serving as politically potent symbols for transforming society. It also underscores the need for a critical gerontology to make explicit such contradictions and reflect on their meaning in the life course as a whole.

OLD AGE AND THE POSTMODERN
LIFE COURSE

An account of the human life course, and specifically what I will call the "postmodern life course," must occupy a strategic position in the reconstruction of theory for critical gerontology. We can begin to define the position of old age in the postmodern life course through two important films. The first is *Make Way for Tomorrow*, a touching portrait of old age. The second is *Cocoon*, a version of the fountain-of-youth story known the world over (Manheimer, 1989).

Make Way for Tomrrow was released in 1937, not long after the passage of the Social Security Act and just before *The Grapes of Wrath*, another film of social commentary. *Make Way for Tomorrow* depicts the plight of an elderly couple who are forced to sell their home and make their way as best they can. Neither member of the couple is able to live with their grown children or fit into any wider social structure. By the end of the movie, the wife is forced to move into an old folks' home, and the couple prepare to part forever, reminiscing about the past but accepting their fate.

By the 1980s decade we are presented, in *Cocoon*, with a very different image of old age. In *Cocoon*, aging actors Hume Cronyn and Don Ameche play residents of a retirement community who accidentally come upon an extraterrestrial rejuvenation technique. At the end of the film aliens from outer space offer the elderly residents an escape from earth and a permanent reversal of old age. Evoking symbols of longevity and immortality, the film offers an image of late life in which past and present are merged, mixed, and transcended. The pessimism of *Make Way for Tomorrow* gives way to a postmodern ethos of playful possibilities and denial of limits.

A half century separates *Make Way for Tomorrow* and *Cocoon*, but the difference between the two films is more than a difference between tragedy and science fiction, social commentary and comic escape. The altered image of old age in these two films reflects a broader reshaping of the human life course. It is a trend described by Bernice Neugarten (1981) as a relativizing of age-based norms for all life stages: the coming of an "age-irrelevant society." Today old age as a period of life is becoming less determinate, less role-governed, and other life stages are moving in that direction as well. What is happening is a restructuring of life-span socialization to match the coming of an "information society," a "postindustrial society," or, more recently, the "postmodern culture."

We can understand the postmodern life course by contrasting it with the modernized life course that was inspired by the industrial revolution and was reinforced by the bureaucratization of the life cycle through the institutions of mass public education and retirement. The bureaucratized or modernized life course was divided into the "three boxes of life": the linear life plan of education, work, and retirement.

The first phase, youth, grew out of a new image of childhood as a protected period of life, a period for investment in human capital in preparation for life (Ariès, 1962). The second phase, adulthood, was defined by the work role, with increasingly bureaucratized institutions for entering and leaving the labor force: the dominance of educational credentialism and formal retirement (Graebner, 1980).

The third phase was old age, formally defined by retirement and supported by pension systems, which promoted a culture of leisure and disengagement.

Today these three phases of life persist, but their forms are changing before our eyes. We are seeing an erosion of the cultural boundaries that separate youth, adulthood, and old age, and we have entered a period in which norms for age-appropriate behavior are in flux. This new ethos reflects the spirit of postmodern culture, dominated by a sense of play and relativity, by a loosening of clear definitions or boundaries. More broadly, the postmodern style reflects a demassification in economy, media, politics, and culture, a society in which the information economy is paramount.

The modernized life course, with its rigid boundaries, was a product of bureaucratic industrialism, which concentrated productivity in the middle years in the name of efficiency. The modernized life course was anchored in the primacy of the economy and the subordination of self to the rationalized requirements of the social order: stay in school, work hard, build up seniority, prepare for retirement. A linear life course reflected that logic.

The postmodern life course, by contrast, with its fluid movement and multiplicity of life-styles, is based not on productivity but on consumerism. The postmodern life course is essentially an extension of the norm of middle age in two directions: downward (the "disappearance of childhood") and upward (the "third age"). Postmodern culture promises an escape from constraints and stereotypes of age-based norms of all kinds. Whether that promise is an illusion or a realistic hope for emancipatory change remains to be seen.

WHAT DO WE KNOW?
THEORY AND EPISTEMOLOGY

Birren and Bengtson (1988) offer a criticism of the impoverishment of empiricism in mainstream gerontology and argue for theory building and new visions. Their line of criticism is echoed by Michael Rose's (1991) attack on conventional biogerontology, an enterprise he calls a "decaying regime" ripe for overthrow and replacement by theories of evolutionary biology. I am not concerned so much with the substantive validity of Rose's critique as I am with the epistemological assumptions that support his line of criticism.

From the standpoint of critical gerontology it is important to see that the graveyard of failed theories in biogerontology reflects a deeper malaise. The "normal" science of biogerontology plods along, patiently accumulating facts, but lacks an adequate framework to make sense of what is discovered about DNA, cell division, protein synthesis, and so on. The impoverishment of empiricism even at the center of prestigious "hard" science, the molecular biology of aging, is paralleled by the failure of theory building in the social and behavioral branches of gerontology.

It is illuminating to contrast the views of Michael Rose and Robert Atchley, who differ sharply in how they see the enterprise of science. On the one hand, Rose (chap. 4, this volume) sees science as akin to a political or ideological struggle. Mainstream biogerontology, as depicted by Rose, is now in a state of "historical crisis" in which domination is exercised by "gatekeepers" of the discipline. Like all insurgents, Rose believes that his own paradigm, evolutionary biology, will eventually prevail in the struggle. But the point to see here is that Rose's account of knowledge building reflects an antiempiricist philosophy of science originally stimulated by Kuhn but given radical expression by Paul Feyerabend (1988).

In sharp contrast, Robert Atchley (chap 1, this volume) has a sunnier view of intellectual inquiry. For Atchley, the presence of competing theories is not a reason for discomfort, nor does it signify crisis leading to paradigm shift. On the contrary, Atchley argues that "the best social gerontologists are quite accustomed to moving back and forth among intellectual paradigms." Atchley offers a vision of gerontology as a cooperative, multidisciplinary field. In terms that evoke Karl Popper's philosophy of science, gerontology is depicted as an "open system," accessible to a wide variety of researchers and with no easily defined center of gravity. It is therefore natural that "cooperation is a more appropriate stance toward this enterprise than intellectual rivalry."

The contrast between Rose and Atchley is not to be understood as a difference between biology and sociology but rather as contrast between a radical and a more mainstream liberal reading of the history of gerontology. Critical gerontology need not promote hostility or polemics, but it ought to be oppositional and deliberately raise uncomfortable questions about the hegemony of theory and methods in mainstream gerontology. The mere presence of contending views— theoretical pluralism—is no assurance that hegemony has been avoided. Pluralism, in other words, is not enough here, any more than the presence of two contending political parties in a democracy means that we actually have achieved conditions of freedom or the ideal of unconstrained communication.

How, then, should we think about knowledge-building in the field of aging? Is it simply a matter of "persuasion, politics and passion," as

Feyerabend (1988), self-proclaimed epistemological anarchist, would tell us? If that were the whole story, then methods of ideology critique are called for. But some facts *do* count. In contrast to the stance deconstructionism might suggest, the reality of old age is not simply a "social construction" of our categories. Gerontology in America, in its half-century history, amounts to something more than a graveyard of failed theories. What we urgently need is an account of the very real, if partial, success of gerontology's struggle to become a science.

We get a very different approach to theory and epistemology in the chapter by Bookstein and Achenbaum in this volume (chap. 2). Their contribution is important because it offers an approach to critical gerontology in terms quite different from the preference for qualitative methods popular among some proponents of critical theory and humanistic gerontology. Bookstein and Achenbaum are explicitly in favor of a quantitative or, as they term it, "biometric" approach to gerontology. Their conclusion is a challenge to proponents of critical gerontology: "It is not enough for those interested in critical gerontology to challenge the status quo; the burden is now upon us to show that the field can be enriched by getting back to basics of measurement."

Bookstein and Achenbaum belong to critical gerontology because they advocate a methodological strategy that attacks the "grand tradition" of empirical research represented by names like Shock, Busse, Birren, and Maddox. They level their attack on the use of calendar age, which amounts to a "reification" of aging and, in their judgment, begs questions in favor of correlations that explain nothing. Their conclusion is that what passes for scientifically rigorous quantitative study of aging amounts to nothing more than "bureaucratic geriatrics."

What is wrong, then, with bureaucratic studies of aging? The answer is that such studies—say, of poverty rates or cancer incidence in people over 65—can't capture the important variations in human development. This claim is more than denouncing the statistics of central tendency in favor of variance. In the end, Bookstein and Achenbaum come down in support of another kind of average: weighted averages constructed by a factor-analytic account designed to disaggregate variables and thereby take individual differences seriously. Under the guise of methodology, they are actually engaged in a subversive agenda to bring back individual differences into the very heartland of quantitative gerontology: a Trojan horse strategy that opens the back door for qualitative methods.

The problem with this disaggregation strategy is that it also amounts to an abdication of theory building in favor of statistics: a more refined and subtle treatment of variations but not a serious explanation of senescence. Praise for biometrics turns out to be a long prolegomena to theory construction. But it is not clear what kind of theory might prove adequate.

What is clear from the critique is that a rigorous approach to critical gerontology needs to rethink modes of scientific measurement. We cannot simply evade questions of methodology and measurement in favor of the narrative study of individual lives. Yet the metrical framework of "normal science" as social gerontology has proved inadequate. Strangely, at just the point when we need to hear more about how theory—or explanation of the facts—stands in relation to the human experience of aging, it turns out that the conceptual strategy of biometry fails us. Such methods, we are told, are no different from those applied to "homogeneous colonies of laboratory animals."

This kind of answer simply won't do. Critical gerontology must begin by recognizing the gap between explanations applied to laboratory animals and those applied to human beings. The point is stressed not out of abstract hostility to reductionism—although Michael Rose's warning against molecular reductionism remains cogent here. The point is rather that when science makes predictions that become known to human agents, then those agents take the predictions into account in forming their plans and intentions. For example, to predict a recession is already to influence the behavior of rational economic agents, whether as self-fulfilling prophecy or as prudent action to avoid disaster. In other words, there is a feedback loop at work here that gives rise to complexities of a different order from what we find with colonies of laboratory animals, no matter how elegant our biometric methods turn out to be.

In calling attention to the difference between rational agents and animals, we are evoking the famous distinction between explanation and understanding as goals for science. For critical gerontology the point of the distinction concerns different *interests* involved in the enterprise of science: on the one hand, prediction and instrumental domination (whether over nature or other human beings); on the other hand, acts of interpretation that open up possibilities of communication, mutual understanding, and coordinated social action. Critical gerontology needs to make explicit different interests at stake in this disjunction between explanation and understanding, science and hermeneutics.

We will not overcome the disjunction simply by adding more humanities disciplines and hoping for an "interdisciplinary" dialogue in gerontology. The reasons that interdisciplinary strategy won't work are made clear by Steven Weiland (chap 5, this volume). As Weiland argues, the prevailing interpretive approach to literature in gerontology has been to use literary texts for referential value without questioning their epistemological status. The ironic result of this interpretive strategy has been to fortify the empiricist habit of gerontology so that the humanities become a handmaiden of empiricism. An alternative approach—one recommended by leading theories of literature today—would reveal a text's gaps, inconsistencies, and contradictions.

In an earlier treatment of critical gerontology I called for "theories of aging that contain self-reflexive rules for their construction, interpretation and application to the life-world" (Moody, 1989). To speak of the "life-world" here is to speak of a prereflective experience of aging eloquently depicted by Gubrium and Kaminsky in chapters 3 and 13, respectively, in this volume. To speak of "self-reflexive rules" is to point to a horizon of consciousness that makes human beings different from laboratory animals. The structure of rational action or intention is unavoidably different from anything that passes for statistical regularities of behavior. But even if this were not the case, even if human beings were just automatons or complicated expert systems, we would still face the problem of explanation left unanswered by the biometric approach. Correlation is not causation, as the saying goes, even if that correlation is exquisitely refined in its regression coefficients.

The problem here does not lie in measurement per se but in interpreting the meaning of what is measured. To think of human beings as variables who bear statistical values is to fall into the trap of imagining people as vessels of experience. On this view, as Gubrium puts it (chap. 3, this volume), the responses to our research questions already lie concealed in the respondent's life experience; the responses need only to be extracted by an adequate "instrument" whose validity can be established.

My argument here is *not* an attack on efforts at measurement. On the contrary, we need measurement—of morale, retirement rates, caregiver burden, and all of the other issues discussed by social gerontology. But we ought not to remain uncritical about what measurements or responses mean. A response by a subject is *both* a variable and a voice, an activity of dialogue, susceptible to interpretation as well as measurement. Life is not simply "there for the asking," any more than a life story exists, ready-made, in memory waiting to be called up by a retrieval program. As with a recursive mathematical function, the telling of the story becomes part of the story itself. Even the hardest of hard data are not simply "there," finished, stored up in the archives. Nietzsche once said that we cannot even imagine what historians yet to be born will discover in events that are, for us, already long in the past.

WHAT SHOULD WE DO?
POLITICAL GERONTOLOGY

One way of characterizing critical gerontology is to see it as a left-wing or adversary position within the field of aging, as "radical gerontology," in Victor Marshall's phrase. But two distinct versions or strategies for radical gerontology present themselves: one approach is to identify with oppressed groups to make their voices known; the second approach is to explain how oppression or injustice occurs. The first leads to overt advocacy; the second, to the perspective of ideology critique and political economy.

Mainstream gerontology has been accustomed to thinking about advocacy based on identification with oppressed groups. Chapter 15 in this volume, by Ovrebo and Minkler, illustrates the tendency, but there are prominent figures such as Maggie Kuhn and Simone de Beauvoir who have practiced this style of advocacy on behalf of the aged. What defines "political" gerontology is not simply passing attention to oppressed or marginalized groups but rather an insistence on political advocacy and social justice as fundamental for gerontology as an enterprise (Myles, 1984; Olson, 1982).

But serious problems arise when gerontology comes to understand itself as a political enterprise in which advocacy takes precedence over inquiry.

Truth and Power

There is a recurrent dilemma about "speaking truth to power," and the dilemma is no less pressing in advocacy for the dispossessed. Most of us take for granted that science and the free communication of ideas are important values. But historical experience shows that whenever politics takes precedence over science or scholarship, there is the temptation to settle differences of opinion by power rather than intellectual persuasion. If truth is merely "fictive" or "socially constructed," then what sense does it make to defend the autonomy of science and freedom of thought? Gerontology has wanted to have it both ways: to be a "union of science and advocacy." But what happens when the facts don't support the advocate's position, when truth and power pull in different directions?

Positive Images of Old Age

The hegemony of instrumental reason and the "failure model" of old age (Kalish, 1979) have largely suppressed serious debate about the philosophic meaning of a "good old age."[2] How then do we give positive content to an "emancipatory" ideal for the last stage of life? To speak of an "ideal" is already to make use of a normative category of better and worse, some lives being more exemplary than others. But making distinctions that way contradicts the fashionable egalitarianism so prevalent in academic life today.

Can we identify normative categories in terms that transcend our own cultural limitations? Ovrebo and Minkler (chap. 15) state that "existential anguish is the product of a Eurocentric worldview, where the individual is the focus and measure of all things. In the Afrocentric worldview, the clan is the focus of survival and the measure of worth." The valorization of Afrocentric culture is increasingly heard today in debates around multicultural education, especially from those who attack so-called elite culture.

But a problem arises when Ovrebo and Minkler argue that "the resolution of the spiritual crises of old age requires great courage. These acts of heroism are seldom observed or noted, except in novels and other works of art. This is one reason why fiction and biography are so important to a culture." The problem here is that these acts of courage and heroism, acts celebrated in fiction and biography, serve to define ideal norms. We may end up concentrating our attention on the lives of exceptional prople as recorded in works of high-quality fiction: a prescription for elitism under another name.

Narrative and Autobiography

In non-Western cultures individualism has not been as highly prized as it has been in West since the Renaissance. No other culture except the modern European has produced widespread examples of the genre of autobiography, a point that Bertram Cohler (chap. 6 in this volume) makes in discussing the role of narrative in the study of lives. Steven Weiland (chap. 5) suggests that the appeal of narrative is compelling because narrative redeems the value of individual lives; narrative becomes "a form of assertion, of maintenance of the self and morale in aging." The alternative prospect—a meaningless life and death—is what haunts Wallace Stegner's novel *Crossing to Safety.*

But is individual narrative the only solution to finding meaning in life? Here we see the importance of the Afrocentric and other non-individualist alternatives to the search for meaning in old age. As

Ovrebo and Minkler (chap. 15) put it, "The resolution of the spiritual crisis for black women resides in becoming a black grandmother." This image of grandmother's wisdom will prove attractive for many. But this nostalgic image is anathema to modern culture, or at least to those inhabiting the "iron cage" of modernity depicted by Max Weber. The traditionalist project of finding meaning in family roles or tribal membership stands in contrast to entire modern Western project of individuality through self-creation. The modern project is also described by Ovrebo and Minkler: "The lesbian quest for meaning calls out for the creation of 'a chosen life.' The heroic archetype for old lesbians is the artist, whose greatest creation is her own life."

The two alternatives stand in sharp contrast: the nonindividualized "tribal" identity versus the individualist project of modernity. Do we favor the self-created life narrative, or do we reject it as "Eurocentric" and a prescription for an alienated old age? The contradiction between these two alternatives is not easily resolved.

Policy Choices

Related to the advocacy posture of gerontology is a recurrent issue about the connection between theory and policy, between knowledge and political action. Chapter 2, by Bookstein and Achenbaum, suggests that their construct of gerontological age may prove to be a "most useful additional criterion for policymakers to allocate limited health care resources in a rapidly aging population." But are we prepared for what adopting gerontological age may entail for our public policy? The concept of gerontological age may turn out to be not merely a methodological device but a weapon in the political struggle over the rights of the aged in the welfare state. Accepting the category of gerontological age would be a move away from chronological age and, if adopted for policy purposes, would probably serve to erode the legitimacy of age-based entitlements.

By using gerontological age as an allocation criterion, we are in effect adopting a technological solution to what is ultimately a problem of ethics and choice, namely, a collective decision about how much to spend supporting people in retirement. This question has a history of its own. As a Marxist might say, "it is not accidental" that what Bookstein and Achenbaum (chap. 2) call "bureaucratic geriatrics" came to prominence in the historical period when age-based entitlements helped to shape the modernized life course. It is not simply that it is conceptually "convenient" (or evasive, depending on your view) to look at averages of people by calendar age. Looking at age in terms of calendar age alone serves an important legitimation function in allocating scarce resources (e.g., if you're over 65, you get Medicare). The problem with using "need" as a basis for entitlement is that "need" is much harder to define or measure than calendar age.

Liberals, understandably, have been skeptical about proposals to replace age-based entitlements by any kind of "needs" test as a basis for benefits or entitlements. Once we move along the slippery slope of gerontological age, it may not be long before we erode the legitimation of all age-based entitlements and put older people at risk, as children proved to be when their means-tested benefits were cut during the 1980s.

Yet Bookstein and Achenbaum are on to something important in their modest proposal. Age-based entitlements aren't what they used to be. Too many elite policymakers have seen that older people, as a group, no longer fit the negative stereotype of *Make Way for the Future*. The emergence of a postmodern life course suddenly puts at risk the framework for aging policy in the American welfare state. The simpleminded response to the generational equity debate is to ask the false question of whether we should adopt an image of old people as the "deserving poor" or as "greedy geezers." Gerontologists may reply that neither image is appropriate, but a critical gerontology must do more to surface the contradictions here.

The need for clarity about the debate is brought out forcefully by the chapter by Nancy Jecker in this volume (chap. 14). Jecker provides a philosophical treatment of the problem of justice between generations. She goes to the heart of the problem when she identifies the social contract theory that underlies John Rawls, Paul Menzel, and Norman Daniels in their account of allocating resources to different age groups. Jecker points out that all of these accounts are based on a methodological principle of mutual disinterestedness, a principle that we take nothing for granted in terms of people's shared commitment to a way of life (an idea of the Good) or mutual care for one another.[3]

It is precisely here, however, that philosophical methodology needs to be complemented by historical and cultural criticism. "Mutual disinterestedness" is not simply a hypothetical construction but a very real description of pervasive alienation in our society. This point has relevance to the generational equity debate. Today the old and young, members of different historical cohorts, know less and less about each other and share little of each other's cultural world. Why then should people care about the needs or claims of members of remote generations—say, Social Security recipients in the year 2030? When we stand in mutual disinterest toward one another, how do we reclaim a sense of solidarity required to share risks or make commitments for the common good?

Nancy Jecker's answer to this question is an effort to erode any sharp distinction between justice and benevolence: between abstract right, on the one hand, and an ethic of caring, on the other. Like Buchanan, Gilligan, and Melden, Jecker wants to rehabilitate an ethic of benevolence and care. Hers is a vision of a "kinder, gentler" justice that could somehow overcome the estrangement between historical cohorts.

It is interesting to note that critical theory, at least in the hands of Habermas, has also dealt with the problem of disinterestedness but has come up with a somewhat different approach to it. Instead of invoking ideals of cultural unity or mutual benevolence, critical theory seeks to reconstruct the social contract on the basis of "communicative ethics," that is, open discourse across generations that constitute themselves in solidarity with their own history, past and future. The hope is that if we have conditions of unconstrained communication we can be free to renegotiate the generational compact according to specific conditions of our history.[4]

A political gerontology is, of necessity, an approach to gerontology grounded in the historical specificity of our situation, which is not the same in 1995 as in 1985, not the same in Britain as in America, and so on. Robert Atchley (chap. 1, this volume) brings out this point when he analyzes current theoretical questions about retirement in the context of changes in the institution of retirement as well as the broader economy and culture.

As Atchley shows, retirement is both a labor force policy and a meaningful stage of human life. As a labor market policy, retirement has its own history and responds to changing imperatives of political economy. As a positive stage of human life, retirement also has a history within elite culture that goes back to Cicero and Montaigne, who have offered a vision of human development in the last stage of life. This positive vision forms part of the emancipatory ideal that belongs on the agenda for a critical gerontology.

From the perspective of critical theory, there remains the question of how to connect these two quite distinct spheres: the imperatives of the labor market and the emancipatory possibilities of later life. We have one narrative from economics and another from culture. How do these two domains interact?

To press the point, there is a gap between the individual and the social system; their *interests* are not the same. Reconciling these competing interests is an ongoing task for politics, but it is also part of the agenda for critical gerontology. The reconciliation or feedback process operating at a society-wide level in systems theory is not the same thing as the process of self-reflection that operates at the level of individual lives or, in principle, among social groups in which free and unconstrained communication flourishes. There is a sharp difference that exists between feedback as a cybernetic process or psychological function and the kind of self-reflexivity that is the basis for human development among individuals or among societies.

Again, this seemingly abstract discussion of feedback, or self-reflexivity, has important methodological consequences for how we approach the phenomenon of aging. Atchley points out that well-educated people are usually surprised to learn that retirement is generally a *positive* growth period. The common assumption is that the elderly become miserable once deprived of work. Atchley's own explanation for this surprise is to invoke the notion of "cultural lag": people simply haven't gotten the word yet.

But from the standpoint of critical gerontology we need to probe more deeply here. Is it possible that a prevailing negative image of retirement plays an important ideological role in the construction of the modernized life course and in our public welfare policies for the aged? If so, what is the latent function of this persisting but mistaken idea? One thinks of Ethel Shanas's comment about that "hydra-headed monster," the persistent belief in family abandonment of the aged. To speak of "myths" or "cultural lag" here is not sufficient. In terms of ideology critique, we need to look more deeply into why academic inquiry, too, fails to confront mistaken beliefs, into the question of whose *interests* are served by the perpetuation of false ideas.

This inquiry is directly related to contemporary critical dialogue about postmodern culture. What Atchley calls "deconceptualizing retirement" is itself an important historical moment in the emergence of the postmodern life course. To the extent that the boundary between work and retirement becomes blurred, some people will gain freedom, but we will also lose the basis of collective legitimation for public pension policies. In postmodern culture, aging and retirement are becoming disconnected, just as youth and education are disconnected by the ethos of lifelong learning. Atchley is correct when he raises the troublesome question: "In the absence of a rationale based on the effects of aging, what morally justifies retirement?" The ethical basis of age-based entitlements is becoming intertwined with the legitimation crisis reflected in the generational equity debate. In terms of communicative ethics, when we lose touch with a shared sense of what retirement is, we lose the capacity to *talk* about it or achieve consensus on social policies.

Atchley charges that, although critical theory can help us understand many things about social development, it "fails to direct us toward the processes that could be expected to bring people together in communicative action." Experience suggests that he may be right about this, but it is important to understand just why.

One reason for the failure of communicative action is the gap between theory and practice, between science and politics. With respect to scientific knowledge, overcoming the gap is a matter of experimental confirmation of theory, on the one hand, and applied science on the other. But from the perspective of critical gerontology, the picture is more complicated. Confirmation and applied science alike may simply end up mystifying what's going on in the first place. Professional control and policy imperatives prove to be another form of domination, as the medicalization of gerontology suggests. Thus, bridging the gap between theory and practice demands more than interventions that apply reified theory intending to bring social practice into harmony with preconceived ideas. Genuine communicative action would mean opening up the dialogue about the experience of old age, for example, incorporating the voices of old people themselves.

The hegemony of instrumental reason alone will not permit this to occur. Professionals and policymakers have a vested interest in seeing the world the way that theory prescribes it to be. Still worse, the professionalization of gerontology means incorporating an abstract language further and further removed from the actual experience of old age. What results is a progressive mystification of lived experience: old people themselves imagine that they are "exceptions" if they fail to conform to the stereotypes (negative or positive) about what late life should be. Once again, the persistence of mistaken images is related to interests that underlie both the production of knowledge and the proliferation of public images of old age.

A second reason for the failure of communicative action is central to Atchley's argument: in a demassified society there are fewer common communication channels. In a world of cable TV, the networks lose market share. There are more options but less consensus. In the political sphere, "sound bites" take the place of rational dialogue or consensus formation. Cultural diversification and ethical relativism conspire to undercut the possibility of intelligible dialogue.

We saw something like this happen in the generational equity debate of the 1980s. That debate was not a mass phenomenon but a dialogue among elites: journalists, executives, legislative staffers, and academics. Atchley may be misreading this debate, as AARP did, by imagining attacks on public benefit programs for older people as a form of "ageism." One can disagree with Callahan's (1987, 1990) proposals for age-based rationing, for example, but it simply doesn't get us very far to throw stones at his proposals by accusing him of ageism.

Thinking about generational equity or the controversy over age-based rationing in terms of "ageism" fails to grasp how deeply these debates are rooted in the emergence of the postmodern life course and the altered status of old age. The generational equity debate was actually far more serious than "ageism." It amounted to a wholesale attack on the legitimacy of age-based entitlements, which reached a climax following the collapse of the Catastrophic Coverage Act of 1988. The issues here involve a serious question about allocation of resources and social justice, as Nancy Jecker's chapter shows. From the standpoint of critical gerontology, the challenge is to acknowledge the contradictions raised by this debate and to situate those contradictions in historical terms that make intelligible the choices before us.

WHAT MAY WE HOPE?
HUMANISTIC GERONTOLOGY

We now come to a third version of critical gerontology, which can be called humanistic or cultural gerontology. This is the perspective defined by the work of humanities scholars active in the field of aging in the disciplines of history, philosophy, and literary criticism. Sometimes directly, sometimes indirectly, such scholarly work has served to criticize or go beyond the methods and conclusions of behavioral sciences; at other times it has served merely to illustrate empirical claims, as Weiland (chap. 5) has noted.

But cultural and literary material, including life narratives, can be used for different purposes, including purposes of social criticism and putting forward alternative images of aging. On the one hand, cultural materials may stand in opposition to the dominant social order; on the other hand, cultural forms serve to integrate lives and celebrate shared meanings. Both elements, the oppositional and the integrative, have been part of humanistic gerontology as practiced gerontology over the past decade or so.

Bertram Cohler's approach (chap. 6) illustrates the integrative style of humanistic gerontology. His work is in the integral tradition of Erikson in the sense that he bridges the gap between fact and value, between science and ethics. For Cohler, as for Erikson, wisdom is

basically an adaptive strength, a coping style for maintaining a coherent narrative and a sense of meaning or morale. The search for
meaning, which Cohler, like Erikson, believes to be universal, is both a
drive and an explanatory factor in human development.

Cohler's meditation on virtue and meaning is historical in its orientation. In common with Erikson's optimism, it is one answer to the
sense of quiet despair that has characterized so much of the social
theory in our time, including the pessimism of Freud and of Max
Weber. In the dialectic between optimism and pessimism, there is a
relationship between the problem of narrative and the modernized or
linear life course. The linear life course, in Erikson's hands, has become a kind of contemporary Pilgrim's Progress, a salvation story.
Instead of salvation we now have the search for ego integrity or
wisdom. The gift of grace comes only after the struggle of the life
review, so it is understandable why "life review" assumes a kind of
mythic power for those who want the linear life story to have a happy
ending, even in old age. Illustrating this point, Cohler cites Erikson's
treatment of Dr. Borg, the celebrated hero of Bergman's film *Wild
Strawberries*. We might also cite his feminine counterpart, Geraldine
Page in *The Trip to Bountiful*. Both *Wild Strawberries* and *The Trip to
Bountiful* are late-life narratives of closure, completeness, ego integrity. They are a cultural response to the despair evoked by *Make Way
for Tomorrow* and an answer to the modernist cul-de-sac that is the
last stage of life.

As Steven Weiland (chap. 5) shows, this same ambiguity in the status
of narrative reappears in a different way at the conclusion of Wallace
Stegner's novel *Crossing to Safety*, where the protagonist, Morgan, has
completed his life review and is able to say, "Now we are finally here.
This, in all its painful ambiguity, is what we came for." This climax is not
exactly "the power that moves the heaven and all the stars," as Dante
might have put it. But it may be the only closure, or salvation, available
to the modern seeker. To achieve more requires faith or a deus ex
machina, as we find in the postmodern fable *Cocoon*.

But should we be satisfied to say that closure or completeness is
just a fairy tale, a happy ending without any basis in fact? Is coherence really the same thing as truth? Is there finally a unified identity
over the life course anyway? A postmodern view of the life course
would point out that longitudinal studies show little correlation between early- and late-life attributes. Between myself in the past and
myself now, there is no continuity, no progress, as Montaigne observed four centuries ago at the threshold of modernity.

Samuel Beckett would have understood. Indeed, recent approaches to the study of lives, Cohler (chap. 6) tells us, have suggested

that chance, not causality, plays the largest role. This conclusion raises disturbing questions about the hermeneutic enterprise we optimistically call the study of lives. Are we left to look at life stories as a sort of inkblot test—a random pattern on which we project our own fantasies, including the happy ending of Dr. Borg? Once we approach the act of interpretation in self-reflexiveness, as Steven Weiland (chap. 5) wants to, then "textuality" becomes a field for multiple, perhaps contradictory readings of the life story. Are we far from epistemological anarchism again?

This whole notion of the "intertextuality" of life interpretations must appear profoundly subversive for what has become the celebration of reminiscence and life review in gerontology (Disch, 1989). Once we take deconstruction seriously, then the popularity of life review in gerontology looks like nothing more than ersatz religion, the "triumph of the therapeutic" without the means of grace (Rieff, 1966). But why ersatz religion; why not the real thing? The answer is that religion remains the great repressed element of modern life. But as Freud himself warned us, the return of the repressed is an inescapable law of psychic life. If recent political experience suggests anything, it is that the return of the sacred is very much a fact of late-20th-century history (Bell, 1980).

One way of reading Erikson's account of the modern life course is to see it as a psychological mirror of the ideology of progress (Lasch, 1991). Erikson's "portrayal of a linear, ordered account of lives" amounts to a reconciliation of opposing forces, where conflict leads us on to a positive outcome. Of course, in this optimistic narrative, the last chapter of the story, old age, obviously presents us with a problem. The solution is to make the pieces whole, to find an inner thread that allows a life story to "make sense." What were once religious categories of self-transcendence or wisdom now become secularized and psychologized. In Erikson's deft hands, spiritual solace was presented in an ideologically acceptable form (Lasch, 1991).

What we have here is a strategy of coherence, and Cohler (chap 6) is very clear on the point. Late-life reminiscence, indeed reminiscence at any stage of life, is "coherence work." Like DNA repair at the cellular level, reminiscence work represents "ego repair," enabling us to cope with life transitions. Reminiscence may involve creating a fictional or metaphoric version of the self (Olney's [1972] term for autobiography). A coherence test of selfhood involves more than objective truth. Life stories are not made up out of whole cloth, but they need not necessarily be completely true to the facts.

The advantage of this approach is that it gives us an account for old age in a postmodern life course. The strategy of coherence is more than a search for consolation in old age. Coherence work is needed when the postmodern life course has rendered unpredictable life transitions of all kinds. Divorce and multiple job changes, new fashions and belief systems follow one another with breathtaking rapidity. In an information economy, all coherence is temporary—provisional, until new boundaries are drawn. What was once a task for the very old—life review, mourning the past—is now demanded of people of all ages. In the face of unpredictable, adverse experience, we rework our life narrative to achieve a new coherence, even if only temporary. What divine providence was to traditional society, coherence now becomes for life-span development psychology.

The problematic status of life narratives turns out to be parallel with the problem of explanation and theory building in the philosophy of science. The grand "modernist" philosophies of positivism and logical empiricism were at bottom based on a correspondence theory of truth. Scientific theories, in the positivist tradition, served to account for "the facts," and mainstream gerontology, as a rule, proceeds from these assumptions, blissfully unaware that "foundationalist" theories of science have fallen apart. So for scientific gerontology, just as for individual life narratives, the task is to maintain coherence if science and the life course are to make sense.

The historical crisis of narrative psychology and scientific explanation must be understood in historical terms. From childhood through old age, we have become accustomed to successively rewriting our life story to create an understandable narrative. Now it turns out that there are important historical connections between economy and culture, between the labor market and the rise of life narrative. Cohler (chap. 6) cites Polanyi and E. P. Thompson, students of economic history, in order to locate the problem of life narratives in the context of economic transformation. The transition to postindustrial or postmodern culture represents the historical context for the study of lives and for interpreting the life course as a totality.

For Erikson, the supreme theorist of the modernized, linear life course, old age presented a soluble problem. But for postmodern culture, all grand narratives have come apart. We can no longer be so confident in Erikson's narrative of a "spiritualized" but still secular life course. In postmodern culture, it becomes increasingly difficult to achieve any sense of wisdom or personal integrity. The problem is not simply that random or unpredictable events disrupt lives. War and economic collapse were present in the Middle Ages no less than today. The problem is that we now have no grand narrative that would legitimate individual sacrifice in the name of a greater good. Lacking a grand narrative, the little narratives by which we give coherence to our lives also become frayed and worn. So by means of the patient work of constructing a life story, we stitch together a coat of many colors: precisely the work of "bricolage" that Barbara Myerhoff described.

This cultural task of life construction is what animated Myerhoff's work and what inspires Marc Kaminsky (chap. 13) in his account of story-telling and definitional ceremonies. The strategy of Kaminsky and of Myerhoff can be grasped by comparing it with a parallel approach of Jay Gubrium (chap. 3). Gubrium, like Kaminsky, has a keen ear for good stories. But for Gubrium the stories remain fragments of cloth, never the magic coat of many colors that Kaminsky finds hidden in the attic of autobiographical memory.

Gubrium, too, insists on the importance of "biographical work." But Gubrium's social landscape is more cheerfully postmodernist. We see the contrast in his touching story of Paul, a demented man who seems like a character drawn from the theater of the absurd. Paul's story is moving in itself. But it is not part of any ritual or definitional ceremony; nursing homes have no such ceremonies. Long-term care facilities run according to the logic of instrumental reason, not shared cultural meaning. For an individual or family, instrumental logic means a loss of opportunity for "biographical work" that can be crucial to sustaining dignity at times of frailty or mental impairment. But recognizing the need for biographical work leads to no social transformation unless that need is anchored in a wider context of what Habermas would call "communicative competence"; for example, as it did in the Alzheimer's movement, which Gubrium has documented.

Kaminsky (chap. 13) sees, all too clearly, that Myerhoff has evaded the ambiguous question about the social and individual functions of life stories. For Kaminsky, as for Myerhoff, individual story and collective ritual stand in a dialectical relationship that resists any simple opposition between individual and society. Kaminsky goes to the heart of the matter when he says that Myerhoff poses the struggle for self-definition as a cultural question. This cultural question also has political significance; hence, the ironical term "depoliticizing" in Kaminsky's title. The aged, whether in Venice, California, or Galveston, Texas, are never simply to be assimilated to some category of "victims" or "oppressed people."[5]

But for critical gerontology, the problem here is that the political economy perspective and the literary evidence still remain apart. In fact, these disparate modes of discourse, economics and culture, reflect deep cleavages in social reality. To unify the broken parts of our experience we may need a revival of shared spiritual meaning or perhaps a new kind of enchantment, a secular ritual.

There is indeed a tour de force in Kaminsky's and Myerhoff's valorization of cultural performance as a solution to *both* epigenetic crises of
human development *and* social conflicts in the wider society. What we
have are two domains—art and social justice—that, alas, move in
different directions. Can we imagine a world where the two are unified,
where the tension is overcome? It is just this temptation to resolve the
tension that Gubrium (chap. 3) resists. He recommends that a critical
gerontology tolerate the tension rather than attempt to integrate voice
and context into an analytically unified vision of aging.

This question about the unity among science, politics, and art is of the
greatest importance in assessing the future for a critical gerontology.
Critical theory in the tradition of the Frankfurt School constantly
sought for unity yet avoided any easygoing resolution. The cleavages
between politics and culture, art and science, remain too wide in modern experience. We see now why Kaminsky resists any simple political
economy critique of Myerhoff's interpretive anthropology, just as he
resists Myerhoff's own (failed) attempt to "depoliticize" her interpretation of the definitional ceremonies of her respondents. What Kaminsky
wants is a far more radical reenchantment of the world than Myerhoff
wanted. He is not willing to seal off the cultural from the political, the
private from the public, the psychological from the economic sphere.
But to imagine a world in which these antinomies are unified is one
thing. It is something else to describe the historical conditions under
which actual unity or transcendence is at all possible.

Here again we see a parallel with Erikson, who brings back the
sacred in subterranean form. Kaminsky, like Myerhoff, accomplishes
"a subtle sacralization of psychological and social experience." The
imperative is nothing less than "to metaphorically connect divinity
with the hidden worth of oppressed people." This is a dazzling image.
Spiritual, artistic, and political imperatives are to be unified, as in an
ecstatic vision or perhaps an impossible dream: "Your young men
shall see visions and your old men shall dream dreams." It is not for
nothing that Marc Kaminsky has spent years laboring to reenchant
the culture of aging.

CONCLUSION:
"THE LAST YEARS MAY MATTER MOST"

I began this account of critical gerontology by sketching the outlines
of the postmodern life course. It may now be clear why the alluring
outlines of postmodern culture prove frustrating for the search for

meaning in later life. The postmodern culture of aging presents itself as freedom from constraint. But, like the imaginary world of *Cocoon*, that freedom is actually a massive form of denial and an escape from history. For the postmodern sensibility, time, aging, and the historical past are not entirely real. They represent a "social construction" that we can change at will, whether in societies or in our individual lives.

There is an optimism here that is at variance with the existential facts and with stubborn political reality. We have been told over and over again that it is time to "reinvent" old age and overcome demeaning stereotypes. A major part of the polemical literature of gerontology is based on just this cultural agenda. The war against ageism, we are assured, will take its place alongside the struggle against racism, sexism, and so on. Individuals can wage the struggle as actress Ruth Gordon does, depicting an octogenarian bohemian in the film *Harold and Maude*, or as Maggie Kuhn or George Burns do in real life. The self-help books advise us that we can all reinvent ourselves if we only get our heads straight. This is America, after all. There's no limit to becoming what you want to be. Even aging begins to look like a form of voluntary action.

But reality is something else again. At the end of his life, W. B. Yeats understood this all too well when he spoke of the "ladders," the artistic constructions by which he, as a poet, attempted to climb out of his situation in life. Now at the end of his days, in "The Circus Animals' Desertion," he writes:

> Now that my ladder's gone,
> I must lie down where all the ladders start,
> In the foul rag-and-bone shop of the heart.

Along similar lines the Japanese novelist Ishiguro offers us a bleak but realistic account of time, history, and finitude. Laurence McCullough, in chapter 9 in this volume, finds Ishiguro's fiction helpful because it reminds us that gerontology must properly be the study of human time. Ishiguro's characters have achieved individuation and unique selfhood at the price of becoming old: "a state of existence without the possibility of novelty . . . because they have no bridge from the past to the future in that they have no present." Against this depressing picture, McCullough juxtaposes a view in which the past is real but also becomes an occasion for responsibility, not a resting place. This second view seems more optimistic, but it also means that old age is charged with new burdens. Florida Scott-Maxwell (1968), in her late-life journal, puts it this way: "Another secret we [old people] carry is that drab outside—wreckage to the eye, mirrors a mortification—inside we flame with a wild life that is almost incommunicable. In silent, hot rebellion we cry silently—'I have lived my life, haven't I? What more is expected of me?'"(p. 32).

Rilke spoke of his fear of dying "with unlived lives in my body." Scott-Maxwell (1968) speaks not of fear but of responsibility, of old age as "more than a disability . . . an intense and varied experience, almost beyond our capacity at times, but something to be carried high" (p. 5). Scott-Maxwell's experience is remote from the postmodernist denial of limits; disability and limits here are very real, but they are not the whole story. Old age is not to be viewed as a stage of life in which the person is simply finished, spent, without emancipatory possibilities. On the contrary, late life can be a period of "late freedom" (*die spaete Freiheit*). As Scott-Maxwell puts it, "The late clarities will be put down to our credit I feel sure. . . . The last years may matter most" (p. 112).

To speak of the freedom or the responsibilities of age is also to speak of normative standards by which we judge our own lives. It is in these terms that McCullough (chap. 9) defines successful aging: "the passage from being an apprentice to the past to becoming master of the past," an apprenticeship that involves "acknowledging one's moral and aesthetic responsibility for the past—in one's personal life, family life, community, nation, and planet—and living out that responsibility in a way that commands respect."

We need desperately to recapture this moral dimension of old age, to see what tremendous possibilities, and also hazards, are at stake. Recapturing the moral dimension of old age means that *unsuccessful* aging is also a possibility, a very real moral hazard. This awareness of the perilousness and the preciousness of life, including the last stage of life, was something taken for granted by the traditional societies. St. Bonaventure described human existence as perched on an "infinite precipice," and the Buddhists speak of human birth as hard to obtain and therefore precious beyond understanding. As the Muslim proverb has it, only the dead understand the worth of life.

We are far removed here from the playful anarchism of postmodern sensibility and equally from the Pilgrim's Progress of the linear life course. The challenge of all normative standards is that we may fail to live up to them: "If we have hardly lived at all, it may be much harder to die. We may have to learn that we failed to live our lives" (Scott-Maxwell, 1968, p. 97). That precisely is the risk of what it means to be human, the "infinite risk" we are in danger of losing once gerontology understands old age exclusively in the categories of instrumental reason. The task of critical gerontology is to keep alive those questions that point toward an emancipatory ideal, to inspire in both old and young a sense of risk and of hope.

NOTES

¹ This presupposition, in fact, is central to Habermas's entire argument. What Habermas describes as a standard of nondistorted communication reflects this fundamental fact about the human situation.

² But for an exception within the discourse of mainstream gerontology, see Sternberg (1990).

³ The argument in favor of disinterestedness is most forcefully expressed by Rawls (1971), the greatest contemporary exponent of the liberal tradition, by means of his device of the "Original Position."

⁴ The solution, as Jecker points out in criticizing Norman Daniels, is not to be found in a more sophisticated version of the "Original Position" device.

⁵ In fact, Ovrebo and Minkler (chap. 15) follow up their catalog of oppression with literary works that end up transcending victimization.

REFERENCES

Achenbaum, W. (in press). *Crossing frontiers: The emergence of gerontology as a field of scientific inquiry in the United States.* New York: Cambridge University Press.

Ariès, P. (1962). (Tr. Robert Baldik) *Centuries of childhood: A social history of family life.* New York: Vintage.

Bell, D. (1980). The return of the sacred? In *The winding passage.* (p. 332ff.). Cambridge, MA: ABT Books.

Birren, J., & Bengtson, V. (1988). *Emergent theories of aging.* New York: Springer Publishing Co.

Braaten, J. (1991). *Habermas's critical theory of society.* Albany: State University of New York Press.

Callahan, D. (1987). *Setting limits: Medical goals in an aging society.* New York: Simon & Schuster.

Callahan, D. (1990). *What kind of life: The limits of medical progress.* New York: Simon & Schuster.

Disch, R. (1989). Introduction and preface to Twenty-five years of the life review: Theoritical and practical considerations. *Journal of Gerontological Social Work, 12* (3).

Estes, C. (1979). *The aging enterprise.* San Francisco: Jossey-Bass.

Estes, C., & Binney, E. (1991). The biomedicalization of aging: Dangers and dilemmas. In M. Minkler & C. L. Estes (Eds.), *Critical perspectives on aging: The political economy of growing old.* New York: Baywood.

Feyerabend, P. (1988). *Against method.* London: Routledge, Chapman, Hall.

Graebner, W. (1980). *A history of retirement: The meaning and function of an American institution, 1885–1978.* New Haven, CT: Yale University Press.

Horkheimer, M., & Adorno, T. (1975). *Dialectic of enlightenment.* New York: Continuum.

Kalish, R. (1979). The new ageism and the failure models: A polemic. *The Gerontologist, 19:*398–402.

Kingson, E., Hirshorn, B., & Cornman, J. (1986). *Ties that bind: the interdependence of generations.* Cabin John, MD: Seven Locks Press.

Lasch, C. (1991). *The true and only Heaven: Progress and its critics.* New York: Norton.

Laslett, P. (1991). *A fresh map of life: The emergence of the Third Age.* Cambridge, MA: Harvard University Press.

Mannheimer, R. (1989). The narrative quest in humanistic gerontology. *Journal of Aging Studies, 3*(3):231–52.

Moody, H. R. (1988). *Abundance of life: Human development policies for an aging society.* New York: Columbia University Press.

Moody, H. R. (1989). Toward a critical gerontology: The contribution of the humanities to theories of aging. In J. Birren & V. Bengston (Eds.), *Emergent theories of aging* (pp. 19–40). New York: Springer Publishing Co.

Myles, J. (1984). *Old age in the welfare state: The political economy of public pensions.* Boston: Little, Brown.

Neugarten, B. (1981). *Age or need?* Beverly Hills, CA: Sage.

Olney, J. (1972). *Metaphors of self: The meaning of autobiography.* Princeton, NJ: Princeton University Press.

Olson, L. (1982). *The political economy of aging: The state, private power, and social welfare.* New York: Columbia University Press.

Pifer, A., & Bronte, L. (Eds.) (1986). *Our aging society: Paradox and promise.* New York: Norton.

Rawls, J. (1971). *Theory of justice.* Cambridge, MA: Harvard University Press.

Rieff, P. (1966). *The triumph of the therapeutic.* New York: Harper & Row.

Rose, M. (1991). *Evolutionary biology of aging.* New York: Oxford University Press.

Scott-Maxwell, F. (1968). *The measure of my days.* New York: Penquin.

Sternberg, J. (1990). *Wisdom: Its nature, origins, and development.* New York: Cambridge University Press.

PART I
Theory/ Epistemology/ Method

1

Critical Perspectives on Retirement

Robert C. Atchley

Critical gerontology seeks to broaden the context of our study of aging by introducing interpretive and emancipatory philosophical questions (Moody, 1988). As advanced by Habermas, critical theory "exposes the prevailing system of domination, expresses its contradictions, assesses its potential for emancipatory change, and criticizes the system to promote that change" (Antonio, 1983, p. 331). A major goal of this chapter is to bring critical perspectives to bear on the social institution, social policies, and life stage we call retirement. It deals with four interconnected issues: (1) retirement in the context of social thought, (2) ways of viewing retirement and their implications for a critical gerontology of retirement, (3) gerontological tools that can be used in a critical gerontology of retirement, and (4) challenges that a critical gerontology of retirement faces from demassification and postmodernism.

A full treatment of retirement from a critical perspective would take a book in itself. This chapter can do no more than sketch the general outline of thought that could be used to bring critical theory to bear on retirement. It is intended as a stimulus for further exploration, not as a definitive treatment.

RETIREMENT IN THE CONTEXT
OF SOCIAL THOUGHT

Retirement is a social invention. It was created through social processes to achieve social aims, and as such, retirement is very much a part of the shifting and changing political, economic, and social fabric of society. From an individualistic perspective, retirement has also come to be seen as a stimulus for human development. Ideas about retirement therefore need to be integrated with our ideas about social structure, social process, and human development. Too much of the literature about retirement has been conceptually isolated from major strains of social thought such as systems theory, political economy theory, critical theory, and human development theory. Much of the literature on causes and consequences of retirement tends to portray retirement in a mechanistic way and conveys little sense of the social dynamics through which social institutions evolve and human development occurs. To achieve a more integrated understanding of retirement, the ways we conceive of retirement need to be conjoined with our more abstract ways of thinking about social life in general so both areas of thought can be enriched. Ideas of retirement can be broadened and deepened, and abstract social thought can be made more concrete, which may allow its improvement. This overall objective permeates the discussion in the remainder of this chapter.

WAYS OF VIEWING RETIREMENT

In many respects, order in the social world is imposed by social action rather than resulting from an unfolding of natural processes. How humans conceive of their world affects profoundly how they anticipate and create their future. In this section we look at three ways that retirement can be conceptualized: as a social institution, as a body of distributional issues, and as a human life stage. Although interconnected, these perspectives on retirement deal with different sets of issues and considerations and therefore present different prospects for the development of a critical gerontology of retirement.

Retirement as a Social Institution

As a social institution, retirement consists of rules of permissible and required exit from the labor force and social arrangements for creating and delivering retirement pensions. Culturally, the retirement institution is a set of general ideas. Operationally, it is accomplished by a huge variety of different types of organizations, some of which do a good job of developing clear and fair policies and procedures and many of which do not. Because retirement policies are created by both employers and government, the structure of retirement parallels the structure of the economy as a whole. In the core private sector of the economy, made up of large corporations, retirement tends to be early and retirement benefits generous. Flexible retirement is common. In the highly competitive private peripheral sector, which by and large supplies the core sector or engages in service employment, small-scale work organizations prevail, and private retirement rules are less likely to exist, private pensions are scarce, and Social Security retirement rules and pension policies tend to govern retirement. In the government sector, retirement policies tend to emphasize years of service, which generally promotes early retirement, and pensions tend to be generous, at least in terms of replacement ratios. Social Security's public retirement pension system provides a base of rules and pension-generating capacity that are built upon by employer-specific retirement systems, both public and private.

The main goals of the retirement institution are to move substantial numbers of mature workers out of the labor force and to avoid the political fallout that would occur from the impoverishment of those displaced. These goals stem from a series of beliefs. First, industrial economies are assumed always to have a shortage of jobs because the use of high-energy production technology means that only a small proportion of able-bodied adults are needed to produce the necessary goods and services, which means, in turn, that ways must be found to reduce the size of the labor force. Second, aging is assumed to cause people to lose their value as workers; therefore, removing aging people from the work force appears to be justified. Third, unemployment is socially disruptive; therefore, movement of older adults out of the labor market must be accompanied by retirement pensions that provide at least a minimum of income security.

Each of the goals and beliefs that form the basis of retirement as a social institution can be challenged on a number of grounds. For example, critical theorists might argue that, although it may be efficient, bureaucratically organized high-energy production, with its job standardization, is constraining and alienating to workers. Therefore, profits (excess productivity) are achieved at the expense of employee growth and development and social solidarity. Taken to its next step, the critical theorist might question the tendency in late capitalism to automate whenever possible.

In the post–World War II era, technology made possible dramatic increases in both capital accumulation and real wages within the core sector of the economy. In this sector, both management and labor have a deep interest in the continued evolution of high-energy production. But as the proportion of the population excluded from this high-income production sector has grown, the political and moral solidarity needed to perpetuate the educational and research activities necessary to this sector has been substantially eroded. Increasingly, the public is rebelling against paying taxes to support institutions that they are excluded from.

One solution to this problem might be to use taxes on core sector economic activity to subsidize public service employment aimed at widely valued public objectives such as preserving the environment or providing affordable long-term care for people who need it. Such a shift of resources would dramatically increase access to productive activity in the population, and it might call into question the assumption that limiting the size of the labor force is to the public good.

The assumption that aging causes people to lose their value as workers can also be challenged on several grounds. For example, underlying industrial employment practices is the Taylorist perspective that only the most desirable workers should be employed by industry (Graebner, 1980). This perspective assumes that society has no obligation to try to find productive places for all of its people who want them, and presumed infirmities of age serve along with lack of education, disability, and racist and sexist assumptions about human capacities to effectively limit the pool of people being considered for scarce jobs. The domination of high-income jobs by highly educated white males under age 60 does not result from natural or even actual group differences in capacity to perform but results instead from a set of inaccurate discriminatory beliefs about the effects of age, gender, race, or disability on capacity to perform. And highly educated white males under 60 occupy the positions of power from which these beliefs can become self-fulfilling prophecies.

A large amount of scientific research has been brought to bear on the issue of the effects of age on employability (Birren, Robinson, & Livingston, 1986; Rosen & Jerdee, 1985; Sterns & Alexander, 1987). In general, this research has shown that older workers perform well in a wide variety of job settings, are quite able to continue to develop on the job, tend to be stable and loyal employees, serve as important sources of organizational memory, continue to be interpersonally competent, and have considerable productive potential even into their late 70s and beyond. There is a decline with age in physical and mental capacity for a significant proportion of employees, but such declines are not caused solely by aging and are not highly correlated with chronological age, nor are they always relevant to work performance. Therefore, physical capacity and health need to be monitored on an individual basis for workers of all ages. These results have been found consistently enough to be considered hard findings that are not widely debated among the scientists working in this area. Yet a large majority of managers continue to relate to older employees based on stereotypes of older workers as having less performance capacity and less potential for development compared to younger workers (Rosen & Jerdee, 1985).

Industrial gerontologists have tended to attribute this behavior to ignorance among managers. Critical theorists, on the other hand, might attribute more weight to the political purposes that such disqualifying stereotypes serve. In our society there remains the vestige of a need to treat our elders with respect. But American managers have difficulty respecting and dominating workers at the same time. It is easier simply to exclude people whose viewpoints challenge management control. The challenge coming from older employees is seldom direct; it more often consists of institutional memory. When the "new brooms" are attempting to "sweep clean," they do not want to be informed about insights gained in the struggle and compromise it took to create that which they blithely seek to destroy. As they attempt to impose rationality through job descriptions and performance appraisals, they do not want to hear about the decades of real-world negotiations that it took to produce a highly effective personalized job for a specific individual. And given the politics of age in the workplace, it is little wonder that most older workers retire at the earliest age possible. As age increases, those who are not at the top of an organization's hierarchy often find themselves being treated in increasingly impersonal, discriminatory, and demeaning ways. This issue should be of considerable interest to critical theorists because in many ways it is the antithesis of the "emancipatory ideal" regardless of how such an ideal might be defined.

The objective of a critical gerontology of the institution of retirement, with its retirement rules, incentives, disincentives, and pension policies, is to expose further the deeper motives behind the institution and to expose the patterns of domination contained within them. Once this has been accomplished, directions for emancipatory change can be identified and criticism can be focused on how such changes could be implemented. One overarching goal of this critical enterprise might be to illuminate a more emancipatory and less manipulative view of retirement. Of course, this argument should be integrated with the general critique of the political economy.

Retirement as a Distributional Issue

As a social institution, retirement involves important distributional issues, particularly the distribution of jobs, income, and retirement chances. Retirement is tied directly to employment and earnings by the eligibility rules and benefit formulas of Social Security and private pensions. Thus, access to jobs and the distribution of income across the labor force are social policy areas that directly affect retirement eligibility and retirement income.

Kohli (1987) pointed out that among German sociologists the term "work society" has taken the place of "industrial society" or "capitalist society" to emphasize the central organizing force of jobs in the lives of people in the developed world. The term "work society" views work

> as a reality not only of the economy but also of culture and life work; it emphasizes how people are engaged into society, in other words, how social life in the broadest sense is regulated. The impact of work goes far beyond simply assuring material survival or organizing economic and political interests; by providing the legitimate basis for the allocation of life chances in most respects, [work] defines the cultural unity of modern society as well as the identity of its members. (p. 128)

Thus, access to jobs represents access to the benefits of the work society, including retirement, and factors such as citizenship or need assume secondary importance.

The notion of organizing the economic life course into preparation, employment, and retirement has existed at least since the time of Plato, but the formal insertion of this life course into laws and rules morally justified the linkage between employment and retirement, especially in terms of social insurance retirement provisions. This linkage of employment and retirement also preserves into retirement the dominant system of status inequality. From this perspective, retirement is a major vehicle for achieving social integration among those who have been employed. But from the point of view of those who have had sporadic or nonexistent access to good jobs, access to retirement is limited.

The bias in favor of providing the most generous retirement benefits to long-term participants in the work force can be seen in a number of government policies in the United States. For example, tax policies create incentives to provide retirement pensions directly in relation to the profitability of the organization. The bigger the profits, the higher the corporate tax liability and the lower the cost of offering private pension coverage. Companies with low profit margins have little or no tax incentive to offer retirement pensions. Such companies also generally pay lower wages, which means that the employees have less income that they can put into tax-sheltered individual retirement savings vehicles. By contrast, employees of companies with high long-term profitability tend to be paid much better in relation to the general standard of living and thus to have greater opportunity to enjoy the tax benefits of saving for retirement. These policies tend to perpetuate class differences in the labor force into retirement.

Administrative retirement rules also tend to give advantages to the already advantaged and to downplay the needs of the disadvantaged. For example, benefit formulas for private pensions tend to give a decided advantage to employees with long service and disproportionately smaller benefits to employees with several different employers. In addition, eligibility requirements, even for Social Security, can discriminate against people whose jobs exist outside formal organizations. For example, in 1980 more than a quarter of African-American women in their early 60s were employed as private household workers. Most of these women's employers did not go through the process of reporting their wages and paying the required Social Security taxes. Thus, among older African-American women there are many who have worked full-time their entire adult lives with no retirement eligibility to show for it. This same situation exists for farm workers in many regions of the country, especially those who are undocumented immigrants.

Employers are not required to provide employees an opportunity to contribute to private pensions in addition to Social Security. This is a national policy. Thus, employees with private pension coverage are concentrated in the core private sector of the economy and in government employment, which in turn means that women and minorities, because of their lower access to employment in these sectors, have much lower incidence of private pension coverage compared to white males.

With their sensitivity to class, gender, and color issues, critical theorists' critiques of the industrial political economy could be extended systematically into a critique of the distributional issues embedded in our retirement policies. This has been done in bits and pieces, especially in relation to gender (Holden, 1989), but the work of developing an integrated critique remains to be done. Indeed, there is a practically open field of opportunity for critical scholars interested in examining and challenging distributional social policies about retirement.

Retirement as a Life Stage

Retirement began as a labor policy designed to handle problems presumed to stem from the effects of aging on employees. It was backed up by a cultural view of the life course in which retirement legitimately followed employment. But this view of the evolution of retirement does not tell the whole story. As large numbers of people experienced retirement as an economically secure and unprescribed stage of life and as American ideals about self-direction and self-improvement permeated popular culture, retirement came to be seen by many as an opportunity to experience a new, emancipatory phase of human development. Retirement for many is an *earned right* to shuck off the yoke of organizational domination that attends dependent employment. Retirement is anticipated and experienced as economic and social freedom.

Apart from the previous point that access to the opportunity to experience this next phase of self-directed development is constrained by the prevailing pattern of economic and social domination, there are at least three issues about retirement as an emancipatory life stage that could concern critical theorists. First, not all people who are eligible to retire are prepared to take advantage of the freedom it represents. Science and mass culture have given us the capacity to live longer, but vocationally oriented education often deflects us from the capacity to see retirement's potential implications for our human and spiritual development. There could be a critique of education's capacity to prepare people both for a commodified labor market and for the freedom of retirement. There may be an inherent contradiction here. Added to this is the possibility that liberal education may be needed periodically throughout the life course and that retirement is an important stimulus for a round of serious liberal education, not just an eight-session "preretirement planning" program. At issue here is the capacity of our educational institutions to conceive of their mission in this way and of the public to support the value of opportunities for liberal education over the entire life course.

A second concern might be the broader social roles that free retired people might play in the general critical enterprise. Retired people may have a freedom to criticize that goes well beyond the boundaries of the narrow old-age interest group. For example, retired people already play important roles in political criticism through involvement in groups such as Common Cause, The Sierra Club, the Gray Panthers, and so on. What might happen if retired people were enlisted and trained for effective roles in helping society to take a critical look at itself?

A third way that critical gerontology might relate to retirement as a life stage concerns identifying the conditions under which coercion might be minimized in the employment and retirement decisions of older employees. If employment were less dependent and promoted development in mature adults, then retirement might be seen as a more optional life stage than is currently the case. The issue for critical gerontology is to look at the process of retirement in terms of coercion, to point us toward policies through which older people might voluntarily remain in the labor force for developmental reasons or voluntarily retire for developmental reasons. People feel that they earn the right to retire, so coercing people to remain in the labor force is politically dangerous. Likewise, coercing capable people to retire deprives organizations of needed human resources. Too often, coercive retirements are misguided efforts to handle issues such as downsizing when a selective employment policy designed to identify the best people for the reorganized work effort might well be the best approach and one that could be age-neutral. An important part of this critique, of course, must be an examination of unconscious age prejudices that harm both older people and organizations (Rosen & Jerdee, 1985).

GERONTOLOGICAL TOOLS FOR A CRITICAL GERONTOLOGY OF RETIREMENT

Already existing work in gerontology contains elements that can usefully be adapted to a critical gerontology of retirement. The main point here is to avoid reinventing the wheel. Critical theorists entering the field of aging should be aware of the many contributions that have already been made that can make their task much easier. For example, Moody's (1988) general piece on critical gerontology lays out an effective meta-theoretical framework, identifying critical theory, interpretive theory in hermeneutics, and analytical scientific theory as important partners in the creation of effective and balanced cognitive understanding of a variety of areas in the field of aging, including retirement. Moody especially sees the involvement of schol-

ars in the humanities as an important part of the integration of
critical theory and hermeneutics into gerontology. There is no question that a critical gerontology of retirement can benefit from the
penetrating questions of philosophers, the capacity of historians to
examine our assumptions about the past, and the questions raised by
literary scholars about the interpretation of texts. An important point
to remember here is that there are people in all of these areas who
have been laboring in the field of aging from some time. The humanist entering the field would do well to search out and learn from
this work.

In the area of human development, there is no shortage of theory,
but there has been little use of human development theory to examine the assumptions embedded in retirement institutional arrangements and social policies. Both stage theories and theories of continuous development could be useful in this enterprise. For example, the
revised stage theory of development in later life described by Erikson,
Erikson, and Kivnick (1986) identifies developmental issues and compromises typical of middle and later life. These ideas could be used to
map the retirement life stage in terms of its compatibility with human
development concerns. It could also be used to critique the developmental assumptions used to justify retirement. On the other hand,
Atchley's (1989) continuity theory emphasizes the constructionist nature of development; that is, people are assumed to create their own
development through the ways they conceive of and anticipate their
futures. The theory is evolutionist; it assumes that development in
later life is built on a base of adaptive skills and structures laid down
and constantly refined by the individual throughout earlier life
stages. Continuity theory is reflexive in that it assumes that feedback
from the results of decisions is used to refine the structures and skills
that produce subsequent rounds of decisions. This theory might be
used, for instance, to critique the discontinuities that are imposed on
aging adults by retirement policies that coerce people to retire. It
could also be used to suggest emanciptory alternatives.

Existing work in gerontology by Achenbaum, (1978), Atchley
(1982), Graebner (1980), Haber (1983), and Quadagno (1988) can help
us understand and critique the evolution of retirement as a social
institution. In this work we see retirement's emergence being affected
by a variety of social issues and social actions. By better understanding how retirement evolved, we can better understand the large array
of social processes and agendas retirement serves. For example, no
single image of retirement fueled its evolution. Indeed, each of the
many images of retirement in the literature has a ring of truth to it.
For Graebner (1980), retirement was simply another means through

which capital exploited and controlled labor. Atchley (1982) saw retirement as an important way to keep down unemployment in tough
economic times by reducing the size of the labor force competing for
scarce jobs. Haber (1983) saw private retirement pensions as a mechanism for discouraging worker mobility. Achenbaum (1978) saw retirement as a way to reduce the incidence of poverty in old age.
Atchley (1982) saw Social Security retirement pensions as protection
for the society from the upheaval that results from age discrimination in the work force in the absence of pensions.

In the period of mass industrialization, the prime function of both
private and public pensions and retirement rules has been to encourage older people to leave the labor force. These systems have been
enormously successful. In advanced industrial economies, regardless
of political or economic philosophy, a strikingly large proportion of
the older population is out of the labor force.

Regardless of the view of what retirement's functions are, there is
also a need for theories that describe and explain the dynamics
through which retirement evolves. For example, cybernetic systems
theory (Atchley, 1970, 1982; Buckley, 1967) focuses on the role that
communications and feedback play in the evolution of social structures and arrangements. According to systems theory, social patterns
develop as a result of choices, which occur in a specific cultural and
historic context.

> Taking into account culturally given preferences and experientially
> given realities, people choose what seems to them the best means of
> achieving a particular goal or set of goals. They then observe the results.
> They may achieve their goals, encounter opposition to their goals, en-
> counter opposition to their means, and so on. By agreement, negotiation,
> or power plays, compromises are gradually reached that endure long
> enough to become customary. (Atchley, 1982, p. 265)

The feedback that is central to systems theory is similar to Moody's
(1988) notion of self-reflection. In systems theory the critical theorist's
concerns over contradiction and paradox are given voice in the feedback that leads to modifications of social structure and process. Systems theory focuses on action alternatives, values, and group processes, including communication and conflict, through which choices
are made. Systems theory acknowledges conflicting values and action
choices. It leads to an understanding of the pragmatic nature of many
choices. For a critical gerontology of retirement, systems theory could
provide a description of the evolutionary process that might be used to
critique pragmatism as the basis for cultural evolution.

To understand the distributional issues raised by retirement as social policy, political economy perspectives have provided important strands of theory that can be used to look at retirement. For example, Myles (1984) used a political economy perspective to look at the relationship between industrialization, politics, and the evolution of the welfare state, including public retirement programs. Myles concluded, among other things, that the degree of labor organization was a major determinant of the generosity of Social Security–type public retirement systems, which he took as support for an intergroup conflict model of Marxian class rivalry.

Quadagno (1988) used a political economy perspective to show how the agrarian interests of the southern states combined with the social structure of the U.S. Congress, which allocated power based on tenure in office, to effectively block attempts to provide adequate retirement income to farm workers in the South in order to perpetuate the extreme labor dependency and exploitation that characterized the sharecropper system. Her research has much to offer a critical gerontology of retirement.

Kohli (1987) used a "moral economy" perspective to examine the historical manner in which German society justified retirement. The main ideas of his argument revolve around (1) the institutionalization of the life course in terms of the preparation/employment/retirement sequence; (2) an assumption that current wages do not fully discharge the employer's and the society's obligations to workers, thereby morally justifying retirement benefits; and (3) the notion that these benefits apply only to those who have been part of the "work society" mentioned earlier. This perspective can be used to critique, as examples, the use of employment as the sole access to benefits and the notion that Social Security retirement benefits are renegotiable.

Thus, many different theoretical perspectives relevant to a critical gerontology of retirement have been used over the past 15 years. However, all of them could benefit from reformulation and integration with the main ideas of the critical enterprise. In addition, all of these perspectives could be enriched by an inclusion of perspectives from the humanities. The goal is not another very abstract social theory to rival that of Habermas. Instead, in the process of translating the ideas of critical theory into a critical gerontology of retirement, we will learn more about retirement, but we will also learn more about critical theory that can be used to improve it.

The final substantive section of this chapter deals with trends in society that will complicate the task of developing a critical gerontology of retirement: demassification and postmodernism.

CHALLENGES CREATED BY DEMASSIFICATION AND POSTMODERNISM

Demassification is the breakup of large-scale social organizations and the mass culture that supported them. C. Wright Mills (1963) described the mass society as one dominated by large political, economic, educational, governmental, and religious organizations. In the large bureaucratic organizations of the mass society, communication takes place top-downward, through established channels of authority or through mass communication media. Either way, dialogue on issues is difficult. Mass institutions stifle the free flow of discussion necessary to the democratic process and replace discussion with opinion implanted through mass media.

The rise in the 1950s of great bureaucratic structures in government, labor, industry, finance, and so on resulted in inaccessibly large organizations that became increasingly administrative and less political (Mills, 1963). Even interest groups such as AARP became mass organizations in which the individual or even organized subgroups have less influence. But a world of large bureaucratic organizations, with their excessive reliance on rules and "rationalized" jobs, is alienating to human beings.

Demassification is a *response* to the mass society dominated by alienating bureaucratic organizations. Although bureaucratic organizations can be very efficient (Perrow, 1986), they have a very poor capacity to meet the needs of individuals in an individualistic society (Bellah et al., 1985). Bureaucratic principles of accountability also easily get out of hand and produce enormous amounts of wasted effort on paperwork, the life blood of the bureaucracy. Dahrendorf (1988) referred to this latter factor as "bureaucratic drag," which saps the productivity of organizations. Thus, to improve worker morale and to eliminate bureaucratic drag, in the 1980s organizations began a process of demassification. This can be seen in industry, the professions, education, unions, and the mass media (Hallinan, Klein, & Glass, 1990).

One of the major elements of demassification is the movement away from universalistic bureaucratic norms toward particularistic norms negotiated and renegotiated to fit the people and the evolving purpose of the organization. A second characteristic of demassification is a sharp reduction in the size of autonomous work units, which improves the capacity for dialogic communication and negotiation. Third, in demassification, horizontal authority relationships increase, and vertical ones decrease. Demassification is nothing short of a rediscovery of interactive community within various social institutions. It generally improves the feelings people have about the group process, and the time formerly spent on bureaucratic accountability often needs to be spent on the communication necessary to retain a sense of group purpose.

As people gain experience with small interactive groups, the capacity of large organizations to attract loyalty declines. People feel that large organizations do not and cannot speak for them, and as a result attachment to mass political parties, voluntary organizations, and labor unions is at an all-time low. The emphasis in American culture in the 1990s is on dialogue within the status group (Gordon, 1964), a group made up of people who consider one another social equals. This trend increases the variety of cultural and normative frameworks in all of our major institutions, including the economy, government, education, and religion. The rise of status groups can also be seen in the proliferation of media segments in cable television and talk radio. Developing clear direction in relation to social issues in such a highly differentiated public is difficult indeed.

Postmodernism is a philosophical shift that gives validity to the diverse normative results of culture making in status groups, and academic and artistic postmodernism are merely specific varieties of postmodernism. Postmodernism is at root a movement aimed at loosening the mental shackles imposed by the technoscientific modern society. Postmodernism, with its antipositivist stance toward knowledge, encourages anarchy in the marketplace of ideas. Sociologists such as Lyotard and Beaudrillard looked at this chaotic picture and saw disintegration (Antonio, 1990), but Habermas (1979) and Klapp (1978) saw instead the loosening of social structure needed for the evolution of adaptive new structural forms.

The evolution of a new world of social structure and process will bring growing pains. While status groups are concentrating on developing their own ideas about how the world should be, what work needs to be done, and how to do it, there is a deemphasis on intergroup negotiation and consensus building. During this time, people tend to revert to their social class, ethnic, gender, age, and color tribes. Prejudice and stereotyping increase.

The challenge for a critical gerontology of retirement is to look at the effects of demassification and postmodernism on retirement as social institution and as social policy. Our current retirement institutions and policies were constructed to fit a society in which mass organizations prevailed. As mass organizations play a smaller and smaller role in terms of organizing the political, economic, and social lives of our population, changes will need to be made in retirement. To participate in this process effectively, critical gerontologists will need to examine the social direction that the demassified postmodern society is taking, develop an emancipatory vision of the future that lies in that direction, and bring effective criticism to bear on the current institution of retirement and retirement social policies in order to promote needed change.

CONCLUSION

There is every reason to be excited about the prospect of creating a critical gerontology of retirement. A good base of work has already been laid in gerontology that can be used in the critical enterprise. As scholars work to introduce critical perspectives from the humanities and the social sciences, it is important to build on what has already been done. This means, of course, that a critical gerontology of retirement must be multidisciplinary even within the area of critical thought.

In developing a critical gerontology of retirement, retirement must be placed in the context of major political, economic, and cultural institutions. To understand retirement and critique it, we must have a good understanding of how society as a whole operates. This means, of course, that a critical gerontology of retirement is an extension of critical theory in its general form. But this must be a creative extension, because critical theory is poorly developed in many areas. Indeed, the development of a critical gerontology of retirement may fill important gaps in critical theory itself.

An adequate critical gerontology of retirement must look not just at the history of retirement, the institutional arrangements, or the social policies that support retirement procedures. It must also look at the human development issues raised by retirement. Human development perspectives are necessary to understand what an emancipatory future would look like in both employment and retirement.

Developing a critical gerontology of retirement in the 1990s will be a challenge because demassification and postmodernism are creating a fast-moving target for critique. In addition, it is more difficult to critique hundreds of status groups than it is to critique monolithic mass institutions.

The infusion of critique into the gerontology of retirement is a vital task. Only a self-reflective society can adapt successfully to dramatic social change, and critical gerontology has a vital part to play in this process. It is important not to be overwhelmed by the complexity and magnitude of the task. Any effort that can be made to introduce emancipatory vision and critique into our thinking about retirement will be an important step.

REFERENCES

Achenbaum, W. A. (1978). *Old age in the new land: The American experience since 1790.* Baltimore: Johns Hopkins University Press.

Antonio, R. J. (1983). The origin, development, and contemporary status of critical theory. *Sociological Quarterly, 24,* 325–351.

Antonio, R. J. (1990). The decline of the Grand Narrative of emancipatory modernity: Crisis or renewal in neo-Marxian theory? In G. Ritzer (Ed.), *Frontiers of social theory: The new syntheses* (pp. 88–116). New York: Columbia University Press.

Atchley, R. C. (1970). *Understanding American society.* Belmont, CA: Wadsworth.

Atchley, R. C. (1982). Retirement as a social institution. *Annual Review of Sociology, 8,* 263–287.

Atchley, R. C. (1985). Social Security-type retirement policies: A cross-national study. In Z. Blau (Ed.), *Current perspectives on aging and the life cycle* (vol. 1, pp. 275–294). Greenwich, CT: JAI Press.

Atchley, R. C. (1989). A continuity theory of normal aging. *Gerontologist, 29,* 183–190.

Bellah, R. N., Madsen, R., Sullivan, W. M., Swidler, A., & Tipton, S. M. (1985). *Habits of the heart: Individualism and commitment in American life.* Berkeley, Calif.: University of California Press.

Birren, J. E., Robinson, P. K., & Livingston, J. E. (Eds.). (1986). *Age, health, and employment.* Englewood Cliffs, NJ: Prentice-Hall.

Buckley, W. (1967). *Sociology and modern systems theory.* Englewood Cliffs, NJ: Prentice-Hall.

Dahrendorf, R. (1988). *The modern social contract.* New York: Weidenfeld & Nicholson.

Erikson, E. H., Erikson, J. M., & Kivnick, H. Q. (1986). *Vital involvement in old age.* New York: W. W. Norton.

Gordon, M. M. (1964). *Assimilation in American life.* New York: Oxford University Press.

Graebner, W. (1980). *A history of retirement.* New Haven, CT: Yale University Press.

Haber, C. (1983). *Beyond sixty-five.* New York: Cambridge University Press.

Habermas, J. (1979). *Communication and the evolution of society.* Boston: Beacon Press.

Hallinan, M. T., Klein, D. M., & Glass, J. (1990). *Change in social institutions.* New York: Plenum Press.

Holden, K. C. (1989). Economic status of older women: A summary of selected research issues. In A. R. Herzog, K. C. Holden, & M. M. Seltzer (Eds.), *Health and economic status of older women* (pp. 92–132). Amityville, NY: Baywood.

Klapp, O. E. (1978). *Opening and closing: Strategies of information adaptation in society.* New York: Cambridge University Press.

Kohli, M. (1987). Retirement and the moral economy: An historical interpretation of the German case. *Journal of Aging Studies, 1,* 125–144.

Mills, C. W. (1963). *Power, politics and people: The collected essays of C. Wright Mills.* New York: Oxford University Press.

Moody, H. R. (1988). Toward a critical gerontology: The contributions of the humanities to theories of aging. In J. E. Birren & V. L. Bengtson (Eds.), *Emergent theories of aging* (pp. 17–40). New York: Springer Publishing Co.

Myles, J. (1984). *Old age in the welfare state.* Boston: Little, Brown.

Perrow, C. (1986). *Complex organizations: A critical essay.* New York: McGraw-Hill.

Quadagno, J. (1988). *The transformation of old age security.* Chicago: University of Chicago Press.

Rosen, B., & Jerdee, T. H. (1985). *Older employees: New roles for valued resources.* Homewood, IL: Dow-Jones Irwin.

Sterns, H. L., & Alexander, R. A. (1987). Industrial gerontology: The aging individual and work. *Annual Review of Gerontology and Geriatrics, 7,* 243–264.

2

Aging as Explanation: How Scientific Measurement Can Advance Critical Gerontology

Fred L. Bookstein and W. Andrew Achenbaum

All sciences of observation follow the same course. One begins by observing a phenomenon, then studies all associated circumstances, and finally, if the results of observation *can be expressed numerically* [sic], estimates the intensity of the causes that concurred in its formation. . . . It is the whole of these laws that appears to me to constitute *social physics*, a science which, while still in its infancy, becomes incontestably more important each day and will eventually rank among those sciences most beneficial to man. (Quetelet, cited in Stigler [1986], p. 195)

It is only since the early part of the last century that science has had the tools to study aging. Quetelet began to study, measure, and document the characteristics of human development and aging—our physiology, behavior, and society—in a manner that formed the basis for creating a science of mankind. (Birren, 1986, p. 265)

Taking for granted that the alternative to art was arithmetic, he plunged deep into statistics, fancying that education would find the surest bottom there; and the study proved the easiest he had ever approached. Even the Government volunteered unlimited statistics, endless columns of figures, bottomless averages merely for the asking. At the Statistical Bureau, Worthington Ford supplied any material that curiosity could imagine for filling vast gaps of ignorance, and methods for applying the plasters of fact. One seemed for a while to be winning ground, and one's averages projected themselves as laws into the future. Perhaps the most perplexing part of the study lay in the attitude of the statisticians, who showed no enthusiastic confidence in their own figures. They should have reached certainty, but they talked like other men who knew less. The method did not result in faith. Indeed, every increase of mass—of volume and velocity—seemed to bring in new elements, and, at last, a scholar, fresh in arithmetic and ignorant of algebra, fell into a superstitious terror of complexity at the sink of facts. Nothing came out as it should. (Adams, 1918/1961, p. 351)

"The ideal of a *critical gerontology*," proposes H. R. Moody (1988), requires scholars to develop "theories of aging that contain . . . rules for their construction, interpretation, and application to the life-world" (p. 33). Moody's call for a "critical gerontology" is provocative, but it does not go far enough. The time *has* come for researchers in aging to assume a more self-critical posture, to elucidate multidisciplinary, longitudinal perspectives on a nexus shared by specialists from many disciplines. We think the focus of critical gerontology should not be limited to what Patrick McKee (1982) calls "the philosophical foundations of gerontology," to establishing the conceptual and normative relationships among different domains of inquiry and distinctive theoretical levels of explanation.

Rather, the sine qua non of critical gerontology must be a critique of existing modes of scientific measurement. Appropriate methodologies cannot be taken for granted in advancing gerontology as a field of inquiry. One's confidence in truth telling and knowledge building is contingent upon the reliability of the evidence under scrutiny. Scientific knowledge depends on accuracy, on getting the basics right. Researchers must believe that the observations that they and their colleagues generate bear close correspondence to the reality they purport to describe. Do currently available measurements enable scholars to grapple with processes of aging as the subject, not just the object, of explanation? We think not.

The theme of this chapter, an essay toward a critical gerontology, emerges out of its epigraphs. Quetelet and Birren, among others, were wrong in urging a unified science of human development that could rely on statistics to remedy failures of measurement. Furthermore, Adams was prescient: he anticipated that Quetelet's view of "social physics"—particularly the tenet that "one's averages projected themselves as laws into the future"—would divert subsequent scientists from more appropriate modes of anthropometric investigation. The disagreement bespoken here largely accounts for the failure of modern biological gerontology to arrive at a scientific structure suitable for describing and explaining basic processes of aging.[1] The present chapter, a collaboration between a statistician and a historian, combines a study in the history of science with a proposal for extending a not particularly new style of multivariate statistics into the heart of gerontology.

The idea that replicated observations of a certain structure could be imagined to represent a "true mean value," about which observations varied by normally distributed "errors," had proved very useful in astronomy and geodesy. Quetelet borrowed the technique for social investigations. (For more on Quetelet's background, see Ackerknecht, 1952.) This reification of averages seemed like an improvement on censuses and earlier notions of *Statistik*, closely tied to the needs of the European state. Participants at the 1937 Woods Hole Conference on Problems of Aging copied this Queteletian tradition of social statistics almost verbatim. We argue that this was an unfortunate choice, an ahistorical reading of the history of statistics. Gerontology's founders introduced an unconformity into normative studies of human aging that has persisted to the present. To understand how this happened, we start by reviewing developments at the beginning of the century.

"THE ALTERNATIVE TO ART WAS ARITHMETIC"

Harvard historian, newspaper correspondent, reformer, editor, and world traveler, Henry Adams (1918/1961) spent much of his maturity trying to explain physical chaos and societal demise in terms of scientific laws of nature. For explanations, Adams turned to physics, geology, and statistics. Such a line of inquiry befitted his 19th-century temperament. Born in 1838, three years after Adolphe Quetelet published his two-volume *Sur l'homme et le developpement de ses fac-*

ultes, ou essai de physique sociale, Adams died in 1918, 4 years after the first American geriatrics textbook was published. Henry Adams's views on statistical reasoning, which took shape prior to gerontology's emergence as a field of inquiry, help to frame the intellectual context in which U.S. pioneers of aging research did their work.

Statistics, Adams discovered, were everywhere to be found. "Numeracy" became increasingly prevalent in 19th-century America. Data were collected in Yankee factories, Southern plantations, and scientific laboratories across the country. Since 1790, the government had been generating data and censuses to keep track of people, goods, and trends (Alonso & Starr, 1987; Cohen, 1982; Conk, 1980). But not all statistics were construed in the same way. In the 18th century, "statistics" meant tabulations of interest to the state: vital statistics such as birth, marriages, and deaths, as well as conventional summaries of the political economy (goods grown, exported, imported; the price of wheat; the state of the exchequer). Statistical methods for keeping track of people and other entities of concern to the state are mentioned in the Bible (Duncan, 1984). John Graunt and William Petty, in the 17th century, applied sampled counts to questions of health and mortality. Bills of mortality were gathered in the late 18th century as evidence for debates over Malthus's and Condorcet's views of the relationship between political health and physical salubrity (Achenbaum, 1978; Rosen, 1952, 1953). In contrast, measurements in geodesy and astronomy, which culminated in the new technique of least-squares, were not designated as "statistics" but rather as a "calculus of observation," a technology of measurement precision (Stigler, 1986). This strand of statistical reasoning had a history independent of the other.

Adolphe Quetelet, descendent of Comte and the physiocrats, was the first to claim that the theory of errors developed for astronomy and geodesy by Gauss and Lagrange by the turn of the 19th century had something to do with understanding human phenomena.[2] The statistical techniques, he felt, could be transferred from the one domain to the other. Thus, Quetelet conflated two statistical traditions into his notion of a unified science, "social physics."

Quetelet's interest in social physics derived from his census work and his collaborations with physicians on questions of public hygiene. If "results of observation can be expressed numerically," then their causes could be understood. Probing human development with statistical methods, Quetelet (1835/1969) declared, should be analogous to studying phenomena in physics or astronomy: One looked for regularities in patterns. "Man is born, grows up, and dies, according to certain laws which have never been properly investigated," he opined in the opening sentence of *A Treatise on Man*. After gathering a variety of physical, intellectual, and social measures from a large number of people at different ages, Quetelet then tried to "determine the average man, amongst different nations, both physical and moral" (p. 9).

This line of reasoning—the pursuit of "l'homme moyen" about whom observed data are normally distributed—was subsequently proved to be fatally flawed in its application to biological phenomena. Among those who challenged the study of unusual distributions by their means—the methodological foundation of "social physics"—were Francis Galton (1822–1911), Karl Pearson (1857–1936), and Sewall Wright (1889–1988). The main line of modern biometrics is founded in direct contradiction to Quetelet's principal reliance on "averages" in explaining social phenomena, a reliance that encapsulates a very serious error in the philosophy of measurement. Techniques of social statistics, according to biometricians, cannot describe true population variation at all; for instance, averages by chronological age wholly beg the problem of reification of "aging," the very phenomenon whose causes and effects we wish to pursue. This is not the place to go into the debate between Quetelet and his later critics in any detail. Yet the crux of the disagreement must be summarized.

Quetelet presumed that distributions of observables about an average in the empirical social sciences were exactly analogous to distributions of physical measurements about a "true value" in the astronomical sciences. There was no such construct as individual variation, only error about the central tendency. In the course of his discovery of biometrical regression, Francis Galton, with the aid of an ingenious analogue device (the quincunx), first noticed that normally distributed data, such as characterize biological measurements of populations, can arise from normal deviations or "errors," not about the population mean but about a multiple less than unity of the appropriate parental score as *it* deviates from the mean. Having observed this phenomenon (which turned out to be universal in biology), Galton left it to others to work into the flexible, general method we know as modern biometrical statistics. In this specialty, "true values" are represented by estimated *factor scores* combining redundantly measured data.

Causation in this context is borne in the interpretation of *path coefficients*, direct contributions of the value of one variable to the expected value of another, first estimated a century ago by F. Y. Edgeworth's method of multiple regression (Stigler, 1986). When biologists discovered the phenomenon of regression in the context of heredity, the social statistician Udny Yule borrowed that idea in 1894 as a justification for averaging ratios of deviations into what are now called "regression coefficients" in "structural equation models." But closing even this escape route, in the early to middle 20th century, the population geneticist Sewall Wright encouraged a radical reformulation of biometric techniques. The reformulation replaced the method of averaging over cases by a much more meaningful arithmetic averaging over variables. The refutation of Quetelet's method in most camps was judged complete. Both the controversy over Quetelet and the existence of alternative models of statistical reasoning seem to have been ignored or overlooked by the founders of modern gerontology.

"METHODS FOR APPLYING
THE PLASTERS OF FACTS"

On the eve of the 1937 Woods Hole Conference on Problems of Aging, those who were to shape the formation of gerontology in the United States thus actually had plenty of latitude in defining the scope of the "problem of aging" and establishing criteria for "scientific" techniques. Methodological pluralism predates the modern era. And it appears that the founders of gerontology tried to position themselves in the mainstream of contemporary scientific orientations and methods. In retrospect, however, they seem to have failed: the methods they adopted "for applying the plasters of facts" resembled a Queteletian mode of analysis.

In his introduction to Cowdry's *Problems of Ageing*, which brought together papers first presented at Woods Hole, John Dewey (1939) stressed that old age was a *"problem . . .* having no precedent in human history." A multidisciplinary perspective was essential: "Biological processes are at the roots of the problems . . . but the biological processes take place in economic, political and cultural contexts" (p. xxvi). If insights from different perspectives were necessary to appreciate the multifaceted features of aging, then many of gerontology's architects felt that some methodological common ground had to be found, but they invoked the less appropriate sense of statistics. To Lawrence K. Frank, an officer of the Macy Foundation, the role of statistics was not the logic of measurement; it was instead to average many bits of data into valid patterns.

Frank's positivist faith complements Quetelet's thinking. Both wanted to grasp the "total" picture, a task facilitated if data could be incorporated from one field to another. But it is worth recalling that before gerontologists achieved professional credibility, they had to dispel a legacy of suspicion in popular and scientific circles. Quackery was rampant: all sorts of palliatives for the woes of old age were for sale (on the relationship of quackery and American science, see Achenbaum, 1978; Burnham, 1987; Haber, 1983; Sorokin, 1956). Though medicine had yet to define a "problem" or disease of advancing years that physicians could cure, in the 1930s many believed that science would soon lead to a significant breakthrough. Thus, they made a conscientious effort to get their facts right. A premium was to be placed on methodological rigor. That way, gerontologic inquiry could have a solid foundation.

Biomedical investigators dominated efforts to give both coherence and weight to the field during the early years. Their methods captured part of a biomedical tradition but not the biometric spirit. The distinction is critical even outside the context of experiment. For instance, the format of choice was that found in biomedical "scientific" journals. Half of the authors of the first 18 investigations in biology published in the *Journal of Gerontology* were associated with three labs devoted to long-range research programs on aging ("Can Research on Aging Flourish?" 1948). Each of these articles rested on phenomena measured at two or more points in time. Papers submitted by physicians on their clinical studies were presented in a similar way. As if to deflect the charge that their work was "soft," social scientists replicated biomedical conventions.[3]

Yet for all of their concern for rigor, pioneers in gerontology had difficulty identifying a statistical approach appropriate for their multifaceted "problem." A fundamental confusion of statistical reasoning in the field through this formative period can be discerned in the contrasting views of two founders. Both James E. Birren and Nathan W. Shock considered themselves basic scientists who took measurement seriously. The former, a psychologist, trained in the lab of the latter, a physiologist.[4]

In his introduction to the *Handbook of Aging and the Individual*, Birren (1959, p. 3) stated that "in scientific discourse the core meaning of 'aging' implies a determinate chain of events occupying a significant portion of the life-span after maturity." Whereas most researchers explained aging "postdictively by statistical relations," Birren observed that some viewed "aging" as a dependent variable, and others, as independent. There was no question, however, that "chronological age is one of the most useful single items of information about an individual if not the *most* useful." Though indubitably "information," however, age per se cannot play any role in explaining a "determinate chain of events" under study. Chronological age is not an "event." It merely indexes events. In fact, what is most surprising about the study of aging is the manner in which chronological age *fails* to predict "determinate chains of events." We expand on this point in our final section. To the extent that aging shows "dynamics," then by Birren's own criterion, his *"most* useful" measure seems unusable for scientific purposes, despite his claims.

Shock's (1961a) handling of these issues differs from Birren's in several ways. Rather than focusing primarily on late-life manifestations, Shock viewed aging as a "process which goes on throughout the life span of the individual." Instead of highlighting the ambiguity inherent in a cross-disciplinary enterprise of treating aging as either an independent or dependent variable, Shock limited his focus: "The basic biological fact of aging is that the probability of death increases with age in a definite mathematical relationship" (p. 654). (In this form the statement is not particularly conducive to advancing biological study, as we shall argue below.) In biogerontology, Shock claimed, "examination of average curves brings to light a number of significant generalizations." Shock put more faith in averages than did Birren, who had long been curious about possible patterns in variance. Shock expected to find decrements, whereas Birren looked for more complex oscillations and interactions. Still, Shock (1961b) was more inclined than Birren to make biological science the core of gerontology:

> Because of wide individual differences in most measurements, average values based on different subjects in each age decade may conceal what is happening in an individual. It is obviously impossible to know what a group of 60-year-olds was like at age 40. Similarly, observations on a group of 40-year-olds may be biased because they include individuals who will die before the group reaches the age of 60. The only solution to this dilemma is to obtain repeated measurements on the same individual as he ages. (p. 16)

The fatal flaw in Shock's position is subtler than Birren's conundrum: it is the Queteletian assumption that averages by a clock calibrated to the earth's rotation are informative about processes not at all driven by that rotation. The average over a set of 65-year-olds is no different, in principle, from one of Quetelet's averages for "Frenchmen." To explicate this problem, and suggest a solution, it is necessary to critique "aging" from a modern biometrical perspective. (For more on Shock's views, see Baker & Achenbaum, in press.)

"ONE'S AVERAGES PROJECTED THEMSELVES AS LAWS INTO THE FUTURE. . . . THE METHOD DID NOT RESULT IN FAITH"

In many particulars, processes of aging do not proceed evenly with respect to the calendar. Some physiological subsystems, even in the health elderly, deteriorate smoothly over the years (in some instances, since birth). Most observed physiological change is episodic, associated with diseases or destructive feedback loops consequent on earlier deterioration. Even chronic diseases change their manifestations sporadically rather than smoothly, as the aging organism finally ceases to struggle with one or another particular form of pain or finds a previously attainable physiological equilibrium to have retreated out of reach. Homeostatic equilibria do not occur like clockwork. Even more is psychological health a jagged adaptation to function of transitional events. Whether or not the consequences of most of these are negative—transitions to widow- or widowhood, retirement, or chronic disability outweigh remarriages, honors, wisdom, active grandparenting, or entry into volunteer careers after retirement— there is nevertheless a major difference between physiological and psychological aging. Physiological aging so much more predictably entails deterioration.

In the language of modern multivariate statistical analysis, gerontological age is then a *latent variable*, a summary of a great diversity of variously correlated changes in physiology and psychology. It will prove convenient for us to tease apart the diverse scientific strategies of gerontology in terms of the manner in which they study age. In particular, we often pay close attention to *aging*, which is the change of this latent *gerontological age* with respect to chronological age (for more formal definitions, see the Appendix). Properly speaking, *neither age nor aging is observable*; instead, they are *estimated* by a joint consideration of all of their consequences.[5] The reader having a background in modern multivariate statistical analysis or psychometric factor analysis might wish to think of aging, in this sense, as analogous to a *factor* underlying the observed patterns of covariation of all of the indicators—"outcome measures"—of a gerontological study. In both factor analysis and latent variable analysis, observed measurements are combined into scores according to *weights* computed statistically. In ordinary factor analysis, observable outcomes are weighted by the extent to which each "explains" the other outcomes (as calibrated by the magnitude of regression coefficients (see the Appendix). In contrast, the latent variable to be called gerontological age instead weights the outcomes by the extent to which they are explicable separately by trends over calendar age.

At root, aging must be modeled as an individually variable process of physiological change, accompanied and modulated by various adjustments and psychosocial compensations. Then it needs to be *measured* individual by individual. *Calendar age—years elapsed since birth—is* inappropriate *as an "independent variable" for studies of normal aging.* It is far too error-prone a measure of the process we seek to adumbrate. The error committed by using calendar age as a proxy for amount of aging is similar to that which would be committed if one studied the maturation of children by correlating IQ scores, attitudes, and the like against physical height. Just as height is a poor measure for a child's developmental age, so too calendar age is a poor measure of gerontological age.

Those who have carried out studies of "normal aging" would find the preceding paragraphs unobjectionable. Rationales for longitudinal analyses of "normal aging" invariably emphasize what investigators often call the "dynamics" of aging: individual differences in the patterns of physiological decline or psychosocial change and the dependence of these patterns on social context and past history. But once such principles arc saluted, they tend to be ignored in operationalizing the research design. The fallacy of the Queteletian approach to aging, which confuses calendar age with a biological cause to be treated biometrically, is clear in reviewing any large-scale study of "normative aging." For illustrative purposes, we discuss here why results from the Duke Longitudinal Study do not really explain processes of aging. To put it bluntly, the study relies too heavily on the application of political and administrative statistics rather than employing appropriate biometric methods.

Our objections are epistemological, not statistical. The study is well done in terms of longitudinal design and sampling. But the tables and figures seem to concentrate on the effect of elapsed years since birth as if somehow that encapsulated the myriad of status measures and physiological markers that change over time in the course of aging.

"The Duke Longitudinal Study of Aging was initiated to investigate processes of aging," notes Erdman Palmore (1970) in his précis of 49 reports from the Duke Longitudinal Study over the period from 1955 through 1969. "The focus has been on the generation of hypotheses" (pp. 4–5). Later we are assured that "the focus of the research is on the *processes* of change as well as on the changes commonly observed among elderly subjects" (p. 18). But throughout the rest of the volume, the operational definition of "normal aging," the title of the volume, goes begging: there is no discussion of the "processes" of aging at all. In the table of contents, the title of report after report invokes phrases such as "the elderly," "the aged," those "senescent," or "older persons." In every chapter, "age groups" are in ranges of years; there is never any attempt to identify the young 65-year-old or the senescent 50-year-old, although the detection and etiology of such cases were to be among the principal research goals.

Such an analysis, even when formally longitudinal in design, is really a "census" in a Queteletian sense of the term, echoing early enumerations done by governments. These summary tabulations of subject characteristics by calendar age are useful to those who might wish to estimate the demand for a new welfare service or the expected effects upon the fisc of changes in cohort demographics. The unfortunate concentration upon "the aged" as an ostensibly discrete group seems most evident in the "systematic summary" of the entire Duke study in the form of 48 "tentative hypotheses" (Palmore, 1970, pp. 419–422). Most of the findings deal with "the aged," or "half the aged," or "most aged," or the "normal aged."[6] Only two of the "summary findings" subdivide "the aged" even by age: those dealing with the frequency of male sexual activity. Otherwise, the summary flatly fails to indicate how to estimate the extent of aging for a particular subject or how to predict future status from measures of the present state. That estimations and predictions are missing from these "summary findings" (e.g., "Most aged have some skin problem" or "Most of the aged have some mild impairment of memory of mild intellectual impairment") illustrates in yet another way an attempt to draw an affinity to social issues that are independent of biological issues. Their omission leaves us with a collection of social indicators, no different in its logic from the percentage of households with indoor plumbing, by age of owner and, let us say, county.

The way evidence is presented in the main text does little to allay this impression. Not surprisingly, most of the many tables and charts in this volume mention calendar age but mainly as a grouping variable, arbitrarily regroupable from study to study. The least effective of these groupings is the contrast of "elderly" versus "young," which probably reveals more about American generational politics than about any biologically based gerontology. Such "groups" could not possibly be homogeneous for outcome variables of any interest. Other subdivisions of age are attempted as well: older or younger than 70, for instance, or more finely broken out by 10-year, 5-year, 3-year, or 6-year intervals.

This approach to "gerontology" has been traduced by the syllable "stat" in "statistics." Of course, no other categorization—ethnicity, gender, race—would be any better for the purposes of a scientific gerontology. It is gerontological age, not calendar age, that has the methodological potential to explain how a collection of physiological and psychosocial indicators cohere in the study of growth, development, and senescence. To omit all attempts at measuring this preeminent explanatory construct vitiates all of the rhetoric of "processes" and "individual differences" in the introductions to reports like this one.

Far fewer are the cross-classifications of outcome measures by any other indicator of aging than years since birth. For a handful of other scores of physiological deterioration—hypertension, EEG anomalies, sensorium deficits, "age feeling," arteriosclerosis, and cardiovascular disease—there is one analysis each, not cross-classified, however, by actual age. These variables are not without interest; indeed, a biometric secondary analysis of data may yet yield the sort of explanatory models we want. But in their present form, each is dependent upon such a great variety of factors in addition to aging—life-style, genetics, history of illnesses, and the like—that the extent to which each serves as proxy for gerontological age is quite modest. The appropriate analysis would be to aggregate these and dozens of others into a summary indicator of "imputed age." This would be precisely the function of the notion of gerontological age as a latent variable.

That this should be the issue is not wholly unexpected. In a chapter in the first edition of the *Handbook of Aging and the Social Sciences*, George Maddox and James Wiley (1976), key participants in the Duke project, acknowledge the problem of measuring aging as follows: "A consensus now exists that age is a very imprecise concept which has distinct biological, psychological, and social components. These components simply do not correlate in a precise way, and this fact must be taken into account in research on aging" (p. 28). So far, so good. But they recommend no procedures, conceptual or statistical, for making this "very imprecise concept" any less imprecise. In their principal statistical model, the only measure of age specified is chronological age. Beyond this, all other determinants of their measured outcomes are explicitly "environmental." Some of the effects of environment on the organism are modeled as instantaneous or concurrent, whereas others are lagged, especially those leading to the onset of chronic disease or frailty. Nevertheless, whereas the text acknowledges that different individuals may be more or less vulnerable to "proximal environmental influences," the variable calibrating this interaction is, once again, chronological age.[7]

The Duke investigators were not alone in failing to measure aging. The 1984 summary publication *Normal Human Aging: The Baltimore Longitudinal Study of Aging*, edited by Nathan Shock, commits exactly the same biometric fallacy. In an appendix, James Schlesselman inadvertently reveals how this study might have gone astray:

> To focus discussion, I will assume that the major goals of a longitudinal investigation include:
> (a) determining means and average rates of change on a number of variables for designated age groups, and detecting differences among these age groups;
> (b) determining individual levels and rates of change in the study participants, and characterizing the magnitude of individual differences. (p. 354)

This is unobjectionable as long as these "individual levels and rates of change" are not aggregated over the age groups whose lability is the essence of those "individual differences." As Schlesselman notes, "one may be interested in groups other than those based upon age. For example, one may have a multiple crossed-classification [sic] based upon various clinical, sociological, and treatment factors." But no such "interests" are evident in the summary volume from which this quotation is taken. That is, there is no acknowledgment anywhere that gerontological age is anything other than calendar age, a quantity measured (without error) in units of years. From such designs it is impossible to inquire as to the the determinants of individual variation in the rate of change of gerontological age; no possibility of reliable individual prediction, let alone intervention, is made accessible by such analyses.

To summarize, neither of the two best-known longitudinal studies of aging attempted to find out *just how aged their subjects were*, how fast they were aging per year, what determines that rate, and what our society might do, either clinically or societally, to slow it down. (We will talk about a third study in the last section of this chapter.) Their failure to model aging as a process is especially regrettable inasmuch as *no additional data would have been required*, only more thoughtful methodological arguments and a different mode of statistical analysis.

"NOTHING CAME OUT AS IT SHOULD"

The main fact about research on aging, to use Adams's (1918/1961) words, is indeed that "nothing [comes] out as it should." Longitudinal studies conducted thus far provide evidence for believing that there are degrees and rates of aging in persons of the same calendar age.

For only a few of us does being 65 "come out as it should"; the rest of us, in the course of our 60s and beyond, will be functionally (much) older or younger than our driver's license or Social Security records show. Gerontologists should concentrate their attention on describing and explaining individual differences in a way that observed measures—from sexuality to frailty—that depend on calendar age cannot measure. Conceptually, how can we manage this, using only the data of the standard longitudinal archives?

Suppose we have a collection of reliably measured biomedical variables and their average values for some population classified by chronological age—perhaps derived from the very tables compiled for the Duke and National Institute of Aging (NIA) longitudinal studies. That is, every subject has a calendar age and a measurement for most of the biomedical indicators at each age. Now, of course, there are individual differences across these variables, otherwise there would be simply no point in measuring more than one person per age prior to the tabulations. But we know more than that these measurements vary; *we know that they vary systematically over age*. The averages *must* change over time. If the typical 50-year-old's value of a cardiac output score, let us say, were the same as the typical value for people aged 51, 52, . . . , 70 as well, then it would make no sense to state that a particular 70-year-old "has the heart of a 50-year-old." We would simply say that he has the heart typical of his age, and that would be the end of it. So the measurements that contribute to a study of aging per se must show systematic trends (increases or decreases) over age if they are to be of any use to a scientific gerontology at all.

Inasmuch as these trends are ubiquitous, it is possible to reverse the logic of the longitudinal studies we have so sharply criticized, all the while continuing to eploit with full efficiency the formation from their marvelous data archives. Those studies consider all measurements to be a function of age and characterize individuals by their deviations from the values typical for their age. Using the same data, *we propose instead that "age" be considered the object of measurement*. The individual's "atypicality" is no longer the deviation of his cardiac output, let us say, from the output typical of his age but the deviation of his age from the age for which his output is the average (or expected) output.

Pursuing this simple logic just one small step further, we arrive at a workable criterion for gerontological age (GA).[8] It should be considered the *average* (in a slightly modified sense, see below) of the "equivalent ages" corresponding to all of the variables measured in a study. Thus, for example, if one subject seen in 1985 has the bones of a 70-year-old (a bone age of 70) and the heart of a 60-year-old (a cardiac age of 60), and if these are the only physiological features measured, then her GA is 65 years, regardless of when she was born. If in 1986 this same subject has a GA of 70, then she aged at the rate of 5 years per year over the 1-year interval between clinical visits. Although the "ideal" 60-, 65-, or 70-year-old with respect to whom this patient is being matched is a function of sampling frame, the dependence of these rates of change upon sampling can be expected to be much less than the dependence of the means themselves, and the nature of the covariances of aging with exogenous factors (such as nutrition) is virtually independent of the choice of the reference population. Therefore, searching for patterns in senescence—what causes them? what happens next?—would be one feasible concern of a scientific gerontology. But first the subject of the patterns must be reified and plotted quantitatively, meaning that a variable serving for GA must be constructed case by case, year by year. Calendar age, a criterion of great importance in bureaucratic studies of aging, cannot capture the salient variations in developmental processes.

We do not mean to imply that such averages are unequivocal. Indeed, names such as "bone age" and "cardiac age" casually presume the existence of *multiple* potential scales of aging, as they are more or less specific to anatomical or functional subsystems. Their declines may be subject to acceleration by different exogenous causes and will manifest a great diversity of synchronous and diachronous correlations. As in factor analysis, so in latent variable analysis a list of attributes (such as all of the alternative indicators of GA) have to be decomposed into more than one "dimension" whenever the patterns by which calendar age fails to predict the indicators severally are found themselves to be correlated. Note, too, that the biometric logic invoked here does not force gerontologists to limit "scientific" attention to biomedical matters. The number of dimensions of this latent variable will surely vary according to the biological, psychological, and social context of a particular gerontological study.[9]

One further refinement will be useful. Statisticians know that some measurements are very much more precise than others. We can measure weight, for instance, much more accurately than we can measure blood pressure or cognitive function. Analogously, in the many different "equivalent ages" that we are combining into the one index of GA, some of the components of age are more precisely measured than others. In the interests of statistical efficiency, our arithmetic should somehow give more weight to the "ages" that are more precisely measured. Consider two variables, for instance, both contributing to GA. Suppose each has a sample range from 5 to 15 (perhaps they are cognitive scores). One of them changes from mean 12 at age 50 to mean 8 at age 70, and the other changes from mean 11 at age 50 to mean 9 at age 70—half as much decline per year. Intuitively, it seems that we learn less about GA from the second variable than from the first: in fact, in some sense it ought to be just half as informative about age. (In the limit, if the mean "changed" from 10 at age 50 to 10 at age 70, we would have learned nothing at all about age from this measure.) In any formula for GA, then, the separate "equivalent ages" ought to enter in proportion to this "precision" of their contribution to GA, which is actually the precision of the effect of calendar age upon *them*. The appropriate statistical maneuver is the *weighted* average. If this were only a study of 50-to-70-year-olds, each component of GA (i.e., the age "equivalent" to each measurement) should be taken proportional to the magnitude of that 50-to-70 difference divided by a suitable measure of the full range of the measurement in question. It turns out that the weight we should be using in the conventional *regression coefficient* of calendar age upon the measurements. This closes a circle with respect to the standard gerontological approaches, which use instead the regression coefficients of the measurements separately upon calendar age but don't add anything up and so cannot ever estimate GA. Note, too, that we have analytically severed our reliance on data derived solely from chronological age.

This formula—GA as a weighted average—is much less important than the conceptual strategy it signifies. To fulfill the express purpose of all of the standard longitudinal studies, we have turned the statistical strategy shared with Quetelet upon its head: not (calendar) age as a predictor of observed biomedical data but the combination of observed biomedical data into an estimator of a useful (gerontological) age. The standard methods use calendar age to "predict" individual outcomes, but they cannot handle individual differences in aging, no matter how fervently they express their devotion to the idea of studying "dynamics." By comparison, the procedure we have sketched above emphasizes the one crucial indicator for which individual differences are the most important—gerontological age—and computes it with the greatest possible precision.

Subsequent investigations may then straightforwardly consider effects upon this crucial central variable. What does the cessation of smoking do to the rate of change of GA? What of remarriage upon the death of a spouse? As it happens, the formula for GA is that for which, on the model of a dominant single dynamic roughly synchronized with age, these subsequent questions—the true concern of the consumers of findings in gerontology—are analyzed as powerfully as possible. Our formula for GA maximizes the observable covariance between the estimate of GA and its contingent causes or effects.[10]

"THEY SHOULD HAVE REACHED CERTAINTY, BUT THEY TALKED LIKE OTHER MEN WHO KNOW LESS"

It is not enough to point out the inadequacy of chronological age as a signpost of biological processes of aging, or to propose an alternative measure, gerontological age. If we are to demonstrate how scientific measurement can advance critical gerontology, then we must be prepared to critique our own analysis. We begin by acknowledging that we are not the first to try to get beyond Queteletian "social physics" in order to measure aging in a great variety of physiological subsystems.

For nearly 50 years, researchers have questioned whether chronological age is an appropriate indicator of physical aging. In the midst of World War II, for instance, Ross McFarland (1973) challenged the prevailing notion that workers past their prime became obsolescent.[11] In a 1951 paper, Dr. I. M. Murray constructed functional measures of aging by combining observations according to several criteria: vision, hearing, blood pressure, and muscle force. At the end of the decade, Clark Tibbitts (1960) differentiated among biological, psychological, situational, and behavioral processes, though he did not provide the algebra necessary to operationalize his construct.[12] Explorations of functional age were also conducted across the Atlantic. From 1959 to 1963, Alastair Heron and Sheila Chown (1967) studied 300 men and 240 women between the ages of 20 and 80. Reporting that there were critical changes in functional capacities *within* humans, the pair concluded that aging was not a unitary process: "functional age must be measured anew for each task in which the investigator is interested, and this age must depend upon pure measures of certain physical and psychological functions" (p. 140). Once again, however, more effort was paid to making a case for an alternative to chronological age for measuring aging than to developing the actual algebra of measurement.

Perhaps the most ambitious early effort to construct a measure of biological aging independent of chronological age came in the course of the Normative Aging Study (NAS) underwritten by the Veterans Administration. About 2,000 male veterans were enrolled for recurring examinations designed to investigate the relationship between normal aging and the natural history of chronic diseases such as diabetes, emphysema, and hypertension. "We were looking for a unifying concept which would enable the measurement of aging in its various aspects, and the relative rates of age change, both across these areas and over the lifespan. . . . The concept of functional age refers to a measure of age other than the chronological" (Bell, 1972, p. 145). Rather than focusing on the number of years since a subject's birth, as the notion of gerontological age implies, the NAS chose instead to gauge proximity to death. In our opinion, this is not the appropriate way to construct statistics to measure gerontological age. Six functional ages were developed: (1) biological assays of blood serum and urine; (2) auditory functioning; (3) anthropometric descriptions; (4) verbal, perceptual, and motor abilities; (5) personality; and (6) life-style. (This last dimension was poorly operationalized.) "The aim of statistical analysis of longitudinal data will be to find clusters of variables which appear to change together and which therefore represent a subsystem" (Dempster, 1972, p. 196). Here too we disagree with the NAS team: their approach would not yield predictions of subsystem-specific rates of aging.

In short, researchers associated with the NAS failed to develop a mathematical model sufficient to represent their notion of "functional" age. The problem, as noted above, was partly methodological. In addition, the group did not address the critical question of whether rates of aging were uniform across different systems. This led to a conceptual issue. Although the NAS did not conflate old age and disease, its concern with time to death as a criterion of functional age made it impossible to disentangle risk factors (like smoking) from "normal" declines in vital capacity, which might have yielded a (composite) unitary rate of aging (Costa & McCrae, 1985).

Unfortunately, few still search for alternatives to chronological age as a measure of biological aging. The concept of "functional age" merits only three paragraphs in the 890-page *Encyclopedia of Aging* (1987). "The construct appears to have little practical utility for research. As an overall summary, chronological age, with all of its problems, is as useful a measure as functional age," concludes Duke's Ilene C. Siegler (1987), who has published in this area. "However, as an early understood construct with broad popular appeal, functional age helps to illustrate the importance of understanding that various abilities age at different rates" (pp. 264–265). Unless we misread her intent, Siegler trivializes the importance of scientific measurement. Surely, she intends to make more than a concession to methodological relativism, given the prevailing belief among gerontologists that chronological age is a poor predictor of aging. Is no alternative possible? Or does she think chronological age *is* an adequate index?

If the deficiencies of chronological age as a measure of aging processes are recognized, then we must go "beyond method" to see that even our modest, present-day knowledge of gerontology demands greater attention to scientific measurement. Reconsider Shock's (1961) comment that increases in the probability of death with age is "the basic biological fact of aging." But for it to be a "basic biological fact," we must turn age into a biological entity. This impulse has encouraged research into biomarkers to assemble a roster of experimentally measurable biochemical titers and ultrastructural factors that express the cumulative effects of having lived in a form useful for forecasting life remaining. The purpose, stated in our terms, is to replace calendar age by a cellular-molecular index of gerontological age calibrated to predicting years until death. As the Appendix argues in more detail, we prefer an index calibrated to years since birth.

Only breakthroughs in measurement can advance our understanding of aging. As we state this, we are keenly aware that some researchers presently are developing more sophisticated techniques for measuring unidirectional physical, chemical, and biological changes that are not necessarily co-linear. Demonstrations that red blood cells of different ages can be identified on the basis of their forward light-scatter and attachment of immunoglobins reinforces our sense of aging processes at the cellular level. Laser technology for plotting changes in molecular composition through senescence enables us to collect better technical data. But advances in technology will not contribute to advances in biogerontology until an alternative is found to chronological age: This refinement in scientific measurement is the most critical.

The search for biometric techniques that capture differential rates in the dynamics of aging processes will have practical as well as theoretical consequences that are bound to be controversial. The policy implications of creating a more reliable indicator of gerontological age are manifest. Although pensions under Social Security and private plans are still linked to definitions of age 65 as the "normal" retirement age, the average set at which most workers have been retiring has been declining since the 1960s. For example, most men who retire do so before age 62, when early-retirement provisions go into effect. How might Social Security operate if people's gerontological, not chronological, age became an eligibility criterion? Or would it merely wreak havoc upon the bureaucracy? Similarly, would Daniel Callahan's (1987) proposals (in *Setting Limits*) concerning elder care be more acceptable if applied only to those whose death seems imminent, rather than to all people who survive past a certain age?

Gerontologists need not replace wholesale one measure (chronological age, which *is* useful in certain contexts) with a new concept. But they must get beyond the fallacy that chronological age is indeed sufficient for all of their purposes. Although we can appreciate why gerontology's pioneers might have found Quetelet's "social physics" appealing, our review indicates that scholars in other disciplines had repudiated Quetelet's methods and assumptions long before gerontology gained acceptance in scientific circles. Still, positive remedies are at hand. "In general, evaluation of any activity is best accomplished by multiple, external, independent, and repetitive analysis," recommends Aaron Wildavsky (1979, p. 172). "The more alternatives the market allows individuals to collectively value, the more information results." We propose that *all* researchers in aging consider using biometric techniques in order to capture differential rates in the dynamic processes of aging. The field must be enriched by getting back to the basics of measurement.

NOTES

[1] This essay is the first of two reviewing the methodological foundations of gerontology as currently practiced. Because the companion piece will deal with measurement issues in "social" or "behavioral" gerontology, we will confine our attention here mainly to trends in the biomedical arena.

[2] For general references to the following material, consult Stigler (1986), Porter (1986), or Mackenzie (1981). The reader should be warned that we are more critical of Quetelet and his legatees than are these sources.

[3] The most frequently cited social science papers tended to be highly statistical in nature: see, for example, "The correlation of intelligence scores and chronological age from early to late maturity," a 1932 article by Catharine and Walter R. Miles. Social scientists who engaged in surveys of older people's attitudes took pains to demonstrate the purported "validity" of their measures; see Havighurst (1951).

[4] The idea of comparing Shock's and Birren's work comes from Michel Philibert (1982).

[5] This nonobservability is a characteristic of most underlying explanatory constructs throughout the biological and social sciences. See Fred L. Bookstein (1982).

[6] We are not concerned in this critique with the conceptualization of "normal" in this style of research. A design limited to those who remain free of chronic diseases as they age clearly induces serious biases of its own, but

as those problems are not related to the more fundamental difficulties of failing to quantify the actual object of research, the quantitative representation of "aging," we reserve discussion of them for another essay.

[7] That the recommended scheme of analysis is very carefully detailed in an appendix to their chapter does not vitiate the literal preposterousness of its models as a matter of quantitative inference: the term that should appear at the end of the equation, "aging," instead appears at the beginning, as "age." The text associated with the full model, in their appendix, again genuflects to the possibility of individual variability; but again, the printed equations omit any terms for individual differences in rates of aging, so there remains no possibility whatever of validly measuring gerontological age. We know, and the authors agree, that calendar age is not the correctly calibrated explanatory variable—thus we know that *all* of the statistical models of the Duke study are systematically misleading, no matter the number of lags over which the "past environment" variable is distributed. In other words, there is nothing quantitative to be explained by an gerontological theory in the entire Duke project corpus.

[8] For a working algebraic definition of this term and others used in this section, see the Appendix.

[9] For instance, *The Ballad of Narayama*, a superb Japanese film of the 1980s, demonstrates a mixed social-biological approach to aging consistent with a one-dimensional definition. The film treats a social system in which all of the observable indicators of aging are forcibly made consistent, by artificial production of the usual signs (loss of teeth, etc.) as necessary, so that the decision that a particular individual is "aged" and thus ought to be left to die can be made without any cultural ambiguity. The film deals explicitly with the problem of presuming that a universal criterion of aging can be measured to yield uniform averages, the very subject we believe should be the core concern of a scientific gerontology.

[10] The technique in this form may be traced back to the early work of Sewall Wright, *Morphometrics in evolutionary biology: The geometry of size and shape change, with examples of fishes*. Academy of Natural Sciences of Philadelphia. For a discussion of its history, see chapter 4 of Fred L. Bookstein, B. Chernoff, R. Elder, J. Humphries, G. Smith, and R. Strauss (1985).

[11] For a different formulation of the same issue but one that eschews biological criteria altogether, see Robert C. Atchley and Linda K. George (1973) and Robert Kastenbaum, Valerie Dubin, Paul Sabatini, and Steven Artt (1972).

[12] A year earlier James Birren (1959) proposed a tripartite division (biological, psychological, and social). Neither man offered a way to operationalize these "abstract" concepts, however.

REFERENCES

Achenbaum, W. A. (1978). *Old age in the new land.* Baltimore: Johns Hopkins University Press.

Ackerknecht, E. (1952). Villerme and Quetelet. *Bulletin of the History of Medicine, 26,* 317–329.

Adams, H. (1961). *The education of Henry Adams.* Boston: Houghton Mifflin. (Original work published 1918)

Atchley, R. C., & George, L. K. (1973). Symptomatic measurement of age. *Gerontologist, 13,* 332–336.

Alonso W., & Starr, P. (Eds.). (1987). *The politics of numbers.* New York: Russell Sage Foundation.

Baker, G. T., III, & Achenbaum, W. A. (in press). A critical, historical analysis of developments in biogerontology. *Experimental Gerontology.*

Bell, B. (1972). Significance of functional age for interdisciplinary and longitudinal research in aging. *Aging and Human Development, 3,* 145–148.

Birren, J. E. (1959). Principles of research on aging. In J. E. Birren (Ed.), *Handbook of aging and the individual* (pp. 18–20). Chicago: University of Chicago Press.

Birren, J. E. (1986). The process of aging. In A. Pifer & L. Bronte (Eds.), *Our aging society* (pp. 263–281). New York: W. W. Norton.

Bookstein, F. L. (1982). Discussion: Modeling and method. In H. Wold & K. Joreskog (Eds.), *Systems under indirect observation: Causality, structure, prediction* (vol. 2, pp. 317–321). Amsterdam, North-Holland: Elsevier.

Bookstein, F. L. (1986). The elements of latent variable models: A cautionary lecture. In M. E. Lamb (Ed.), *Advances in developmental psychology* (vol. 4, pp. 240–230). Hillsdale, NJ: Lawrence Erlbaum.

Burnham, J. (1987). *How superstition won and science lost.* New Brunswick, NJ: Rutgers University Press.

Callahan, D. (1987). *Setting limits.* New York: Simon & Schuster.

Can Research on Aging Flourish? (1948). *Journal of Gerontology, 3,* 141–142.

Cohen, P. C. (1982). *A calculating people.* Chicago: University of Chicago Press.

Conk, M. (1980). *The United States census and labor force change.* Ann Arbor, MI: UMI Research Press.

Costa, P. T., Jr., & McCrae, R. R. (1985). Concepts of functional or biological age: A critical view. In R. Andres, D. L. Bierman, & W. R. Hazzard (Eds.), *Principles of geriatric medicine* (pp. 30–37). New York: McGraw-Hill.

Dempster, A. P. (1972). Functional age and age-related measures. *Aging and Human Development, 3,* 195–196.

Dewey, J. (1939). Introduction. In E. V. Cowdry (Ed.), *Problems of ageing* (pp. xix–xvii). Baltimore: Williams & Wilkins Co.

Duncan, O. D. (1984). *Notes on social measurement: Historical and critical.* New York: Russell Sage Foundation.

Edelman, C. D., & Siegler, I. C. (1978). *Federal age discrimination in employment law.* Charlottesville, VA: Mitchie Co.

Haber, C. (1983). *Beyond sixty-five.* New York: Cambridge University Press.

Havighurst, R. J. (1951). Validity of the Chicago Attitude Inventory as a measure of personal adjustment in old age. *Journal of Abnormal and Social Psychology, 46,* 24–29.

Heron, A., & Chown, S. (1967). *Age and function.* Boston: Little, Brown.

Kastenbaum, R., Dabin, V., Sabatini, P., & Artt, S. (1972). "The ages of me": Toward personal and interpersonal definitions of functional aging. *Aging and Human Development, 3,* 197–212.

Mackenzie, D. A. (1981). *Statistics in Britain, 1986–1930.* Edinburgh: Edinburgh University Press.

Maddox, G., & Wiley, J. (1976). Scope, concepts, and methods in the study of aging. In R. H. Binstock & E. Shanas (Eds.), *Handbook of aging and the social sciences.* New York: Van Nostrand Reinhold.

McKee, P. L. (Ed.). (1982). *Philosophical foundations of gerontology.* New York: Human Sciences Press.

McFarland, R. (1973). The need for functional age measurements in industrial gerontology. *Industrial Gerontology,* old series; no. 19, 1–20.

Miles, C., & Miles, W. R. (1932). The correlation of intelligence scores and chronological age from early to late maturity. *American Journal of Psychology, 44,* 44–78.

Moody, H. R. (1988). Toward a critical gerontology: The contribution of the humanities to theories of aging. In J. E. Birren & V. L. Bengtson (Eds.), *Emergent theories of aging* (pp. 19–40). New York: Springer Publishing Co.

Murray, I. M. (1951). Assessment of physiologic age by combination of several criteria—vision, hearing, blood pressure, and muscle force. *Journal of Gerontology, 6,* 120–126.

Palmore, E. (Ed.). (1970). *Normal aging.* Durham, NC: Duke University Press.

Philibert, M. (1982). The phenomenological approach to images of aging. In P. L. McKee, (Ed.), *Philosophical foundations of gerontology* (pp. 252–266). New York: Human Sciences Press.

Porter, T. M. (1986). *The rise of statistical thinking.* Princeton: Princeton University Press.

Quetelet, L. A. (1969). *A treatise on man and the development of his faculties.* Gainesville, FL: Scholars' Facsimiles and Reprints. (Original work published 1835/1842)

Rosen, G. (1952). Political order and human health in Jeffersonian thought. *Bulletin of the History of Medicine, 28,* 23–36.

Rosen, G. (1953). Problems in the application of statistical analysis to questions of health, 1700–1880. *Bulletin of the History of Medicine, 29,* 27–45.

Shock, N. W. (1961a). Current concepts of the aging process. *Journal of the American Medical Association, 175,* 654.

Shock, N. W. (1961b). The role of research in solving the problems of the aged. *Gerontologist, 1,* 14–16.

Siegler, I. C. (1987). Functional age. In G. L. Maddox, L. W. Poon, G. S. Roth, I. C. Siegler, R. Steinberg, & R. J. Corsini (Eds.), *The encyclopedia of aging* (pp. 264–265). New York: Springer Publishing Co.

Sorokin, P. A. (1956). *Fads and foibles in modern sociology and related sciences.* Chicago: H. Regnery Co.

Stigler, S. M. (1986). *The history of statistics.* Cambridge, MA: Harvard University Press.

Tibbitts, C. (Ed.). (1960). Origin, scope, and fields of gerontology. In *Handbook of social gerontology* (pp. 3–26). Chicago: University of Chicago Press.
Wildavsky, A. (1979). *Speaking truth to power.* Boston: Little, Brown.

APPENDIX: A Brief Glossary of Some Concepts in Critical Gerontology

We characterize gerontology as the scientific study of aging. We insist that the words *scientific* and *aging* be taken *sensu stricto*. In this Appendix we assemble a series of definitions of which this characterization is the ultimate import. A first series of definitions will result in a characterization of "aging"; a second series, in a narrow characterization of "scientific" as it applies to quantitative data. The resulting view of gerontology is not for everyone—it is, in fact, intentionally exclusionary—but, after all, this chapter is about *critical gerontology*, and the critic ought to begin from first principles.

Numerical attribute of an *entity*. A logical primitive, a quantitative "variable." A *quantitative study* is the conscientious collection of some numerical attributes over a list of entities. Entities and attributes of a study must have been assembled as a coherent suite of indirect manifestations of underlying processes that elicit our scientific interest. For instance, the various measures of a large gerontological study ought to be diverse manifestations of "aging" among a sample of subjects chosen so as to vary substantially in their underlying gerontological age.

Regression coefficient. A formula $\beta_{Y.X} = \Sigma_j X_j Y_j / \Sigma_j X_j^2$ referring to pairs $(X_j Y_j)$ of numerical attributes over the entities j of a list (cases of a sample). Regression coefficients calibrate one numerical attribute in relation to another; they are the crucial construct for grounding quantitative scientific inferences upon nonexperimental data.

Latent variable (Bookstein, 1986). A linear combination $LV = \Sigma \beta_{Y.X_i} X_i$ of observed numerical attributes X_i (a list of "variables") each multiplied by a regression coefficient referring it to the same numerical attribute Y. The value LV of the formula, case by case, is what the attributes X_i of the list "have in common" in respect of explaining or being explained by Y.

Calendar age. Years since birth.

Gerontological age. A latent variable for which the role of Y in the definition is played by calendar age: the sum of all of the inverse regressions $\beta_{\text{CalAge}.X_i} X_i$, each of which approximates calendar age as a multiple of one of the numerical attributes X_i in a gerontological study. Gerontological age, like calendar age, is expressed in units of calendar years. To an indicator X_i that deteriorates with age corresponds a coefficient β that is negative (the lower the subject's score, the older he is expected to be); to an indicator increasing with age, a positive coefficient β; to one that is trendless over age, a value of β equal to zero (so that it has no influence on gerontological age). This formulation is modifiable to account for nonlinearities in the trends of the indicators over time or the interactions of age with environmental variables, events, and the like in their determination.

Aging. The principal explanandum of gerontology: change of gerontological age, in years, or rate of change of gerontological age with respect to calendar age, in years per year. This is the crucial entry in the present glossary.

To explain *how* the gerontologist is supposed to study aging, we need to erect another series of subordinate definitions.

(A) Measurement. A regression coefficient having an agreed-upon standard error, that is, a posterior probability distribution; a calibration of an attribute to known precision.

Quantitative theory. The assertion that two measurements based in different data repeatedly result in the same numerical value, to within their standard errors, particularly as improvements in instrumentation (broadly construed) reduce those standard errors over time. Quantitative theories have to do with the reality and precision of regression coefficients based in different data. Example: "The speed of light is a universal constant." Example: "The effect of smoking on lung cancer incidence is about X% per pack per day per decade regardless of race."

Census. Counts or totals of attributes within the cells of a classification of the entities of one's sample according to one or more other attributes.

Statistic. The quantities of a census, or any algebraic function of them, such as a regression coefficient.

Bureaucratic. Referring to censuses or their statistics.

Bureaucratic geriatrics. Compilation of statistics from a census of persons cross-classified by calendar age, for any useful governmental purpose. Compare *Scientific.*

Scientific. Having to do with investigation of the possibility of quantitative theories, usually involving a suite of numerical attributes. The ideal quantitative scientific studies are those concerned with true values of regression coefficients.

Finally, combining the two main themes of this semantic thrust, the quantification of aging and the structure of a scientific study, we arrive at the normative definition with which we began:

Gerontology. The scientific study of aging. Gerontological studies involve the subtle construction of measures of gerontological age (and its subordinate dimensions) and careful scrutiny of the independent determinants of its observed changes, including, but not limited to, the passage of time (increase in calendar age).

3

Voice and Context in a New Gerontology

Jaber F. Gubrium

In this chapter, I am concerned with how social researchers, particularly gerontologists, hear what their subjects or respondents tell them about their lives. The focus is not technical communication but the question of how to conceptualize the manner by which experience is given voice. I draw on observational and open-ended interview data from several studies of older people and aging to argue that context, not just individual thought and sentiment, gives voice to experience and that a new gerontology can be built on the understanding. The outcome is a critical empiricism that makes visible the practice and situatedness of aging.

VOICE AND CONTEXT

As in social research in general, gerontology is preoccupied with respondents' answers, not their questions. The gerontologist assesses morale or life satisfaction by asking respondents to indicate, on scales of opinion, the degree to which they are satisfied with life as a whole. Alternatively, respondents may be required to mark questionnaire items dealing with particular qualities of life as they apply to themselves (Gubrium & Lynott 1983). Growing interest in home care targets the caregiver's perception of the impairment cared for, the stress or felt burden associated with caregiving, and attitude toward institutionalization, among related variables such as the degree of social support available and the interpersonal relationship between the caregiver and the care receiver (Gubrium & Lynott, 1987). Answers feed the search for pattern or regularity in the aging experience.

Careful attention to the research process suggests that respondents may formulate answers in the course of dealing with pertinent questions of their own. While doing research on caregivers of Alzheimer's disease victims (Gubrium, 1986a), I was particularly struck by how often adult sons, daughters, elderly spouses, and significant others stated that they did not know what was going on in their lives nor how they felt about it. I had heard similar remarks and questions in other field settings, but because they now were so forceful and I was simultaneously concerned with how experience is given voice, the comments took on a special relevance.

Some of the questions and remarks referenced the afflicted family member. Caregivers wondered whether it was possible that, despite the forgetfulness and confusion, there was a semblance of sensibility underneath it all (Gubrium, 1988). In support groups, caregivers routinely asked for help in sorting through the meaning of responsibility and voicing the emotions appropriate to their situations. As an elderly caregiving spouse once tenderly noted:

> You know, it's kinda hard to face up to it, seeing his mind just going like it is. He's just not the same Harold that he used to be. He was always sharp as a tack. And you'd never find a kinder and more loving husband. [Weeps.] Oh, I'm sorry, but I just don't know what to do or think. My state of mind now . . . I'm empty. I don't know what I feel. I don't even know if I feel anything. I'm just numb. And what does he feel, the poor guy? Do you think he knows? Does he feel anything at all? Maybe you can tell me. Am I different or something? I'm really frightened . . . of not knowing how to feel. Should I be feeling something that I'm not? Or not feeling the way I seem to be? God knows, I must be a sight! Excuse me, please. (Gubrium, 1989a, p. 261)

Other field sites provided occasions for raising questions about general morale and aspects of life satisfaction. Open-ended interviews in community settings, focused on the meaning of house and home among the aged, told of a connection in respondents' questions between life satisfaction and encounters with varied images of neighborhood and residency. For example, responding to an interview item dealing with satisfaction with his neighborhood, an 80-year-old man remarked:

> I'm not sure about that one. I've been thinking a lot about that. What I've been hearing lately on TV and the radio about all the crime and other stuff makes me feel that maybe it ain't so good and I should be scared. But everyone around here says it's all exaggerated and that I don't have anything to worry about. So, what *should* I think? You tell me. You're the expert.

Needless to say, we did discuss the matter, which was inconclusive. He never did decide during the interview whether he was satisfied or dissatisfied with the neighborhood, but it was clear that he had been thinking about it. The important thing about the response was that his answer evidently was in the making. I later considered that the social organization of this answer-in-the-making might tell me a great deal about how experience is given voice.

Hazan's (1990) recently published field study of community formation in Israel can be read as suggesting that what satisfaction with one's environs mean does not simply arise from personal experience but is mediated by the categories used to assess satisfaction. A new language of community helped to form a sense of integration where there was no sentiment of belonging. The experience of "neighborhood" satisfaction (or dissatisfaction) virtually emerged with a new category—community—for evaluating residential contacts. The question of belonging depended on how one categorized the locale.

I often have heard respondents preface their remarks to me about their lives by saying, "It depends." The it-depends quality of answers indicates that respondents precede their answers with questions of their own about experiential contingencies and that answers to these questions affect what is eventually conveyed as responses to inquiries. The it-depends quality of answers implies that the respondent can voice diverse senses of the personal experiences being studied, varying by narrative context (Gubrium & Lynott, 1983). The caregiver who bothers to explain that she feels burdened only in relation to very specific bodily tasks but otherwise thinks about caregiving completely in terms of familial responsibility offers a seemingly contradictory response (Gubrium, 1991). When the caregiver explains further that these specific "burdensome" bodily tasks change in character as she thinks about it and compares her situation with others, her experience "depends" too much to be captured by a standardized methodology.

Perhaps the most intriguing concern of all is the response that one has not thought about the matter addressed in a particular research item. This does not mean that the respondent refuses to answer but only that he or she may prefer to think about the matter before an answer is formulated.

An interesting, possibly unfortunate twist on such a response occurred during my Alzheimer's disease fieldwork (Gubrium, 1986a). In exchange for free day care in a geriatric clinic for Alzheimer's disease victims, family members were asked to participate in the clinic's research program on the burdens of home care. Standard burden-of-care assessments were administered along with subjective evaluations of the patient's impairment, the caregiver's general well-being, and related topics of interest. Family members often discussed their assessment experiences in the clinic's support group for caregivers. Some, especially the newcomers, commented that they had not considered some of the issues presented in the assessments. Group discussions indicated that their answers grew out of their encounters with the assessments as much as answers represented what they had felt all along. Indeed, and this was the possibly unfortunate side of the process, several indicated that assessment items made them think something possibly was wrong with what they were doing and that one could feel very badly about the burdens of caregiving. Assessment items framed the home care experience in terms of stress, strain, burden, and resentment, not commitment, love, familial responsibility, mixed feelings, or companionship, among other complications and ways of thinking about care and caring. One might say that, in some sense, the caregivers learned how to be particular respondents in the very process of answering assessment items.

It occurred to me that such ordinary questions and concerns were as important for the study of aging as the systematic answers that elderly regularly provide those who study them. I have become particularly acute about listening for such questions or related concerns, not dismissing explicit references or clues to them as so much research debris. When a respondent states that his or her feelings or thoughts about something "depends," I pay as much attention to the "what" it depends on and the "how" of the connection as to the eventual answer. When someone asks me what I mean by a particular question, I believe it important to zero in on how that meaning is mutually worked out. When a respondent states or marks that she both agrees and disagrees with a particular questionnaire item, such as might be presented in a caregiver burden inventory, it is important to probe how a single question can have such a seemingly contradictory response. Rather than treat the response as methodologically meaningless, I wonder what kinds of questions could make such ostensible contradictions reasonable.

A growing interest in how experience is given voice now tells me that expressions such as "It depends" and "I've never thought about that before" are signs of savvy people, rather different in general character from the "judgmental dope" regularly imaged as the respondent (Garfinkel, 1967). According to Garfinkel, the respondent as judgmental dope is tacitly imagined to be the virtual vessel of his or her experience. Answers to research questions lie dormant in the respondent's experience, to be secured by an objective and, one hopes, standardized methodology. Least of all is the judgmental dope permitted to constitute the substantive references of the methodology, even while the dope may be allowed to express sentiments such as how strongly he or she feels about some predefined matter.

Seriously taking account of how the elderly give voice to experience requires that context be given its due. The savvy respondent does not simply break out into a response. Even under the best conditions, her comments can suggest that she thinks about, or thinks over for the first time, the diverse contingencies of everyday life that can specify the meaning of an answer. At the same time, if context figures significantly in how the elderly give voice to experience, it is important that theory entertain the question of what voice is heard when we study aging.

LOCAL CULTURE

Adapted from Geertz's (1983) ideas of local knowledge, the concept of "local culture" (Gubrium 1989b) provides a way of conceptualizing how circumscribed domains of understanding situate the meaning of aging. Just as organizational researchers are taking account of traditions, stories, and local symbols to shed light on organizational decision making (Jones, Moore, & Snyder, 1988), the cultures of friendship circles, residential settings, and support groups provide contexts for assigning meaning to matters such as life satisfaction, felt burden, and sense of future.

As part of the Alzheimer's disease research, support groups for caregivers were observed in two cities over a period of 3 years. Some groups were composed of caregiving spouses, mainly the elderly wives of dementia victims cared for at home. A few groups were limited to the adult children of demented parents, usually caregiving daughters. Most groups were attended by a mixture of family care-givers and significant others, including the rare sibling or friend who provided care.

Support groups may be classified by function and leadership. Some groups have a didactic mission, and others are more socioemotional. The didactic group aims to teach and guide participants to think and feel in particular ways about their troubles and situations. The socio-emotional group offers a formal opportunity to express and share feelings. Some groups are facilitated by experienced members at large; others are led by professional service providers. The support groups observed in the Alzheimer's disease study combined the func-tions and leadership styles. On occasion, some groups were didactic; at other times, they were socioemotional. Leadership style could vary by discussion topic. Any group could become antiprofessional and member-guided when professional ignorance of home care compli-cations was at issue; the same group could become decidedly atten-tive to expert opinion when so-called medical breakthroughs were being discussed.

Each group had a local culture that, despite function and leader-ship style, served to frame the experiences that participants brought to each other's attention. A support group's interpersonal history was a configuration of categories for comparing and assessing individual caregiving experiences. In one group, the notion of the "really" ideal caregiver was an especially persistent background concern of partici-pants, presenting them with a local standard for evaluating caregiv-ing responsibilities. One caregiver in particular, Jessica, who no longer attended but was influential in community Alzheimer's disease service activities, was a virtual exemplar of "total devotion" to the home care of a demented family member. Jessica presented partici-pants with a basis of comparison for the evaluation of their own caregiving activity, felt strain, and sentiments about possible institu-tionalization. For example, participants used Jessica's legendary expe-rience to assess whether their individual contributions were "all that great" compared to "what Jessica does for her husband." The hus-band was a so-called living vegetable, who presented Jessica with an ostensible "36-hour day" burden of care.

Jessica's status as the ideal caregiver was not always positive. When a condition known as "denial" was entertained, believed to be a tacit refusal to acknowledge the reality of an event or experience, Jessica became an exemplar of overdevotion, which brought to bear a differ-ent context for interpreting filial responsibility. She was still an ideal caregiver of sorts but one not to be emulated. In the context of denial, Jessica was used to evaluate whether, in comparison, one was being realistic about continued home care. The question now was whether one had gone "too far," that is, to a point where a totally devoted caregiver becomes the disease's so-called second victim, caught in a spiral of overconcern and the denial of personal and familial strain.

Against the background of the support group's local culture, the issue-linked quality of Jessica's exemplary status offered support for diametrically opposed decisions regarding institutional placement. When Jessica presented the positive ideal, participants hesitated to speak of the possibility of placing their demented loved ones in a nursing home. It was not uncommon for those considered too (coldly) rational in assessing their home situation to be thought of as rushing to judgment in deciding "it's time," a common expression referring to the time it is appropriate to consider an alternative to home care. When Jessica portrayed the negative ideal, participants discussed at length the indirect and insidious impact of dementia on the caregiver and other members of the household. On such occasions, one was likely to hear participants entertain denial as underpinning overdevotion.

From this support group we learn that ostensibly measurable entities, such as the perceived degree of impairment, felt stress, and the inclination to institutionalize the patient, do what Silverman (1989) calls "escaping." Depending on the issue under consideration, either devotion or denial, Jessica's legendary status cognitively shifts (escapes) from a positive to a negative standard of comparison. Paralleling this, participants who use Jessica as a basis for evaluating their own caregiving stand to experience rather dramatic alterations in understanding their circumstances, thoughts, and feelings.

Not all support groups had such singularly prominent exemplars. Prominent exemplars tended to homogenize the meaning of the burden of care over time, as diametrically opposite as their details might be. Support groups lacking such exemplars provided a wider spectrum of evaluative categories for the interpretation of individual experiences and engaged participants in more intensive efforts to designate standards of comparison.

The local cultures of the groups were not simply given. In communicating caregiving experiences to the group, each participant contributed to the group's changing or growing local culture. The process of interpersonal comparison was not just a chain of interindividual contrasts against a stable evaluative background, but comparisons simultaneously entered the exemplary background for further comparison. Each comparison and resulting judgment became, in its recollection, a local basis for subsequent contrast and judgment. To that extent, the local culture of each support group always was both old and new, continually ramifying the context available for designating the personal meaning of caregiving.

INTERLOCUTORS

To limit the voice of elderly to individuals is to overlook the public or social quality of discourse. When I speak about myself, I am both subject and object. As subject, I describe; as object, I am described. Just as two speakers can agree or disagree with each other, I similarly can concede to or disagree with myself about my thoughts and sentiments. By the same token, the individual is not necessarily privy to what he or others otherwise take to be his "own" discourse. The psychiatric or casual rhetoric of denial certainly challenges claims to personal knowledge, just as the weeping caregiver and the 80-year-old man in the earlier extracts asked others to specify their inner voices for them, especially their sentiments. We not only speak for ourselves, to ourselves, and about ourselves, but others speak for us, to us, and about us. No one, it seems, just speaks. We all are, with and among ourselves, interlocutors of our thoughts and feelings (Todorov, 1984).

As interlocutors, we bring a variety of understandings and conceptual schemes to descriptions of ourselves or others. In one support group, Jessica's exemplification provided a basis for speaking about and interpreting the caregiving experience. Other support groups provided different understandings and subsequent "readings." The innermost privacies of participants took on different meanings in the context of alternative local cultures, what Kristiva (see Giddens, 1979, chap. 1; Hawkes, 1977, chap. 4) has called the "intertextuality" of discourse. The interlocutor even provides a basis for preserving the mind of the mindless, a substantial subset of whom are represented by senile dementia (Gubrium, 1986b). What is more, the mind of the mindless is preserved according to the context ("text") in which the interlocutor's related experience is embedded.

Although I do not argue that behavior is a mere text, consider dementia victim Paul's social relations as a way of showing how context, through the interlocutor, gives voice to experience even among those presumed not to have much, if any, mind at all (Gubrium, 1991). Paul is a nursing home patient with Alzheimer's disease. He occupies a room adjacent to the nurses' station because the staff likes to "keep an eye on him." Paul is a so-called wanderer, which means that he loses track of his whereabouts and "wanders off." He occasionally enters others' rooms and, in the words of some women on the floor, "scares us half to death." Less commonly, he finds his way to another unit and temporarily is lost. Paul's wandering and "restlessness" can cause the staff to restrain him. At times, he is found secured in a geriatric chair, a precaution against stumbling. Occasionally, he is fastened to his bed with arm and leg restraints. Paul tends to be very loud when restrained. Neither the other patients nor staff are sure if it is better to tolerate a restrained Paul yelling or a quiet Paul who, at any moment, might wander into someone's room.

There are various opinions about Paul's intrusions into others' lives. Some patients cannot understand why the nursing home admits what they take to be mental patients. To them, Paul is the peak of physical health: wiry, strong, energetic, ambulatory, "ruggedly good-looking." As an LPN once remarked, "To look at him, you'd think absolutely nothing was wrong with him." This suggests only one thing: Paul has "completely lost his marbles." At the same time, Paul occasionally is the source of much hilarity. His good looks are the butt of jokes and gossip among some patients about how certain women on the unit "really" want Paul to sneak into their rooms "for a good see." Paul's "antics" cause an equal amount of gossip and joking among staff members. To the staff, he basically is harmless, not at all violent, and, in his own confused way, a "gentle giant." In Paul, the staff sees a man who, when he is not being too difficult, brings variety to their work lives.

Paul exudes incoherent conviviality. He regularly ambles to the nurses' station and wants to "talk over" things. When staff members take the time, particularly in the relative quiet of the afternoon, they pretend to gossip with him about whatever they attribute to being on his mind. Although they cannot understand him, it is evident to them that he thoroughly enjoys their company. When he laughs, they laugh with him. In doing fieldwork on Paul's unit, I fondly recall the many times Paul would casually place his elbow on top of the nurses' station, chest-high for him, and in his affable manner ask glowingly, "How's life, partner?" From previous experience, I knew that whatever I said in response would probably not be followed by anything comprehensible. Nonetheless, partly through courtesy and partly because his greeting was so charming, I regularly responded in kind: "Fine, partner. How's life been treating you?"

I once poured him a plastic cup of water in the process because he seemed a bit parched. I had been drinking water while taking field notes. He took the cup, half toasted me, and slugged it back, as if it were a stiff drink. He immediately smiled, gently slammed the cup on the top of the station, and stated with apparent pleasure, "That hit the spot." I poured him another. After that, we made a habit of this for a time, combining what seemed to be the semblance of conviviality with the non sequiturs of his dementia. For me, it was a tender and welcome exchange each time it occurred. For the staff, it was a source of good-natured teasing about how Paul and Jay went drinking every afternoon.

Paul's wife, Adele, often "spoke" with and for Paul during her frequent visits to the nursing home. As with my own participation in Paul's self-presentation and self-management while drinking, Adele not only spoke her own mind to Paul but audibly conveyed for him what she believed to be his thoughts and sentiments. When she found him restrained, she sometimes approached the nurses' station and, sympathizing with the staff about the occasional need for this in Paul's case, asked whether they knew how he must be feeling, tied to his chair or bed. As she once explained:

> I know the poor fellow doesn't like it. You can just hear him. He feels like you've put him in jail. He doesn't understand how this could happen to him. When I'm in there, I know that deep down inside, he's asking how anyone could do this to him. Can't we maybe let him stand up and stretch a bit? I know he was pretty bad this morning. I'll watch him.

I overheard and actually participated in a number of "conversations" that Adele had with Paul. Joining in, I found myself embellishing the discursive logic that she, by speaking for him, articulated as his. In turn, Adele spoke for herself. One time, in one of these conversations, Adele indicated that Paul was bothered about his relations with others on the floor. I found it reasonable to ask him whether his relations with certain patients were causing him to be annoyed. Adele responded for him in a manner that seemed to follow. I then answered in a compatible fashion. These "conversations" were not always consensual. There were disagreements, such as when Adele inferred that I was misinterpreting what Paul was thinking. The disagreements led to corrections that were comprehensible in the flow of their exchanges. The organization of discourse itself gave a minimally lucid tone to all contributions (Heritage, 1984; Sudnow, 1972).

Yet this was not just a discursive ritual. It had a moral imperative. The staff knew that when Paul allegedly felt wronged, Adele complained bitterly. They knew Paul was sorrowful because Adele informed them of it. They realized when Paul was being left alone too much and that he, like any human being, needed company and affection from others because Adele spoke for him. With others' discursive support and conversational indulgence, Adele kept Paul's voice and spirit socially alive and working.

Paul's ascribed thoughts and feelings reflected the local cultural contradictions of the nursing home. Adele expressed distress for him when she "knew" Paul felt frightened in the company of strangers. She wanted him to feel that this was home, not a hospital, or at least as much like home as possible under the circumstances. She repeatedly reminded others, both staff and patients, that Paul had a past and thus she stood as his sentry against the overwhelming institutional claims of the present. She spoke of what he was, what he had accomplished in life, and how much others admired him for it. She recounted his foibles and transgressions, too, and used the information to account for his present conduct. In practice, Paul had a living past. Adele made sure of that. She publicly maintained his biography, using it to dilute the thrust of the organization into daily living.

Although, administratively, Paul was an individual, experientially he could not be separated from those around him. This, of course, is true for all of us. What made Paul's situation particularly significant in this regard was that it vividly showed that voice does not belong to individuals but is assigned to them. What is more, the voice Adele presented was practical, organized within the concrete context of speech and its related actions.

LIFE NARRATIVE

To give voice to experience presumably is to speak of one's life. Gerontologists regularly ask the elderly about their lives as if life simply were there for the asking; although, perhaps more than other researchers, they are alert to problems of communicative competence. As noted earlier, the competent respondent reaches back and into life to obtain answers to questions about it. Experience, in effect, coincides with life. But is life itself simply there for the asking, containing and giving shape to personal experience, even under the best of methodological and communicative conditions?

Consider some preliminary findings from a study of life narrative among nursing home patients suggesting that life may be separated from experience. The separation is significant for understanding what is voiced in studies of aging. Early in the research, I became intrigued by a peculiar kind of qualification, used to signal the separation, that sometimes followed open-ended discussions with patients about the quality of life in the nursing home. The discussions centered on the personal articulation of a prominent cultural tension of nursing home life, whether it is experienced as home or a hospital.

Focal were the meaning of home and the extent to which "this place," meaning the nursing facility, was or was not like home and why.

Eighty-six-year-old patient Ida's remarks initially highlighted the manner in which a discussion about the quality of life in the facility could be qualified. Our discussion began with an extended conversation about the meaning of home. Home to Ida meant what it did to others. It was linked with family, notably with bonds of trust and love. Ida spoke at length of growing up in poverty on a farm some distance from the nearest town. She clearly noted that "even if we was poor, we didn't know it," touchingly describing how her mother made them all feel wanted and "rich" in the important things of life. Ida traced the warm and loving atmosphere of her early life into the home she eventually made for her own husband and children. Theirs, too, was not a life very well off, but it was loving, and as she emphasized, their modest abode was a home. In speaking of home, Ida seemed to savor the word, as if its bare sound was pleasing to her ears. She wasn't different from many other patients in this regard. Asked to recount the meaning of home, Ida would linger on the word, slowly drawing it out, with a facial expression seeming to suggest that home was swirling around in her head with total abandon. She seemed momentarily intoxicated by the word.

We gradually turned to life in the nursing home. Ida spoke at length about other patients, the staff, the so-called atmosphere, families, the food, and other services. Having just discussed the meaning of home, she compared what was offered in the facility with her understanding of the trusting and loving household. Although the food in the facility was not bad, she explained that it was not like home. The staff, particularly two "very sweet aides," were nice to her and treated her like a mother. Ida complained that the staff sometimes could be flip and uncaring, but she understood that "the girls," meaning the nursing staff, had jobs requiring them to be more than just friendly to patients. Evaluating the facility's atmosphere, Ida remarked that "they" try to make it as much like home as possible, noting that she had been in worse places. She remarked that there were very sick people in the facility, and it was difficult to think of the place as a home; in that regard, it was more like a hospital. Still, Ida lived there, and, to the extent that "they" tried, she reported that it was homelike. We spent considerable time discussing such matters. Some of my questions sounded like quality-of-care inquiries; others dealt with overall life satisfaction. It was evident that Ida felt the facility to be adequate for what it was. She was not totally disgusted with the nursing staff, as some patients were, nor was she completely satisfied, as a few seemed to be. According to Ida, all told, living in this particular facility was satisfactory, not nearly as terrible as she had expected it might be.

As I continued to probe, attempting to understand what I assumed to be the current experiential connections of her life, several times she stated, "It doesn't matter anyway." At first, I took this as a shorthand way of not being too harsh in judging the facility, unfairly singling it out for what characterized nursing homes in general. I had typified Ida as the kind of person who does not ask life to be perfect but only acceptable and livable, as she repeatedly reminded me her poverty had taught her.

But Ida persisted. No, the food was not that bad, but it didn't matter anyway. No, the staff didn't spend as much time as they could with each patient, but it really did not matter. Yes, by and large, she was satisfied under the circumstances, but what did it matter? I eventually bothered to address the qualification and asked her why it did not matter. She answered, "Because my life's over."

In retrospect, I cannot say that this answer itself caused me to begin contemplating that life could be separated from experience, that Ida, in effect, was telling me that while she was giving voice to experience, it was not about her life. A theoretical interest in the relation between voice and context itself was alerting me to the need to listen for the experiential bounds and meaningful backgrounds of what the aged or others say about elderly lives. The combination came to bear on the possibility that life was not just something lived but was to be considered an object that one could look upon, inspect, think back on, look ahead to, close off, and open up to experience. It occurred to me that when Ida and, later, other patients spoke about daily living, they were not necessarily telling me anything about a life—their lives—even though they could describe current living conditions in considerable detail and with reasoned judgment. I considered that when I asked Ida how satisfied she was with her life now, she was telling me more about now than she was speaking about her life. Indeed, I wondered if what we gerontologists knew about life satisfaction "in general" was a conglomeration of life and "just living," as some patients distinguished what they once were from what they now withstood.

As a personal object, *the* life has a story that is more or less communicable. If the differentiation of life from experience tells us anything, the chapters of a life story might inform us of life's bounds and contours. We might expect, for example, that if we asked Ida to tell her life story, the last chapter would not include her current nursing home experience, because, according to Ida, her life is over. By the same token, we might hypothesize that the patient whose last chapter was about the nursing home experience might be informing us that his or her life was *not* over. We might even guess that, for some, the life before placement has ended and a new one inside the nursing home has begun, as preliminary analysis of the life narrative material suggests is a possibility. Conversion and recovery experiences certainly can be narratively conveyed in this fashion.

The narrative material is beginning to show that, as a basis for undertaking personal evaluations of quality of care, it is important to consider patients in terms of their life orientations to the nursing home. For the patient who orients to the nursing home experience as part of his or her life, one might guess that it would seriously matter what the overall quality of care is in the facility. Among those who lives are claimed to be over, the quality of care would have a different meaning and urgency.

A comparative sample of life stories and related narrative materials collected in adult congregate-living facilities shows that few consider their lives to be over. Last chapters are about the present, not the past. In contrast, sorting through the life stories of the nursing home sample suggests that there are several different orientations to the nursing home experience. There are those, like Ida, who see their lives as over and say that they are now "just living" or existing; others see life as yet to come in a world after living. Some see the life in this world as being extended beyond where it might have ended if they had remained on their own. Some make a new life for themselves in the nursing home; the last chapter of their stories is about the present.

These are preliminary results. There are as yet many complications to take into account. For example, respondents differ in understanding what is meant by conveying life in terms of chapters. Weekly fluctuations in health status seem to affect the bounds of the life story, as the longitudinal analysis of repeated waves of interviews suggests. I have tried to limit the study to the so-called classic nursing home patient, comparing his or her life narrative to short-stay rehabilitation patients. The differences between them are not clear-cut in terms of nursing home orientation. For example, it is possible that even after residing in a facility for as long as 5 years, a few elderly patients show that one can still think of the experience as rehabilitative and hope to *return* to one's life, not move forward to a new life in the facility or in the beyond or forbear a life that is now over.

A NEW GERONTOLOGY

Gerontology has come a long way in its short 40-odd years. Prescientific bromides and maxims of successful aging have given way to hypotheses about and systematic observations of the aging experience. Alternative theories have been formulated for why variables pertinent to growing old go together the way they do. Observations have been extended not only beyond Grandma's house and the town's crone but to comparisons of city with village, culture with subculture, and industrial with developing nations. Methods have been developed to sort experiences, from standardized measurement devices for attitudes and sentiments to indicators of quality of care. The aim has been to engage objectively the process of aging so as to systematically trace its organization.

Yet for some, this is a story of scientization as much as the growth of a scientific gerontology. Against scientization, there has been a decided surge of interest in the place of personal meaning, the unstandardized, and the emergent in everyday life. Gergen (1980) has underscored the need to take account of what he calls the aleatoric, that is, the experientially contingent and accidental qualities of life change, not limiting research to predefined experiential categories. More recently, Bruner (1986) has set forth a narrative mode for cognitive development to teach us that human imagination is an essential feature of action. Anthropologists Myerhoff (1978) and Kaufman (1986) have shown how elaborately storied indeed are the lives of the elderly, which are assigned meaning in accordance with diverse cultural codes. Cursory examination of the proceedings of recent annual conferences of the Gerontological Society of America suggests that there is a solid concern with subjectivity: the categories and qualities of growing older, being old, associating with the aged, and caring for frail elderly.

Luborsky (1990) refers to this development in the field of aging as "the romance with personal meaning and lived experience." The so-called romance is part of a broader thrust, what Silverman (1985) features as the search for authenticity in reaction to the overwhelming rationalization of everyday life. For example, Silverman and Bloor (1990) view patient-centered medicine as a kind of romantic reaction to body-centered medicine, shifting the so-called medical gaze from lesions and physiological systems to include the patient's understanding of his or her illness. Overall, the aim has been to get beyond the (overrationalized) languages of scientific discourse to the actual voices of experience.

Drawing on Foucault (1973, 1979), Silverman (1985) and Gubrium and Silverman (1989) present both ethnographic and conversation-analytic evidence to argue that the romance with personal meaning is itself a kind of language, as potentially rationalized and rational as its objective scientific nemesis. Personal meaning and aleatoric change are understood, communicated, and described in language, the language of feeling, and as such they are as subject to the rules and concrete conditions of communication as any object of experience. In relation to Alzheimer's disease, Gubrium (1988, 1989a) has shown that the incommunicable—experiences that some say cannot be put into words—are conveyed according to culturally recognizable codes, such as through the ordinary poetry used to communicate what "it's like" to witness the mental demise of a loved one.

The point is that if we are to take account of how experience is given voice in a new gerontology, the rush to discover and trace personal meaning must not discount the social organization of voicing, that is, the various and diverse contexts within which speakers and listeners formulate, communicate, and respond to interpretations of life. Attending to voice without context is tantamount to looking upon Derrida's (1981) "continuous play of difference" or experience without organization (Denzin, 1990), which I cannot accept. The world of literary interpretation might imagine, even encourage, this form of whirling textuality, but the world of everyday life has tradition, formal organization, and political surroundings that, in practice, concretely enter into and shape the voicing of experience. I have tried to show in this chapter that although local cultures are not fixed, they nonetheless provide discernible categories for assigning meaning to self, to convey who one is and is not in some regard. As Paul's story suggests, interlocutors present, or harbor, meaningful contexts within which to preserve the thoughts and feelings of those diagnostically bereft of reason. And as life narratives seem to indicate, the orienting framework of stories about matters such as nursing home living can cast living as life for some and unchaptered for others, not just more or less authentic personal sentiments about institutionalization.

In my analytic of experience, voice and context stand in dynamic tension. One—voice—focuses our attention on subjective relevancies, and the other—context—informs us that voice is ineluctably part of language and communication, things essentially situated and shared. Scientism would have us drown voice in objective context, transforming context into conditions without voice or, as is scientific habit, into standardized and measurable equivalents. The romance with personal meaning would dissolve context in the voicing of "authentic" experience, trivializing the public markers, resources, and available categories of everyday life. In contrast, just as the subjects, respondents, and informants whose lives gerontologists study must wend their way between the varied voices and contexts of experience in the "real world," a new gerontology might best tolerate the tension rather than attempting to integrate voice and context into an analytically unified vision of aging, totalizing experience.

This new gerontology, then, is against theoretical integration. Rather than attempting, through some system of propositions, to logically link and contain voice and context as categories for analysis, it emphasizes the practice of everyday life, being attuned to life's distinct voices and their situatedness, akin to Bourdieu's (1977) idea of "habitus," where life is invented in discourse but "within limits." The goal is a critical empiricism; its aim, on the one hand, is to make visible the variety, contingency, and inventiveness in any and all efforts to present life and, on the other hand, to resist the temptation to put it all together into an analytically consistent and comprehensive framework privileging certain voices and silencing others.

REFERENCES

Bourdieu, P. (1977). *Outline of a theory of practice.* Cambridge: Cambridge University Press.

Bruner, J. (1986). *Actual minds, possible worlds.* Cambridge, MA: Harvard University Press.

Denzin, N. K. (1990). Reading cultural texts: Comment on Griswold. *American Journal of Sociology, 95,* 1577–1580.

Derrida, J. (1981). *Positions.* Chicago: University of Chicago Press.

Foucault, M. (1973). *The birth of the clinic.* London: Tavistock.

Foucault, M. (1979). *The history of sexuality* (Vol. 1). London: Allen Lane.

Garfinkel, H. (1967). *Studies in ethnomethodology.* Englewood Cliffs, NJ: Prentice-Hall.

Geertz, C. (1983). *Local knowledge.* New York: Basic Books.

Gergen, K. L. (1980). The emerging crisis in life-span developmental theory. In P. Baltes & O. Brim (Eds.), *Life-span development and behavior.* New York: Academic Press.

Giddens, A. (1979). *Central problems of social theory.* Berkeley: University of California Press.

Gubrium, J. F. (1986a). *Oldtimers and Alzheimer's: The descriptive organization of senility.* Greenwich, CT: JAI Press.

Gubrium, J. F. (1986b). The social preservation of mind: The Alzheimer's disease experience. *Symbolic Interaction, 6,* 37–51.

Gubrium, J. F. (1988). Incommunicables and poetic documentation in the Alzheimer's disease experience. *Semiotica, 72,* 235–253.

Gubrium, J. F. (1989a). Emotion work and emotive discourse in the Alzheimer's disease experience. In D. Unruh & G. S. Livings (Eds.), *Current perspectives on aging and the life cycle* (Vol. 3, pp. 243–268). Greenwich, CT: JAI Press.

Gubrium, J. F. (1989b). Local cultures and service policy. In J. F. Gubrium & D. Silverman (Eds.), *The politics of field research* (pp. 94–112). London: Sage.

Gubrium, J. F. (1991). *The mosaic of care.* New York: Springer Publishing Co.

Gubrium, J. F., & Lynott, R. J. (1983). Rethinking life satisfaction. *Human Organization, 42,* 30–38.

Gubrium, J. F., & Lynott, R. J. (1987). Measurement and the interpretation of burden in the Alzheimer's disease experience. *Journal of Aging Studies, 1,* 265–285.

Gubrium, J. F., & Silverman, D. (1989). *The politics of field research: Sociology beyond enlightenment.* London: Sage.

Hawkes, T. (1977). *Structuralism and semiotics.* Berkeley: University of California Press.

Hazan, H. (1990). *A paradoxical community: The emergence of a social world in an urban renewal setting.* Greenwich, CT: JAI Press.

Heritage, J. (1984). *Garfinkel and ethnomethodology.* Cambridge: Polity Press.

Jones, M. O., Moore, M. D., & Snyder, R. C. (Eds.). (1988). *Inside organizations.* Newbury Park, CA: Sage.

Kaufman, S. R. (1986). *The ageless self.* Madison: University of Wisconsin Press.

Luborsky, M. (1990, November). *The romance with personal meaning and lived experience.* Paper presented at the 43rd annual conference of the Gerontological Society of America, Boston.

Myerhoff, B. (1978). *Number our days.* New York: Simon and Schuster.

Silverman, D. (1985). *Qualitative methodology and sociology.* Aldershot, UK: Gower House.

Silverman, D. (1989). Six rules of qualitative research: A post-romantic argument. *Symbolic Interaction, 12,* 215–230.

Silverman, D., & Bloor, M. (1990). Patient-centered medicine: Some sociological observations on its constitution, penetration, and cultural assonance. *Advances in Medical Sociology, 1,* 3–25.

Sudnow, D. (Ed.). (1972). *Studies in social interaction.* New York: Free Press.

Todorov, T. (1984). *Mikhail Bakhtin: The dialogical principle.* Minneapolis: University of Minnesota Press.

4

Evolutionary Gerontology and Critical Gerontology: Let's Just Be Friends

Michael R. Rose

Two new intellectual movements are beginning to have an impact on mainstream gerontology: critical gerontology and evolutionary gerontology. This chapter is intended to serve as an introduction to evolutionary gerontology for those from the field of critical gerontology. It is argued that evolutionary gerontology and critical gerontology should be kept apart because of the potential for vastly destructive interactions arising from the commingling of ideology with evolutionary biology. However, this potential problem does not in any way imply that the two intellectual movements are invalid or malformed when kept separate.

I am grateful to W. A. Achenbaum, M. Djawdan, and J. L. Graves for their comments on an earlier version of the manuscript.

Evolutionary gerontology should be of interest to all gerontologists because it is about to foment a revolution in the theoretical foundations and experimental programs of biological gerontology, a revolution that will change the position of the discipline radically. This changed position will have effects upon both the scientific standing of gerontology, considered from a purely academic perspective, and the practical standing of gerontology, considered from a medical perspective. For example, the problem of postponing human aging will be transformed from a mystery mostly discussed by quacks into a technological project with delimitable methods, costs, and benefits.

Below, in the first major section of the chapter, this view of evolutionary gerontology is presented in more detail. First, the state of conventional gerontology will be reviewed, to define the historical background for the forthcoming transformation. Second, the new evolutionary gerontology will be outlined. Third, the potential scientific impact of evolutionary gerontology will be discussed. Fourth, the potential significance of evolutionary gerontology for medical practice will be discussed.

In the next section, the relationship between evolutionary thinking and humanistic gerontology transformed by critical theory will be discussed. The discussion will not be concerned with the intellectual validity of any such relationship. Rather, it will focus upon the potential hazards arising from the introduction of explicitly ideological elements into evolutionary biology, particularly in the application of evolutionary biology to social policies concerning the elderly.

INTRODUCTION TO
EVOLUTIONARY GERONTOLOGY

Conventional Gerontology

The present-day scientific gerontologist, considered in terms of the modal phenotypes, performs one of two different kinds of experiments. The first is the longitudinal study of some particular biological attribute in a cohort of aging organisms, usually rodents but often humans, flies, or nematodes. These attributes might be DNA content, somatic mutation, and protein activity, or they might be features of cell or tissue function, such as cell turnover in liver. All of this research tests whether or not a particular biological attribute declines in an age-correlated manner. A problem with this type of research is that, by itself, it offers no means of evaluating the causal significance of any such correlated decline for aging itself. On the other hand, one area where this work has been useful is in testing the many failed theories of conventional gerontology. For example, the error catastrophe theory of Orgel (1963) proposed that aging arises, at least in part, because of errors in the synthesis of constituents of the protein translation machinery feeding back on themselves, causing progressive deterioration in the accuracy of protein synthesis. This theory can be tested by estimating the accuracy of protein synthesis as a function of age. When this is done, the evidence against any sort of error catastrophe in protein synthesis is overwhelming (e.g., Rothstein, 1987). Thus, although the aging-cohort approach has led to little in the way of useful positive results, it has been valuable in destroying many of the contending theories of conventional gerontology.

The second type of experiment that our generic biological gerontologist performs is in vitro culture of vertebrate cells. The basis for the relevance of this research to aging is Hayflick's (1965) classic demonstration of the finite replicative capacity of in vitro cell cultures when they are allowed to multiply rapidly and have not undergone tumorous transformation. That is, in vitro cultures tend to stop replicating eventually. This has been offered as one of the fundamental biological constraints upon organismal survival. Moreover, the life span of a number of mammals correlates well with the replicative capacity of their in vitro cells (Röhme, 1981). The only difficulty is that it is hard to argue that research on this system has progressed one millimeter toward explaining organismal aging. One of the problems is that cells from extremely senescent organisms still have replicative potential (e.g., Martin, Sprague, & Epstein, 1970). Another is that many of the pathologies of senescent organisms involve postmitotic cells that continue to live (Finch, 1990). In fact, a vast array of species have cells that do not usually undergo mitosis in the adult, from insects to nematodes to rotifers. Many of these cells hardly even synthesize new protein after the onset of adulthood.

There are still other types of experiments that are occasionally performed and still more obscure theories. The provision of antioxidants to resist molecular deterioration has been popular, but the results have been strikingly equivocal (Sohal, 1987). Genetic studies of inbred lines (e.g., Watson, Gelman, Williams, & Yunis, 1990) are vitiated by the fact that the pathologies of inbred lines are not representative of those in older outbred organisms, when the inbreeding is artificially imposed (see Johnson & Wood, 1982; Rose, 1984a).

The many physiological theories of aging that have proliferated through the century, from the autotoxification theory of Metchnikoff (1904) to the death hormone theory of Denckla (1975), have been strikingly out of keeping with the range of biological detail concerning aging (Finch, 1990; Rose, 1991). In 1979, Comfort proposed that the history of gerontological research cannot be written as a tale of progression toward one or two "highly probable" main theories. In 1991, this judgment would still seem to be valid where conventional biological gerontology is concerned. Although there has been a feast of gerontological funding, research and publications, the nutritive value of the banquet has been limited.

Evolutionary Gerontology

Let me say here that I am a partisan of evolutionary gerontology, and I have recently published a kind of manifesto for the movement (Rose, 1991). Science is certainly not a meeting of dispassionate minds arguing the merits of their respective theses in an objective fashion. As Feyerabend (1975) discussed so colorfully, it is much more a matter of conviction and persuasion. My favorite analogy is that science is just like politics—like American politics, when you are dealing with co-dominant oligarchies that have as their major difference who is going to be in charge; like revolutionary politics, when small intellectual movements propose to overthrow the existing scientific order. What we are about in evolutionary gerontology is revolutionary politics. For us, conventional biological gerontology represents an intellectual regime in florid decay, one that we wish to transform completely.

The basis for our choice of scientific politics is our conviction that the fundamental cause of aging has nothing whatsoever to do with any ineluctable biochemical mechanism. There are potentially immortal organisms, both unicellular *and* multicellular, organisms like fissile sea anemones, which have never been found to age (Rose, 1991). Moreover, we are all produced by eukaryotic cell lineages that have been alive continuously for hundreds of millions of years. To us, the search for biomedical or cellular theories that might fundamentally explain aging is as cogent as quantum mechanical theories of linguistics.

Instead, evolutionary biologists explain aging in terms of the declining force of natural selection with age. This theoretical analysis is strictly apodictic; starting from genetic variation affecting characters in a somewhat age-dependent manner, the evolution of aging follows necessarily for species that have an adult that does not reproduce by fission. This idea began as an intuition of such biological luminaries as R. A. Fisher and J. B. S. Haldane but achieved full mathematical development in the hands of W. D. Hamilton (1966) and Brian Charlesworth (1980). For the history and a gentle mathematical treatment of the theory, see Rose (1991).

The basic logic of this theory is as follows. We begin with the assumption that natural selection alone, not a deity or cosmic force, is responsible for the physiological efficiency of organisms. That is, it is the action of natural selection that brings about adaptations from initially random genetic variation. The key step in the evolutionary analysis of aging is determining the effect on organismal fitness of an age-specific change in survival. For simplicity, consider a genetic change that kills the organism. If such a change occurs before the onset of the population's reproduction, then any such genetic change will be strongly selected against because it precludes that genetic change being represented in the next generation. Next consider a genetic change that kills after all individuals in the population have ceased reproduction. Any such change will have no effect upon the net reproduction of individuals carrying it, and it can be represented in the next generation. Quantitatively, the mathematical result is one of a high level in the "force of natural selection" before the start of reproduction, with a fall in this force once reproduction begins, such that the force of selection reaches zero after the cessation of reproduction. In anthropomorphic terms, natural selection stops caring as you get older. On the theory of evolution, this then implies that aging is inevitable for organisms like ourselves.

Over the years, this basic theory has been grudgingly accepted by more and more gerontologists. However, it generally has been regarded more as background or window dressing. What has not been understood as widely is that this theory provides the foundation for a powerful experimental program of research. Experimental evolutionary research on aging tends to be of two kinds. The first is population-genetic, focusing on the nature and number of the genes that underlie the evolution of aging. A crucial debate has concerned the pattern of genetic effects on aging, specifically whether fitness trades off against later survival or is independent of it (e.g., Rose & Charlesworth, 1980). Recent evidence indicates that both possibilities arise (Service, Hutchinson, & Rose, 1988). Another controversial point has been the number of genes that control aging, early low estimates (Luckinbill, Clare, Krell, Cirocco, & Richards, 1987) now giving way to high estimates (Hutchinson & Rose, 1990). This work is fundamental to evaluating the prospects for any molecular analysis of aging because a large number of loci with complex effects are going to render any simple reductionist approach largely futile.

The second experimental approach has been to postpone aging, using the guidance of the evolutionary theory, and then proceed to analyze biologically how aging has been postponed. One of the most powerful corollaries of the evolutionary theory of aging is that it should be feasible to postpone aging if one alters patterns of natural selection, given the rejection of any simple biochemically determinate aging. This has now been done several times with *Drosophila* species (e.g., Luckinbill & Clare, 1985; Rose, 1984b, 1991). Indeed, it is almost an embarrassingly easy experiment.

It might be instructive to describe in general terms how this kind of experiment proceeds in evolutionary gerontology. One begins with a large outbred population that is generally fit and genetically polymorphic. This population is then used to found two sets of experimental populations. All of these experimental populations are reproduced using discrete generations: eggs are laid en masse, the adults are discarded, and the eggs grow up through larval and pupal stages as a discrete cohort, mating among each other, the way it used to happen at liberal arts colleges. The whole cycle begins again when these adults are used to lay a batch of eggs to start the next generation. The two groups of populations (the individual is not an experimental unit in population genetics) differ only in the timing used to determine when the eggs for the next generation are laid. One group of populations will be allowed to lay eggs only as young adults; the other group of populations will be allowed to lay eggs only as older adults. Evidently, these two groups differ strikingly with respect to the age at first reproduction, and thus they differ with respect to the point at which the force of selection declines with age. In the early-reproduction populations, the force of selection declines early; in the later-reproduction populations, the force of selection declines late. Thus, on the evolutionary theory of aging, we predict that the latter group will eventually evolve postponed aging relative to the former. And this is indeed the generic finding.

With the creation of populations with postponed aging, research has since proceeded to analyze the biology of such evolutionarily postponed aging, from morphology (Rose, Dorey, Coyle, & Service, 1984) to physiology (Service, 1987). Indeed, this work is expanding very rapidly now, with new breakthrough findings available almost by the week.

To recap, evolutionary gerontology has a general mathematical theory that makes concrete testable predictions. Those predictions have in fact been experimentally corroborated. Specifically, it has been possible to use the evolutionary theory to create populations with postponed aging, populations that constitute excellent systems for other types of experimental research. In addition, a point that has not been discussed here is that the evolutionary theory of aging can, in turn, be used to explain a great deal of the natural history of aging, especially its comparative distribution (Rose, 1991) and organismal physiology (Rose, 1990).

Scientific Significance of Evolutionary Gerontology

From the vantage point of evolutionary gerontology, aging is not merely scientifically explicable; it is one of the most readily explicable phenomena in all of biology. The equations that underlie the evolutionary theory of aging, particularly those giving the decline in the force of natural selection with age, are among the most powerful in biological theory. They indicate that selection falls from full intensity at the onset of life to zero at some finite age after the onset of reproduction. Moreover, the theory makes an absolute comparative prediction: aging should evolve whenever reproduction is not fissile but not when reproduction is fissile. This type of prediction allows the use of fairly naive falsification (Popper, 1959), an unusual situation in experimental science (pace Popper, 1959; cf. Lakatos, 1970), particularly biology. To date, falsification has not occurred.

   In addition, it is possible to use the methods of evolutionary gerontology, particularly the creation of populations with genetically postponed aging, to test, refine, or demolish the theories of conventional biological gerontology. To give an example of refinement, one of the classic theories of gerontology is Pearl's (1928) "rate of living" theory. This theory supposes that more rapid metabolism trades off against longevity so that a roughly fixed total amount of "living" is experienced. The best evidence for this was the relationship between ambient temperature and life span in poikilotherms, the latter varying inversely with the former. Indeed, direct measures of the total metabolic activity over a lifetime in *Drosophila* indicate rough constancy over a range of temperatures (Miquel, Lundgren, Bensch, & Atlan, 1976). Evolutionary refinement of this hypothesis is provided by the concept of "antagonistic pleiotropy" (Rose, 1985; Williams, 1957), in which genes enhancing early reproduction have pleiotropic (additional) effects that decrease the likelihood of later survival. That is, "rate of living" generalizes as an evolutionary theory of antagonism between benefits at one stage and penalties at another stage (cf. Rose, 1991). Experimentally, this is manifest as a reduction in early fecundity among flies selected for postponed aging (Rose, 1984b). Indeed, considerable detailed work is being performed on this physiological antagonism in *Drosophila* (e.g., Service, 1987; Service et al., 1988; Service & Rose, 1985).

Perhaps of greater value is the outright demolition of conventional gerontological theories concerning the biology of aging. If such a theory puts forward claims to general applicability, then the biological basis of postponed aging in the stocks that evolutionary gerontologists have produced should reflect the mechanisms posited by that theory. For example, if the theory in question is error catastrophe theory, then flies that live up to twice as long as normal flies should have higher rates of translation fidelity, as well as reduced translation errors. This example is actually somewhat superfluous because it is well known that translation fidelity is hardly affected by aging (Rothstein, 1987), but it illustrates the principle. Systems developed by evolutionary gerontology can thus be used to clear out the underbrush of dead foliage made up of the many failed theories of conventional gerontology.

Finally, the status of aging as a biological research problem will be transformed from marginal respectability to mainstream acceptance. All of the working parts of successful science will be in place, hard theory and hard experimentation. It would remain only to inform the rest of the scientific community of the new state of affairs.

Medical Significance of Evolutionary Gerontology

The postponement of aging is now a trivial problem, at least where basic scientific research is concerned. If you were a fruit fly or a guppy or a mouse, then the development of genetic and other tools for the postponement of your aging would be straightforward, given the machinery of evolutionary gerontology. But—and this is the key "but"—the evolutionary theory indicates that the mechanistic control of aging in different taxonomic groups will be no more universal than the mechanisms of sight are (Rose, 1991). That is, one would not want human ophthamologists to train only on the eyes of octopi, still less only on the eyes of fruit flies. The function of sight may be analogous, but the visual mechanisms are not always homologous (they do not necessarily share a common genetic basis). Therefore, there is not a single physiological mechanism that could be supportably generalized from postponed aging in fruit flies to postponed aging in humans without further experimental test.

To make progress at unraveling aging in humans, and to postpone it, research must be performed that uses homologous experimental systems. Ideally, these would be organisms like chimpanzees; that is, ideally where medical applicability is concerned. Ethically, much of the research required would be repugnant in the extreme if it were performed upon chimpanzees. An intermediate alternative might be to use a rodent.

The research strategy would be as follows (for more detail, see Rose, 1988, 1990). Using *Drosophila* and other simple invertebrates, we would develop a deep understanding of the physiological and genetic mechanisms that underlie evolutionarily postponed aging. As this proceeds, we would simultaneously select a short-lived rodent, like *Mus musculus*, for postponement of aging. Using the insights developed with simpler systems, we would unravel postponed aging in the rodent system. In particular, methods should be discovered that postpone aging by intervening directly in those physiological processes that control aging. Such means of intervention could then be tested using systems like dogs or cats. Finally, with the development of means of directly postponing aging in mammals generally, trials with humans could be initiated using these methods of direct intervention.

Nothing about this research program is particularly easy. Even selection for postponed aging in mice, which is not intellectually difficult, would be extremely time- and resource-consuming. However, the strategy is broadly feasible. Given enough time and resource, there is no reason to doubt that eventually we will be able to postpone human aging, at least to some extent. With an open-ended research program, there is the further possibility that increases in the human "health span" could likewise be open-ended. Moreover, it is important to understand that evolutionarily postponed aging involves an enhancement in performance at later ages, not an extended period of debility. The long-term prospect, then, is more of an extension of youth than an increase in longevity, though the latter does occur.

SCIENTISTIC FASCISM

It is not difficult to concede that all scientists approach their work with attitudes quite far from the ideal objectivity that is supposedly the coin of natural science. Rather, scientists tend to behave more like squabbling children, each group tearfully convinced of the rightness of its own particular claims. But it is another phenomenon altogether when scientists use their scientific ideas as the basis for advancing their own particular ideological views.

Evolutionary biology, unfortunately, has been particularly exploited by ideological movements, from Marxism to eugenics to Herbert Spencer's laissez-faire to various strains of racism and fascism.

This is too depressing, and sometimes grisly, a list to bear examination in detail. I think that the problem has been obvious enough. My concern here is to argue that this problem cannot be regarded as irrelevant history, even for such a seemingly innocent concern as the relationship between evolutionary and critical gerontologies.

The problem persists because evolution is internally teleological. That is, natural selection acts on the relative value, in fitness currency, of individuals within populations. Selection acts to reduce the frequency of low-fitness genotypes, usually, and to increase the average fitness of the population. The intuitive affinities between this process and doctrines of racial competition, class struggle, or market competition are self-evident. When evolutionary biologists go out of their way to propound eugenic or other scientistic proposals (e.g., Fisher, 1930), the entire brew can only become more poisonous.

If one takes critical gerontology broadly to denote a humanistically sensitive and programmatically motivated style of gerontology, then it is obvious that there must be assertions of values and ideals inherent in it. Yet, as I have just argued, explicit programs and values tend to mix poisonously with evolutionary biology. One might imagine some kind of ageist ideology coming out of a marriage between critical gerontology and evolutionary gerontology, an ideology that might advocate the compulsory euthanasia of the retired on the grounds of their evolutionary unimportance. Or there might be an exact reversal of this, with a program of suppressing early reproduction so that we would evolve progressively greater longevities as a species. Either would be a nightmare, an abomination.

Accordingly, I conclude that evolutionary gerontology should strictly avoid taking on the imperatives of critical gerontology, and critical gerontologists should take pains not to develop "evolutionary ethics" concerning the treatment of the elderly. This is not a criticism of the programs of critical gerontology; there is obvious value in a sensitivity to the humanistic and valuational aspects of the problems of aging. But let's just appreciate each other from a safe distance.

REFERENCES

Charlesworth, B. (1980). *Evolution in age-structured populations*. London: Cambridge University Press.

Comfort, A. (1979). *The biology of senescence* (3rd ed.). Edinburgh: Churchill Livingstone.

Denckla, W. D. (1975). A time to die. *Life Science, 16,* 31–44.

Feyerabend, P. (1975). *Against method.* London: New Left Books.

Finch, C. E. (1990). *Longevity, senescence, and the genome.* Chicago: University of Chicago Press.

Fisher, R. A. (1930). *The genetical theory of natural selection.* Oxford: Clarendon Press.

Hamilton, W. D. (1966). The moulding of senescence by natural selection. *Journal of Theoretical Biology, 12,* 12–45.

Hanawalt, P. C. (1987). On the role of DNA damage and repair processes in aging: Evidence for and against. In H. R. Warner, R. N. Butler, R. L. Sprott, & E. L. Schneider (Eds.), *Modern biological theories of aging* (pp. 183–198). New York: Raven Press.

Hayflick, L. (1965). The limited *in vitro* lifetime of human diploid cell strains. *Experimental Cell Research 37,* 614–636.

Hutchinson, E. W., & Rose, M. R. (1990). Quantitative genetic analysis of *Drosophila* stocks with postponed aging. In D. E. Harrison (Ed.), *Genetic effects on aging II* (pp. 66–87). Caldwell, NJ: Telford Press.

Johnson, T. E., & Wood, W. B. (1982). Genetic analysis of life-span in *Caenorhabditis elegans. Proceedings of the National Academy of the Sciences of the United States of America, 79,* 6603–6607.

Lakatos, I. (1970). Falsification and the methodology of scientific research programmes. In I. Lakatos & A. Musgrave (Eds.), *Criticism and the growth of knowledge* (pp. 91–196). Cambridge: Cambridge University Press.

Luckinbill, L. S., & Clare, M. J. (1985). Selection for lifespan in *Drosophila melanogaster. Heredity, 55,* 9–18.

Luckinbill, L. S., Clare, M. J., Krell, W. L., Cirocco, W.C., & Richards, P. A. (1987). Estimating the number of genetic elements that defer senescence in *Drosophila. Evolutionary Ecology, 1,* 37–46.

Martin, G. M., Sprague, C. A., & Epstein, C. J. (1970). Replicative lifespan of cultivated human cells: Effect of donor's age, tissue and genotype. *Laboratory Investigation, 23,* 86–92.

Metchnikoff, E. (1904). *The nature of man.* London: Heinemann.

Miquel, J., Lundgren, P. R., Bensch, K. G., & Atlan, H. (1976). Effects of temperature on the life span, vitality and fine structure of *Drosophila melanogaster. Mechanisms of Ageing and Development, 5,* 347–370.

Orgel, L. E. (1963). The maintenance of the accuracy of protein synthesis and its relevance to ageing. *Proceedings of the National Academy of the Sciences of the United States of America, 49,* 517–521.

Pearl, R. (1928). *The rate of living.* New York: Alfred A. Knopf.

Popper, K. R. (1959). *The logic of scientific discovery.* London: Hutchinson.

Röhme, D. (1981). Evidence for a relationship between longevity of mammalian species and life spans of normal fibroblasts *in vitro* and erythrocytes *in vivo. Proceedings of the National Academy of the Sciences of the United States of America, 78,* 5009–5013.

Rose, M. R. (1984a). Genetic covariation in *Drosophila* life history: Untangling the data. *American Naturalist 123,* 565–569.

Rose, M. R. (1984b). Laboratory evolution of postponed senescence in *Drosophila melanogaster. Evolution, 38,* 1004–1010.

Rose, M. R. (1985). Life history evolution with antagonistic pleiotropy and overlapping generations. *Theoretical Population Biology, 28,* 342–358.

Rose, M. R. (1988). Response to "Thoughts on the selection of longer-lived rodents"—rejoinders. *Growth, Development and Aging, 52,* 209–211.

Rose, M. R. (1990). Should mice be selected for postponed aging? A workshop summary. *Growth, Development and Aging, 54,* 7–17.

Rose, M. R. (1991). *Evolutionary biology of aging.* New York: Oxford University Press.

Rose, M., & Charlesworth, B. (1980). A test of evolutionary theories of senescence. *Nature, 287,* 141–142.

Rose, M. R., Dorey, M. L., Coyle, A. M., & Service, P. M. (1984). The morphology of postponed senescence in *Drosophila melanogaster. Canadian Journal of Zoology, 62,* 1576–1580.

Rose, M. R., & Service, P. M. (1985). The evolution of aging. *Review of Biological Research in Aging, 2,* 85–98.

Rothstein, M. (1987). Evidence for and against the error catastrophe hypothesis. In H. R. Warner, R. N. Butler, R. L. Sprott, & E. L. Schneider (Eds.), *Modern biological theories of aging* (pp. 139–154). New York: Raven Press.

Service, P. M. (1987). Physiological mechanisms of increased stress resistance in *Drosophila melanogaster* selected for postponed senescence. *Physiological Zoology, 60,* 321–326.

Service, P. M., Hutchinson, E. W., & Rose, M. R. (1988). Multiple genetic mechanisms for the evolution of senescence in *Drosophila melanogaster. Evolution, 42,* 708–716.

Service, P. M., & Rose, M. R. (1985). Genetic co-variation among life-history components: The effects of novel environments. *Evolution, 39,* 943–945.

Sohal, R. S. (1987). The free-radical theory of aging: A critique. *Review of Biological Research in Aging, 3,* 431–449.

Watson, A. L. M., Gelman, R. S., Williams, R. M., & Yunis, E. J. (1990). Murine chromosomal regions influencing life span. In D. E. Harrison (Ed.), *Genetic effects on aging II* (pp. 473–488). Caldwell, NJ: Telford Press.

Williams, G. C. (1957). Pleiotropy, natural selection, and the evolution of senescence. *Evolution, 11,* 398–411.

Criticism between Literature and Gerontology

Steven Weiland

The tragic character of thought—as any perspective will show—is that it takes a rigid mold too soon; chooses destiny like a Calvinist, in infancy, instead of waiting slowly for old age, and hence for the most part works against the world, good sense, and its own object.
—R. P. Blackmur, "A Critic's Job of Work"

The form of life to which narrative discourse belongs is our historical condition itself.
—Paul Ricoeur, "The Nature of Narrative"

Has gerontology come too late to literary studies, now perhaps the most morbid of disciplines? An essay by the influential French critic Roland Barthes (1977) announced "The Death of the Author." Literary historian Alvin Kernan has gone further and named his recent book *The Death of Literature.* The critic too is gone, or so it is proposed for at least the kind of criticism represented by renowned figures like Edmund Wilson or Lionel Trilling, their practice having disappeared in the specializations of academic life (Jacoby, 1987; Pells, 1985). Nonetheless, literary theory and textual criticism flourish in a paradox: uncertainty about literary tradition and the authority of the canon has brought about new potential for interpretive careers, based as they often are now on the application of complex interpretive techniques with specialized vocabularies to literary and nonliterary texts (or to texts now defined as literature). With the perception of an abundance of textuality across the disciplines, literary studies and rhetoric have new scholarly and curricular priority.[1]

The thematic richness of literary studies is a sign, too, of its infiltration by adjacent disciplines in the humanities (philosophy and anthropology, for example) as well as of its intentions, in turn, to claim considerable interpretive authority in scholarship outside English (Robbins, 1987). Gerontology, a field made of many kinds of inquiry, has only unevenly pursued its epistemic foundations, its textuality and vocabulary, and other critical and rhetorical themes. Hence, literature and criticism's role in the study of aging may be constrained by stereotyping: gerontologists finding literary studies ambitious, hermetic (or relativistic), and inaccessible, and literary critics finding gerontology parochial, pragmatic (or positivist), and even anti-intellectual.

In what follows I begin with an account of some problems of literary theory and a model for a critical center, a metaphor whose popularity itself suggests the rifts in the current scene.[2] As its uses are defined, the center entails primary attention to narrative, whose psychological and gerontological manifestations in the now famous idea of the life review I take up next. Narrative is the surest point of connection between literature and gerontology. I turn then to Wallace Stegner's (1988) recent novel *Crossing to Safety,* certain to be a classic for its presentation of individual and historical dimensions of aging. *Crossing to Safety* is a story of aging in a career in which developmental themes unfold in the world of academic, intellectual, and creative work. It presents the relations between a personal narrative and a professional or disciplinary one, conveniently enough in this case the problem of a critical vocation. As Harry Moody (1988) claims in his call for a critical gerontology: "The *ideal* old age is not an uncritical subjective preference but depends on concrete historical possibilities" (p. 28).

RIFT AND REFERENCE

Without pragmatic claims, and in a field as demographically urgent as gerontology, imaginative literature has an uncertain relation to the empirical findings of science and social science. Accordingly, the impact of literature on gerontology may have to come as much from attention to the problems of theory and its proposals about language, epistemology, and the social meanings of literature as from the literary demonstration of aging. That is to say that theory and criticism are themselves now part of the object they inquire into and that their uses in gerontology, in the centrist format I suggest below, must be added to developmental narratives of aging and other formal attributes of literature that gerontologists have found to be useful.

Gerontology has shown a steady interest in imaginative literature, largely ignoring developments in literary theory and instead accumulating accounts of what are often called "images of aging." Studies of this kind represent the historical mainstream of literary inquiry and the belief in referential value. Accordingly, literature is used to illustrate negative or (less often) positive stereotypes of aging or to provide an aging character in a short story, novel, play, or film as an example of resignation, wisdom, or another quality understood to be unique to the experience of growing old.[3]

Though it derives from humanistic motives and practices, this interpretive program may also (and paradoxically so, given my statement above) have the effect of fortifying the empirical habits of gerontology. Literary case studies may be seen as standing side by side, albeit in a different vocabulary, with objects of scientific research to demonstrate the consequences of aging in cognitive and personality development, family relations, and social attitudes. For obvious reasons this approach favors fiction and drama in which human character appears in recognizable situations over time. Poetry, with its lack of narrative (generally) and allusive verbal structure has been less useful, except in the theme of the character of the aging poet.

Valuable as they are, studies of literary images of aging rarely interrogate (to use a term from contemporary literary theory) the premises of this form of gerontological inquiry, either in skepticism about its representational assumptions or in curiosity about the dense network of historical, textual, institutional, and other sources from which many theorists now understand works of literature to have emerged; valuable exceptions include Hendricks and Leedham (1987) and Woodward and Schwartz (1986). Perhaps there are good reasons for such thematic selectivity. Geoffrey Hartman (1980), an influential deconstructionist, has proposed that the goal of criticism is to reveal contradictions and equivocations, in effect making fiction "interpretable by making it less readable" (p. 32). The academic community of critics might welcome such a result, but those who write about literature with gerontologists as their audience could hardly argue for its utility by proclaiming its inaccessibility. Still, recent studies of literature and gerontology are unduly isolated from the conflicts that may impede or, conversely, give greater meaning to literary applications.

There is a rift in English departments over the role of literary theory and the seeming marginalization of literature itself as an object of study. Theorists argue not only for value of their work in understanding canonical and neglected texts but for the autonomy of theory, reflecting its aspiration to the merger of philosophic, social, linguistic, and material interests that could not be contained by the older styles of textual analysis. For example, according to Michel Foucault (1972), a philosopher of history with a strong following in literary studies,

> The frontiers of a book are never clear-cut; beyond the title, the first lines, and the last full stop, beyond its internal configuration and its autonomous form, it is caught up in a system of references to other books, other texts, other sentences: it is a node within a network. (p. 24)

The book being read is not the one the reader holds in his or her hands. For any inquiry into it shows that its unity and meanings are variable and relative and that its construction reflects a vast and complex "field of discourse." Foucault has in mind the many institutional and disciplinary discourses of history, regulatory ones in his view, that structure, distribute, and maintain power through textuality. Paradoxically, Foucault's rival, Jacques Derrida, and his followers in deconstruction (especially in America) narrow the interpretive "field" in order to expand it again on behalf of attention to the complexities and concealments of language, producing a doctrine of textuality based on deliberate "misreading."

By showing a text's gaps, inconsistencies, and contradictions, deconstruction expresses skepticism about its referential uses or even its intention to be about the world outside the text. Though it would surprise Dickens (for example) to know it, there is now disagreement about how far the activity in language traditionally called literature can also be assumed to be accurately or even recognizably about other forms of human experience in history and society. Dickens thought that language fortified—in its cruelty, bombast, and circumlocutions—the dehumanizing activities of the schools, the courts, and the welfare system. But he believed in the power of literary discourse to consolidate or even tame all others on behalf of representations of Victorian society that were convincing enough to prompt change in it. His novels can now be situated in their "networks," but the literary culture that sustains such historical endeavors in criticism is prone to find the most value in the textual rather than the political space they occupy. For many expert readers, Dickens's novels (and those of others, of course) have gone, to use a popular formulation from Barthes (1977), from being works to texts. Partisans of this critical transformation find greater elasticity in the kinds of interpretations available, even ones that perhaps ratify the original political intention. But skeptics of skepticism, including influential critics otherwise loyal to postmodern ideas (like Edward Said, discussed below), see in the rift in literary studies signs of neglect of criticism's most durable task—a secondary rift, as it were, in advanced theorizing, where, of course, there are also strong political purposes (for well-regarded examples, see Eagleton, 1983, 1984; Lentricchia, 1983).

The uses of literature and criticism are also problematized (another favorite term of theorists) by a rift in gerontology, one reflecting the tired but still true "two cultures" debate (science vs. humanities) and another uncertainty within humanistic gerontology itself. For even as some humanistically oriented gerontologists are calling for pursuit of "methodological heresies" (including literary ones), others, equally humanistic, lament the fragmentation of efforts and the difficulty of mounting a critical gerontology that would gain power from consensus about the role of social transformation. Their mutual impatience with science and positivism apparently cannot seal an agreement about the ends of gerontological inquiry generally, perhaps a typical and temporary strain of "boundary work."[4] Transformational or emancipatory intentions, often relying on the theorists of the Frankfurt School, compete with more traditional or meliorative ideals of academic scholarship.[5] The diverse discourses of gerontology show that as many gerontologists want to understand as to change individual and social ideas about aging.

The study of aging through literature meets the demands for methodological pluralism in gerontology, but so too does it carry the burden of epistemological skepticism and other critical themes. The impact of such skepticism, including its ahistorical tendency, has produced efforts to find a critical position that shelters referential textuality while it shows how the linguistic surface is much more than just that. For gerontologists, the question may be put more directly: If literature, as many postmodernists propose, is only about literature (or even just language), then what use is it in an enterprise like social gerontology, where the claims of aging as human and social experiences must be fitted to complex problems of economics, health care, transportation, and other areas of public policy? Has the novelty of theory, as enemies of deconstruction assert, obscured the reasons for attention to literature in the first place? And are arcane readings of texts, reflecting the antifoundationalism of postmodern theorizing, obstacles to seeing how literature can provide a reasonably accurate record of individual and social experience, one that is helpful in understanding aging?

THE SITUATED CRITIC

In an important book of synthesis, Edward Said (1983a, p. 182) has asked for "critical consciousness" as the product of literary study. Its task is to do more than describe texts and seek insights about them in teaching and scholarship, for it is "to occupy itself with the intrinsic conditions on which knowledge is made possible." Said looks closely at the examples of Derrida and Foucault, finding in their seminal work and its attention to the processes of textual knowledge "a conscious effort to release a very specialized sort of textual *discovery* from the mass of material, habits, conventions, and institutions constituting an immediate historical pressure" (pp. 182–183). Both believe in a kind of "involuntarism," the author never being the sufficient cause of a text. Hence, their ideas "have a special interest for critics today who may wish to place themselves skeptically between culture as a massive body of self-congratulating ideas and system or method, anything resembling a sovereign technique that claims to be free of history, subjectivity, or circumstance" (p. 202). This is a timely stance even for gerontologists uninterested in literature.

Said favors Foucault, at least insofar as Derrida's exclusive interest in what is undecidable in a text means that he and his followers cannot reach into the actual historical power of ideas. "The search *within* a text for the conditions of textuality," Said (1983a) reminds us, "will falter at that very point where the text's historical presentation to the reader is put into question and made an issue for the critic" (p. 212).[6] Foucault occupies a more favorable "geopolitical" position, exemplifying the critic who stands between the dominant culture and any impersonal system of disciplines (now including, presumably, the techniques of Derrida made into an academic orthodoxy). "For Foucault," Said claims in what turns out to be qualified admiration, "where there is knowledge and discourse, there must criticism also be, to reveal the exact places—and displacements—of the text, thereby to see the text as a process signifying an effective historical will to be present, an effective desire to be a text and to be a position taken" (p. 221).[7] But despite Foucault's insight into the formation of discourses (their *location* in history) he does not, in Said's view, show enough interest in why such developments take place or in the problem of historical change.

I have recounted Said's adept reading of the conflict of theories and borrowed his spatial ("between") metaphor because, in the work of theory today, figures like Derrida and Foucault have become coordinates around which a personal statement like Said's must be organized, one that itself resists popular forms of resistance to orthodox literary study. Such is the way theory vies with literature as a site for specifying critical values, the vocabularies and forms of philosophic work now holding as much or even more interest than recent fiction or poetry; and hence, so original and forthright a thinker as Said offers a binary account of essentials in order to express his own desire to be "present," to be a critic of the oppositional theorists who dominate academic criticism.

I understand Said's (1983a) metaphor to convey "between-ness" of two kinds, perhaps yielding an oxymoronic plural center. First there are the justifiably appealing theories of Derrida and Foucault, positioned between the sovereignties of the academic disciplines and of the state and the reigning national culture. Said grants them this position, one that appears to have prompted an account of his own. Said himself is less hostile to the activities of the disciplines (he is a self-proclaimed conservative in matters of scholarship), so he proposes a second way to be "between." It incorporates from Derrida, Foucalt, and others recognition of the multilayered and networked textuality of literature, of the role of language in constituting social realities and institutions, and of the virtues of misreading in revealing covert meanings. But it is skeptical of totalizing theories and the interests and options they foreclose. Said insists on the "worldliness" of literature and criticism. He believes in the latter's obligation to history, to human variability and change, and to moral judgment and statement.

Said puts himself between old and new critical attitudes, and he insists on a role for criticism that, with the bias of tradition, puts it between the text and the world. In his definition of "secular criticism," Said (1983b) stresses how individual consciousness makes itself truly critical:

> On the one hand, the individual mind registers and is very much aware of the collective whole, context, or situation in which it finds itself. On

the other hand, precisely because of this awareness—a worldly self-situating, a sensitive response to the dominant culture—the individual consciousness is not naturally and easily a mere child of the culture, but a historical and social actor in it. And because of that perspective, which introduces circumstance and distinction where there only had been conformity and belonging, there is distance, or what we might also call criticism. (p. 15)

For my purposes, Said's use of another metaphor—the "mere child"—itself indicates how the figurative habits of discourse can reveal where critical progress can be made. For as I propose below, processes of aging also disclose the uses of criticism. The view that Said terms "collective" is very different from the totalizing he finds in the systems of Derrida and Foucault. The perspective he endorses—situated and historical—is the subject and object of narrative, where gerontology too has located important discursive meanings.

LIFE REVIEW, NARRATIVE, AND COVERT EXPRESSION

When Erik H. Erikson (1978) concluded his commentary on Ingmar Bergman's film *Wild Strawberries* with the remark that "a good story does not need a chart to come alive and . . . a chart [like the familiar one illustrating Erikson's own eight-stage theory] can use a good story" (p. 30), he recognized that a psychological theory depends on its implied narrative. He was also, I think, being coy, if not merely modest, about what might be added to the imaginative account of a life—a fictional one or a real one artistically presented—by a theory that could help to explain its inner logic and external meanings. Erikson is the self-declared psychologist of the "outer world." He has sought to overcome the emphasis on early childhood in classic psychoanalysis (what he called the habit of "originology") in favor of a more complete view of developmental stages, including their historical and social dimensions. And although he may have contributed to the mythologizing of aging in the form of a progressive and hopeful life cycle, he has, as a developmental theorist and biographer, also helped to make stories of aging demonstrate the alignment of empirical and humanistic methods.

The discovery of narrative in the many discourses of aging has had the effect of giving primacy to what amount to literary criteria in joining the data from personal narrative to other kinds of gerontological inquiry (Manheimer, 1989). For example, Robert Butler's (1963) argument in his pathmaking essay on the life review, which helped to initiate the application of narrative models to gerontology, offers as much literary as clinical evidence. But it neglects, perhaps deliberately, important distinctions. Butler presents the actual voices of the aged (some are patients) and the fictional ones of a story by Henry James with seemingly equal authority. By blurring the differences between them, he suggests that it is expressive power and utility (often the same thing) that give value to narratives of aging. Literary study tells us that the meaning is *in* the narration, not as information to container but as an activity having its own traditions and uses.[8]

That is the conclusion, too, of important recent work on the role of narrative in developmental psychology and psychoanalysis (see Cohler & Freeman, 1988; Freeman, 1984; Sarbin, 1986; Schafer, 1980; Spence, 1982). Both have been called primarily narrative activities, the former for reasons that are plain and the latter because its therapeutic action depends on making a coherent and meaningful story (or "construction," in Freud's term) from the discursiveness or free associations of the clinical encounter. Analyst and patient share, verbally and in the transference, in the telling and gradual retelling of the events in a life and their relations and meanings (another point Butler [1963] ignores, though he recognizes the problem of point of view in literature). And if the facts of experience are inaccessible and the act of biographical reconstruction or personal narrative autonomous, then fictional narrative too may be granted a kind of clinical authority.

Where truth is allied to the prospect of clinical results or to the satisfying aging that is the goal of the life review, debates over what actually happened in relation to how it is perceived to have happened can indeed seem unfruitful. The patient or life reviewer, after all, is not looking for a complete or historically accurate record of his or her past but an account of it (naively thought to be a historical representation) that is convincing and useful in the present.[9] Narratives of aging, with their intrapsychic principles of selection and order, present this goal to their interpreters, to developmental psychologists or literary critics who find overlapping cognitive, adaptive, formal, and aesthetic results. Hans Loewald (1972) stated these as possibilities in the idiosyncratic chronology of personal narratives:

> Past, present, and future present themselves in psychic life not primarily as one preceding or following the other, but as modes of time which determine and shape each other, which differentiate out of and articulate a pure now. There is no irreversibility on a linear continuum, as in the common concept of time as succession, but a reciprocal relationship

whereby one time mode cannot be experienced or thought about without the other and whereby they continually modify each other. (p. 407)[10]

The process of adding meaning is part of the definition of adulthood and old age. Indeed, Jerome Bruner (1990) has sought to redefine the project of cognitive psychology, which he helped to invent, as a "meaning making" enterprise with narrative understanding at *its* center, even invoking psychoanalytic contributions (no doubt to the displeasure of orthodox cognitivists). Poised as it is at the border of clinical and interpretive work, and with its unique life cycle resources, gerontology is a site where the study of how narrative meaning is made, maintained, and altered has unusual urgency. Even as it holds to referential meanings, it can use literary study and ideas about narrative (including, again, psychoanalytic influences) to activate recognition of contingency and to prompt enough "misreading" to represent the complex relations between imaginative and scientific discourses.

Of course, Wallace Stegner (1988) knows the problems entailed in the personal narrative. "Recollection . . . is usually about half invention," he says in *Crossing to Safety*, and he warns of "what memory reports plausibly but not necessarily truly" (p. 64). But his casual statement of this cognitive and artistic dilemma is a sign, too, of Stegner's surprising distrust of psycholgoy and of psychoanalysis in particular. He dismisses it as a "belittling" theory based on "distortions" and "half-truths," a case of the mind "infecting" the emotions. Undeterred by the "half-truth" of memory, *Crossing to Safety*'s narrator Larry Morgan (himself a novelist) sees only what is unproved in the partialities of psychology, not what insight may derive from its fruitfully inexact methods.

Morgan's judgment might be welcome as an irony but not as a sign of how fiction works for writers and readers who have always been preoccupied with the inner life and conflicts of character. Memory organized into narrative is selective according to complex and (often) competing principles of cognition and art, again a point missing from Butler's (1963) otherwise compelling proposal. Where experimental, clinical, and imaginative methods intersect and where there may be opportunities for greater interpretive density and rigor is now a preoccupation of literary theorists who, like Bruner (1990), turn to narrative as an instrument of centering in a fragmented field.

But as Said (1983a, 1983b) reminds us, however necessary it is for literature to retain its referential qualities via the tasks of criticism, it remains literature, the object, too, of legitimate deconstructive inquiry. For developmentalists and gerontologists apt to rely on the example of literature and even on the reflexive and narrative models of historiography, anthropology, and other scholarly discourses, the problem of indirection is essential. No doubt Bernice Neugarten (1979) did not intend to give comfort to disciples of Derrida or Foucault when she urged paying more attention to "covert expression" in the study of developmental themes.[11] Narrative interpretation in gerontology may show how surface and covert meanings can be combined (or reconfigured in the freedom of postmodern interpretations) to reveal critical intentions.

THE POUR OF HISTORY

The theme of the life review, with its collapsed chronology and interwoven past and present, could hardly have a better exemplar than Stegner's (1988) *Crossing to Safety*. Most of the novel is devoted to an account of marriage, career, and friendship over four decades.[12] But the review proceeds only after this meditation:

> If you could forget mortality . . . you could really believe that time is circular, and not linear and progressive as our culture is bent on proving. Seen in geological perspective, we are fossils in the making, to be buried and eventually exposed again for the puzzlement of creatures of later eras. Seen in either geological or biological terms, we don't warrant attention as individuals. (p. 4)

Said notes that deconstruction is weak before the novel because the author has already deconstructed the text by presenting it through the voice of a narrator. Stegner thus invites us at the outset to be skeptics before his own assertions of narrative identity. For mortality cannot be "forgotten." The narrative element in literature and psychology can be said to be the form of inquiry best suited to undermine geological and biological perspectives. It is a form of assertion, of maintenance of the self and morale in aging (Cohler & Galatzer-Levy, 1990).

Thinking ahead to the novel that will unfold, and retrospectively about what he had to learn in order to write it, the narrator Morgan is rueful and relativistic, positioned now 180 degrees from his temporary geological perspective and inserted into history: "What ever happened to the passion we all had to improve ourselves, live up to our potential, leave a mark on the world? . . . Instead, the world has left marks on us. We got older. Life chastened us so that now we lie waiting to die, or walk on canes, or sit on porches where once the young juices flowed strongly, and feel old and inept and confused" (Stegner, 1988, p. 13). Having presented himself as a self-conscious life reviewer, Morgan shows how memory produces principles of reminiscence as it is shaped by them. Inclined to judge himself and his friends harshly, he recognizes too that the unique knowledge he has of their personal history is all that is really needed to see that their lives also had productive and benevolent effects. But neither, I think, does he wish for their lives to be judged by mere relativism or "It might have been worse." And the novel turns out to belie its narrator's thoughts of incapacity and disengagement.

A new arrival in 1937 at the University of Wisconsin's English Department, fresh from Berkeley's graduate school, Morgan has hopes for a conventional academic career despite having been offered only a 1-year fill-in appointment. He undertakes an exhausting program of writing: "When I hear the contemporary disparagement of ambition and the work ethic I bristle. I can't help it" (Stegner, 1988, p. 103). But equal satisfaction comes from a friendship he and his wife share with another academic couple. A narrative with four actors unfolds, demonstrating for Morgan his belief that, faced with the choice of Seneca's *De Senectute* and *De Amicitia* (as he was in a classically oriented Albuquerque high school), it would not be resigned wisdom he might aspire to but friendship.

Morgan and Sid Lang, and their wives Sally and Charity, are "braided and plaited" into a friendship. To simplify a complex subject, Morgan says: "It is a relationship that has no formal shape, there are no rules or obligations or bonds as in marriage or the family, it is held together by neither law nor property nor blood, there is no glue in it but mutual liking" (Stegner, 1988, p. 102).[13] Friendship is the still point in a turning political world.

> We weren't indifferent. We lived in our time, which were hard times. We had our interests, which were mainly literary and intellectual and only occasionally, inescapably political. But what memory brings back from there is not politics, or the meagerness of living on a hundred and fifty dollars a month, or even the writing I was doing, but the details of friendship—parties, picnics, walks, midnight conversations, glimpses from the occasional unencumbered hours. *Amicita* lasts better than *res publica*, and at least as well as *ars poetica.* Or so it seems now. (p. 109)

Of course, the hint of doubt in the last few words reminds us of how truth is refracted in memory and how the ratio of commitments changes over the life course.

Their close relationship sees the two couples through the birth of children, Morgan's departure from Madison (his contract is not renewed but Lang's is), a successful new career as an editor and writer, and then the crippling illness of Sally. Her condition does not, however, prevent their travel from their New Mexico home, and it is in Florence that the life review comes to focus, not only on the mingled family histories but on experiences of intense meaning, at once private and historical. "Anyone who reads," Morgan proclaims,

> even one from the remote Southwest at the far end of an attenuated tradition, is to some extent a citizen of the world. . . . I could not look up the Arno without feelings of recognition, as if, somewhere off downstream, the river drained into the Rio Grande. I knew names, books, some of the art. I was myself the product of ideas that had been formulated right here. (Stegner, 1988, p. 266)

But it is the sight of a simple street procession that inspires the novel's most evocative passages. Detached from all but the visual presence of the locale itself, the forward narrative impulse yields to feelings of historical connection and meaning. "It was like looking upriver into the pour of history, seeing backward toward the beginnings of modern civilization" (p. 256).

Crossing to Safety reaches far back into cultural history—admirably conscious of its ethnocentrism—even as it compresses the actual experience of the narrator. It exploits the cognitive dimension of the life review, whose uses in the present also give meaning to the cultural narrative, one that stands, like the professional one I address below, between endless geological time and a finite personal history. These forms of narrative deepening are Morgan's stay against Lang's "identity diffusion," to borrow Erikson's terms from the psychology of late adolescence. And structurally, these cultural and professional narratives underline the compact chronology of the novel proper, which lasts but a single day. It opens with the Morgans' return to the Langs' isolated summer home in northern New York State, where Charity is near death from cancer. When it closes, after the lengthy life review, they have seen Charity depart for the hospital and have guided Sid toward reengagement with life. Getting ready for the day, Morgan reconstructs their 34 years of friendship. He does so to prepare for the end of it in its present form and also to reconcile conflicting feelings about what will remain.

THE SUNSHINE ABOVE THE SMOKE

The life review features warm memories of companionship. But it is summarized in unexpected terms in the concluding sentence of the novel's first half: "Good fortune, contentment, peace, happiness, have never been able to deceive me finally. I expected the worse [his wife's illness], and I was right. So much for the dream of man" (Stegner, 1988, p. 205). As an image of aging, this statement is a familiar sign of resignation. But in a second round of review prompted by awareness of the proximity of the dying Charity, Morgan reflects on the fate of Lang in his marriage and career.[14]

Just as personal narrative conveys its origins and uses against the backdrop of developmental or life cycle theory, a career can be assimilated to a larger story that helps to define the border between private and public meaning, between text and history, the territory of Said's critical consciousness. Erikson (1958) asserted that work was the most neglected theme in his field.[15] His biographies derive from his belief that the choice and pursuit of a vocation is part of a dual narrative, of the developmental path of the person and of the historical form of work itself. As a social structure of particular ideals and images and of professional responsibilities and constraints, a vocation is a format for aging—in late adolescent identity formation, where Erikson located the crisis of early adulthood, and certainly in middle and old age, when the consequences of having taken up work of a particular kind are expressed in normative developmental trends. Moody (1988a) identified the problem when, again, he names what is needed for a critical theory of aging: "Historicizing the content of emancipation means looking at concrete lived experience: at the life events and the life chances of particular age cohorts" (pp. 28–29). (See also Riegel, 1975).

Early in *Crossing to Safety*, Morgan presents the image of English departments that prompted people like himself and Lang to choose careers in literary study:

> They used to look like high serene lamaseries where the elect lived in both comfort and grace. Up there, scholars as learned and harmless as Chaucer's Clerk of Oxenford moved among books and ideas, eating and drinking well, sleeping soft, having three-month summer vacations during which they had only to cultivate their inclinations and their "fields." Freed by tenure, by an assured salary, by modest wants, by an inherited competence, or by all four, they were untouched by the scrabbling and scuffling that went on outside the walls, or down in the warrens where we aspirants worked and hoped. (Stegner, 1988, p. 40)

Morgan knows that such a view idealizes the past and that not all professors were people of learning and goodwill. "But still there they were, up in the sunshine above the smoke, a patched elbowed, tweedy elite that we might never improve when we joined it but that we never questioned. Especially during the Depression, when every frog of us was lustful for a lily pad" (pp. 40–41).

It is precisely the academic cohort effects produced by the 1930s that give the psychology of vocation unusual meaning in *Crossing to Safety*.[16] Lang is, oddly enough, a man of independent wealth, with the freedom to choose not to work. He became a professor because he had wanted to be a poet, the classroom being the place where the limits of his creative talent are not an impediment to a life among books. But by entering the academic profession in the late 1930s, he cannot avoid its historical conflicts. "Those were not the most logical years to be advocating philosophical retirement," Morgan says, "even for poets. Poetic speech in those days was supposed to be public speech, and bring thousands to the barricades. Literature was for mobilizing the masses (the middle-class masses), Doing Good, and Righting Wrong" (Stegner, 1988, p. 90).

Of course, the parenthetical sneer and capitalized words suggest Morgan's own skepticism about this literary program, also asserted at this time by academic leaders like Robert Maynard Hutchins at the University of Chicago. But Lang's own "vague disinclination to become engaged in social betterment," his preference for the habits of perception and poetry, is the source of his family's belief that he is a "defeatist," a person "in retreat." He needn't have become a reformer, but his "vagueness" is a debilitating attribute of its own. To his wife, Lang often seems a person without purpose or ambition, at least the usual academic kind. It is the source, too, of his historical dislocation and psychological diffusion. It makes him "aimless" in late life, the object of Morgan's nascent critical understanding of aging.

SAFETY FIRST

Lang cannot write the scholarly essays and books his colleagues (and his wife) demand, and he loses his Wisconsin post. Thinking about Lang's preferences, Morgan says, "What he'd probably like best of all would be to move up here [to the summer retreat] the year around and write poems and dig in the local history and folklore and jot down in his journal when the Jack-in-the-pulpit and Calypso orchids come out, and how the crows get through the winter" (Stegner, 1988, p. 188). Lang ultimately takes a post at Dartmouth, where the work culture of the liberal arts college and the post–World War II expansion of the faculty meet to provide just the opportunity he needs. But as he ages, he simply renews his dedication to the detachment—an inability to meet the world—seemingly enabled and justified by his wide (but shapeless) reading and his poetry. Observing his workshop in Morgan's company, Lang's daughter expresses her disappointment: "He never gets past preparing. Preparing has been his life's work. He prepares, and then he cleans up" (p. 216).

Indeed, Morgan is not reluctant to present the Langs as part of a social and economic formation with its peculiar problems of generativity.

> The people we are talking about are hangovers from a quieter time. They have been able to buy quiet, and distance themselves from industrial ugliness. They live behind university walls part of the year, and in a green garden the rest of it. Their intelligence and their civilized tradition protect them from most of the temptations, indiscretions, vulgarities, and passionate errors that pester and perturb most of us. They fascinate their children because they are so decent, so gracious, so compassionate and understanding and cultivated and well-meaning. They baffle their children because in spite of all they have and are, in spite of being to most eyes an ideal couple, they are remote, unreliable, even harsh. And they have missed something, and show it. (Stegner, 1988, p. 241)

Morgan's own preparation in academic work—and then his rejection of it—produces enough sympathy to define the role structuring that makes their aging so unsatisfying: "Why are they so helplessly who they are?" (p. 242).

The answers are in their individual developmental histories and, in Lang's case, in the history of the teaching of English, which must provide the rudiments of an identity no less than his marriage and friendship. The purity of his dedication to literature reflects both the origins of literary study in the 19th century as a protest against industrialization and urbanization and the modern (and even postmodern) professional culture that emerged from the crucible of Victorian letters—ironically enough, a form of literary work that isolated it from society and politics. Morgan and Lang both understand themselves to have been trained as graduate students in an American version of literature as protest *and* retreat, at least partly traceable to the movement called New Humanism and its legacy at leading graduate schools in the 1920s and 1930s.[17] While they are in Italy, Lang supplies to them a motto (from Dante) for their preoccupation with art: "Think who you are. You were not made to live like brutes, but to pursue virtue and knowledge" (Stegner, 1988, p. 269).

And although they shared in the New Humanism's loyalty to literature as a classical pursuit and in its distrust of science and modernity, they made their careers at a time when only extraordinary discipline could fully preserve such an ideal. In Morgan's view, Lang approximates it but at the cost of "missing something." He is not so ineffective as his wife and daughter think, but he is less effective than he might have been had he been more engaged in the public issues of his time. And he would benefit now from being as self-conscious as Morgan is about the historical dynamics of his profession. Lang's vocation may be pure, but it was incomplete. In the 1940s and 1950s, literary study helped to forge a style of cultural criticism—it sought a public audience—that often flourished outside the university. The "New York Intellectuals" and the British intellectual style represented by Raymond Williams, Richard Hoggart, and others are well-known examples. Stegner himself, as an essayist and novelist, and his hero the historian and critic Bernard DeVoto represent a Western version, as does Said in comparative literature and culture.[18]

The problem a half century ago (as now) for professors of literature and other humanists was not only personal but institutional. Arriving in academic life at the time they did, Morgan and Lang were part of a debate about the uses of liberal learning that came also to define the organization of academic careers. Indeed, the year Stegner has Morgan arrive in Madison (1937), John Dewey (1961) criticized Hutchins's proposals for higher education—based on study of the Great Books—as needlessly remote from the problems of modern society. "The policy of aloofness," Dewey says, "amounts fundamentally to acceptance of a popular American slogan, 'Safety First'" (p. 951). Many humanities departments in public universities—even within the land grant ethos for which Wisconsin was famous—adopted standards reflected or inspired by Hutchins. They have been especially durable at the liberal arts college (like Lang's Dartmouth).

In the postwar years, for different and mainly political reasons, there was a general consensus about the need for detachment in scholarship and teaching. In the 1960s, of course, this professional tradition was challenged. And although "relevance" was often more a slogan than a program of ideas about how academic inquiry could bind private and public life, new fields of research, teaching, and practice emerged (or were strengthened) carrying such potential. Gerontology is one, especially for its obligations at the borders of biology, social science, public policy, and the humanities. Literary study can contribute timely images of aging, even as "critical consciousness" prompts examination of the *aging of images* of the academic profession itself in the life course of its practitioners.[19] *Crossing to Safety* displays both themes, the second, as it were, a sign of the limits of the first.

HERE AND THERE

With his wife's death near as the novel draws to a close, Lang is left to struggle with the fate of his domestic dependence and historical displacement. Morgan remembers his asking about the prospects of living without Charity, and he thinks intensely about his friend's survival as he searches for Lang in the novel's last pages: "Where is he? Out in the woods somewhere debating between what he has lost and what he can't give up, wandering without guidance in a freedom he has never learned to use?" (Stegner, 1988, p. 340). Morgan himself has used narrative and life review to provide meaning, including critical reflections (however fragmented) on his profession. But in a suggestive exchange with Lang's children, eager as they are for a satisfying narrative to be made of their parent's lives or perhaps a story more pleasing to them than the real one, Morgan rejects the idea of a book about his old friends. "You've got the wrong idea of what writers do," he tells them. "They don't understand any more than other people. They invent only plots they can resolve. They ask questions they can answer. Those aren't people that you see in books, those are constructs. Novels or biographies, it makes no difference" (pp. 240–241).

In registering his skepticism about referential literature—with considerable irony, I think—Stegner (1988) also knows that what is typically called criticism in English is even more mechanically constructed by the habits of the profession. In his rejection of a version of the "images of aging" method, Lang recounts his wife's advice on critical professionalism: take a single idea ("perfectability" is the one that a departmental colleague had chosen years ago) and "lay out a whole string of thinkers and writers on that bed" (p. 56). Lang's resistance is without benefit to his professional identity of aesthetic purity and, we can add now, his historical innocence. Morgan's artfully calibrated life review puts into relief Lang's inability to hold his life together with a critical account of its development and structure. With his domestic and professional affiliations deriving from the need for dependence and safety, he "wanders without guidance."

But Stegner invokes the generosity of experience and the perspective of aging to grant Lang the virtues of his weakness. For he conveys ambivalence about Lang's desires and optimism about his fate in the choice of the novel's title. The phrase comes from a poem by Robert Frost (1967), but only the last stanza is quoted in the novel's epigraph. Here is the whole of "I Could Give All to Time":

To Time it never seems that he is brave
To set himself against the peaks of snow
To lay them level with the sunning wave,
Nor is he overjoyed when they lie low,
But only grave, contemplative and grave.

What now is inland shall be ocean isle,
Then eddies playing round a sunken reef
Like the curl at the corner of a smile;
And I could share Time's lack of joy or grief
At such a planetary change of style.

I could give all to Time except—except
What I myself have held. But why declare
The things forbidden that while the Customs slept
I have crossed to Safety with? For I am There,
And what I would not part with I have kept. (pp. 334–335)

The first two stanzas convey the same geological long view with which the novel opens: individuals seem to count for little in the grand scheme of things. The stanzas are absent from the novel, as Derrida would note, as a form of presence, pointing to the ambivalence and fear of aging that is otherwise so carefully modulated in the narration. They underline the security-minded affirmation that is signified by Stegner's (1988) citation of the final stanza and its valorization in the title. In a reversal, the poem asserts the constraints of endless geological time and the freedom of (mortal) human time, which, although it overlaps with all physical change, can be "kept" or "saved" in the form of narrative, memory, and life review. Time and history appear to happen to us; we justifiably strive to be safe, and we deserve the small fruits of mortality, especially love and friendship but also our language making, poetry, and story-telling.

"Why is it so important to be safe?" Charity Lang asks in wondering about the tepidness of academic life and inviting us to contemplate the unhappy fate of criticism. We cannot be certain which of the characters may be said to be representing Frost's encouragement to keep and to be safe: Lang in his need for his wife and a pure vocation, Charity in her dying wish to maintain a particular image of her husband, or even Morgan himself in his friendship for Lang that overcomes whatever disdain derives from their professional differences. Ernst Kris (1975) calls the "personal myth" a "treasured possession" for its "passionate collector" (pp. 273–295). Morgan's approximation of critical consciousness, after all, defines what is missing in Lang's life but also what might be recovered, however attenuated, in the construction of a narrative.

Contemplating the geological abstraction that opens Frost's poem from the point of view of an actual life means recognizing—within the commonplace but still effective metaphor of the traveler—choice within change, the prospects for human agency. Still, the dominant metaphor of safety makes Stegner, too, a centrist of a kind. It invokes (as I proposed earlier) the values of "safety first" and of "playing it safe" even while it is a consoling metaphor for mortality. Stegner's confidence in his novel's title resembles Said's in critical consciousness as a site of theoretical mediation. But metaphor is no more reliable than narrative, and literature is a volatile resource for gerontology. As Paul de Man (1978), deconstruction's chief American spokesman, claimed: "Contrary to common belief, literature is not the place where the unstable epistemology of metaphor is suspended by aesthetic pleasure, although this attempt is a constituative moment of its system. It is rather the place where the possible convergence of rigor and pleasure is shown to be a delusion" (p. 30).

In a parallel consideration of the consequences of narrative, philosopher Paul Ricoeur (1981) shows more confidence in the historical or worldly utility and durability of literature. The "references" of "true history" and "fictional history," he says, "*cross* upon the basic historicity of human experience." But by doing so they do not cancel out what distinguishes them from one another. Crossing makes the two "function as a difference" on behalf of greater realization of "the potentialities of the present" (pp. 294–295).[20]

The last line of Frost's poem suggests Erikson's epigenetic principle of development: the overlapping of stages and the gradual transformation, in the "outer world," of the building blocks of personality from the genetic ground plan. The past persists in the present, as developmental psychology, psychoanalysis, and narrative each demonstrate. A situated life review, Ricoeur (1981) implies, could be recast according to the aims of history or literature stressing again (with Said) "potentialities" in the world that each can usefully represent.[21] Frost (1967) resists fatalism in welcoming the one life cycle each of us lives. Hence, *Crossing to Safety* ends on a note of apparent simplicity and affirmation:

And now I see the figure, dusty-gold in the moonlight, coming steadily up the road from the stable. It is blurred, its shadow encumbers its feet, but it comes without pause, as if timing itself to meet the family coming down from the hill.
    "Sid?" I say.
    "Yes," he says. (Stegner, 1988, p. 341)

CONCLUSION: AN EGG

Gerontology might be inclined to say of such lines that they reaffirm Lang's relations with family and friends even if they do not directly assert his recognition of the meaning of professional diffusion as well. But literary theory would say more, or as the French critic Helene Cixous (1990) has put it in the poetmodern hermetic style that is aimed at widening the meanings of literature: "The text signifies massively; it is an egg" (p. 3).

Gerontologists (and others) are justifiably tempted by literature for its referential qualities, perhaps the most problematic of its significations for today's leading theorists and unsteady ground for a humanistic gerontological synthesis. And even in developmental psychology theoretical advances may come from antitheoretical pursuits. Recalling his ground-breaking inquiry into the concept of "ego identity," Erikson (1956/1980) acknowledged that his use of the term "reflected the dilemma of a psychoanalyst who was led to a new concept not by theoretical preoccupation but rather through the expansion of his clinical awareness to other fields" (p. 108).

The expansion offered to gerontology by literary inquiry comes in the form of narrative contextualizing, including the story of literary study itself and how it has shaped a professional discourse with uncertain or even conflicting ideals. Said (1983a) presents the problem in its contemporary form and as a historically recurrent opportunity for worldly criticism. "The power of discourse is that it is at once the object of struggle and the tool by which the struggle is conducted" (p. 216). Accordingly, *Crossing to Safety* signifies its own role in this history with braided narratives, to borrow another of Stegner's metaphors: lives woven together in family and friendship and personal experience structured within professional cultures. That it does so without Said's theoretical force is only to say that it is a novel. And that Said's critical consciousness can appear to be but another positon in the academic battle over the uses of theory is to say that he has not aspired to the narrative appeal of fiction. Indeed, he emphasizes the role of the essay for polemical goals. Said defines a position from which the novel can be read. He and Stegner together suggest how criticism might assume a place between the literary text and the sciences of aging.

They force us, too, to think about literary studies within literary studies' own unfolding narrative. Or how do its socializing practices, theoretical divisions, and model practitioners—its cohort effects, in the language of gerontology—define a life course in the discipline and the potential for critical ideas about aging? These are questions for critical gerontology, as it turns to the study of gerontological discourses, from the life review to more complicated (or conflicted) forms in literary and other narratives of aging. In all of them the meaning is often in the telling, in the language that *is* experience even as it is about living and aging. As *Crossing to Safety* moves toward its conclusion, and after Morgan has completed his life review, he says, speaking of both: "Now we are finally here. This, in all its painful ambiguity, is what we came for" (Stegner, 1988, p. 284).

NOTES

[1] Vocabulary has become perhaps the great sign of difference between critical generations (see Letricchia & McLaughlin, 1990). Oddly enough, the term *criticism* does not earn an essay in this volume. Itself a complex term, its uses in the phrase "literary criticism" may, for some users, be very different indeed from the meaning of the first term in the phrase "critical gerontology." Signs of overlap, difference, and potential for applications to gerontology that might supplement the approach proposed by Harry R. Moody (1988a) appear in Terry Eagleton (1984) and in Michael Walzer (1988). I return to this theme in later sections of my essay. Thanks to the university presses, there are many places to observe the varieties of literary criticism. A comprehensive historical survey is available in Vincent B. Leitch (1988).

[2] See, for example, Wayne Booth's (1983) presidential address to the Modern Language Association. Psychologist Jerome Bruner (1990) says of his own field, "It has lost its center and risks losing the cohesion needed to assure the internal exchange that might justify a division of labor among its parts" (p. ix).

[3] See, for example, E. F. Ansello (1977) and Mary Sohngen (1977). A useful compendium of sources is Robert E. Yahnke and Richard M. Eastman (1990). The durability of this approach is evident in Herbert F. Donow (1990). My brief essay, "Gerontology and Literary Studies," appears in the same issue of *The Gerontologist* as an instance of friendly counterpoint. A well-organized and thoroughly documented survey can be found in Anne M. Wyatt-Brown (1990).

[4] See Thomas Gieryn (1983). Gieryn suggests that "boundary-work" can be observed in the "stylistic resources" of a profession seeking to explain or justify expanding its authority (p. 791).

[5] The category "methodological heresies" appears in Nancy Datan, Dean Rodeheaver, and Fergus Hughes (1987). See also Moody's essay (1988a) and others in the volume in which it appeared, and W. Andrew Achenbaum (1987). The problem is not just one of the late 1980s: "We have become as specialized, as objective, as fragmented as any other field. And we function within a cultural milieu that matches very well this model of efficient, industrious activity that lacks a unifying frame of reference" (Kastenbaum, 1978, p. 62).

[6] Said adds that Derrida "has chosen the lucidity of the undecidable in a text, so to speak, over the identifiable power of a text" and that his work "has [not] demanded from its disciples any binding engagement on matters pertaining to discovery and knowledge, freedom, oppression, or injustice" (p. 214).

[7] For an account of changes in criticism along the lines proposed by Said and an argument for an adaptive postmodernism, see David Simpson (1988). Jim Merod (1987) acknowledges the influence of Said on his *Political Responsibility of the Critic*.

[8] I mean here to endorse Harry Moody's (1988b) suggestion that the life review itself needs critical appraisal and support from "categories" of inquiry other than psychotherapy (he cites literature as one). See also Kathleen Woodward (1986).

[9] Examples of expressive and functional success can be found in Sharon Kaufman (1986). The problem of verifiability, of course, is at the center of the controversy surrounding Adolf Grunbaum's philosophical study of psychoanalysis. A convenient place to observe it is in Grunbaum's (1986) own summary of his book and then the extensive comments pro and con from many scholars across the disciplines of the sciences and humanities.

[10] Ernst Kris (1975) put the matter this way in his well-known essay "The Personal Myth": "The dynamics of memory function suggest that our autobiographical memory is in constant flux, is instantly being reorganized, and is constantly subject to changes which *the tensions of the present tend to impose*" (p. 299; emphasis added). One might argue that when the life review is presented as a response to mortality or as a search for meaning or coherence, it loses some of the historical specificity that Moody and others always identify as needed in critical reflection. My discussion of *Crossing to Safety* (Stegner, 1988) is meant to provide a literary example.

[11] Also standing behind literary study of the kind offered here is Neugarten's (1984) proposal that the goal of interpreting the life course "is not to discover universals, not to make predictions that will hold good over time, and certainly not to control; but, instead, to explicate contexts and thereby to achieve new insights and new understandings" (p. 292).

[12] For important views on the life review (including skepticism), see Victor Molinari and Robert E. Reichlin (1984–1985) and Robert Disch (1988).

[13] See also Sarah H. Matthews (1986). She stresses "noninstitutional" relationships. Morgan and Lang, of course, are also bound by intellectual colleagueship. Matthews, who values the spontaneous and unrevised truthfulness of the interview, also underlines the differences that derive from the study of oral and written sources, a point of view that threatens the utility of any literary text to gerontology.

[14] Whether he does so on behalf of Stegner, too, in the matter of how a career is shaped, as I believe he does, is a question for biography. I don't mean to be coy—many details in *Crossing to Safety* are clearly autobiographical, including the narrator's arrival in Madison in 1937, the birth of a first child, and the publication of a first book. Stegner was also a student of Norman

Foerster, one of the leading New Humanists (discussed below in the text) while at the University of Iowa. Stegner's success as a novelist and his career as a teacher of creative writing, mainly at Stanford, provided him with a good position from which to think as a kind of insider/outsider about orthodox academic careers in literature. For a biographical account, which is (alas) thin on Stegner's earliest professional years, see Forrest G. Robinson and Margaret G. Robinson, (1977).

[15] A review a few years after Erikson's concurred with his view; see Walter S. Neff (1965). In his account of the life review, Butler (1963) refers to "the customary defense operations provided by work" (p. 66). But at the end of "The Personal Myth," Kris (1975) notes the developmental significance of "patterns of biography supplied by cultural sources, patterns frequently related to the tradition of a special vocation" (p. 300). Kaufman's (1986) informants all valued "activity" and "productivity" but not always the "work role". See also Susan S. Whitburne (1986). She concentrates on the literature of vocational psychology. Richard L. Ochberg (1988) addresses the question of professional "career culture." But each culture has its special features. The career path of academic life—flat after the promotion to full professor, usually in midcareer—belies his emphasis on "constant advancement." Within the uniformities of the academic career I believe there to be important disciplinary differences. See note 19, below.

[16] K. Warner Schaie (1984) notes that "developmentalists have often treated historical time and generational effects as confounds to be controlled and explained away" (pp. 1–2). Schaie urges greater subtlety in the designation of cohorts. But that is a problem in the humanities when the "events" giving academic cohorts historical definition are such things as the advent of particular theories and critical styles. Morgan and Lang, for example, are uncertain about where they stand in relation to the New Humanists.

[17] This two-sentence account reflects, of course, a complex group of events and ideas. I rely on Terry Eagleton's versions of the "Rise of English" (1983) and *The Function of Criticism* (1984). The American case is presented by Gerald Graff in *Professing Literature: An Institutional History* (1987). Graff says this of the late 1930s, when the professors of *Crossing to Safety* are being socialized into English: "The argument that the politics of literature should be seen as part of its form modulated subtly into the idea that literature had no politics, except as an irrelevant extrinsic concern" (p. 150). By this time there are only echoes of the New Humanism, but Morgan and Lang sense its reverberations. It has been summarized thus:

> Against the decline of philosophical absolutism in the nineteenth century and the rise of romantic individualism and naturalistic pragmatism, the [New] Humanists found the essence of their challenge in defending a view of life that could uphold general universal standards and values without recourse to metaphysics or religious dogma. (Hoeveler, 1977, p. 25)

Based on Lang's "visceral" connection with nature, Morgan says of him, "If there was ever a romantic who should not have studied with Irving Babbitt [a leading New Humanist], he is the one" (Stegner, 1988, p. 81). Butler (1970) too has something to contribute to this problem: "Some behavior is on time in terms of both individual and social perspectives. Some is outdated, anachronistic; some ahead of time, which we could call proleptic. Thus, we might endeavor to control the relations of culture and the individual" (p. 126).

[18] On the fate of "cultural criticism," see Pells (1985) and Jacoby (1987) and Giles Gunn (1987). For the British, see Lesley Johnson (1979). See also Wallace Stegner (1974) and Edward Said (1978). I consider this theme in the introduction to my own study of postwar intellectuals, where I rely on the example of sociologist C. Wright Mills (Weiland, 1991). Stegner's (1974) feelings about academic scholarship focused on method or theory can be observed in DeVoto's comment (1932) that under such conditions literature "ceases to be an art, it ceases to have any bearing on human life, and becomes only a despised corpse, a cadaver without worth except as material for the practice of a barren but technically expert dissection" (p. 96). The "New York Intellectuals" (and Mills) made a similar assumption, as does Said throughout *The World, the Text, and the Critic* (1983a). The postwar intellectual style described above has not always aged happily; see Sanford Pinsker (1990).

[19] The matter of academic aging has had considerable attention with regard to scholarly productivity (now more often called "vitality") across the life span, especially in the sciences. For a sample of themes and methods on the generic academic career, see Peter M. Newton (1983), Janet Lawrence and Robert Blackburn (1985), and Roger G. Baldwin (1990). I emphasize the matter of the "disciplinary accent" in *Faculty Seniority*. (Weiland, 1992).

[20] Ricoeur provides an important reflection on the life review:

> The "true" histories of the past uncover the buried potentialities of the present. Croce said that there is only the history of the present. That is true, provided we add: *there is only a history of the potentialities of the present.* History, in this sense, explores the field of "imaginative" variations which surround the present and the real that we take for granted in everyday life. (p. 295)

[21] For a developmental perspective emphasizing the "optimal" rather than the normal, see Dale Dannefer and Marion Perlmutter (1990). They propose that "instead of reifying what exists at one particular historical moment or in one particular cultural setting, the focus should be on understanding the range of expression of human possibilities and the social arrangements that facilitate those possibilities" (p. 132).

REFERENCES

Achenbaum, W. A. (1987). Can gerontology be a science? *Journal of Aging Studies, 1,* 3–18.

Ansello, E. F. (1977). Old age and literature: An overview. *Educational Gerontology, 2,* 211–218.

Baldwin, Roger G. (1990). Faculty career stages and implications for professional development. In J. Schuster & D. Wheeler (Eds.), *Enhancing faculty careers* (pp. 20–40). San Francisco: Jossey-Bass.

Barthes, R. (1977). *Image—music—text* (Trans. S. Heath). New York: Hill and Wang.

Booth, W. (1983). Arts and scandals, 1982. *PMLA, 98*, 312–322.

Butler, R. N. (1963). The life review: An interpretation of reminiscence of the aged. *Psychiatry, 26*, 65–76.

Butler, R. N. (1970). Looking forward to what? The life review, legacy, and excessive identity versus change. *American Behavioral Scientist, 14*, 126.

Bruner, J. (1990). *Acts of meaning*. Cambridge, MA: Harvard University Press.

Cixous, H. (1990). *Reading with Clarice Lispector* (Ed. and Trans. V. A. Conley). Minneapolis: University of Minnesota Press.

Cohler, B., & Freeman, M. (1988). Psychoanalysis and developmental narrative. In S. Greenspan & G. Pollack (Eds.), *The course of life* (rev. ed.). New York: International Universities Press.

Cohler, B. J., & Galatzer-Levy, R. M. (1990). Self, meaning, and morale across the second half of life. In R. A. Nemiroff & C. A. Colarusso (Eds.), *New dimensions in adult development* (pp. 214–263). New York: Basic Books.

Dannefer, D., & Perlmutter, M. (1990). Development as a multidimensional process: Individual and social constituents. *Human Development, 33*, 108–37.

Datan, N., Rodeheaver, D., & Hughes, F. (1987). Adult development and aging. *Annual Review of Psychology, 38*, 153–180.

De Man, P. (1978). The epistemology of metaphor. *Critical Inquiry, 5*, 30.

Dewey, J. (1961). President Hutchins' Proposals to Remake Higher Education. In R. Hofstadter & W. Smith (Eds.), *American higher education: A documentary history* (Vol. 2, pp. 949–953) Chicago: University of Chicago Press.

Disch, R. (Ed.). (1988). *Twenty-five years of the life review: Theoretical and practical considerations*. New York: Haworth.

Donow, H. F. (1990). Two approaches to the care of an elder parent. *Gerontologist, 30*, 486–490.

Eagleton, T. (1984). *The function of criticism: From* The Spectator *to post-structuralism*. London: Verso.

Eagleton, T. (1983). Rise of English. In *Literary theory: An introduction*. Minneapolis: University of Minnesota Press.

Erikson, E. H. (1980). The problem of ego identity. In *Identity and the life cycle*. New York: Norton. (Original work published 1956)

Erikson, E. H. (1978). Reflections on Dr. Borg's life cycle. In E. H. Erikson (Ed.), *Adulthood* (pp. 1–31). New York: Norton.

Erikson, E. H. (1958). *Young man Luther*. New York: Norton.

Foucault, M. (1972). *The archaeology of knowledge* (Trans. A. M. S. Smith). New York: Pantheon.

Freeman, M. (1984). History, narrative, and life-span developmental knowledge. *Human Development, 27*, 1–19.

Gieryn, T. (1983). Boundary-work and the demarcation of science from non-science: Strains and interests in professional ideologies of scientists. *American Sociological Review, 48,* 781–795.

Graff, G. (1987). *Professing literature: An institutional history.* Chicago: University of Chicago Press.

Grunbaum, A. (1986). Precis of *The foundations of psychoanalysis: A philosophical critique. Behavioral and Brain Sciences, 9,* 217–284.

Gunn, G. (1987). *The culture of criticism and the criticism of culture.* New York: Oxford University Press.

Hartman, G. (1980). *Criticism in the wilderness: The study of literature today.* New Haven, CT: Yale University Press.

Hendricks, J., & Leedham, C. A. (1987). Making sense of literary aging: Relevance of recent gerontological theory. *Journal of Aging Studies, 1,* 187–208.

Hoeveler, J. D. Jr. (1977). *The new humanism: A critique of modern America, 1900–1940.* Charlottesville: University Press of Virginia.

Jacoby, R. (1987). *The last intellectuals: American culture in the age of academe.* New York: Basic Books.

Johnson, L. (1979). *The cultural critics: From Matthew Arnold to Raymond Williams.* London: Routledge and Kegan Paul.

Kastenbaum, R. (1978). Gerontology's search for understanding. *Gerontologist, 18,* 62.

Kaufman, S. (1986). *The ageless self: Sources of meaning in late life.* Madison: University of Wisconsin Press.

Kris, E. (1975). The personal myth. In *Selected papers of Ernst Kris.* New Haven, CT: Yale University Press.

Lawrence, J., & Blackburn, R. (1985). Faculty careers: Maturation, demographic, and historical effects. *Research in Higher Education, 22,* 135–154.

Leitch, V. B. (1988). *American literary criticism from the 30s to the 80s.* New York: Columbia University Press.

Lentricchia, F. (1983). *Criticism and social change.* Chicago: University of Chicago Press.

Lentricchia, F., & McLaughlin, T. (Eds.). (1900). *Critical terms for literary study.* Chicago: University of Chicago Press.

Loewald, H. W. (1972). The experience of time. *Psychoanalytic Study of the Child, 27,* 407.

Manheimer, R. J. (1989). The narrative quest in qualitative gerontology. *Journal of Aging Studies, 3,* 231–252.

Matthews, S. H. (1986). *Friendships through the life course: Oral biographies in old age.* Beverly Hills, CA: Sage.

Merod, J. (1987). *The political responsibility of the critic.* Ithaca, NY: Cornell University Press.

Molinari, V., & Reichlin, R. E. (1984–1985). Life review reminiscence in the elderly: A review of the literature. *International Journal of Aging and Human Development, 20,* 81–92.

Moody, H. R. (1988a). Toward a critical gerontology: The contributions of the humanities to theories of aging. In J. E. Birren & V. L. Bengston (Eds.), *Emergent theories of aging.* New York: Springer Publishing Co.

Moody, H. R. (1988b). Twenty-five years of the life review: Where did we come from? Where are we going? *Journal of Gerontological Social Work, 12,* 19.

Neff, W. S. (1965). Psychoanalytic conceptions of the meaning of work. *Psychiatry, 28,* 324–333.

Neugarten, B. (1984). Interpretive social science and research on aging. In A. A. Rossi (Ed.), *Gender and the life course.* Chicago: Aldine.

Neugarten, B. (1979). Time, age and the life cycle. *American Journal of Psychiatry, 136,* 887–894.

Newton, P. M. (1983). Periods in the adult development of faculty member. *Human Relations, 36,* 441–458.

Ochberg, R. L. (1988). Life stories and the psychosocial construction of careers. *Journal of Personality, 56,* 173–205.

Pells, R. (1985). *The liberal mind in a conservative age: American intellectuals in the 1940s and 1950s.* New York: Harper and Row.

Pinsker, S. J. (1990). Revisionist thought, academic power, and the aging American intellectual. *Gettysburg Review, 3,* 417–426.

The Poetry of Robert Frost. (1967). (Ed. E. C. Latham). New York: Holt, Rinehart and Winston.

Ricoeur, P. (1981). The function of narrative. In J. B. Thompson (Ed. and Trans.), *Hermeneutics and the human sciences.* New York: Cambridge University Press.

Riegel, K. F. (1975). Adult life crises: A dialectical interpretation of development. In N. Datan & L. Ginsburg (Eds.), *Life-span developmental psychology: Normative life crises* (pp. 99–128). New York: Academic Press.

Robbins, B. (1987). "Poaching off the disciplines. *Raritan, 6,* 81–96.

Robinson, F. G., & Robinson, M. G. (1977). *Wallace Stegner.* Boston: Twayne.

Said, E. (1983a). Criticism between culture and system. In *The world, the text, and the critic.* Cambridge, MA: Harvard University Press.

Said, E. (1983b). Secular criticism. In *The world, the text, and the critic.* Cambridge, MA: Harvard University Press.

Said, E. (1978). *Orientalism.* New York: Pantheon.

Sarbin, T. (Ed.). (1986). *Narrative psychology: The storied nature of human conduct.* New York: Praeger.

Schafer, R. (1980). Narration in the psychoanalytic dialogue. In W. J. T. Mitchell (Ed.), *On narrative.* Chicago: University of Chicago Press.

Schaie, K. W. (1984). Historical time and cohort effects. In K. A. McCluskey & H. W. Reese (Eds.), *Life-span developmental psychology: Historical and generational effects.* Orlando, FL: Academic Press.

Simpson, D. (1988). Literary criticism and the return to history. *Critical Inquiry, 14,* 721–747.

Sohngen, M. (1977). The experience of old age as depicted in novels. *Gerontologist, 17,* 70–78.

Spence, D. (1982). *Narrative truth and historical truth.* New York: Norton.

Stegner, W. (1988). *Crossing to safety.* New York: Penguin.

Stegner, W. (1974). *The uneasy chair: A biography of Bernard DeVoto.* New York: Doubleday.

Walzer, M. (1988). *The company of critics: Social criticism and political commitment in the twentieth century.* New York: Basic Books.

Weiland, S. (1990). Gerontology and literary studies. *Gerontologist, 30,* 435–436.

Weiland, S. (1991). Scholars, intellectuals, craftsmen. In S. Weiland (Ed.), *Intellectual craftsmen: Works and ways in American scholarship, 1935–1990* (pp. 1–17). New Brunswick, NJ: Transaction.

Weiland, S. (1992). *Faculty senority: Aging, academic vitality, and disciplinary cultures.* Washington, DC: American Association for the Study of Higher Education.

Whitburne, S. S. (1986). Work and identity. In *Adult development* (2nd ed.; pp. 357–397). New York: Praeger.

Woodward, K. (1986). Reminiscence and the life review: Prospects and retrospects. In S. Gadow & T. R. Cole (Eds.), *What does it mean to grow old? Reflections from the humanities* (pp. 137–161). Durham, NC: Duke University Press.

Woodward, K., & Schwartz, M. M. (Eds.). (1986). *Memory and desire: Aging—literature—psychoanalysis.* Bloomington: Indiana University Press.

Wyatt-Brown, A. M. (1990). The coming of age of literary gerontology. *Journal of Aging Studies, 4,* 299–315.

Yahnke, R. E., & Eastman, R. M. (1990). *Aging in literature: A reader's guide.* Chicago: American Library Association Books.

PART II
Humanistic Gerontology

6

Aging, Morale, and Meaning: The Nexus of Narrative

Bertram J. Cohler

A very old woman lies in her bed in a university hospital, her frailty in stark contrast to the equipment surrounding her. Pumps, tubes, and bottles are arrayed around her bed in a forest of high technology. Formerly she was a vital, energetic musician and community leader in the arts, but age and infirmity have deprived her of the energy and enthusiasm that had marked more than half a century of her working life. She asks the doctor to sit beside her. In a voice little more than a whisper, as the doctor leans over to hear her better, she wheezes, "There is no meaning. It is a cruel joke." Her eyes close and she sinks into an indistinct state between life and death.

This elderly woman, searching for meaning and purpose in her own life as she lies near death, reflects one of the most significant chal-

Revision of paper presented at the Institute for the Medical Humanities, The University of Texas Medical Branch at Galveston, January 1991. Pioneering contributions to the study of adult development and aging by my colleagues Bernice Neugarten, Morton A. Lieberman, and Sehldon S. Tobin have informed my own study of the course of lives over time.

lenges of our high-tech, postmodern society: how can people maintain their morale and their sense of themselves throughout the course of their lives? Although the problem is not new—it has been faced by all generations—our present-day society exacerbates it in two ways. First, our new technologies pose a threat of enormously destructive power, enough to end our collective existence, and also the possibility of ecological disaster. Second, our increasingly secular society has called into question many of the traditional belief systems that provided a supportive framework within which we could preserve a sense of personal integrity and continuity over time.

Today, the advance of medical science has lent a new urgency to the question by its ability to prolong the life of the elderly and the seriously ill by heroic measures. Older adults and their families are increasingly confronted with the most difficult bioethical question: whether or not to prolong life and under what circumstances. In a rapidly aging society, with those over the age of 85 constituting the most rapidly growing segment of the population, the necessity of considering what life means and what constitutes an acceptable quality of life is likely to increase rather than diminish.

For instance, most people periodically evaluate their own lives in terms of experience, coherence, and integrity. Psychological changes in later life, however, including the increasing awareness of mortality, lead older adults to be more explicitly concerned with this issue than are adults prior to middle age (Butler, 1963; Munnichs, 1966; Tobin, 1991). A sense of psychological well-being in later life is assumed to be associated with enhanced preservation of meaning, expressed as a purposive or coherent life story. Failure to maintain this coherent life story leads to feelings of lowered morale and a sense of personal depletion, as exemplified by the older patient who had lost her sense of personal significance.

This increased appreciation of the significance of the life story as a source of personal coherence has become an opportunity for increased interdisciplinary study across the disciplines of the humanities and the social sciences and an important point of connection between humanistic study and the disciplines of medicine. Indeed, examination of the life-story construct, using the concepts of interpretation and criticism developed by the humanities, together with the methods and findings from social science studies of lives over time, has brought about a renewed appreciation of the significance of meaning and coherence, as well as the role of memory and present experience, in laying the foundations for an individual's life-story construct, or personal narrative.

ADVERSITY AND THE MANAGEMENT
OF MEANING IN CONTEMPORARY CULTURE

Writing at the beginning of the 20th century, Max Weber (1904–1905/ 1955) examined the search for certainty and assurance of personal significance in our own time, especially in terms of the important changes in religious and secular thought that had taken place during the preceding two centuries. Weber suggested that the changed relationship of man to God that took place in the Occident following the Reformation laid the foundation for a crisis of meaning that has continued to the present. He contended that after Luther, who removed the priest as mediator between man and God, and after Calvin, who removed all certainty regarding "election," the secure sense of salvation and inherent meaning enjoyed earlier was replaced by indecision and doubt. At first, this doubt was confined to religious matters, but a Protestant revolution developed that ultimately fostered the emergence of an ethic of aesthetic conduct *in the world* (Thompson, 1966, 1967) that required a continuing demonstration of worldly success in order to gain a personal conviction that one was of the elect, that one was saved rather than damned.

This Protestant revolution, and its ultimate transformation from religious to secular, fostered feelings of doubt and despair that went far beyond concern with election. With the loss of a clearly defined guide to conduct, such as had characterized Europe prior to the Reformation, concern with meaning and teleological intent became uppermost. Homans (1989) has argued that much of contemporary philosophy and psychology, particularly psychoanalysis, is a response to the breakdown of traditional guides for living. One result of Protestant concern for this-worldly asceticism, which "slammed the door of the monastery behind it, and strode in the market-place of life," (Weber, 1904–1905) has been the separation of reason and passion, with reason and a means-ends rationality deemed essential for enacting a mode of life that would provide assurance of election and a sense of fitness.

Concern with the issue of meaning, along with the maintenance of a sense of personal coherence or integrity, has also been heightened by changes in the relationship to the means of production, beginning about the middle of the 18th century and continuing down to the present time. As Karl Marx (and critical theory within the social sciences) emphasized, the emergence of capitalist modes of production threatened the earlier satisfaction workers had obtained from an immediate and personal relationship to the fruits of their labor, which was to a large degree the result of their own efforts and skills. Such cultural and social changes were certainly instrumental in bringing about an enhanced concern with personal coherence and a strengthening of interest in the personal narrative or life-story construct.

Although management of personal continuity over time is a problem posed for all cultures, concern with maintenance of coherence within the life-history construct may be unique to the West. Within many traditional cultures, the source of personal integrity is founded within a larger, corporate family group. The Rudolphs (1978) have well portrayed this issue in their description of the adult life of an Indian nobleman. At midlife, Amar Singh derived a sense of coherence for his own life and that of his family from his participation within an extended family that had for many decades provided leadership for a province. Singh's response to middle age was to experience enhanced confirmation from family membership. There is little evidence that Singh was ever concerned with the issues of personal integrity that are so common among men and women during their middle years within our own culture (Marshall, 1975, 1981; Neugarten, 1979; Neugarten & Datan, 1974a).

All cultures have evolved a worldview linking past, present, and future (Geertz, 1973a; Levi-Strauss, 1966), although there are no cultures other than the Western that are so explicitly concerned with a linear time perspective. The West is also distinctive in its concern with the individual life apart from that of others; this Western concept of person leads to concern with the history of the particular life, represented in autobiography, memoir, diary, and other personal documents (Frank, 1974, 1979; Hallowell, 1955; Langness & Frank, 1981; Lejeune, 1989; Mauss, 1938/1985; Weintraub, 1975, 1978). The concept of a personal narrative or life history constitutes the presently recounted record of the personal past that orders and makes sense of lived experience.

The present time is one of particular fascination with the life-history construct, ranging from interest in the study of autobiographical accounts (Weintraub, 1975, 1978) to the psychological cast study (Allport, 1929; Runyan, 1982; R. W. White, 1966). Weintraub (1975, 1978) notes that genuine autobiography is guided by "a desire to discern and assign meaning to a life" (1975, p. 824).[1] Weintraub argues that the issue of meaning is intrinsic to Christianity, with its emphasis upon inner life. However, the concept of a narrative of the course of life, focusing on the search after meaning, is distinctive of Western culture from the Renaissance to the present. Increased focus on individuality, stressing the significance of self-consciousness (Weintraub, 1978), has accompanied this narrative turn.

Weintraub's analysis supports Weber's (1904–1905/1955) emphasis upon Calvinism and, more generally, the Reformation as a unique time of social and historical change enhancing concern with preservation of a sense of meaning across the course of life. However, Weintraub (1975) argues that it was only in the late 18th century that the contemporary autobiography emerged in something resembling its present sense. Vico's (1725/1968) discussion of his struggle to construct the New Science; Rousseau's (1782–1789/1960) autobiography, "The Confessions"; Wordsworth's (1850/1979) poetic musing regarding his own life story; Adams's (1907/1961) *Education*; and Henry James's (1913–1917/1983) autobiography are among the "ideal types" of this personal narrative, designed to render an account of the course of one's own life, integrating diverse themes into an overall "unity thema," and providing meaning for life (Murray & Associates, 1938). Indeed, from earliest childhood through oldest age, individuals successively rewrite their life-story constructs or personal narratives, striving to maintain meaning through preservation of continuity of self over time (Ricoeur, 1977). The life-story construct provides integration of presently experienced past and present and anticipated future and includes both expected and eruptive life changes, woven into an integrated account of the course of life (Cohler, 1982).

A fundamental issue in studying lives over time concerns the manner in which individuals attribute meanings to their presently experienced past and present and their anticipated future, allowing them to construct a personal narrative or life history that, at any one point across the course of their lifetimes, concerns the manner in which is defined the self (Kohut, 1981). Although the specific criteria for an acceptable life history vary across cultures (the distinction between history and fiction may be important only in the modern West), the need for a narrative of the course of one's life that "makes sense" in the terms specified by a particular culture appears to be universal.

Present interest in the narrative or life-story construct within our own society may largely reflect changes that have led to a crisis of meaning in our time, as evidenced in such recent intellectual developments as chaos theory in the physical sciences or the aleatoric perspective in the psychological sciences (Gergen, 1977). This focus upon unexpected, largely adverse factors that pose problems for maintaining a sense of personal continuity over time suggests that change rather than continuity is the most significant factor in the study of life history and that presently experienced continuity is a consequence of a continually revised life story designed to organize the presently experienced past and present and the anticipated future into a linear story in which chance factors are given meanings in an effort to maintain a sense of coherent self (Bandura, 1982; Gergen, 1977, 1982).[2]

Studies by Elder and his colleagues regarding the impact of both the Great Depression and, more recently, military service in World War II upon middle-aged and older adults have shown the importance of understanding lives in terms of the meanings attributed to prior experiences (Elder, 1979, 1986; Elder, Liker & Cross, 1984; Elder & Rockwell, 1978, 1979). Freeman (1985) and Cohler and Freeman (in press) have suggested that lives may be considered as analogous to texts: individuals successively rewrite stories of their own development to take into account unpredictable, often adverse experiences that require sense to be made of them in order to preserve personal coherence over time.

LIFE HISTORY AS A "GOOD" STORY

The life-history construct, like all historical accounts within our own culture, may be understood as a narrative (H. White, 1987) that is composed of a sequence of events reflecting particular intentions and covering a presently remembered past, experienced present, and expected or assumed future and that is organized according to socially constructed understandings of time and space (Carr, 1986; Macintyre, 1984; Ricoeur, 1977). Bruner (1990) has extended Kenneth Burke's (1945/1969, 1950/1969) discussion in defining a narrative as (1) referring inherently to a sequence of events in which people are featured as actors; (2) evaluated in terms of an internal plot or story line rather than an extralinguistic reality; (3) providing points of connection between the exceptional and the ordinary that render ordinary that which is exceptional; and (4) showing a literary quality or, phrased in terms of the life-story construct, portraying some dramatic quality or "tension" relating to a problem that needs to be resolved. Events constituting a narrative, like historical events more generally, are of little significance or meaning apart from their placement within the overall story (Mink, 1968; H. White, 1980, 1981, 1987). The task of both the author and reader or listener of the narrative is to construct an emerging "plot" or "story line" based on this sequence of recounted events.[3]

Starting from somewhat different theoretical positions, Geertz (1973b, 1983), Elder and Rockwell (1979), Bertaux (1981), Bertaux and Kohli (1984), Jean Mandler (1984), Polkinghorne (1983, 1988), and Jerome Bruner (1990) all have maintained that a central concern of the human sciences of social studies (Cohler, 1988) is to understand the personal narrative or life-story construct both in terms of an ordered sequence and in terms of the context, frame, or plot the author employs to provide coherence or narrative integrity for a particular story (Labov & Waletzky, 1967). In addition, in order to evaluate truly the "followability" of the life-story construct, one must evince an appreciation of the shared symbolic understandings, historical events, modes of production, and dominant idea systems of the society from which the construct arose. Ricoeur (1977) has noted that "narrative intelligibility implies something more than the subjective accountability of one's own life-story. It comes to terms with the general condition of acceptability that we apply when we read any story, be it historical or fictional . . . a story has to be 'followable' and, in this sense, 'self-explanatory'" (p. 869).

Ricoeur's (1977) discussion of narrative also identifies narrative intelligibility as leading to an increased experience of personal integrity or coherence. Freud (1937/1964) likewise referred to an enhanced sense of conviction as the test of the adequacy of the life-history reconstructions within clinical psychoanalysis. The experience of fragmentation, or loss of personal integrity, may be understood as the failure to maintain an acceptable or "followable" personal historical narrative or life story (Klein, 1976; Kohut, 1975, 1977; Ricoeur, 1977; Schafer, 1980, 1981, 1992). Schafer (1980, 1981) has maintained that analyst and analysand actively collaborate in constructing a new life story that is more convincing, or more "followable," coherent and integrated, than that told by the analysand at the beginning of analysis.[4]

Life-story constructs are narratives that must be evaluated by the same criteria as other narratives (Mandler, 1984; Mandler & Johnson, 1977; Peterson & McCabe, 1983, 1991; Stein & Policastro, 1984),[5] meeting the same test of coherence and internal consistency as other narratives (Cohler, 1982; Freeman, 1885; Ricoeur, 1977). Methods of criticism applicable generally to stories within our own culture (Booth, 1983; Crane, 1953) are equally applicable in the evaluation of the life-story constructs and implicitly inform judgment of the adequacy of accounts concerning both one's own life and that of others. Bruner (1986, 1987, 1990) additionally notes that any good story or narrative presents the reader or listener with a situation of tension or a problem that engages the reader's or listener's psychological curiosity.

This perspective on the personal narrative or life history as story provides an important means for linking humanistic and social science studies and is reflected in much contemporary inquiry, from developmental psychology through the studies of history and literature. L. Polanyi (1985) has defined a story as "events that took place in particular circumstances, involved particular characters, and gave rise to states of affairs which contrast in some way with the situation obtaining in the story world at the beginning of the story" (pp. 22–23). She notes that we must be provided with sufficient detail to understand the nature of changes that have taken place and to understand relations among the events in the story. Formal aspects of the story, including the manner in which it is told, are implicitly evaluated in terms of their contributions to a narrative that is coherent, culturally acceptable, and as a consequence, "followable" in the terms used by Ricoeur (1977) or Schafer (1980, 1981). Stein and Policastro (1984) have reviewed more than 20 definitions of the concept of story in our own culture. Much of this debate regarding the concept of story concerns the role of intention and novelty, or unexpected complicating events, as defining characteristics. In a similar manner, adequate resolution of problems posed by unanticipated adversity may be important as a defining element of the life-story construct.

Whereas Mandler and Johnson (1977) maintain that the presence of a protagonist with an intention may not be an essential element in the concept of a story, Stein and her colleagues (Stein & Glenn, 1979, Stein & Policastro, 1984) maintain that, within our own culture, essential elements of a story do include a protagonist who intends to carry out some action and an outcome, ending, or statement of the consequences of the intended action. Further, although, as Stein and Policastro (1984) show, it is possible for young children to construct a story with only one event, a story that is viewed as "good" characteristically includes at least three event units organized in a temporal manner. Within our own culture, at least, this story is experienced by the reader or listener as reflecting a causal relationship. The inclusion of an ending or outcome, as well as reference to intention, is important for our culture in evaluating both life-story constructs and stories in general.

The ability to construct a "followable" life story is evident from early childhood. Farnham-Diggory (1966), Engel (1986), and Fivush, Gray, and Fromhoff (1987) all have shown that children as young as 2 years are able to maintain a linear time perspective; and reports by Sachs (1980, 1983) and by Miller and her colleagues (Miller, Potts, Fung Hoogstra, & Mintz, 1990; Miller & Sperry, 1988) have shown that even 2-year-olds are able to tell stories about the past. Mandler and Johnson (1977), Stein and Glenn (1979), and Peterson and McCabe (1983, 1991) have shown that children beginning school are capable of understanding complex stories. Children are able to evaluate the adequacy or "goodness" of a story, including its ability to foster a sense of conviction regarding the relationship between episodes. Employing the linear time perspective characteristic of our culture, portrayed by Ricoeur (1977) and by Peterson and McCabe (1983), children learn to tell stories about their own experiences that are modeled after adult conceptions of time and to make these cultural accounts of time and person constituent elements of their own successively constructed life stories. Once learned, these criteria for evaluating the adequacy of any story are applied both to their own life stories and to those of others, either as recounted in discourse or as in a formal biography (Lejeune, 1989).[6]

Significantly, a major concern in emerging life-story constructs seems to involve a focus on adversity and on the means for resolving unexpected disruptions among previously ordered events. Indeed, distress seems to be a major organizing factor in the life-story construct within our own culture: Miller and Sperry (1988) report that recounting of adversity and difficulty is among the earliest uses that children make of the past in their own life stories. Peterson and McCabe (1983) report that narratives of young children judged as "good" most often (75%) referred to sad and unpleasant events rather than to happy ones, although no such difference was found among narratives judged as "bad." It is common for those seeking intervention for psychological distress to "blame" their past and to seek explanations for their present difficulties in their earlier adversity. This reliance upon past adversity as the basis of the narrative account is also reflected in much of psychological theorizing regarding critical or sensitive periods early in life that are presumed to shape later life outcomes (Erikson, 1950/1963; Lorenz, 1937/1965).

Stories dealing with a response to affliction provide a means for integrating the presently remembered past experience, present, and anticipated future into an account that makes sense of lived time. They provide a basis for studying both continuity and change across the course of life and also a basis for therapeutic intervention (Jaspers, 1963). The life-story construct based on a "narrative of affliction," may provide increased coherence at a particular time but at the cost of satisfactory adjustment to subsequent life experiences (Mass & Kuypers, 1974), particularly at crisis times that challenge present maintenance of meaning and personal integrity (Butler, 1963; Lieberman & Tobin, 1983). For example, Henry Adams (1907/1961) portrays his own life in terms of two periods of crisis (unanticipated adversity) that require reconsideration of the story of his life as previously understood, all of which results in feelings of increased integrity and narrative certainty. It is clear from Adams's account that personal adversity represents a challenge to the story of one's life, which in turn demands increased narrative clarity.

LIFE STORY, AGING, AND MAINTENANCE OF PERSONAL INTEGRITY

Ontological anxiety, or concern with death and afterlife (Weber, 1904–1905/1955) is particularly emphasized within our culture and is perhaps best express in existential philosophy. Millenarian aspects of Christianity also reflect the Western linear organization of time, presenting death as an end, with the possibility of an afterlife promised at some time in the unknowable future. Consistent with this linear organization of time, our culture is also unique in the extent to which death remains a preoccupation across the course of life. The narrative of the personal life history is seen as a story constructed in early childhood, sometime after about the third year of life (Farnham-Diggory, 1966) and successively rewritten across the course of life, as long as there is capacity for remembering (Cohler & Freeman, in press; Schafer, 1981).

"Good" lives and "good" stories are both presumed to have a beginning, a middle, and a definite ending (Ricoeur, 1977); later life becomes the testing ground for the success of our personal and collective search for narrative integrity. Preparation for what is expected to be a "good" death, with its attendant record of accomplishment in life and satisfaction with life as lived, is believed critical for the maintenance of morale at the end of life. The need for maintaining a coherent and followable life story over time appears to be particularly important in later life, when individuals prepare for settling accounts through the process described by Butler (1963) as the "life-review." As one older man awaiting death from a chronic disease observed, "It is absurd that we spend eighty years waiting for the last few minutes of life, rather than living each day as it comes."

This Western preoccupation with the construction of meaning across the course of life reflects the shift from a traditional, spontaneous life to one guided by preoccupation with maintenance of a followable life story (Ricoeur, 1977). It also reflects our concern regarding the availability of others as a source of solace and support at those times when a breakdown in narrative coherence becomes a threat. As individuals grow older, they look increasingly for personal consistency over time, reflected in their preoccupation within the longitudinal study of lives of finding evidence of continuity rather than change in lives over time. Significant in this regard, it was only those more personally troubled older adults in mass and Kuypers's (1974) study who expressed concern with maintenance of such consistency over periods of several decades.

THE COHERENT LIFE STORY AND THE WISE ELDER: DR. BORG AS IDEAL TYPE

Erikson (1978, 1982) assumes that later life endows persons with particular sagacity and understanding that permits them unique perspective on the course of life. However, even among a psychologically robust group of elders, Erikson, Erikson, and Kivnick (1986) have difficulty identifying the unique perspective on self and others that is believed to uniquely characterize old age. Gutmann (1987) has also provided a somewhat glorified picture of the wise elder in which time and aging combine to endow older adults with particular insight. Birren (1980), Clayton and Birren (1980), and Mannheimer (1988) have outlined at least some of the factors qualifying this assumption of inherent wisdom according to later life. In truth, we know little about the factors leading one person to succumb to adversity while another is able to rise above it and to use it in the service of a revised life story, thus maintaining a sense of meaning and purpose even when confronted by a challenge to the previously existing account of the life story. The vignette at the beginning of this chapter, of the older adult confronting death with the sense of a life lacking in meaning, reflects the breakdown of the coherent life story and attendant loss of meaning constructed by self from the experiences of a lifetime. The fear of death arriving in the context of personal fragmentation may well represent the ultimate terror confronting the older adult in our postmodern society.

Erik Erikson's (1978, 1982) portrayal of Dr. Borg in Ingmar Bergman's film *Wild Strawberries* well characterizes many of the issues in the study of personal integrity and the realization of wisdom in later life. Dr. Borg is the "ideal type"[7] of the "postmodern" elder: the very symbol of the bourgeois, this elderly professor, a doctor, a Swede, was possessed by feelings of doubt and despair as he reflected upon his own life story, which he saw as his retreating into rational study and forsaking the smell of spring and the joy of the fields for a life's work devoted to science and its application to the healing arts. The film is particularly significant in light of Erikson's frequent discussion of Dr. Borg's struggles for wisdom (Erikson, 1958, 1978, 1982; Erikson et al., 1986) as the ideal type of encounter with and resolution of the epigenetic "crisis" of "integrity versus despair." Erikson notes particularly Dr. Borg's struggle for wisdom, culminating in the process of grieving over the past and yet making peace with the accomplishments and disappointments of a lifetime. Indeed, one cannot read Erikson's moving account without wondering whether, in his fascination with Borg's personal journey, Erikson sees himself reflected in the mirror of his fellow Scandinavian!

Bergman's film portrays events culminating in the celebration of a half-century of service to the medical profession and the people. Rejecting the possibility of an airplane trip from his retirement home to the place where he is to be honored, Borg elects to travel by auto, using the journey as an opportunity for revisiting places significant across the course of his life. He is accompanied by his daughter-in-law and, in the course of his journey, acquires other passengers, each of whom plays a role of symbolic significance in this story in which dream, reminiscence, and present life are intermingled. The film ends with the jubilee celebration, which is less significant than the increased self-understanding or wisdom that Borg obtains in the course of the day's journey. Just as with Faust before him, Dr. Borg's experience of his own aging is marked by a disappointment over pleasures forsworn in the continuing search for sense of personal integrity through rational pursuit of knowledge.

Only late in life is Dr. Borg finally able to see an "extraordinary logic" to life. Wisdom transcends history, and Borg experiences himself as totally embraced and comforted by the totality of his culture. Bergman's portrayal of Dr. Borg's attainment of wisdom and his triumph of integrity over despair reflects the old doctor's grieving at his dispassionate scientific inquiry at the expense of passionate intimate relationships. Parenthetically, it might be observed that this regret about a life devoted to reason and excluding passion reflects a fundamental dichotomy within our culture, which, as Weber (1904–1905/1955) notes, is unique in its emphasis upon a necessary tension between these two modes of being.

The great challenge of later life that Bergman portrays in the film is to integrate a linear past now experienced as part of the present, to find, as it were, the capacity in oneself to be comforted by those memories of the past that, in turn, make possible a life review and a preparation for a peaceful death.[8] In this respect, the film's scene in the strawberry patch has become the dramatic realization of the basis of much of our contemporary understanding of the problems of aging, the role of reminiscence in later life, and the need for maintaining a sense of personal coherence and integrity.

Erikson's (1978, 1982) account of Dr. Borg reflects two problems endemic in much social science theorizing regarding aging and the course of life. In the first place, Erikson assumes that continuity in lives over time is inherent in the concept of life cycle. However, this itself is a major problem for study in the human sciences. In the second place, Erikson assumes that the cumulative effect of aging across the course of life results in increased wisdom and integrity, which is a problematic conclusion at best. At present there is much controversy regarding issues of continuity and change in the study of a life course. Although some investigators, such as McCrae and Costa (1984), believe that they can demonstrate this continuity through reliance upon factor-analytic approaches, findings reported from the majority of longitudinal studies across the past two decades have shown very low relationships between earlier and later-life attributes. Indeed, Neugarten (1969) has suggested that many of these longitudinal studies failed to realize their initial promise by assuming rather than studying the factors associated with variation in continuity within lives over time.

This critique is consistent with more recent approaches to the study of lives (Bandura, 1982; Gergen, 1977, 1980), which suggests that chance may play the largest role in determining change over time; the function of the life-story construct or personal narrative is to "emplot" (Ricoeur, 1977) these chance events with meanings that render the presently remembered course of life as a coherent or integrated account using the same template as other stories in our own culture. The best method for studying this continuing search after meaning is to regard the life-story construct as a text and to use methods for the analysis of this text that are used more generally in humanistic study of narratives (Ricoeur, 1971, 1977; Schafer, 1980, 1981, 1992; H. White, 1972, 1978, 1980, 1981).

WISDOM AND COHERENCE IN THE LIFE STORY ACROSS THE SECOND HALF OF LIFE

From this perspective, the so-called wisdom achieved in later life consists of the ability to maintain a coherent narrative of the course of life in which the presently remembered past, experienced present, and anticipated future are understood as problems to be studied rather than as outcomes to be assumed. The question is not whether older adults are able to realize wisdom but rather how these older adults are able to continue to experience a sense of coherence while confronting factors associated with the loss of personal integrity, as well as feelings of fragmentation and disruption of the life story across the course of their lives. In this instance, the life-story construct of the first half of adulthood may be less viable in providing a continuing sense of coherence across the second half of life. As the elderly come to a stronger sense of the finitude of life (Munnichs, 1966) or experience a personalization of death (Neugarten & Datan, 1974a), they may need to change the manner in which they use time and memory to order their life-story construct.

For instance, confronted by increased awareness of their own mortality, older adults live much more in the present than do younger adults. In the words of one older man: "I take each day as it comes. Who can predict the future?" Although loss through death is a reality confronting all of us across the course of life, beginning at about middle age it is expected that we will be confronted first with the deaths of our parents and then of relatives and close friends. In this manner, as Neugarten and Datan (1974b) have observed, death becomes increasingly personalized. With the death of parents, we become the oldest generation within the family, heightening the experience of the finitude of life and the reality of our own mortality (Munnichs, 1966; Marshall, 1975). Increased awareness of finitude, particularly in the context of the deaths of parents and friends, fosters a mode of reminiscence most characteristic of later life, when memory becomes more important than present continuing social contacts as a means of realizing increased solace and morale. As Erikson, Erikson, & Kivnick (1986) observe about Dr. Borg:

> Whenever he is restless or sad, he tries *now*, he tells us, to "recall memories of his childhood to calm down." That night, he wanders back again to the strawberry patch and to everything that he "dreamed or remembered or experienced" that day. It sounds like a visual lullaby that he now imagines; a "warm, sunny day" with "a mild breeze coming through the birches." (p. 262)

Erikson (1978) highlights the significance of reminiscence in later life as a source of the comfort and solace that were once available through relationships with others. Over time, memory increasingly serves the functions previously realized through being with others. Reminiscence both fosters comfort through the ability to recall important experiences of a lifetime and provides the resource of a storehouse of memories that can continually be reordered over time to preserve sense of meaning and purpose even when confronted by such adversity as relocation into long-term care in later adulthood. Across the course of later life, reminiscence is increasingly used more in the service of life review (Butler, 1963)—that is, as a settling of accounts with the entire prior course of life—than as a guide to present actions, as it generally is in middle age (Lieberman & Falk, 1971).

Erikson's (1978) observation with respect to the significance of reminiscence and personal review of the life story points out the importance of the remembered past for the maintenance of morale in later life. Butler (1963) has noted the significance of the life review for the reintegration of the remembered past as part of making sense of life as lived. Myerhoff (1979) has shown the significance of the life review both within the community of older adults and in the maintenance of personal integrity, and Kaminsky (1984) and his colleagues have shown the value of fostering life review and reminiscence as an important part of the psychotherapy of older adults. These reports show the significance of the life-story construct as a source of soothing and comfort across the course of life and particularly in later life. Cohler and Galatzer-Levy (1990) have suggested that memories of the past may largely replace interpersonal contact as a source of solace during times of distress. The loss through death of a spouse or close friends, problems in moving about, and limitations on personal energy all contribute to an increased preference in the elderly for the memory of past satisfactions at being with others rather than actually being with them. Recalling the past through recounting the presently experienced life-story construct, as in the life of Dr. Borg, contributes to a sense of personal well-being across the second half of life in ways that may be quite different from the use of the past in either early adulthood or middle-age (Lieberman & Falk, 1971; Lieberman & Tobin, 1983).

The life review has received much attention in studies of mental health and aging since Butler's (1963) initial report (Cohler & Freeman, in press). The life review may be seen as the presently recounted life-story construct that is successively revised across the life according to principles not yet clearly understood. Indeed, emerging interest in the concept of the life-story construct within the narrative tradition provides an important new means for studying such factors associated with variation in the life review as aging, cohort, and life changes. The contributions of criticism within literature (Booth, 1983; Scholes, 1989), the concept of the story within developmental psycholinguistics (Peterson & McCabe, 1983, 1991), and the ethnographic approach to the study of late-life narratives (Luborsky, 1989, 1990a, 1990b), all point the way toward a systematic study of the life-story construct across the course of life. This study must address such questions as whether the same criteria for a "good" story that are relevant in childhood are also relevant for the life story of the adult years (Miller & Sperry, 1988; Peterson & McCabe, 1983) and whether the role of adversity or other departures from the expected course of life plays a role in the maintenance of a coherent life story across the second half of life different from that across the first half of life.

The particular problems posed by memory impairment in recounting the life-story construct may contribute to our understanding of the marked increase in depression observed in the early phases of Alzheimer's disease (Lazarus et al., 1987). Part of this depression may be related to the awareness of loss of functions, but we must consider whether the depression isn't markedly worsened by memory loss and the inability to recall the past, which is so essential for being able to use the life-story construct as a continuing source of solace and comfort. To date much of the study of life story as narrative has been devoted to the age at which children first begin to tell a good or coherent life story. The concepts and methods of this narrative study should be extended to a study of the life-story construct across the course of life up to oldest age. This is implicitly the task that Erikson (1978) poses in his analysis of Dr. Borg's personal journey in Bergman's film.

Further, this human science study of aging must account for the complex interplay of sociohistorical events and individual life changes, either related to these larger events or due to otherwise unpredictable circumstances. Indeed, as Gergen (1977) and Bandura (1982) have noted, many of the most important life changes are relatively unpredictable and accountable largely on a chance basis. These eruptive changes pose a fundamental threat to the maintenance of meaning, which is essential for a continued sense of high morale and well-being experienced across the course of life.

CONCLUSION

The study of aging in our postindustrial society has led to a significant reconsideration of both the methods of study most appropriate for the life-history construct and the questions that it is most important for us to study. The epochal work of Weber (1904–1905/1955) has traced this intense concern with meaning in our time back to the Reformation. It is clear, however, that socioeconomic changes introduced in the 19th century have led in our own time of particularly rapid change to an enhanced appreciation of the importance of maintaining a sense of personal continuity over time. It is particularly important to focus on the means by which individuals construct meaning in their lives and on the complex interplay between the process of constructing meaning in particular lives and social and historical change. Across the course of life, individuals rely upon others as a source of both meaning and solace in their lives. From the initial experience of the infant, comforted by his mother's very presence, to the older adult maintaining continuity of past and present through memories of a lifetime of relating to significant others, the psychological significance of relationships is intertwined in the remembered story of a life that answers the question of meaning posed by Weber and that works to preserve morale.

Increased attention must be paid to critiques such as those of Ricoeur (1971, 1977), Hayden White (1987), and others, who have begun to address the problems of method posed by narrative study and are thus providing a new basis for human science inquiry (Polkinghorne, 1988). Explication of the assumptions underlying the human studies may, in turn, lead to greater understanding of the maintenance of meaning and sense of personal continuity across the course of life, in the context of both aging and continuing social change (Tobin, 1991). Study of the personal narrative of older adults, of the factors associated with change over time in this narrative, and of the complex interplay between presently realized and remembered experience of others, all with respect to maintenance of morale and personal integrity over time, will add greatly to our understanding of mental health across the course of life.

NOTES

[1] Weintraub (1975) dates the use of the term *autobiography* to the early 19th century, when it is first used in both English and German dictionaries. He also notes that the genre of recorded lives as lived by the writer includes true autobiographies, with memoirs, or recounting of particular events with a certain assumed objectivity; and autobiographies that focus on a recounting of deeds done, sorting out the past and assigning meaning to it as a part of the present. In neither instance is there explicit concern with personal justification with these deeds.

[2] This emerging sense of self founded on the capacity for maintaining a coherent narrative of experience has been portrayed in quite similar ways by theorists from quite different traditions (Carr, 1986; Macintyre, 1984;

Ricoeur, 1983). Within psychoanalysis, E. Kris (1956) initially referred to this capacity for narrative coherence as an attribute of ego strength, using the term "personal myth" to refer to the capacity to maintain a coherent story of the course of life. The extension of this concept into contemporary psychoanalytic theory and practice is reflected in the recent edited volume by Hartocollis and Graham (1991). This term was subsequently extended in the work of Potamianou (1985) and Feinstein (1979) within psychodynamic psychology. Crapanzano (1989) has used the term "self characterization" in his psychoanalytically and linguistically informed comparative ethnographic and literary study of the capacity for complex portrayal of self and other. Within cognitive psychology, capacity for experiencing a coherent life story is described as "autobiographical memory" (Greenwald, 1980; Rubin, 1986). The study of personal coherence has long been the focus of social psychology, including Goldstein's (1939) observations of the importance of the capacity to organize and represent a coherent life story, Lecky's (1945/1969) discussion of the concept of self-consistency, Syngg and Combs's (1953) discussion of the preservation of the "phenomenal self," and Rogers's (1951) discussion of "self-actualization" in personality development and in psychotherapy. Concern with this concept has assumed particular importance in health psychology, particularly as represented by Antonovsky's (1979, 1987) concept of a "sense of coherence," and Epstein's (1981) discussion of a "unity principle" in personality. The concern is seen as well in more explicitly social-psychological discussions, such as Mancuso and Sarbin's (1983) concept of "self-narrative," Epstein's (1981) and Sirgy's (1986) discussions of "self-congruity," McAdams's (1985a, 1985b) description of the "imago" in the construction of a life story, and Kerby's (1991) discussion of self as constructed from narrative. Consistent with a human studies approach, Kaufman (1986), Moody (1986), and Bruner (1986, 1987, 1990) have showed the importance of studying the manner in which individuals create meaning in their lives, emphasizing the reflexive quality of the personal narrative in which the narrator and the central figure of the narration are the same.

[3] The critic Hirsch (1976) has pleaded for recognition of "authoritorial intent" or recognition of the author's intended meaning for a text. Presumably, the author arranges events in a particular sequence telling a particular story in a particular manner to achieve some intended goal. Hirsch is concerned that this intent fails to emerge when the task of constructing meaning is placed on the reader (Mink, 1981; Schafer, 1980, 1981, 1992). In a similar manner, listeners to a life story, as in the clinical psychoanalytic encounter, strive to understand the principles leading the analysand to place events together within a particular fabric or "story." However, as Ricoeur (1971) and Freeman (1985) have observed, there is a continuing and open dialogue between text and reader, with the very significance or meaning of an account shifting over time, in the context of additional elements of the story, new means for understanding stories, and such changes external to the text as additional life experiences or the theory used to help make sense of the story line. Appeal to such authoritorial intent is understandable in terms of the

anxiety generated by the lack of certainty and a fixed point of departure for interpretation (Devereux, 1967). It is important that we recognize this anxiety in order that we may be free to attend to the sequences of events comprising the text and focus on the task of interpretation in a manner akin to Freud's (1912/1958) concept of "evenly suspended attention."

[4] Kohut (1959/1978) has noted the significance of empathy, or vicarious introspection, as the single most important element in the psychoanalytic "cure." The experience of telling the life story to another, who struggles to understand this account, has positive therapeutic value although not sufficient to bring about resolution of personal distress apart from interpretation of emergent transference enactments.

[5] Peterson and McCabe (1983) have provided a systematic comparison between three modes of evaluating narratives, showing that young children are able to tell narratives that may be judged according the criteria outlined by Bruner (1990), but they found that coding systems yield somewhat different findings. Systematic study of the good narrative requires study from more than one perspective.

[6] Innovative study of the narrative or story reported by Stein and Glenn (1979), (Labov and Waletsky, (1967), Labov and Fanshel (1977) and Deese (1965, 1984) and extended more recently through systematic studies such as those reported by Peterson and McCabe (1983) and Luborsky (1989, 1990) has provided systematic means for portraying dimensions intrinsic to the "good" story and for evaluating changes in life stories over time. These approaches go well beyond linguistic codes to represent changes in narratives as a consequence of time, aging, and experience with and response to affliction.

[7] the concept of the ideal type was formulated by Max Weber (1904–1905/1955), who noted that particular individuals, such as the citizens of Calvin's Geneva, had the advantage of "artificial simplicity . . . as they could at best but seldom be found in history" (p. 98) and thus are portrayed—and are portrayable—in terms of their most consistent and logical forms.

[8] It may be that the depression accompanying the onset of Alzheimer's disease (Lazarus, Newton, Cohler, Lesser, & Schweon, 1987) stems in part from the realization of loss of memory, which is so essential for maintaining this personal narrative and for maintaining solace derived from memories such as that of Dr. Borg about the time of his youth in the strawberry patch.

REFERENCES

Adams, H. (1961). *The education of Henry Adams.* Boston: Houghton-Mifflin. (Original work published 1907)

Allport, G. (1929). The study of personality by the intuitive method: An experiment in teaching from *The Locomotive God. The Journal of Abnormal and Social Psychology, 24,* 14–27.

Antonovsky, A. (1979). *Health, stress, and coping: New perspectives on mental and physical well being.* San Francisco: Jossey-Bass.

Antonovksy, A. (1987). *Unraveling the mystery of health: How people manage stress and stay well.* San Francisco: Jossey-Bass.

Bandura, A. (1982). The psychology of chance encounters and life-paths. *American Psychologist, 37,* 747–755.

Bertaux, D., & Kohli, M. (1984). The life-story approach: A continental view. *Annual Review of Sociology, 10,* 215–237.

Birren, J. (1980). Progress in research on aging in the behavioral and social sciences. *Human Development, 23,* 33–45.

Booth, W. (1983). *The rhetoric of fiction* (2nd ed.). Chicago: University of Chicago Press.

Bruner, J. (1986). *Actual minds, possible worlds.* Cambridge, MA: Harvard University Press.

Bruner, J. (1987). Life as narrative. *Social Research, 54,* 11–32.

Bruner, J. (1990). *Acts of meaning.* Cambridge, MA: Harvard University Press.

Burke, K. (1969). *A grammar of motives.* Berkeley: University of California Press. (Original work published 1945)

Burke, K. (1969). *A rhetoric of motives.* Berkeley: University of California Press. (Original work published 1950)

Butler, R. (1963). The life review: An interpretation of reminiscence in the aged. *Psychiatry, 26,* 65–76.

Carr, D. (1986). *Time, narrative, and history.* Bloomington: Indiana University Press.

Clayton, V., & Brinnen, J. (1980). The development of wisdom across the lifespan: A reexamination of an ancient topic. In P. Baltes & O. G. Brim, Jr. (Eds.), *Life-span development and behavior* (Vol. 3, pp. 103–135). New York: Academic Press.

Cohler, B. (1982). Personal narrative and life-course. In P. Baltes & O. G. Brim, Jr. (Eds.), *Life-span development and behavior* (Vol. 4, pp. 205–241). New York: Academic Press.

Cohler, B. (1988). The human studies and the life history. *Social Service Review, 62,* 552–576.

Cohler, B., & Freeman, M. (in press). Psychoanalysis and the developmental narrative. In G. Pollack & S. Greenspan (Eds.), *The course of life* (rev. ed.). New York: International Universities Press.

Cohler, B., & Galatzer-Levy, R. (1990). Self, meaning and morale across the second half of life. In R. Nemiroff & C. Colarusso (Eds.), *New dimensions in adult development* (pp. 214–259). New York: Basic Books.

Crane, R. D. (1953). *The language of criticism and the structure of poetry.* Toronto: University of Toronto Press.

Crapanzano, V. (1989). On self characterization. In J. Stigler, R. Shweder, & G. Herdt (Eds.), *Cultural psychology* (pp. 401–426). Cambridge: Cambridge University Press.

Deese, J. (1965). *Structure of associations in language and thought.* Baltimore: Johns Hopkins University Press.

Deese, J. (1984). *Thought into speech: The psychology of language.* New York: Prentice-Hall.

Devereux, G. (1967). *From anxiety to method in the behavioral sciences.* The Hague: Mouton.

Elder, G. (1979). Historical change in life patterns and personality. In P. Baltes & O. G. Brim (Eds.), *Life-span development and behavior* (Vol. 1, pp. 117–159). New York: Academic Press.

Elder, G. (1986). Military times and turning points in men's lives. *Developmental Psychology, 22,* 233–245.

Elder, G., Jr., Liker, J., & Cross, C. (1984). Parent-child behavior in the great depression: Life-course and intergenerational influences. In P. Baltes & O. G. Brim, Jr. (Eds.), *Life-span development and behavior* (Vol. 6, pp. 111–158). New York: Academic Press.

Elder, G., & Rockwell, R. (1978). Economic depression and post-war opportunity: A study of life patterns and health. In R. Simmons (Ed.), *Research in community and mental health* (pp. 249–304). Greenwich, CT: JAL Press.

Elder, G., & Rockwell, R. (1979). The life course and human development: An ecological perspective. *International Journal of Behavioral Development, 2,* 1–21.

Engel, S. (1986). Learning to reminiscence: A developmental study of how young children talk about the past. *Dissertation Abstracts, 47B,* 1294.

Epstein, S. (1981). The unity principle versus the reality and pleasure principles, *or* the talc of the scorpion and the frog. In M. Lynch, A. Norem-Hebeisen, & K. Gergen (Eds.), *Self-concept: Advances in theory and research* (pp. 27–37). Cambridge, MA: Ballinger-Harper and Row.

Erikson, E. H. (1958). *Young man Luther: A study in psychoanalysis and history.* New York: Norton.

Erikson, E. H. (1963). *Childhood and society* (rev. ed.). New York: Norton. (Original work published 1950)

Erikson, E. (1978). Reflections on Dr. Borg's life cycle. In E. Erikson (Ed.), *Adulthood* (pp. 1–32). New York: Norton.

Erikson, E. (1982). *The life-cycle completed: A review.* New York: Norton.

Erikson, E., Erikson, J., & Kivnick, H. (1986). *Vital involvement in old age.* New York: Norton.

Farnham-Diggory, S. (1966). Self, future, and time: A developmental study of the concepts of psychotic, brain-damaged, and normal children. *Monographs of the Society for Research in Child Development, 31* (Whole No. 1).

Feinstein, A. D. (1979). Personal mythology as a paradigm for a holistic public psychology. *American Journal of Orthopsychiatry, 49,* 198–217.

Fivush, R., Gray, J., & Fromhoff, F. (1987). Two-year-olds talk about the past. *Cognitive Psychology, 2,* 393–409.

Frank, G. (1974). Life history model of adaptation to disability: The case of a "congenital amputee." *Social Science in Medicine, 19,* 639–645.

Frank, G. (1979). Finding the common denominator: A phenomonological critique of the life history method. *Ethos, 7,* 68–94.

Freeman, M. (1985). Paul Ricoeur on interpretation: The model of the text and the idea of development. *Human Development, 28,* 295–312.

Freud, S. (1958). Recommendations to physicians practicing psychoanalysis. In J. Strachey (Ed. and Trans.), *The standard edition of the complete psychological works of Sigmund Freud* (Vol. 12, pp. 109–120). London: Hogarth Press. (Original work published 1912)

Freud, S. (1964). Constructions in analysis. In J. Strachey (Ed. and Trans.) *The standard edition of the complete psychological works of Sigmund Freud* (Vol. 23, pp. 255–270). London: Hogarth Press. (Original work published 1957)

Geertz, C. (1973a). Person, time and conduct in Bali. In C. Geertz (Ed.), *The interpretation of cultures* (pp. 360–411). New York: Basic Books.

Geertz, C. (1973b). Thick description: Toward an interpretive theory of culture. In C. Geertz (Ed.), *The interpretation of cultures* (pp. 3–30). New York: Basic Books.

Geertz, C. (1983). "From the native's point of view": On the nature of antropological understanding. In C. Geertz (Ed.), *Local knowledge: Further essays in interpretive anthropology* (pp. 55–72). New York: Basic Books.

Gergen, K. (1977). Stability, change and chance in understanding human development. In N. Datan & H. Reese (Eds.), *Life-span developmental psychology: Dialectical perspectives on experimental research* (pp. 32–65). New York: Academic Press.

Gergen, K. (1980). The emerging crisis in life-span development theory. In P. Baltes & O. G. brim, Jr. (Eds.), *Life-span development and behavior* (Vol. 3, pp. 32–65). New York: Academic Press.

Gergen, K. (1982). From self to science: What is there to know? In J. Suls (Ed.), *Psychological perspectives on the self* (Vol. 1, pp. 129–149). Hillsdale, NJ: Erlbaum.

Goldstein, K. (1939). *The organism.* New York: American Book Co.

Greenwald, A. (1980). The totalitarian ego: Fabrication and revision of personal history. *American Psychologist, 35,* 603–618.

Gutmann, D. (1987). *Reclaimed powers: Towards a psychology of men and women in later life.* New York: Basic Books.

Hallowell, A. I. (1955). The self and its behvioral environment. In A. I. Hallowell (Ed.), *Culture and experience* (pp. 75–110). Philadelphia: University of Pennsylvania Press.

Hartocollis, P., & Graham, I. (Eds.). (1991). *The personal myth in psychoanalytic theory.* Madison, CT: International Universities Press.

Hirsch, E. D. (1976). *The aims of interpretation.* Chicago: University of Chicago Press.

Homans, P. (1989). *The ability to mourn: Disillusionment and the social origins of psychoanalysis.* Chicago: University of Chicago Press.

James, H. (1983). *Autobiography.* (Ed. F. W. Dupee). Princeton, NJ: Princeton University Press. (Original work published 1913–1917)

Jaspers, K. (1963). *General psychopathology.* (Trans. J. Hoenig & M. W. Hamilton). Chicago: University of Chicago Press.

Kaminsky, M. (1984). *The uses of reminiscence: New ways of working with older adults.* New York: Haworth Press.

Kaufman, S. (1986). *The ageless self: Sources of meaning in late life.* Madison: University of Wisconsin Press.

Kerby, A. P. (1991). *Narrative and the self.* Bloomington: Indiana University Press.

Klein, G. (1976). *Psychoanalytic theory: An exploration of essentials.* Madison, CT: International Universities Press.

Kohut, H. (1978). Introspection, empathy and psychoanalysis: An examination of the relationship between mode of observation and theory. In P. Ornstein (Ed.), *The search for the self: Selected writings of Heinz Kohut, 1950–1978* (Vol. 1, pp. 205–232). New York: International Universities Press. (Original work published 1959)

Kohut, H. (1975). The self in history. In C. Strozier (Ed.), *Self psychology and the humanities: Reflections on a new psychoanalytic approach by Heinz Kohut* (pp. 161–170). New York: Norton.

Kohut, H. (1977). *The restoration of the self.* New York: International Universities Press.

Kohut, H. (1981). On the continuity of the self and cultural self objects. In C. Strozier (Ed.), *Self psychology and the humanities: Reflections on a new psychoanalytic approach by Heinz Kohut* (pp. 232–243). New York: Norton.

Kris, E. (1956). The personal myth: A problem in psychoanalytic technique. *Journal of the American Psychoanalytic Association, 4,* 653–681.

Labov, W., & Fanshel, D. (1977). *Therapeutic discourse: Psychotherapy as discourse.* New York: Academic Press.

Labov, W., & Waletzky, J. (1967). Narrative analysis: Oral versions of personal experience. In J. Helm (Ed.), *Essays on the verbal and visual arts* (pp. 12–44). Seattle: University of Washington Press and American Ethnological Society.

Langness, L. L., & Frank, G. (1981). *Lives: An autobiographical approach to biography.* Novato, CA: Chandler and Sharp.

Lazarus, L., Newton, N., Cohler, B., Lesser, J., & Schweon, C. (1987). Frequency and presentation of depressive symptoms in patients with primary degenerative dementia. *American Journal of Psychiatry, 144,* 41–45.

Lecky, P. (1969). *Self-consistency: A theory of personality.* New York: Doubleday-Anchor. (Original work published 1945)

Lejeune, P. (1989). *On autobiography.* (Trans. K. Leary). Minneapolis: University of Minnesota Press.

Levi-Strauss, C. (1966). *The savage mind.* Chicago: University of Chicago Press.

Lieberman, M., & Falk, J. (1971). The remembered past as a source of data for research on the life cycle. *Human Development, 14,* 132–141.

Lieberman, M., & Tobin, S. (1983). *The experience of old age: Stress, coping and survival.* New York: Basic Books.

Lorenz, K. (1965). *Evolution and modification of behavior.* Chicago: University of Chicago Press. (Original work published 1937)

Luborsky, M. (1989, November). *Structures for affect self-report: A discourse perspective.* Paper presented at annual meeting of the Gerontological Society of North America, Minneapolis.

Luborsky, M. (1990a). Alchemists' visions: Cultural norms in eliciting and analyzing life history narratives. *Journal of Aging Studies, 4,* 17–29.

Luborsky, M. (1990b). *In whose image does the life history empower?* Paper presented at the annual meeting of the Gerontological Society of North America, Boston.

Maas, H., & Kuypers, J. (1974). *From thirty to seventy: A forty year longitudinal study of adult life-styles and personality.* San Francisco: Jossey-Bass.

MacIntyre, A. (1984). *After virtue: A study in moral theory.* Notre Dame, IN: University of Notre Dame Press.

Mancuso, J., & Sarbin, T. (1983). The self-narrative in the enactment of social roles. In T. Sarbin & K. Scheibe (Eds.), *Studies in social identity* (pp. 233–253). New York: Praeger.

Mandler, J. (1984). *Stories, scripts, and scenes: Aspects of schema theory.* Hillsdale, NJ: Erlbaum.

Mandler, J., & Johnson, N. (1977). Remembrance of things passed: Story structure and recall. *Cognitive Psychology, 9,* 111–151.

Mannheimer, R. (1992). Wisdom and method: Philosophical contributions to gerontology. In T. Cole, D. Van Tassel, & R. Kastenbaum (Eds.), *The handbook of aging and the humanities.* New York: Springer Publishing Co.

Marshall, V. (1975). Age and awareness of finitude in developmental gerontology. *Omega, 6,* 113–129.

Marshall, V. (1981). *Last chapters: A sociology of death and dying.* Belmont, CA: Wadsworth.

Mauss, M. (1985). A category of the human mind: The notion of person; the notion of self. (Trans. W. D. Halls). In M. Carrithers, S. Collin, & S. Lukes (Eds.), *The category of the person: Anthropology, philosophy, history* (pp. 1–25). New York: Cambridge University Press. (Original work published 1938)

McAdams, D. (1985a). The "imago." In P. Shaver (Ed.), *Self, situations, and social behavior: Review of personality and social psychology* (pp. 115–141). Newbury Park, CA: Sage Publications.

McAdams, D. (1985b). *Power, intimacy, and the life-story: Personological inquires into identity.* Homewood, IL: Dorsey Press.

McCrae, R., & Costa, P. (1984). *Emerging lives, enduring dispositions: Personality in adulthood.* Boston: Little, Brown.

Miller, P., Potts, R., Fund, H., Hoogstra, L., & Mintz, J. (1990). Narrative practices and the social construction of self in childhood. *American Ethnologist, 17,* 292–311.

Miller, P., & Sperry, L. (1988). Early talk about the past: The origins of conversational stories of personal experience. *Journal of Child Language, 15,* 293–315.

Mink, L. O. (1968). Philosophical analysis and historical understanding. *Review of Metaphysics, 20,* 667–698.

Mink, L. O. (1981). Everyman his or her own analyst. *Critical Inquiry, 7*, 777–792.

Moody, H. (1986). The meaning of life and the meaning of old age. In T. Cole & S. Gadow (Eds.), *What does it mean to grow old: Reflections from the humanities*, (pp. 9–40). Durham, NC: Duke University Press.

Munnichs, J. (1966). *Old age and finitude: A contribution to psychogerontology.* New York: Karger.

Murray, H., & Associates. (1938). *Explorations in personality.* New York: Oxford University Press.

Myerhoff, B. (1979). *Number our days.* New York: Dutton.

Neugarten, B. (1969). Continuities and discontinuities of psychological issues into adult life. *Human Development, 12*, 121–130.

Neugarten, B. (1979). Time, age, and the life-cycle. *American Journal of Psychiatry, 136*, 887–894.

Neugarten, B., & Datan, N. (1974a). The middle years. In S. Arieti (Ed.), *American handbook of psychiatry: 1. The foundations of psychiatry* (pp. 592–606). New York: Basic Books.

Neugarten, B., & Datan, N. (1974b). Sociological perspectives on the life cycle. In P. Baltes & K. W. Schaie (Eds.), *Life-span developmental psychology: Personality and socialization* (pp. 53–69). New York: Academic Press.

Peterson, C., & McCabe, A. (1983). *Developmental psycholinguistics: Three ways of looking at a child's narrative.* New York: Plenum.

Peterson, C., & McCabe, A. (1991). Linking children's connective use and narrative macrostructure. In A. McCabe & C. Peterson (Eds.), *Developing narrative structure* (pp. 29–54). Hillsdale, NJ: Lawrence Erlbaum Associates.

Polanyi, L. (1985). *Telling the American story.* Norwood, NJ: Ablex.

Polkinghorne, D. (1983). *Methodology for the human sciences: Systems of inquiry.* Albany, NY: Press of the State University of New York.

Polkinghorne, D. (1988). *Narrative knowing and the human sciences.* Albany, NY: State University of New York Press.

Potamianou, A. (1985). The personal myth: Points of counterpoints. *The Psychoanalytic Study of the Child, 40*, 285–297.

Ricoeur, P. (1971). The model of the text: Meaningful action considered as a text. *Social Research, 38*, 562–569.

Ricoeur, P. (1977). The question of proof in Freud's psychoanalytic writings. *Journal of the American Psychoanalytic Association, 25*, 835–872.

Ricoeur, P. (1983). Can fictional narratives be true? *Analecta Husserliana, 14*, 3–19.

Rogers, C. (1951). *Client-centered psychology: Its current practice, implications, and theory.* Boston: Houghton-Mifflin.

Rousseau, J. J. (1960). *The confessions.* (Trans. J. M. Cohen). Baltimore: Johns Hopkins University Press. (Original work published 1782–1789).

Rubin, D. (Ed.). (1986). *Autobiographical memory.* Cambridge: Cambridge University Press.

Rudolph, S., & Rudolph, L. (1978). Rajput adulthood: Reflections on the Amar

Singh diary. In E. Erikson (Ed.), *Adulthood* (pp. 149–172). New York: Norton.

Runyan, W. McK. (1982). *Life histories and psychobiography: Explorations in theory and method.* New York: Oxford University Press.

Sachs, J. (1980). Topic selection in parent-child discourse. *Discourse Processes, 2,* 145–153.

Sachs, J. (1983). Talking about the there and then: The emergence of displaced reference in parent-child discourse. In K. Nelson (Ed.), *Children's language* (Vol. 4, pp. 1–27). New York: Gardner Press.

Schafer, R. (1980). Narration in the psychoanalytic dialogue. *Critical Inquiry, 7,* 29–53.

Schafer, R. (1981). *Narrative actions in psychoanalysis.* Worcester, MA: Clark University Press. (Vol. 14 of the Heinz Werner Lecture Series).

Schafer, R. (1992). *Retelling a life: Narration and dialogue in psychoanalysis.* New York: Basic Books.

Scholes, R. (1989). *Protocols of reading.* New Haven, CT: Yale University Press.

Sirgy, M. J. (1986). *Self-congruity: Toward a theory of personality and cybernetics.* New York: Praeger.

Stein, N., & Glenn, C. (1979). An analysis of story comprehension in elementary school children. In R. Freedle (Ed.), *New directions in discourse processing* (Vol 2 of *Advances in Discourse Processes,* pp. 53–120). Norwood, NJ: Ablex.

Stein, N., & Policastro, M. (1984). The concept of a story: A comparison between children's and teacher's viewpoints. In H. Mandl, N. Stein, & T. Trabasso (Eds.), *Language and comprehension of text* (pp. 113–158). Hillsdale, NJ: Erlbaum.

Syngg, D., & Coombs, A. W. (1953). *Individual behavior.* Chicago: University of Chicago Press.

Thompson, E. P. (1966). *The making of the English working class.* New York: Random House/Vintage Books.

Thompson, E. P. (1967). Time, work, and industrial capitalism. *Past and Present: Journal of Historical Studies,* no. 38, 56–97.

Tobin, S. (1991). *Personhood in advanced old age: Implications for practice.* New York: Springer Publishing Co.

Vico, G. (1968). *The new science* (3rd ed. of 1744; trans. and ed. T. G. Bergin & M. H. Fisch). Ithaca, NY: Cornell University Press. (Original work published 1725).

Weber, M. (1955). *The Protestant ethic and the spirit of capitalism.* (Trans. T. Parsons). New York: Charles Scribner. (Original work published 1904–1905)

Weintraub, K. (1975). Autobiography and historical consciousness. *Critical Inquiry, 1,* 821–848.

Weintraub, K. (1978). *The value of the individual: Self and circumstance in autobiography.* Chicago: University of Chicago Press.

White, H. (1972). The structure of historical narrative. *Clio, 1,* 5–19.

White, H. (1978). Interpretation in history. In H. White (Ed.), *Tropics of discourse: Essays in cultural criticism* (pp. 51–80). Baltimore: Johns Hopkins University Press.

White, H. (1980). The value of narrativity in the representation of reality. *Critical Inquiry, 7,* 5–29.

White, H. (1981). Critical response: 3. The narrativization of real events. *Critical Inquiry, 7,* 793–789.

White, H. (1987). The question of narrative in contemporary historical theory. In H. White (Ed.), *The content of the form: Narrative discourse and historical representation* (pp. 26–58). Baltimore: Johns Hopkins University Press.

White, R. W. (1966). *Lives in progress* (2nd ed.). New York: Holt, Rinehart, and Winston.

Wordsworth, W. (1979). *The prelude.* (Ed. J. Wordsworth, M. Abrams, & S. Gill). New York: Norton Critical Editions. (Original work published 1850)

7

Rethinking Industrialization: Old Age and the Family Economy*

Brian Gratton and Carole Haber

In the history of old age, the effects of industrialization upon the old have been clearly and repeatedly outlined. As explained by early 20th-century analysts, modern sociological critiques, and several recent historians, with the advent of the factory, the status of the old underwent a dramatic decline.[1] According to this perspective, the preindustrial economy provided the greatest supports for the elderly: the family guaranteed their economic survival, and dependent and subservient kin relied upon their elders' experience and knowledge. With industrialization, however, the dominant role of the old was assumed

*The authors would like to thank Frances M. Rotondo for her contributions to this essay.

to have been transformed. Impoverished by an economy that provided wages based on speed, and deserted by children who found better opportunities elsewhere, the old were left in fragmented households, struggling to survive and ultimately destined to become paupers in the almshouse's wards.

In this chapter we offer a very different critique of industrialization's effects upon the elderly and their families. In contrast to traditional views that assume that the factory debased the old and forced them into both impoverishment and isolated households, we suggest that the economic growth that occurred in the United States between 1880 and 1930 had radically different consequences for older Americans. Rather than impoverishment, industrialization brought with it real gains in the per capita wealth of the average American; by the end of the industrial era, most old persons possessed wealth and assets that had been attainable only to a small minority of preindustrial elders. Moreover, industrialization hardly destroyed the bonds among family members. At the end of the 19th century, the elderly often established complex households.[2] Such living arrangements fostered a family economy that provided for the needs of family members and allowed the old to attain substantial level of affluence. The phenomena of complex households and increasing wealth, as we shall see, were intricately related. In sharing their households and establishing a "family fund," the elderly were able to protect themselves against impoverishment.

Yet, while assuring the economic success of the old, such households did not necessarily engender harmony. In industrial America, the family economy demanded numerous sacrifices from family members. For the support of aging kin, children were forced into the labor market, marriages were postponed, and generations were obliged to reside together. By the end of the industrial era, a bifurcated pattern of family life began to emerge. With increasing affluence, working-class families moved to combine households, wealth, and resources; in contrast, even wealthier middle-class families began to move away from such complex arrangements. Encouraged by social commentators who praised the private, two-generational home, relatively prosperous elders and their children began to establish separate households. This pattern, however, was a reflection of neither the disruption of industrialization nor its denigration of old age. Rather, it was based on the growing prosperity of a large segment of the old and on their ability to establish the widely preferred model of independent households. Social Security permitted a still larger number of the elderly to realize this ideal.

THE FAMILY ECONOMY
IN THE INDUSTRIAL ERA

At the turn of the 20th century, social commentators often remarked upon the elderly's decline in status. Individuals such as Lee Welling Squier (1912) and Abraham Epstein (1922) argued that, with old age, most workers faced increasing desperation. Apt to experience a decrease in wages, they found themselves unemployed and unemployable. Their fate was then determined: They would end their lives in squalor, abandoned by their kin and discarded by employers onto the "scrap heap" of industrial society. According to this narrative, America's urban and industrial growth had transformed well-knit and prosperous families into isolated and impoverished individuals (For some examples of this argument, see Devine, 1909; Epstein, 1922, 1928; Rubinow, 1934; Squier, 1912; Todd, 1915; Warner, 1894).

This depiction of old age has had broad ramifications. Influential in the rhetoric of the early-20th-century pension movement, it has become central to many contemporary sociological theories about the effect of industrialization upon old age. Nevertheless, individuals such as Epstein greatly overstated the negative effects of modernization upon the elderly. Despite their prediction that all elderly individuals would be discarded on the industrial scrap heap, only a small minority of the old met this dire fate. In the period between 1860 and 1930, the great majority of the elderly were clearly neither abandoned by their young nor faced with increasing impoverishment. As several family historians have discovered, industrialization hardly destroyed the family. Residence in a large industrialized city, in fact, *increased* the tendency of the elderly to live with other family members. In Massachusetts, for example, increasing urban and industrial growth in the cities of Salem, Lawrence, and Lynn strengthened, rather than weakened, ties among generations. In 1880, a greater percentage of the elderly headed households inhabited by adult children than had their counterparts in 1860. Moreover, a higher percentage of the urban elders lived with their children than did their rural peers. In Salem, Lawrence, and Lynn, 64% of men and 61% of women aged 55 and over lived with children; in nonurban areas of Essex County, the corresponding proportions were 47% and 35%, respectively (Chudacoff & Hareven, 1977, 1978).[3]

Nor was this urban extended family limited to late-19th-century Massachusetts. In New York, in the early 20th century, the elderly in the city, rather than in the countryside, resided in complex households. They, instead of the rural old, were likely to share a dwelling with their children. In the 1920s, 40% of the state's rural elderly lived with children in their homes; in the cities, 60% resided with off-spring.[4]

In all likelihood, the tendency toward extended families among the elderly was based on two significant factors. First, 19th-century de-clines in child mortality and increases in longevity made it demo-graphically more likely that adult children and aged parents would live long enough to form such households. In the preindustrial era, the possibilities for the formation of three-generation households had been extremely limited (Ruggles, 1987; Laslett & Wall, 1972). Second, extended family arrangements came to serve critical functions for both the old and their children. At the turn of the century, the estab-lishment of such families brought measurable benefits to both gener-ations: highly desirable living space could be shared, and income could be combined. With the wages of numerous family members, persons who individually might experience a decline in income re-mained solidly in the middle classes. Moreover, in cities, where the elderly were far more likely to own property than were the young, the adult children were able to shelter themselves in the homes already established by the older generation (Anderson, 1971; U.S. Bureau of the Census, 1895).

The discovery of an increase in extended and complex households argues strongly against the notion that industrialization led to the destruction of the family unit or the isolation of older people. Rather, industrialization clearly encouraged workers to rely upon family members and to exchange family-shared resources (Bodnar, 1982, 1985; Bodnar, Simon, & Weber, 1982). This strategy depended heav-ily on the paid and unpaid labor of all members of the family. Along with the head of household, the labors of both women and mature children contributed to the economic well-being of the household. Although married women rarely worked outside the home, their unpaid labor played an essential role in the success of the family strategies. Their failure to seek outside employment could have been based on rational considerations. As historian Ruth Cowan (1987, p. 170) has noted, such work would have been "a threat to the families' standard of living." As wives and mothers, women per-formed arduous and essential work within the home that sustained the family and thus ensured that their children would survive to become productive members of the family enterprise (see also Haines, 1979, 1985).

These maturing "useful children" fit the needs of working-class families well. Encouraged to work by parents who wished to increase the income of the household, they dutifully turned their wages over to their elders and added to the family's financial success. Parents then wielded great authority over the lives of their children. They planned their careers, often directing them toward objectives that would favor the family as a whole (Stern, 1987; Zelizer, 1985). In part, such behavior was based on the children's sense of responsibility and obligation to the family fund. For most young workers, little question existed as to the control of their wages; upon being paid, they relinquished the money to their parents. "When you worked," explained one immigrant, "you used to bring your pay home and give it to your parents. And whatever they feel they want to give you, they decide" (Bodnar, 1985, p. 73). Another working-class girl recalled that her "parents wanted fifteen dollars a month from me. . . . They wanted it every month" (Bodnar, 1982, p. 22).

In most analyses of family strategies, such patterns of behavior have been explained as part of the working class's struggle to survive. Several historians have argued that individuals who coerced their children into the labor market or relied upon their wages simply had little choice. Without such actions, the old would have faced overwhelming destitution. Summarizing working-class oral histories, John Bodnar (1982, p. 180) concluded that, prior to 1930, workers were "primarily concerned with survival." Their family fund merely allowed them exist; they "achieved little in the way of savings." Like Bodnar, Mark Stern (1987) also emphasized the close margin of existence in working-class families. Families headed by persons in late middle age with older working children did well, but the loss of children's wages was devastating. "With all the children gone," wrote Stern, "the old couple would again be impoverished" (p. 41).[5]

The family fund, however, actually did far more than merely allow the old to exist; it served to ensure the security and often the relative prosperity of the elderly couple's final years (Morawska, 1985). By the end of the industrial era, in fact, the wealth and well-being of the working-class old had significantly increased. By their sixth decade, their reliance upon family-based strategies allowed them to accumulate property and assets far greater than the young or middle aged were able to amass. For a majority of older people, therefore, industrialization brought great economic benefits.

These conclusions are based on evidence drawn from cost-of-living surveys of blue-collar workers conducted in 1889–1890 and 1917–1919.[6] Each survey recorded income and expenditure for families, rather than for individuals. Because surveyors excluded the very rich and the very poor, as well as all farmers, the data do not represent the entire population, but they permit close study across the stages of the life course of the working-class—the very group contemporary analysts concluded were destined to be impoverished in old age. The analyses presented here use data for 6,314 households headed by males 25 and over in 1889-1890, and 12,327 such homes in 1917–1919. To enhance comparisons between the surveys, all 1889-1890 money values have been converted to 1918 dollars, and eight groups have been defined by the age of the household head: 25–29, 30–34, 35–39, 40–44, 45–49, 50–54, and 60 and over.[7]

In contrast to the assumptions of turn-of-the-century analysts, the studies reveal the potential for success in family-based economies, the positive effects of industrialization for all age groups, and in particular, the ability of older couples to accumulate considerable assets across the life course. The surveys also reveal the paradox of the elderly's economic status. In one sense, advocates for the elderly had indeed been correct. With industrialization, the long years of experience of the old rarely translated into high earnings; individuals in their 20s or 30s earned substantially more than did elderly men. Using medians for the eight age groups in each survey, Figure 7.1 displays the earnings of the male heads of household, as well as total household income from all sources. In each period, the highest earnings were reported by men in their middle to late 30s; men 60 and over earned less than 70% of the peak. Such a notable decline in individual income was probably the result of a complex array of factors. Many older workers reduced their labor force activity as they grew older; some were judged to be less productive and paid accordingly; still others were employed in less lucrative fields; whereas young workers entered new and higher-paying occupations.

Despite this decline in earnings, the elderly did not become impoverished; their total household income, in fact, revealed a radically different pattern from that of their individual wages. In each survey, household income reached its peak in households headed by men aged 55 to 59. Although, individually, such elderly men earned less than the young did, they attained greater total income. The difference was the result of a kin-based strategy that relied upon the labor, wages, and assets of the entire family. Figure 7.2 displays the composition of mean family income: in 1889–1890, at least one-quarter of mean household income for all households headed by men over 45 was the result of an upward intergenerational flow from their children. For household heads over 60, children's earnings made up approximately one-third of household income, and "other" sources made up another fifth. By 1917–1919, reliance on children's wages had declined for most age groups. For households headed by men in their 60s, however, children still provided about 30% of the total household income.

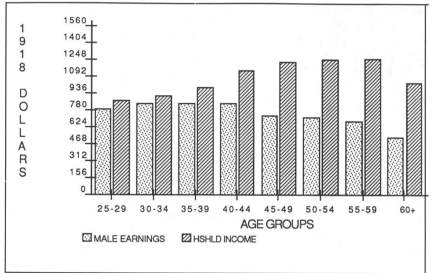

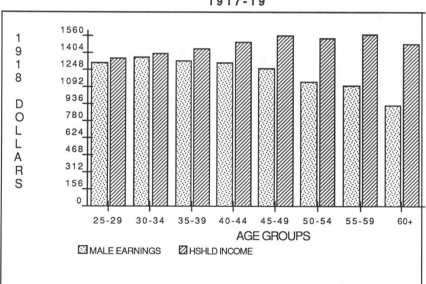

FIGURE 7.1 Median male earnings and household income.

1889-90

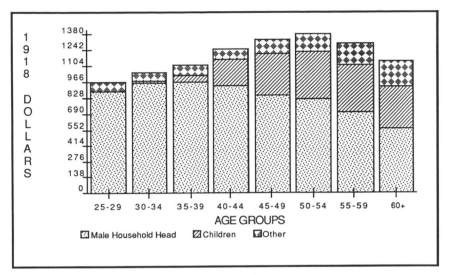

1917-19

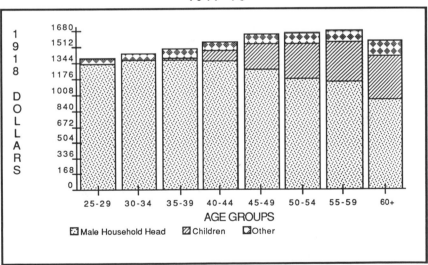

FIGURE 7.2 Composition of family income.

To some degree, this extra revenue was necessary because older families had to meet the needs of both additional and more mature members. In 1917–1919, households headed by men 40 to 44 had an average household size of 5.4, versus the mean in all households of 4.9. Per capita statistics indicate, however, that despite the size of the household, persons in older households maintained excellent standards of consumption. In 1889–1890, per capital expenditure in families headed by men over 60 equaled $231, the fourth-highest level among the age groups; in 1917–1919, households headed by elderly men were in the third-highest group, spending $319 per member.

Both household and per capita measures demonstrate industrialization's positive effect upon the economic welfare of most blue-collar workers over the course of three decades. In 1917–1919, the earnings of males 60 and over was 75% higher than it had been in 1889–1890. Median household income and expenditure for all age groups rose by more than 40%; the oldest households reported even greater income and expenditure gains. Mean expenditure per person rose 38% for all household members and an equal amount for persons in households headed by men over 60. Following a cohort approach, in 1889–1890, an individual in a household headed by a man 25–29 consumed $255 in goods and services annually; in 1917–1919, the same person, living in a household headed by a man 55–59, enjoyed $342 in expenditure per year.

Given such experience, working-class people had little reason to expect that their old age would be filled with impoverishment or destitution. The majority of elderly individuals were unlikely to face their last days deprived of all necessities. Industrialization and rising wealth not only allowed the old to have greater average expenditure but even provided them "luxury" items; a smaller proportion of the budgets had to be spent on necessities. For the first time, many working-class elderly could support the purchase of nonessential items in their budgets. In the 19th century, 47% of an individual's consumption in families headed by men over 60 was allocated for food; in the 20th century, however, such individuals spent only 39% on food. Yet the decline in expenses was not based on intense austerity. In 1917–1919, on average, the families of elderly household heads spent more on amusements, vacations, books, and newspapers than did their younger counterparts.

Such high consumption was not the only benefit of the elderly's family-based tactics; they also allowed the old to amass significant savings. In both surveys, older households attained larger annual surpluses of income over expenditures than did the young. As shown in Figure 7.3, in 1889–1890, median surpluses were greatest for

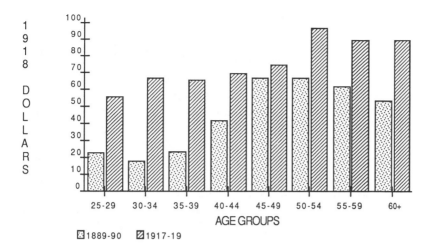

FIGURE 7.3 Median annual surplus.

households headed by men 45–59 and 50–54; in households headed by men over 60, surpluses, although not as high as those in middle-aged families, were still well above the average. In 1917–1919, the oldest households had a median annual surplus of $89, the second highest among all age groups and well above the average of $67. These yearly savings could have a significant effect; through the life course, individuals could amass valuable assets (Rotella & Alter, 1989). Workers who managed simply to accrue the median annual savings reflected in the 1889–1890 study amassed at least $1,745 between age 25 and 65. In 1917–1919, the same calculation yielded $3,015. If mean surpluses are used, the savings accumulated to about $5,000 in each of the cost-of-living studies.

The potential for accumulation of assets corresponds quite well with the amount of wealth actually held by older people in industrial states in the mid-1920s. In surveys taken during this decade, more than 40% of persons 65 and over possessed wealth in excess of $5,000; another 20% owned between $1,000 and $5,000.[8] These levels of accumulation promised an important source of security in old age. An annuity based on the 1889–1890 accumulation of $1,745 would provide only about 8 years of the $231 average expenditure for one person in the oldest households in that period. By 1917–1919, the median of $3,015 could provide a 10-year annuity at $317, the much higher per capita expenditure in households headed by men over 60 in that survey. The $5,000 accumulation—available to at least 40% of the aged in the 1920s surveys—could provide an elderly couple 10 years of their expenditure needs.

Formal annuitization, of course, was impractical for the elderly: certainties never exist for length of life or for the safety of investments. Moreover, the elderly's assets, often concentrated in home ownership, were not always readily converted into income (Binstock, 1983). These economic uncertainties help to explain the continued, if increasingly intermittent, labor force activity of older men in the era before the guaranteed retirement benefits of Social Security. Although older men reduced their work activity and some endured long periods of joblessness, they endeavored to maintain some connection to gainful employment. Without the support of a guaranteed pension, elderly workers were unable to predict with confidence that their savings would last the remainder of their lives. In comparison to later decades, then, full retirement among the old was rare. Moreover, when such decisions were made, they were formulated within the context of the family economy, rather than being based solely upon a socially determined retirement age.

As the family economy helps to illuminate work and retirement decisions among the aged, it also explains why the elderly often chose to concentrate a large proportion of their assets in home ownership. Although not always readily converted into income, houses provided the old with a highly valued asset that conformed to and supported family strategies (Bushman, 1981). By owning their houses, the elderly set the stage for the kin-based economy from which income and savings were generated. The residence also provided shelter for working children and, in time, promised a worthy inheritance for faithful sons and daughters.

Perhaps not surprisingly, then, complex and extended families were not common among society's most impoverished. Rather, they were formed by those who could afford to live together and efficiently pool their labor and assets. As Daniel Scott Smith (1979, 1982) has observed, the poorest of the old had the least opportunity to sustain independent, complex households.[9] Older people of greater means had the resources necessary to support additional kin; working-class elders had the greatest reason to encourage adult children to remain unmarried and contribute to the family income. In 1900, 68% of all urban middle-class individuals age 55 and older resided with at least one offspring; among the urban working class, the proportion was 61% (Smith, 1986).[10] Richer people had the wealth—especially in the ownership of real estate—necessary to bring others into their households. For the most affluent, their actions may have been charity; for those of lesser means, the arrangement was a way of using resources in realty to combine income and reduce per capita expenditures (Ruggles, 1987).

For the poorest of the old, however, the family economy had little meaning and brought few benefits. Although the great majority of the elderly increased their wealth and well-being during the industrial era, a small percentage remained impoverished. Early-20th-century surveys of the elderly reported that about 17% of the old had no income or property (Massachusetts Commission on Pensions, 1925; National Civil Federation, 1925). To a large degree, this poverty-stricken group proved the importance of the family economy in the late 19th and early 20th centuries. Dominated by single and widowed older women, the most impoverished of the old lacked the potential to amass assets over the course of a lifetime or the ability to exchange resources with family members. Having exhausted their savings, and with limited job opportunities, they were generally dependent upon their children or, as a last resort, were forced to rely upon public or private charities. Not surprisingly, widows were disproportionately represented in the caseloads of welfare workers, who were all too well acquainted with their desperate plight.[11] Other groups faced hard times in old age as well. Immigrants had a better than average chance of ending their days in the almshouse. Having accumulated few resources during their lives, they possessed little with which to support themselves in old age. Blacks, as well, generally failed to amass any material wealth. Unlike their white counterparts, their economic status did not improve with age; many simply remained impoverished throughout their lives (Atack & Bateman, 1987; Blumin, 1982; Gratton, 1986a, 1986b).

Clearly, despite the real-income growth of the industrial era, these segments of the elderly population were vulnerable and impoverished. Their presence in the almshouse, in newly established old age homes, and on outdoor relief rolls were well noted by social advocates, who assumed they were emblematic of the growing impoverishment and abandonment of all of the elderly. In reality, however, the lives of most middle- and working-class elderly bore little resemblance to the characterizations of social analysts. Although the wages of older male workers did appear low, they could be labeled neither impoverished nor abandoned; their household incomes not only sustained higher standards of living but enabled a large proportion of the elderly to realize considerable affluence. As the demographic realities of longer life allowed elderly parents to reside with adult children, the economic benefits of such residential patterns were clear: the old could ensure their own prosperity through control of the family's earnings.

THE CRISIS OF THE FAMILY ECONOMY

Although the demographic conditions upon which these new house-hold structures were built did not disappear after 1900, the household structure of elderly Americans subsequently became increasingly less complex and extended. By the second decade of 20th century, the tendency for the middle class to extend households to accommodate older or younger generations began to weaken. Between 1900 and 1940, the proportion of men aged 65 and over who lived as dependents in their children's homes declined from 16% to 11%; for women the percentage fell from 34 to 23 (Smith, 1982). But this decline was hardly due to neglect on the part of the young nor to a sudden dislike of their elders. Rather, such living arrangements were the result of economic prosperity; increased wages and additional wealth allowed these families to realize another traditional ideal of autonomous households in separate dwellings. Among the more prosperous families, elderly individuals could amass sufficient wealth in the course of a lifetime to live independently, without depending on their children's wages. Their more prosperous children could also afford to obtain housing and reside by themselves. By 1915, in fact, a new pattern began to emerge: whereas increasing proportions of the working class turned to family extension, fewer middle-class families resorted to complex households.[12]

One explanation for this bifurcated pattern, we would suggest, may be found in part in the economic conditions of industrialization. The average income levels of the working class rose to the standards that the middle class had achieved decades before. As a result, the more prosperous workers secured wealth sufficient to provide housing and support for relatives. The "luxury" of kinship co-residence, once available only to the middle class and skilled workers, now became a pattern among laborers. Moreover, the additional high wages of family members increased the financial well-being of the group. In 1880, in Erie County, New York, for instance, the inclusion of extended family among the unskilled generally diminished family wealth. By 1915, this loss of average income was no longer the case. The extended family, in fact, was likely to lead to an improvement in the economic status of the unskilled worker (Ruggles, 1987).

The middle class, on the other hand, now began to follow a different pattern. Before 1900, even white-collar workers were impoverished, by present-day standards. Despite their comparatively higher wages, they were often unable to establish separate living quarters for their aged relatives. In the 20th century, however, their increased wages allowed them to live independently. This arrangement was not entirely new: it had long been followed by the upper class and had emerged in the late 19th century among the elderly who resided in the villages of America. (On the importance of the autonomous household in the villages of America, see Haber & Gratton, in press.)

The growing isolation of the middle-class household not only reflected a transformation in its economic basis but was supported as well by evolving cultural expectations. In the mid-19th century, middle-class sentiment proclaimed the family to be the foundation of all social order, responsible for the development of an individual's personality, values, and character (Deglar, 1980). Few questioned then, that the family was ultimately accountable for the needs of its members. The care of the dependent relative, especially the widowed mother, was an moral obligation that went beyond economic considerations.[13] In dealing with their own families, as well as in defining the correct welfare policy for the poor, the 19th-century middle class continually espoused the primary importance of family responsibility.

Despite such beliefs, co-residence with an elderly relative did not always imply peaceful coexistence. Within complex households, the lines of authority often led to conflict and dissension.[14] In the mid-19th century, for example, Julia and Bildad Merrill, Jr., of Utica, New York, moved into the household of Bildad's elderly parents. Faced with growing disability, Bildad Merrill, Sr., and his wife, Nancy, traded their autonomy for the support of the younger generation. But this economic strategy did not translate into harmonious relations; the elderly found it difficult to relinquish their authority to their offspring. Both mother and daughter-in-law claimed command over the servants and preeminence with the children. Ultimately, their dispute led to an outbreak of violence between the two women and an ignominious church trial. After public apologies and resolutions, they returned to share the same abode—and many of the same intergenerational tensions (Ryan, 1981).

The Merrills' household arrangements reflected a threshold of affluence that allowed middle-class families to support the elderly in times of need, as well as to sustain the belief that the family was fulfilling its ethical responsibility. For such individuals, the neglect of relatives showed lack of breeding or refinement; to share possessions and space was part of the moral code of the bourgeoisie. Like the Merrills, therefore, few middle-class individuals would have questioned the importance of assisting kin if such assistance was required. Before the advent of the welfare state, resorting to public welfare was viewed as ultimate failure; the family, rather than the state, was responsible for the well-being of its relatives (Hareven, 1986). Thus, despite the significant decline in family size that occurred throughout the 19th century, small middle-class families did not necessarily desert their kin. According to the 1900 census, in fact, it mattered little whether the old had one child or five; aging widows would almost always find offspring with whom to reside, even if it meant instigating generational conflicts.[15]

By the early 20th century, however, declines in fertility placed greater burdens on the children, presenting an increasing share with the Merrills' often difficult living arrangements. With fewer children, both the elderly and their offspring lost the privilege of choice. As the number of offspring decreased, the risk of burden for the existing children increased; the predicament of how to provide for the needs of the elderly parent was shared by more Americans (Gratton, 1986b).[16] The aged could not select the most congenial environment, nor could the children decide which of many siblings might remain in the household of the old. Especially for urban daughters, care of the old became an obligation they were more likely to face as they themselves entered middle age.

Thus, although the 19th-century decline in family size did not lead to the abandonment of the old, it may have caused even greater tensions within the family group. As the birthrate continued to fall in the 20th century, the risk of burden for the existing children increased. In the early 1930s, an anonymous female writer recalled the problems of three-generational households. "When I was a child," she wrote:

> I took it for granted that a grandmother or grandfather should live in the house of nearly everyone of my playmates. Soon I came to take it for granted, also, that these houses should be full of friction. The association of grandparents with friction took such a hold in my mind that I called myself lucky because my own were dead! ("Old Age Intestate," 1931, p. 715).[17]

Despite her antagonism to such residence patterns, in her own adulthood the author found herself with little choice but to accept her aging mother into her household. The results, she reported, were disastrous. "[H]armony is gone. Rest has vanished" ("Old Age Intestate," 1931, p. 712). Her daily routine, the lives of her children, and the stability of her marriage, she asserted, had been severely upset. Nor, she argued, was she alone. Numerous friends and acquaintances reported the disruption of family harmony and the demise of social life upon the coresidence of an aging parent. "The intrusion," she argued, "is probably a common cause of divorce, and most certainly of marital unhappiness and problems in children" ("Old Age Intestate," 1931, p. 714).

The anonymous author's complaints reflected her struggle over opposing values and norms. Her conviction that her elderly mother could not be abandoned conflicted with her strong desire to reside only with her husband and children. Although she felt obligated to open her home to her widowed mother, she strongly objected to the constraints it imposed. The only happy families, she concluded, were those who were financially secure enough to allow aging parent and adult children to live in separate residences ("Old Age Intestate," 1931).

The author's expressed desire for different dwellings hardly marked her as unique—although she did not feel comfortable enough to provide her real name. Even in 18th-century England, elderly individuals who were financially able chose to live apart from their offspring. Great wealth allowed both the old and their adult children the luxury of separate existences (Laslett, 1977). In the 20th century, as the middle class began to attain a high level of affluence, the old norm of extension and modification faded, and the preference for separate residences began to find expression as a "modern" cultural prescription. Although the ideology of supporting the old was never rejected, social critics and advocates of proper family behavior began to stress the centrality of the small private household. For this new paradigm, they drew upon an old ideal. The values that urged that the elderly be sheltered in children's homes had always conflicted with a similarly enduring and powerful norm among Americans: the preference for separate residences, an objective shared by the elderly and their adult children (Hareven, 1982; Heaton & Hoppe, 1987).

Even in the 19th century, the nuclear family can be found at the center of the kindship ideology; the father, the mother, and the children, rather than maiden aunts or mothers-in-law, comprised the central elements in the kinship circle. Despite their admonition that families should help their kin, social theorists had also expressed concern that the addition of relatives into the hallowed circle could not fail to bring dissension and turmoil. The author Samuel Butler was only one of many English and American analysts who expressed concern. "I believe," he wrote in 1885,

> that more unhappiness comes from this source than from any other—I mean from the attempt to prolong the family connection unduly and to make people hang together artificially who would never naturally do so. The mischief among the lower classes is not so great, but among the middle and upper classes it is killing a large number daily. And the old people do not really like it so much better than the young. (cited in Ruggles, 1987, p. 3)

Butler's pronouncement prefigured three pressing middle-class concerns that would be expressed with increasing vehemence in the early 20th century. First, scores of social analysts were convinced that the enclosed nuclear family was the ideal—and most congenial—arrangement for all family members. Pension proponent and expert on aging Abraham Epstein (1928) argued that the happiest families were those without extended kin. In 1928, in words that were echoed by the anonymous magazine writer only 3 years later, Epstein declared that "We all know among our acquaintances, some people whose young lives have been made pitiably wretched, and in some instances totally ruined, by the constant 'pestering' of an old father-in-law or mother-in-law" (p. 147). Both the elderly and their children, he seemed confident, would be far happier if they could afford to live in separate dwellings.[18]

Second, family experts viewed nuclear households as the proper environment for raising children and ensuring their moral upbringing. Nowhere was this concern expressed with greater intensity than in the early-20th-century attack on the practice of boarding. According to a 1910 report of the U.S. Bureau of Labor (cited in Modell & Hareven, 1978), for example, the custom of boarding had little proper place in the American home. The practice, the report explained, was extremely detrimental to family members: "[T]he close quarters often destroy all privacy, and the lodger or boarder becomes practically a member of the family" (p. 53). The institution, which so for so long had been an accepted part of middle-class life and an important source of revenue to the aging, was now seen as a sign of working-class immorality. It was, social analysts declared, an outright attack on the primacy of insular kinship relations.

Finally, welfare advocates were concerned about the economic impact of extended families because they understood how family economies operated to sustain older people. Middle-aged adults, they feared, were constantly being forced to make irreconcilable economic judgments over the allocation of valued resources. In supporting their elders, they robbed the young; in providing for their children, they dismissed the traditional obligations they owed to their elders. According to welfare authorities, members of extended families seemed to be faced with an insurmountable predicament: either they provided for their children's growth and education, or they saved the old from the almshouse. "It seems cruel," wrote Abraham Epstein in 1928,

> to force any father or mother in this twentieth century to decide between supporting old parents and contenting themselves with a little less

food, less room, less clothing, and the curtailment of their children's education, or sending their parents to the poorhouse or to charitable agencies to accept the stigma of pauperism, and thus assure themselves of more food, more room, more clothing and a better education for their children. (p. 147)

Even politicians accepted this dictum. According to David I. Walsh (1927), senator from Massachusetts, the family economy itself created a vicious cycle of impoverishment. By depriving the children in order to prosper, the elders limited their offspring's future; without proper education or training, the unprepared young adults would only repeat the errors of their fathers. "Many married sons and daughters," he declared in 1927, "in order to spare their aged parents the disgrace and bitterness of pauperism, assume burdens which cannot be borne except at the cost of depriving their own children of the rights of childhood and the opportunities of success, and of dooming themselves in turn to an old age of helpless dependence" (p. 224).

Given such fears, family experts and welfare advocates came to view the family economy and its extended and complex households with increasing hostility. Although the working class still relied upon the wages of the young and accepted the belief that "a child ought to sacrifice his own interest or ambition to promote the welfare of the family," the middle class began to object to this integenerational transfer of funds.[19] Not surprisingly perhaps, their criticisms grew increasingly strident as more middle-class individuals moved away from the need to rely upon family resources and blue-collar workers grew prosperous enough to capitalize on a family-based strategy. For the affluent middle class, however, the extended family no longer seemed a sanctuary of love and affection; it represented the assumed impoverishment of the working class. Only the degraded elderly, they argued, would choose to live in crowded households with adult children; all others would follow the model of independent residences.

CONCLUSION

Social advocates were clearly mistaken about the impact of industrialization upon the elderly. Rather than creating impoverishment, economic growth greatly enhanced the real income, level of consumption, and savings of most Americans. Despite relative declines in males' earnings across the life cycle, the old did not suddenly become poverty-stricken. By relying upon a family-based economic scheme, they were often able to accumulate considerable assets and savings. Moreover, changing demographic conditions allowed greater numbers to form complex family structures that allowed for the intergenerational exchange of resources.

In the 19th century, complex households received widespread social support, even from the middle class. The addition of a widowed parent to the home or the continued residence of a mature child seemed to reflect kinship responsibility and concern. Yet, despite cultural approval, such family arrangements may have reflected necessity more than desire. Both middle- and working-class families turned to extended family arrangements as a means of meeting the vicissitudes of the industrial environment. The family system, however, was not without its limitations. Despite its potential for accumulation of assets, it could never guarantee protection against every possible eventuality in old age. Thus, family members found themselves forced into accepting numerous responsibilities and compromises. Children were obliged to maintain their financial contributions to the household, wives had to assume the domestic toil of keeping workers in the labor force, and aging workers had little choice but to strive to remain employed. Nor could the family economy assure peace among the family members. Although not all extended families repeated the humiliating history of the Merrills, co-residence often led to unresolved family tensions and disagreements.

As their wealth increased, therefore, members of the middle class sought to establish separate residence patterns. Greater affluence allowed them to create distinct households that simultaneously maintained relationships between generations while guaranteeing autonomy. Broad cultural norms that insisted on family members' responsibility to one another did not preclude a preference for another ideal, "intimacy at a distance." As that preference came within the reach of classes that dominated cultural prescription and advice, autonomous households were proclaimed the "correct" arrangement.

The opportunity to form such households was clearly broadened after the establishment of Social Security. Even in its earliest form, the welfare system guaranteed a stable retirement income, making older blue-collar workers more confident that their savings would support them in old age. As a result, they no longer felt compelled to rely upon their children's financial or residential assistance. Decisions to retire that had once been based on family strategies began to yield to mass retirement at the specified Social Security age of 65. Generations within families maintained close attachments, but did not live with one another.

After World War II, a majority of elderly persons followed the residential and work patterns once limited to the elite. Most now retire and reside by themselves or with a spouse in the "empty nest" of a household without children. This isolated existence marks a dramatic break with the past. Whereas less than 10% of the elderly lived alone in 1900, more than 40% of women and 15% of men now do so (Heaton & Hoppe, 1987; Kobrin, 1976). Many contemporary critics charge that these statistics reveal the disintegration of the modern family.[20] The elderly who live alone, they claim, have been neglected and abandoned by irresponsible younger relatives. The present-day living arrangements of older people, however, may be based on far different motives. Even in the past, affluent individuals seemed to prefer separate residences. Although Americans always believed that family members had a duty to support each other, extension or modification of the nuclear household provoked tension and dispute among kin. Although complex households met a strong cultural belief, they violated another which held that the generations should maintain separate residences, and that family relations might be injured rather than enhanced by joint living arrangements. In recent decades, Social Security and the increasing wealth of the old have transformed the complex household—and reliance on the family fund—into the modern-day pattern of the elderly's autonomous residences and age-based retirement. For the first time, most elderly people have the capacity to withdraw from work and live in separate households.

Given such contemporary choices, the effects of industrialization on the old must be reconsidered. The economic transformation of the nation improved the economic well-being of all the aged. Greater wealth led the middle classes to establish separate residences for the elderly and their adult children. The working class, however, still relied upon family strategies to meet the challenges of the industrial era. High standards of living and a secure old age demanded continued exchange and support within the household. Social Security's guarantee of a retirement income finally released kin from these responsibilities. Abandoning complex households, the old and the young achieved the long-standing objective of both intimacy and separation.

NOTES

[1] Even very recent accounts contend that industrialization deprived older people of economic security and close family relationships common to agricultural societies (Markides & Cooper, 1987).

[2] In our discussion, the term "extended" is used for households that include three generations in a family; "complex" will denote these as well as various other arrangements such as the inclusion of siblings, cousins, fictive kin, or non-kin, as well as households in which older persons retain headship, but adult children reside.

[3] These findings replicate Michael Anderson's (1971) famous contention about the industrial period in Great Britain.

[4] To some degree, this difference reflected the ethnic origins of the elderly. As in the countryside, the foreign-born old were more likely to live in simple nuclear families with at least one offspring in their residence. Their strong presence in urban areas, then, clearly influenced the proportion of old who continued to reside with their children. Yet even among the native-born elderly, those who lived in the city were more likely than their rural counterparts to inhabit the same home as their children. In New York in the early 20th century, over 50% of the urban, American-born elderly lived with at least one offspring; in the countryside, however, only 30% resided with a child (Weiler, 1986).

[5] For a historian who takes a more optimistic view of the family economy, see Ewa Morawska (1985).

[6] The data for *Cost of Living of Industrial Workers in the United States and Europe, 1889–1890* (ICPSR 7711) were originally collected by the Bureau of Labor. *Cost of Living in the United States, 1917–1919* (ICPSR 8299) was a project of the Department of Labor, Bureau of Labor Statistics. Each is now available in machine-readable format from the Inter-University Consortium for Political and Social Research, Ann Arbor, MI. Neither the collector of the original data nor the consortium bears any responsibility for the analysis or interpretation here. For a fuller description of the data sets and more extensive analyses, see Brian Gratton and Frances M. Rotondo (1992).

[7] The spectrum of ages among respondents allows researchers to consider life-cycle effects—to observe income, expenditure, and savings across age groups and to estimate the consequences for the economic well-being of older persons. Unlike cohort data, cross-sectional evidence does not display the train of events experienced by individuals during their lifetimes but compares individuals at different ages at a single point in time. Thus, lower earnings for older men may not mean that their wages have fallen but that younger cohorts have entered higher-paid occuptions. To contemporary observers, however, age differences probably did appear to represent what the future offered. In addition, the remarkable similarity between the two surveys in age-based patterns strongly suggests that life-cycle effects, as well as cohort differences, had impact.

[8] Such findings probably represent conservative estimates of the level and range of wealth holdings in the older population in the 1920s because assets tend to be underreported (see Palmer, Smeeding, & Jencks, 1988). The surveys did not divide married couples' assets between husband and wife. Although this inflates individual averages, it is equivalent to the household measurement in the cost of living surveys.

[9] Smith's study of the 1900 census showed that complex families were more often formed by middle-class persons. He concludes that the larger roles of extension in more affluent households proves false the "notion that co-residence of old people with their children . . . was primarily forced by economic dependency" (Smith, 1979, p. 297). Smith interprets the results as a function of cultural values, a theme he has elaborated in "'All in Some Degree Related to Each Other'" (1989). This thesis exaggerates the prosperity of the middle class and ignores the role economics play in co-residence. For the middle class, the creation of complex families may have been a rational economic response to change: as the income of the elderly declined or as death or marriage robbed the family of a significant wage earner, other family members or boarders entered the home to ensure its continued financial well-being. For a critique of the cultural argument, see Brian Gratton, (1986b).

[10] Smith (1986) finds the least co-residence in a third locale: in places of less than 25,000 population, only 56% had a child in the home.

[11] The proportion of widows who reported no property was about twice the level of all other women (Massachusetts Commission on Pensions, 1925; National Civil Federation, 1928).

[12] According to Ruggles (1987), in Erie County, New York, in 1880, 41% of all families with servants lived with extended kin; by 1915, the proportion was only 20%.

[13] In the 1930s, in an article in *Harper's Magazine*, an anonymous female author denounced the long-standing tradition of having the widowed mother enter the home of the married daughter. Her own friends and relatives, she stated, reacted with disbelief and shame when she advocated placing her mother in an "Old Ladies Home." Despite the fact that her mother's presence created great strains in the family, she yielded and allowed her mother to remain. "So strong is the tradition," she wrote, "so strong the sense of duty which we carry on for generation to generation," that she found herself with little choice. ("Old Age Intestate" 1931, p. 715). See also Tamara K. Hareven and Randolph Langenback (1978).

[14] On such tensions, see especially the work of John Bodnar (1982, 1985). In *Family Time and Industrial Time*, Tamara Hareven (1982) notes that disputes between generations over the dual ideals of assistance and autonomy "often generated conflicts of interests within the family" (p. 185).

[15] According to Daniel Scott Smith (1979), a woman with one child was nearly as likely to live with a child as was a woman with five children (79% to 89%). For a slightly modified position, see Smith (1989). For some scholars, this phenomenon, and the greater likelihood that the middle class would provide extended household shelter, show that cultural norms, largely lost today, strongly influenced behavior.

[16] On a recognition of this problem in the first decades of the 20th century, see, I. M. Rubinow (1930/1972), pp. 8–9.

[17] The author, of course, was not alone in her view. See Tim B. Heaton and Caroline Hoppe (1987).

[18] Epstein argued that the family had, in any case, largely disintegrated in modern times and that state pensions "would increase filial affection and respect for parents" (p. 210) because they would no longer be burdens to their children. Such a perception was not limited to "experts." Even the old themselves reported that they would have been far happier in separate households. In an article published in the *Saturday Evening Post* and reprinted in *Reader's Digest* ("I Am the Mother-in-Law," 1937) the anonymous author, a women aged 73, wrote: "When declining health and declining finances left me no alternative but to live with my daughter, my first feeling was one of bitterness." The author pledged to make herself as little of a burden as possible through numerous rules: "I must not be around when she was getting her work done, or when she had her friends in. I must ask no questions and give no unasked advice. I resolved to spend the greater part of each day alone in my room" (p. 12).

[19] Carolyn F. Ware Collection, Boxes 51–55, Franklin Delano Roosevelt Library, Hyde Park, NY; see also Ware (1935).

[20] Even in the late 19th century, critics charged that such a value was lost. See "Twenty-ninth Annual Report" (1887).

REFERENCES

Anderson, M. (1971). *Family structure in nineteenth-century Lancashire.* Cambridge: Cambridge University Press.

Atack, J., & Bateman F. (1987). *To their own soil.* Ames: Iowa State University Press.

Binstock, R. H. (1983). The aged as scapegoat. *Gerontologist, 23,* 136–143.

Blumin, S. (1982). Age and equality in antebellum America. *Social Science History, 6*(3), 369–379.

Bodnar, J. (1982). *Workers' world: Kinship, community and protest in an industrial society, 1900–1940.* Baltimore: Johns Hopkins University.

Bodnar, J. (1985). *The transplanted: A history of immigrants in urban America.* Bloomington: Indiana University Press.

Bodnar, J., Simon, R., & Weber, M. (1982). *Lives of their own: Blacks, Italians, and Poles in Pittsburgh, 1900–1960.* Urbana: University of Illinois Press.

Bushman, R. L. (1981). Family security in the transition from farm to city, 1750–1850. *Journal of Family History, 6,* 238–256.

Chudacoff, H. & Hareven, T. (1979). From the empty nest to family dissolution. *Journal of Family History, 4,* 69–83.

Chudacoff, H., & Hareven, T. (1978). Family transitions into old age. In T. Hareven (Ed.), *Transitions.* New York: Academic Press.

Cowan, R. (1987). Women's work, housework, and history: The historical roots of inequality in work-force participation. In N. Gerstel & H. Gross (Eds.), *Families and work.* Philadelphia: Temple University Press.

Deglar, C. (1980). *At odds: Women and the family in America from the revolution to the present.* New York: Oxford University Press.

Devine, E. T. (1909). *Misery and its causes*. New York: Macmillan.

Epstein, A. (1922). *Facing old age: A study of old age dependency in the United States and old age pensions*. New York: Alfred A. Knopf.

Epstein, A. (1928). *The challenge of the aged*. New York: Vanguard Press.

Gratton, B. (1986a). The labor force participation of older men: 1890–1950. *Journal of Social History, 20*(4), 689–710.

Gratton, B. (1986b). *Urban elders: Family, work, and welfare among Boston's aged, 1890–1950*. Philadelphia: Temple University Press.

Gratton, B., & Rotondo, F. M. (1992). The "family fund": Strategies for security in old age in the industrial era. In M. Szinovacz, D. J. Ekerdt, & B. H. Vinick (Eds.), *Families and retirement*. Beverly Hills: CA: Sage Press.

Haber, C., & Gratton, B. (in press). *Chronicles of the elderly: A social history of old age in America*. Bloomington: Indiana University Press.

Haines, M. R. (1979). Industrial work and the family life cycle, 1889–1890. *Research in Economic History, 4,* 289–356.

Haines, M. R. (1985). The life cycle, savings, and demographic adaptation: Some historical evidence for the United States and Europe. In A. S. Rossi (Ed.), *Gender and the life course*. New York: Aldine.

Hareven, T. (1982). *Family time and industrial time*. Cambridge: Cambridge University Press.

Hareven, T. (1986). Life-course transitions and kin assistance in old age: A cohort comparison. In D. Van Tassel & P. N. Stearns (Eds.), *Old age in a bureaucratic society: The elderly, the experts, and the state in American history* (pp. 110–125). New York: Greenwood Press.

Hareven, T. K. & Langenback, R. (1978). *Amoskeog: Life and work in an American factory city*. New York: Pantheon Press.

Heaton, T. B., & Hoppe, C. (1987). Widowed and married: Comparative change in living arrangements, 1900–1980. *Social Science History, 11,* 261–280.

I Am the Mother-in-Law in the Home. (1937). *Reader's Digest, 31,* 11–14.

Kobrin, F. E. (1976). The fall in household size and the rise of the primary individual in the United States. *Demography, 13,* 127–138.

Laslett, P. (1977). *Family life and illicit love*. Cambridge: Cambridge University Press.

Laslett, P., & Wall, R. (1972). *Household and family in past time*. Cambridge: Cambridge University Press.

Markides, K. S., & Cooper, C. L. (1987). (Eds.). Industrialization and retirement. In *Retirement in industrialized societies*. New York: John Wiley and Sons.

Massachusetts Commission on Pensions. (1925). *Report*. Boston: Commonwealth of Massachusetts.

Modell, J., & Hareven, T. K. (1978). Urbanization and the malleable household: An examination of boarding and lodging in American families. In M. Gordon (Ed.), *The American family in social-historical perspective*, 2nd ed. New York: St. Martin's Press.

Morawska, E. (1985). *For bread with butter: The life-worlds of East Central*

Europeans in Johnstown, Pennsylvania, 1900–1940. Cambridge: Cambridge University Press.

National Civil Federation. (1928). *Extent of old age dependency.* New York: Author.

Old age intestate. (1931). *Harper's Magazine. 162,* 712–715.

Palmer, J. L., Smeeding, T., & Jencks, C. (1988). The uses and limits of income comparison. In J. Palmer, T. Smeeding, & B. B. Torrey (Eds.), *The vulnerable.* Washington, DC: Urban Institute Press.

Rotella, E., & Alter, A. (1989). *Working class debt in the late nineteenth century.* Bloomington: Indiana University, Economic History Workshop.

Rubinow, I. M. (1934). *Social insurance.* New York: Henry Holt & Co.

Rubinow, I. M. (1972). *The care of the aged.* In D. J. Rothman (Ed.), *The aged and the Depression.* New York: Arno Press. (Original work published 1930)

Ruggles, S. (1987). *Prolonged connections: The rise of the extended family in nineteenth-century England and America.* Madison: University of Wisconsin Press.

Ryan, M. (1981). *Cradle of the middle class.* Cambridge: Cambridge University Press.

Smith, D. S. (1979). Life course, norms, and the family system of older Americans in 1900. *Journal of Family History, 4,* 285–298.

Smith, D. S. (1982a). The elderly in economically developed countries. In P. N. Stearns (Ed.), *Old age in preindustrial society.* New York: Holmes & Meier.

Smith, D. S. (1982b) Historical change in the household structure of the elderly in economically developed societies. In P. N. Stearns (Ed.), *Old age in preindustrial society.* New York: Holmes & Meier.

Smith, D. S. (1989). All in some degree related to each other. A demographic and comparative resolution of the anomaly of New England kinship. *American Historical Review, 94*(1), 44–79.

Smith, D. S. (1986). Accounting for change in the families of the elderly in the United States, 1900–present. In D. Van Tassel & P. N. Stearns (Eds.), *Old age in a bureaucratic society: The elderly, the experts, and the state in American History* (pp. 87–109). New York: Greenwood Press.

Squier, L. W. (1912). *Old age dependency in the United States.* New York: Macmillan.

Stern, M. J. (1987). *Society and family strategy: Erie County, New York, 1850–1920.* Albany: State University of New York Press.

Todd, A. J. (1915). Old age and the industrial scrap heap. *American Statistical Association, 14*(110), 550–557.

Twenty-ninth annual report of the Board of Directors for Public Institutions. (1887). *Documents of the City of Boston, 1886, 1*(16), 34.

U.S. Bureau of the Census. (1895). *Eleventh census of the United States (1890): Housing,* Report on farms and homes: Proprietorship and indebtedness. Washington DC: Government Printing Office.

Walsh, D. I. (1927, September). *American Labor Legislation Review.*

Ware, C. (1935). *Greenwich Village, 1920–1930.* Boston: Houghton Mifflin.
Warner, A. (1894). The causes of poverty further considered. *American Statistical Association, 4*(27), 46–48.
Weiler, N. S. (1986). Family security or Social Security? The family and the elderly in New York State during the 1920s. *Journal of Family History, 22*(1), 77–95.
Zelizer, V. (1985). *Pricing the priceless child: The changing social value of children.* New York: Basic Books.

8

Encrusted Elders: Arizona and the Political Spirit of Postmodern Aging

Robert Kastenbaum

But, alas, emotion without thought is unstable. It rises like the tide and subsides like the tide irrespective of what it has accomplished. It is easily diverted into any side channel dug by old habits or provided by cool cunning, or it disperses itself aimlessly. Then comes the reaction of disillusionment, and men turn all the more fiercely to the pursuit of narrow ends where they are habituated to use observation and planning and where they have acquired some control of conditions. The separation of warm emotion and cool intelligence is the great moral tragedy.
—*John Dewey (1922)*

There are no items of clothing or of food or of other practical use which we do not seize

> upon as theatrical props to dramatize the
> way we want to present our roles and the
> scene we are playing in. Everything we do is
> significant, nothing is without its conscious
> symbolic load. Moreover, nothing is lost on
> the audience.
> —*Mary Douglas (1966)*

> If we speak of the mind's withdrawal as the
> necessary condition of all mental activities,
> we can hardly avoid raising the question of
> the place or region toward which the move-
> ment of absenting oneself is directed.
> —*Hannah Arendt (1971)*

This withdrawal of the mind. This symbolic load. This separation of warm emotion and cool intelligence. this business of good little boys and girls growing old in the postmodern world. This critical voice that is starting to find itself but has yet to find its audience.

Dare we give ourselves permission to listen? No application of critical theory to gerontology is likely to match the intensity and verisimilitude one can hear in the words and observe in the actions of an increasing number of old people. In this chapter I make a first attempt to articulate some facets of this indigenous and implicit critical theory and to suggest how/why this view is arising from its internal and external milieu. At the least, I hope to encourage further attention to the aging person's own critique of self and society as a counterbalance and corrective to academic formulations. Perhaps it is not too much to seek a further goal as well: a keener awareness of both the disturbing reality and the redemptive potential inherent in the encrustation of spirit in the postmodern aged.

We begin with a set of observations based on the discourse and behavior of senior adults in the political sphere. Our example is the response of Arizona's older voters to the ballot issue of establishing a paid state holiday in honor of Martin Luther King, Jr. This sampling will help to particularize and ground the later discussion.

RACISM OR ENLIGHTENED SELF-INTEREST?

Arizona attracts many senior adults. Over the years, this attraction has led to the development of residential areas planned especially for the comfort and convenience of couples who wish to exchange the icy blasts of Illinois or Minnesota for the sunned desert. Whether choosing to live in adult-only communities or integrating themselves into heterogeneous neighborhoods, senior adults are numerous enough to wield considerable economic and political power.

Nevertheless, one should not hasten to form a stereotype of the Arizona elder. The spectrum includes some Native Ameircans, Hispanic Americans, and Asian Americans who live securely within their ethnic orbits, as well as others with dual-culture identities and lifestyles. There are a few elders within the relatively small African American population. The Anglo who has lived in Arizona since childhood's hour enjoys special status as one of the rare old-timers. Those who emigrated in their adult years are far more numerous. The solitary old man in Apache Junction or Carefree, just barely getting by on a limited fixed income, and the impoverished widow who wanders ghostlike through Tucson or Phoenix do not fit the popular image of a prosperous, gregarious, golf-playing couple in Sun City West or Leisure World. Each of these people brings a different life story into old age and therefore a different perspective for generation of critical theory. This diversity should be kept in mind to deter overgeneralization from the more limited band of the spectrum that we are able to explore here.

We will be focusing primarily on Anglo men and women who moved to Arizona in their later years and chose to purchase homes in adult communities. Most came to Arizona as married couples. They had some money from savings, pension plans, and the sale of their previous homes. Although leaving some friends and relatives behind, many also had "advance scouts" among those already resettled in Arizona. In turn, once established in Arizona, they might themselves try to persuade others to join them in Sun Lakes or Sun City. The adult community they selected was likely to have appealed to them for several reasons: the homes were sparkling new, the streets clean and well maintained, amenities and shopping within access, and their neighbors likely to be much like themselves. The place had a civilized look about it yet was not in the middle of a congested and noisy city. The palm trees (themselves immigrants) and southwestern touches in architecture and decor offered a pleasurable difference from their previous residential areas, yet all exuded a familiar and conforting middle-class ambience.

And one thing more:

"We feel safe here," the Chamberlains[1] told me. "It's a hell of a note," said Mister. "You live in a place practically all your life, and just when you should really be enjoying yourself, you feel like a stranger.

You lock your doors. You lock your car. You lock up everything you have, and even then you worry."

"I never had any trouble myself," said Missus. "But I know people who did." She described rude talk on the streets, a home burglary in which an old widow was injured, and another incident in which a man accidentally shot his own son, mistaking him for an intruder. "Our neighborhood was just not the pleasant place it had always been. I never thought I'd want to leave it, but the time came when I did. That [she smiled] and the unholy desire to be drenched by sun instead of cold rain."

A DIVISIVE ISSUE: A MARTIN LUTHER KING HOLIDAY FOR ARIZONA?

Arizona has had at least its share of hot political issues. There had already been considerable turmoil by the time a statewide election was scheduled to give voters the opportunity to decide for themselves the question of a paid holiday to honor Martin Luther King, Jr., and the civil rights movement. Then-governor Bruce Babbitt had announced the establishment of such a holiday prior to exiting state politics in order to run for the presidential nomination. The new governor, a populist outsider to the state political establishment, gave his first priority to revoking this holiday, citing an opinion from the attorney general's office that Babbitt's action did not conform to the necessary legal procedures. This stance pleased some Arizonans and enraged others. The tension soon broadened and intensified. Governor Evan Mecham was perceived by some both as a racist and as a person who lacked the necessary skills to manage state government. Others became devoted to Mecham as a person who would stand up to the establishment, represent good old-fashioned morality, and bring the state, if not the nation, back to its senses.

Charges. Countercharges. Scandals. For months the "Mecham situation" and the "King holiday situation" not only dominated the media but made politics an unusually salient concern. Before very long, Governor Mecham had been impeached and also defeated in an attempt to regain office. Still unresolved and become increasingly complex, the King holiday issue was placed on the November 1990 statewide ballot. Although our major interest here is the way that senior adults interpreted and responded to this issue, we must first set forth some of the factors that made the process far from simple:

1. A substitute holiday was already on the books but almost completely ignored. Mecham had specified a Sunday holiday. No special observations were planned for this unpaid holiday. Civil rights advocates refused to take this alternative seriously, and those on the other side of the fence took no notice of it except when it seemed strategic to say, "We already have a holiday for him—what more do you want?"

2. Some other public and private agencies had in the meantime created their own MLK holidays (e.g., both Arizona State University and its host city, Tempe).

3. Prospective voters had more to contend with than the MLK holiday. A close gubernatorial race was (accurately) predicted, and the ballot included 11 propositions that dealt with other issues. Much attention, controversy, and confusion had centered around three of these propositions that offered different approaches to automobile insurance rules and rates (all three were rejected at the polls).

4. Not one but two MLK propositions appeared on the ballot. Proposition 301 would have eliminated Columbus Day as a paid holiday to make way for the MLK observance. This proposition found very little favor among either the public or the media and was roundly attacked by people claiming to represent Italian-American sensitivities. Nevertheless, 301 had won a place on the ballot and added a degree of confusion to the proceedings. The real contender was 302, a proposition that would have added a paid holiday in the name of Martin Luther King, Jr., without touching Columbus Day.

There was an expected scenario. Most observers judged that the voters of Arizona were eager to approve the MLK holiday if only to put behind them all of the rancor and adverse national publicity that had been stirred up. Business leaders urged passage for the economic benefits in continuing to attract tourists, commercial investments, sports franchises, and so on. Economic concerns had also been emphasized by opponents: why should state employees have another day off at public expense? However, surveys as well as informed opinion suggested that 302 would pass with a few percentage points to spare.

However, an unanticipated development was introduced shortly before the election. Viewers at a CBS Sunday sports program heard a report that the National Football League (NFL) had decided to withdraw the 1993 Superbowl game from Phoenix if the King holiday were to be rejected that coming Tuesday. No source was credited, and it was up to viewers to judge the credibility of the report.

Both MLK proposals were rejected at the polls. The defeat of 301, with its unpopular assault on Columbus Day, was expected. However, many were surprised by the defeat of 302. This measure had been supported by a broad coalition of community leaders and endorsed by most media representatives. The demographics of Proposition 302's defeat were provocative. From a statewide perspective, the MLK initiative had fallen short by only 17,000 votes in an election that had drawn more than a million to the polls. The measure had carried in Arizona's two largest urban areas (Maricopa County, including Phoenix, and Pima County, including Tucson), as well as in three other counties. Voters in 10 predominately rural counties had rejected the proposition. The margin of defeat was substantial in these rural areas, going 3–1 against the proposition in Mohave County, which was a stronghold of support for ex-governor Mecham.

What about the senior adults of Arizona? The results are clear and striking if we exclude the more-difficult-to-identify elders who live in age-integrated urban or suburban settings.[2] The rural areas, whose preference at the polls has already been noted, have a higher proportion of elderly people than does the state at large. There is considerable overlap, then, between the rural vote and the senior vote. But the picture is even clearer when we review voting behavior in precincts that serve residents of adult communities (among the largest: Leisure World, Sun Lakes, Sun City, Sun City West, Youngtown). Voters representing communities that exclude children and young adults rejected Proposition 302 far more decisively than did the electorate in general. In fact, excluding the adult community vote would have resulted in passage of the proposed MLK holiday.

Precincts whose registration consisted primarily of senior adults rejected Proposition 302 by margins ranging from 2 to 1 to 4 to 1. That geography alone had little hand in the matter was demonstrated by the fact that adjoining communities often voted in support of the MLK holiday. For example, Sun City, the largest adult community, is neighbored by the Hispanic enclave of El Mirage and the predominately Anglo, age-heterogeneous town of Glendale. Voters in El Mirage and Glendale approved Proposition 302; those in Sun City shot it down in flames.

A PRELIMINARY INTERPRETATION

For some time previous to this ballot I had wondered about a blank chapter in "Everybody's Book of Gerontology." This is the chapter that might have followed the familiar and impressive treatise on victims of ageism. All gerontologists worth their sodium chloride know this chapter by heart. People are still being denied access, opportunity, companionship, services, and respect on the basis of age. Chances are that gerontologists will continue to find employment in exposing and combating ageism for a long time to come. But one never reads or hears about older adults as themselves practitioners of bigotry, racism, discrimination. Literature reviews prove to be exercises in futility. The topic does not appear in syllabi or texts. The topic does not come up at gerontology conferences or congressional hearings. And nobody seems to miss it.

The MLK holiday issue and the discussion it engendered before and after the balloting provided an opportunity to make some observations about the public-oriented side of this missing chapter. The opportunity would be limited, imperfect, and with little depth. Yet this private participation in a public ritual did have the value of forcing thoughts, feelings, and dispositions into decisive action. On a specified day, senior adults would exercise their rights of citizenship by entering a polling place, drawing a curtain about them if they so chose, and punching a small hole into a card.

In proposing a preliminary interpretation of the MLK holiday results, I formulated three racism-related models, giving them the provisional labels *proactive racism, pragmatic self-interest,* and *fortress mentality* (Kastenbaum, 1991). In proactive racism, a person's life is organized around antagonism toward other sets of people. It is often a predatory orientation that seeks out "enemies" and attempts to do them harm. Proactive racists have been responsible for the most blatant acts of aggression against person and property. Observers who speak of racism as a type of mental/emotional illness usually have the proactivists in mind. Unlike the vicious proactivist, many people engage in racist thought, language, and behavior that is incidental to their otherwise responsible and balanced life-styles:

Mr. Potter: I don't have a thing against them—not a blessed thing.
Mrs. Potter: God made every last one of us. But He made us different.
Mr. Potter: I give some of them a great deal of credit for what they have accomplished. But nobody's given me a good reason why I have to keep paying the bills for all of them on welfare. Nobody pays my bills for me. Let them work or let them take the consequences.
Mrs. Potter: And that's the truth.

Those who see themselves as simply functioning in pursuit of their own pragmatic self-interest do not usually go out of their way to oppress or humiliate people of other racial, ethnic, or religious backgrounds. Furthermore, they are apt to be appalled by crude and violent behavior that is directed against "them." Nevertheless, they tend to perpetuate patterns of discrimination that have become so habitual to themselves and to much of society that they seem "just natural."

The fortress mentality is an orientation that requires constant vigilance. The world is not a safe place. There are forces at work that would invade our inner citadel of privacy and autonomy and steal all that we have remaining to us.

MRS. McKINNON (*widow*): We came out here for the weather but not just for the weather. We needed a little sanity, too. [Did you find it?] Up to a point. But our days might be numbered, from what we keep hearing about. [What do you mean?] Oh my. Don't you read the newspapers? They want to open the doors for just anybody to live here. Anybody and everybody. First, it will be young families with children. Then, anybody and everybody.

MRS. ELDRIDGE: I still have my old man. But all Mackie has is her home and her sanity—

MRS. McKINNON: —and my Plymouth.

MRS. ELDRIDGE: They want her to stop driving. But Mackie has been driving for years and never an accident. Wouldn't that be the glorious day—take away our wheels and open the Sun Cities to people who don't belong here.

MRS. McKINNON: That day will never come if I have anything to say about it.

MRS. ELDRIDGE: Oh, Mackie, you have lots to say about everything!

Reviewing "research conversations," radio talk-show call-ins, newspaper and television coverage, and the election results themselves, it seemed to me that the proactive racism model had little to do with the proceedings. It was difficult to find examples of raw, obsessed, predatory racism. Two factors appeared to mitigate against this extreme form of bigotry: (a) limited interracial contact and (b) the centralist, socially integrated position of senior citizens who relocated to Arizona.

Most residents of rural Arizona had experienced very little contact with African Americans, either in the past or in their current situation. Hispanic Americans and native Americans comprised the largest share of the non-Anglo population. Competition, distrust, misunderstanding, and downright meanness have disfigured the relationships among these groups ever since Arizona's territorial days. The local Anglo racists had only an indirect, abstracted, and stereotype-mediated orientation toward the African Americans who had so little to do with their own lives. Virulent proactive racists tended to seek out the more available Hispanics and Native Americans as targets of their rage.

The middle-class, establishment-type couples who set up housekeeping in Arizona's adult communities also were isolated from African Americans in their everyday lives. Only people with white faces picked up the morning newspapers from their doorsteps or motored along in a golf cart en route to lunching at a popular restaurant. But most residents of adult communities had a more positive reason for eschewing proactive racism. These were people who had worked hard and followed the rules all of their lives. A pleasant and secure place in the sun was their well earned reward. This fulfillment of the American dream required a sense of moderation and perspective. And, perhaps most essential, its continued actualization also required that people not interfere with each other, not violate their privacy, not disrupt their routines. Behavior that was pushy, tasteless, and extreme just would not be tolerated.

MR. FINNDAHL: We have a certain understanding here. Most of us do. "You don't bug me; I won't bug you." But it goes beyond that. I need to put it more positively. "I will do my part to make Sun City the best place you can think of to live, and I expect you to do the same."

The out-and-out racist, like the drunk or the person "dressed up like a hippopotamus on stilts," is an embarrassment to the community and is likely to be shunned or snapped at as the citizenry seeks to protect itself from the unhinged or irresponsible.

By contrast, the pragmatic self-interest model had much to recommend it. Senior adults were conspicuous among the callers to radio talk shows prior to the election. I would hear one after another characterize him/herself as a person who had nothing against civil rights but who objected to the cost of an additional paid state holiday. Typically, the caller would speak about having worked hard, being on a fixed income now, and being faced with rising costs of living in a state that didn't know how to balance its budget. All of these points are both relevant and reasonable. From the caller's perspective, voting down the MLK holiday propositions was a practical and justifiable necessity based securely upon the hard facts of the situation. But there was also a typicaly temporal pattern to be discerned if we divided the caller's discourse into two segments: the spontaneous statement and the response to questions or comments by the radio host. Frequently, the hosts would introduce facts or ideas that were somewhat discordant with the caller's position. For example, the host might point out that the costs of the proposed holiday would be a very small budget item that would be more than compensated for by regaining convention and other commercial revenues. I never heard a caller respond to such comments; invariably, the senior adult caller would simply repeat what he/she had said a moment before.

This dogged persistence, this disconfirmation and dismissal of another person's viewpoint seems to take a little of the shine off the image of rational self-interest. A Sun City source noticed this for himself:

MR. FINNDAHL: A lot of old coots are having the times of their lives with this. Last time I turned the radio on, there was another batch, sawing away about the election. [Have you called in?] No, enough is enough. That holiday doesn't have a Chinaman's chance, not in Sun City, anyways. But the old coots are kidding themselves when they keep saying it's all about money. I know some of those fellows. They'd never miss the money. It's the idea of it that's killing them. [The idea?] The idea is they are being told to kiss a black man's ass and they just won't do it. [I've never heard it put that way.] You won't. Not on the radio. [How would you put it?] Kids in the sandbox. Throwing sand at each other and screaming. You can't make people into saints; you can't even make them into grown-ups by making up a holiday. Better if this whole thing had never come up. But here it is, and most of us are making fools of ourselves, one way or another.

Mr. Finndahl could not have known it at the time, but the "don't tell me what to do" theme would become even more operative as the election approached. As noted above, a television sportscaster chose to pass along the unverified report that the NFL would pull the 1993 Superbowl Game from Phoenix unless the voters approved the MLK holiday proposition. There was an explosive reaction throughout the state. By far the most common response was outrage directed at the NFL for what was seen as a crude attempt at blackmail. Differences between the urban and the rural, the Republican and the Democrat, and the young and the old suddenly became less important than the unacceptable threat by an outside force. The whole point of the election was altered in the minds of many people. Without question, many thousands of voters decided that their number-one priority had to be the rejection of the MLK holiday in order to tell the NFL where it could get off. Those who had any doubts about which way to go on the MLK issue now made up their minds to express their indignation with a no vote.

This development had the effect of emphasizing the strong advocacy of those who did vote in favor of the holiday, given the near-universal impulse to defy the NFL. Rejection of the MLK holiday would have been understandable on the basis of indignation alone. But this sudden and general arousal of resentment galvanized a pre-existing attitudinal structure in which a passive, almost idle form of racism nested along with the belief that one was only acting in one's own legitimate and reasonable self-interests. After crediting the case for pragmatic self-interest, we were still left with the impression that a deeper set of personal and social forces had expressed themselves within the ranks of senior adults. The fortress mentality model seemed to provide a useful point of departure for exploring these forces, but our interest goes far beyond a one-time political happening. For a transition between this example of voting behavior and the larger question of the fortress mentality in later adulthood, let's look briefly at one facet of the follow-up research that has been engaging my attention.

"TO THE EDITOR" AND TO THE BARRICADES

Subsequent to the election I have been collecting and analyzing examples of discourse by senior adults, especially those who reside in adult communities. One sample of discourse has been derived from letters to the editor of a daily newspaper that serves the area with the highest concentration of adult communities (Sun City, Sun City West, Youngtown). The sampling frame encompasses a total of 6 months, divided equally between the last quarter of 1990 and the first quarter of 1991 (as noted, the election took place in November 1990). The editors of *The Daily News Sun* have told me that they printed virtually all of the letters submitted to the newspaper during that time frame. A letter would have been rejected for publication only if it were considered obscene of libelous or if the writer did not include his/her name. This would have been a rare occurrence, according to the editors; therefore, this sample should provide a useful if limited source of information.

The focus here is upon one facet of the open letters that stands out in two contexts: the MLK holiday and perceived threats to the age-segregated status of the adult communities. (This means that for present purposes we are neglecting the wider variety of substance and style that occurs within the total sample of letters to the editor.) As might be expected, the MLK issue was a major topic for letter writers during this time frame. However, there was also considerable interest in the "adults only" issue. This is an issue that had come up numerous times prior to the MLK holiday situation. The adult community of Youngtown had been especially prominent in this controversy. As the nation's first "retirement community," Youngtown had established a policy of restricting residency to adults beyond a certain age (reset from 60 to 55 in 1989). Early in the sampling time frame (September 15, 1990), the U. S. Department of Justice dismissed a set of protests against this policy by seven families with children under the age of 18.

What emerges as an obvious theme in both contexts is the impulse to barricade against physical or symbolic invasion. This is a salient concern that even divides one elderly neighbor from another. One letter, for example, quotes part of another in advocating that a recreation center toughen its policy of restricted use:

> However, it is important to notice that it is the homeowners of Sun City who are the members of the organization and it is the members who are entitled to use the facilities. Nothing in the agreed upon Statement of Facts indicates that nonmembers from Youngtown, Peoria or El Mirage may use the facilities.

This lawyerish communication hardens the barricade against senior adults from Youngtown as well as Peoria's mixed crew and El Mirage's low-income Hispanics. For their part, a number of Youngtown residents spoke in support of preserving their own age-based exclusionary policy. "I like the idea that there is place for people our age and that there are no children" is how one woman put it. Another confides that "the age restrictions were part of what appealed to me. When people get older, they still like children, but they can't stand having them around 24 hours a day." A 30-year-old woman who cleans houses in Sun City heard a comment at a Youngtown Town Council meeting "that it was about time to get young people out of the town and that equated youth with the plague." She added: "It's clear the hatred is there. I should have kept a list of all the hurtful comments." Although no letters appeared on this topic, a Hispanic man, age 32, with a wife and three children, was quoted as questioning Youngtown's motives in proceeding against his family because they had violated Youngtown's age-restrictive ordinance. "What bothers me is that I see only Mexicans going to court."

The sense of being "coerced and blackmailed" was already being expressed before the NFL inflamed the scene. "Equal rights groups" were depicted as oral invaders "who would cram it down your throat, like it or not." But when the NFL did enter the fray, some readers concluded that they had come under attack from almost all quarters: "Blackmail seems to be a word that our politicians, the business community and even the sports community have used to threaten the Valley with the most dire economical and financial situations." Singled out for criticism "is the well funded out of state campaign for an MLK holiday." The same writer bristles at complaints about senior citizens voting against bond issues and other costly social programs. "Continuous threats about 'the Sun Cities voting record' may cause those 'Old Folks' to suddenly hibernate and reduce or in some cases stop spending for more than the bare minimums." A counterthreat is issued: "Also our astute legislators should consider that if the Grey [*sic*] Panthers migration to Arizona slows or stops, the influx of migratory people will be a greater percentage of street people, illegals from Mexico, the Caribbean, Central and South America very few of whom contribute to our ever-growing budget."

Metaphors of attack and invasion often come to the surface. The implicit message appears to be "There are people out there who want what we have. But we won't let them in. They can't fool us, and you can't fool us either. We are intelligent and tough-minded. We will fight to keep what's ours and what we have coming to us."

This siege mentality can contribute to an identification with other embattled people: "With sanctions applied against us, we can now empathize with the people of South Africa, who have endured unfair American trade restrictions because of their internal affairs. Maybe Arizona should secede before we deteriorate into a Third World country where voting rights are a joke. Or, are we already there?"

The above passage is also typical in its selection of the economic sphere of discourse. Most of the letters (like most of the radio call-ins) formulated the issue in terms of two components: (a) money and (b) law and order. Money talk operated as an implicit code that referred not only to financial matters but also to a variety of other fears and concerns. The very substance of life that might be bled away from them by fools, scoundrels, and opportunists—this was "money." The often passionate defense of rights, liberty, and freedom sounded like a plea for reinforcing and guaranteeing law and order in the broadest sense. Safe—but for how long—in their enclaves, some adult community residents sought their continued security by invoking the principles of equity and fairness. They were the ones who had kept the American Way of Life going with their hard work and good citizenship. Now it was time to call upon the equity they had built up in the system. Now was the time to be treated fairly in recognition of their past services and residual value. But this legitimate return upon their investments depended upon the health and reliability of the system as a whole. Dissolution of law and order would make them vulnerable to the depradations of unworthy and unscrupulous people. And under these circumstances, it is enraging to be criticized as though they were the ones who were not playing by the rules (e.g., through age-exclusionary ordinaces) or not carrying their share of responsibilities (e.g., by voting against school bond issues). Who made America strong in the first place if not the diligent, churchgoing, law-abiding people who now ask only to have the opportunity to enjoy their last years in peace and security?

The barricade themes of economic survival and protection through law and order have a firm basis in consensual reality. But it is my impression that some senior adults have pressed these themes into service well beyond their primary spheres of meaning. In exploring the metaphoric connotations we will also wander a little way across the heretofore blank pages of that missing chapter in which elderly people step outside of their assigned role as victims of discrimination.

ENCRUSTATION: THEN AND NOW

In passing from innocence to experience, something is gained and something is lost. Among the reasons that babies are perceived as "sweet," "precious," and "adorable" are their lack of guile and their need for protection. They are fresh little selves who have everything to see for the first time, everything to learn. Not jaded, not cynical, not guided by a hidden agenda, babies provide us with an opportunity to revisit that world of intimacy, immediacy, and spontaneity that we long ago exited in search of adult gratifications.

This situation is short-lived. Babies quickly become interpreters and organizers of their own experience. For example, the ability to distinguish between "old" and "boring" signals and "new" and "exciting" signals makes its appearance within the first weeks of postnatal life and develops rapidly thereafter. Infants who reject repetitious environmental signals as irrelevant and stultifying are practicing what might be called *critical neonatology*: "World, you will just have to do better; this story is worn out and, I might add, oppressive and exploitative." Habituation to signals that have already yielded their meanings makes it possible to construct one's own version of self and world, influenced by but not completely under the control of the sociophysical environment.

Following the habituation process from infancy through the total life course can offer us insights regarding the metamorphosis of eager and wondering baby eyes into the guarded and calculating squint of the adult (Kastenbaum, 1980–1981, 1984; Norris-Baker & Scheidt, 1989; Reich & Zautra, 1991). Lost are such appealing characteristics as openness, spontaneity, and holistic response. Gained are the efficient characteristics of information filtering and processing, planful action, and self-sustained viability.

Ambivalence shades society's attitudes toward the residues of early experiential styles. Our "childish" or even "infantile" moments can bring us disgrace: "Why don't you grow up! Why don't you act your age!" But we also have a soft spot for characters in cartoons or real life whose childish nature comes through and connects with our own. As individuals we differ markedly in our tolerance for such insufficiently socialized traits as idle curiosity, activity for activity's sake, impulsive shifts of mood and desire, and seeing just how far we can go with something by going a little too far. The mainstream compromise is to become a predictable and responsible worker who relaxes by watching or engaging in juvenile forms of behavior.

The child who is precocious in extruding a quasi-adult crust is often well rewarded and proposed as an example to others. Passages to subsequent adult roles are accompanied by further surrender of wonder, curiosity, and spontaneity. Taken to its extreme, life-span development is a process of fossilization. Where protean babe was, petrified elder is. Fortunately, this *is* an extreme. Many adults are relatively "settled" people who have learned to moderate their desires and expectations and to take evasive actions when necessary. Nevertheless, they retain a permeability to new experience and a flickering sense of possibility and potential.

There is a level of encrustation, however, that goes beyond ordinary "settledness." What is often taken as a natural consequence of aging can be seen instead as a self-protective hardening process, reinforcing the barricades against actual or perceived threats. This process occurs relatively early in some people and not at all in others. There is an empirical but noncausal association with age: with increased exposure to loss and stress, there is more provocation for becoming a fortress self. For this outcome we should not blame either the passage of time per se nor the many substantive sequences that are subsumed under the rubric of "aging." In fact, it would be inappropriate to place any blame whatsoever. Encrustation of the spirit in old age is a kind of achievement, a kind of triumph, a kind of creative gesture. As I hope to suggest below, this is not the best kind of achievement, triumph, or gesture, but it deserves our respect and understanding.

Let us first take a step backward in time. Two steps would send us reeling into premodern society, where flourishing into old age the individual too crusty or rusty to survive didn't. There was little insulation for those who were not keen enough to meet the challenges of a still untamed natural world, as well as the threats that humans seem always to have presented to each other. We will limit our retrotraversal to the more familiar turf of modern times and will not fret about its precise boundaries, which, like many other boundaries, are the subject of interminable dispute. And because our stay must be brief, we will select a narrow ring of time/place that continues to have resonance for us today.

New York City. Turn of the century. Throngs of men, women, and children, shimmering in hope and fear, reach the harbor. They are greeted, also in hope and fear, by relatives who are themselves still "greenhorns" trying to find their way. Focus now upon those who were already well along in years. Consider how they are marked—by their geographical origins, by the reputation of their ancestors, by their place in a rigidly stratified society, by their religion, by their language, and by the animosities that have accompanied all of these characteristics like a swarm of hornets. Above all, they are marked by the accelerating, exhilarating, and annihilating pressures of the industrial revolution as it rumbles along in high gear.

These people can feel both the pain of being torn from their roots and the excitement of breaking away. Tension, confusion, and uncertainty do not quite swallow them whole, for they possess an internal guidance mechanism. They know who they are. "I am the tailor from Minsk." "I am the midwife from Parma." "I am the fix-it man from Belfast." They bring forward a marked identity that will both ease and obstruct their family's progress. "Where did you say you were from?" "That's no kind of job for a Jew." "If you ask me, they're all socialists and troublemakers." They have strong allegiances and reliable enemies. They can be fierce and they can be patient. They can be stubborn and they can be overbearing, and they can sacrifice everything for their vision of progeny who will "make it" in America.

We will notice some hardened and embittered characters here and there. They have been subjected to indignities and betrayals, deprivations and sorrows. The world will have a difficult time hurting them again because they have closed up the most likely points of invasion and because, given a chance, they will strike first. These tough old birds do not write letters to the editor or give themselves over to self-pity. Instead, they are fierce, alert, and direct in their defense of what must be defended. We see them in an alternating double image: fortress and tower of strength. Yes, they have invested much of their energies in self-protection against a world that has repeatedly demonstrated its cruelty and malice. But no, it is not just self that is being protected. It is a family, a past, a future, a people.

Furthermore, there is no question about the persistence and location of spirit. It's there, all right. Shining through. Glaring through. All of that stubbornness, all of that meanness, all of that static, layered violence is the extrusion of spirit and the protection of spirit. Anyone can see it. Anyone can feel it. However, this transformation has not occurred with all of the elders. Some remain open, vulnerable, at a loss, dependent. Others try to weather the storm of change inside a soft shell that has been assembled from available materials. Maria won't leave the house. Zdenek hides in his books. Rose cultivates her symptoms; and Brendan, his version of the past.

There is a difference today—actually, a set of differences.

Contextual Differences

Back then, many people were seeking the opportunity to improve their situation within the parameters of industrializing society. In the time/place sample taken above, immigrant generations hoped to get their share of the goods, privileges, and amenities that were being produced at such a great human cost and at such a tantalizing reach from the average person. Some also sought to place their own hands on the great levers of power. The seething Socialists, Communists, Nihilists, and even the nameless malcontents came up with variant scenarios but did not propose to abolish the mechanical horn of plenty.

The young expected to offer their strenuous exertions in return for a respected place in a thriving and growing system. Their elders not only wished them well but often lived for the success of the younger generation. For themselves, however, they were defined, preserved, and limited by their deeply marked identities and by their bone memories of life within feudal, priestish, and stratified societies. They faced the challenge of integrating two sets of life rules: the obedient underclass person who survived by not making waves and the competitive, aggressive risk taker who might reach the top of the heap. The immigrant youths would eventually grow old themselves, striving every step of the way to become secure, respected, and prosperous insiders.

Although the resonances live on, the actual political and social context had changed radically by the time that the Potters, the MacKinnons, and thousands of others resettled themselves in Arizona. Born into the system, they had always been insiders. In fact, they were what the system was all about. And it was the system that was now the problem—or so it seemed. Up to a point, the system had worked. They had their pensions, their savings, their place in the community. However, there were problems on all sides. The community was not what it used to be. The wrong kind of people had intruded upon the scene. (No racism here, of course; it's just that property values would be negatively affected.) And even the right people were doing the wrong things: living together out of wedlock, having abortions, smoking pot, and even—how could they?—taking a casual attitude toward schooling and work. Furthermore, things were getting rundown on Main Street, and the old place did not have the same energy and pizzazz, as aging factories shut their doors and young people drifted away or just hung around to no particular purpose. Technology had also slipped its leash. Industrial fervor generated air pollution and gridlock traffic. Computerization invited anonymity and alienation. No, progress certainly wasn't what it used to be. That gurgling sound was modern times going down the drain.

Some elderly couples could shrug off these blights and remain in the haven of their familiar neighborhoods. Some took to the bottle behind closed doors. Some took the initiative in liberating themselves from past rules and strictures and rediscovered urges and talents that had long been shackled through family and occupational responsibilities. Others chose to relocate to Arizona, Florida, or other Sunbelt areas for the obvious attractions of climate, weather and adventure.

But of particular interest to us here are those who formed the vanguard of a new crusade. They sought and to some extent found an alternative to the dismal proposition of growing old within a decaying realm that had lost faith in its gods and respected not its elders. Re-created in the desert is that promised land. Here nobody is old because everybody is. Here law, order, predictability, sanity, and decency reign. Here what has eroded in Kansas, turned savage in Illinois, and become foreign in New York has returned to life with a welcoming smile on its face. Pre–World War II America, its depression lifted, expressed itself again through the values and virtues of the adult community.

Encrustation of the spirit is relatively inconspicuous as long as the taxes stay down, the streets remain inviolate, and one's own grip on the wheel is firm and steady. The community not only stands as bulwark against the barbarians but also as a holographic projection of the vital, competent, going-on-forever inner self. Deteriorating neighborhoods back east may have whispered harshly of one's own inevitable decline. By grateful contrast, the new stage setting calls for lively and confident players. This effect was especially striking in the early years of adult communities as the very absence of nursing homes and other harbingers of frail age suggested that corrupting time had been banned from the city limits.

Time? Sun City time is the time of busy and robust adults in their prime years, although the roles are enacted by a senior cast. Punctuality is highly valued. Meetings must begin and end promptly. There is never enough time to do all that one has planned. Primary attention is focused on the events that fill one's life today and tomorrow. And there is a normative insistence that these hours and days be filled to brimming. "We are busy people" is the message transmitted in words and action, and indeed, they are active, doing people whose industrious schedules bear little resemblance to the stereotyped image of old folks nodding in the rocking chair.

It's a funny kind of time, though.

Psychoanalyst J. A. M. Meerloo (1954) observed that "the person who seems always to be in such a great hurry does not really wish to save time—he wishes time to have no real duration. Actually through his hurry, he seeks to evade time or to by-pass it." He also remarks on "a normal fear of the empty unknown time, in which we shall no longer love or be loved." In Sun City, time is a precious but also a volatile and dangerous substance. Allowed to escape from its glass container, what harm it might do the fragile ecology of a waking dreamland! And so people race with time as though to make the sun stand forever still between dawn and set. And people fill time so that they will not themselves be swallowed by emptiness. And they avert their eyes when the ragged tooth marks of time begin to appear around the edges of a neighbor's mind or body.

The retired hairdresser from Des Moines and the former insurance agent from Duluth do not have to read Habermas's (1991) explications of Husserl and Derrida. Since leaving Des Moines and Duluth, they have themselves become the experts. They have learned to hold the repetition structure of their experiences in balance by a flashing interplay of symbolic and concrete interactions. If only everybody can keep up the act! If only the reciprocal construction of reality can continue to flutter, without a pause, through the urgent beating of wings that dare not tire. If only the art of the detour can support a "timelessly temporalizing internesting of the past, present, and future." If only.

But not likely. Sooner or later there is failure. And before the whizzing illusion shatters, there is fear and foreknowledge of failure. It's not going to work forever. The barbarians will storm the gates. The invisible wolf will steal my time and eat my dreams.

Embodied Differences

With this background we can be very brief in our preliminary description of the encrusted spirit, postmodern version. To be more precise, this is the transition-to-postmodern version. Its unique perils of passage will be replaced by other tribulations in subsequent generations.

The tanned golfers and gardeners of Sun City are unlike the marked, embittered, hardened, and dedicated aged of the immigrant generation. As well-socialized and successful citizens they have no ready answer for the evils that threaten to engulf them. There has been no history of abuse and injustice to prepare them for exclusion, scapegoating, degradation, and collapse. They have every right to expect the good life. Every right. How can this be happening to them? The story was not supposed to take this turn. It's just not fair!

It is a confused and fearful spirit that seeks sanctuary. Why am I being mocked, forgotten, and rejected by the society I helped to perfect? Why are these values being rejected both by the younger generation and by the political establishment? Why have the rules changed? Why do I sense an impending loss of control over my own life? Am I to end up as an outsider, a prisoner in my own land?

A preliminary and incomplete description of the encrustation process would include the following:

1. The felt need for additional self-protection emerges fairly late in adult life. Previously, the person had become well adapted to a society that lived by known rules and values and that required competencies that one had developed and refined over many years.

2. A sense of impending catastrophe gradually arises, fed by anxieties from divergent sources: financial, environmental, interpersonal, phenomenological, and biological. Common to these anxieties is the apprehension of losing all that one has left and therefore becoming one's antiself: a failed, helpless, abandoned, unloved waif.

3. There will be individual differences in symbolizing and expressing this dilemma. Two of the more accessible and acceptable modalities are to dress the fears in either financial or somatic guise. Men, tending more toward externalization and the denial of physical distress, prefer economic metaphors. Women are more likely to call upon somatic metaphors. Whatever the individual choice, one is inclined to select a realm of discourse that is familiar and potent enough to preempt the surfacing of even more disturbing images.

4. All will seek a concrete enemy to face. Identification of the enemy makes it possible to orient one's fortress in the most strategic direction. Furthermore, one can then work effectively to defeat or hold off the foe instead of yielding to free-floating anxiety and confusion. One does not have to plunge into the abyss of doubt: "Am I slipping away from the world or the world from me?" Instead, one shrewdly constructs the necessary defense works, making adroit use of available materials.

5. Social stereotypes are among the most enticing of available

materials. We have been exposed to them since childhood. The world is divided into our kind of people and those others. As a rule, those others don't measure up to our fine qualities, and they should be kept in their place. These stereotypes have always seen heavy duty when people have had difficulty in explaining disasters and hard times. And such can be the experience of people who have grown up in late modern times and old in the early postmodern period. Discriminatory attitudes and practices came along for the ride but did not figure prominently in the life-styles of most people who are now resident in adult communities. Now, however, these residuals prove their value. The wolf of time that sucks the memory from our tongues and the blood from our bones will not really be fooled or deterred, but we can keep ourselves directed and energized by resisting "those people." All of the grand old animosities awaken from their slumber. Markers of race, origin, ethnicity, and religion serve to identify the enemy. Age discrimination also plays its role within the community of the aged: both the young and the enfeebled old are set apart, although for different reasons. Furthermore, as the larger society transmits disrespectful and hostile messages to the besieged elders, they are now able to convert these negative inputs into their own discriminatory transformations.

6. The reactivation of bigotry in old age is especially useful to those whose information-processing abilities have become atrophied or compromised. These include people who have neglected continued self-education during their adult years and brought ineffective habits of mind forward with them. Challenges that require analyzing new situations or coming up with solutions to familiar problems find them cognitively impoverished and rigid. The heavy drinkers have further diminished their ability to deal with complex and shifting circumstances. Reliance upon stereotypes reduces the need to think things through for ourselves and therefore also diminishes confusion, uncertainty, and doubts about one's own intellectual competence. Bigotry is a gift to people whose minds are not in good working order and who are faced with circumstances that challenge the best of minds.

ENCRUSTATION, CO-CREATIVITY, AND CRITICAL GERONTOLOGY

Encrustation is a survival strategy that has become increasingly common as senior adults find themselves in a world that does not seem to understand and respect the values they had so long cherished. Fears of collapse from the inside and assault from the outside are transformed into a new scenario that includes significant "theatrical props" (Douglas, 1966, p. 121) and stage directions. The mind is saved from itself (Arendt, 1971) and given the opportunity to reengage with a supporting cast of co-creators. The adult community, with its manicured streets and pulsing schedules, eliminates the need for individuals to take all of the weight of desperation fantasy upon their own shoulders. In other words, the encrustation is to some extent consensual and palpable, not merely a trick that individuals have played upon themselves. This haven, this alternative universe, is a product of co-creation and can succeed only if a great many people "keep pedaling." Having enemies helps in this regard. Beating back threats through votes, letters, hearings, and other legitimate actions affirms both the common strength and the continued viability of law and order. Articulate, alert, and feisty, the adult community is not itself to be stereotyped but to be appreciated as a still-evolving response to changing conditions. If we would prefer a cohort that is warmer, fuzzier, and less defended, then perhaps we should co-create a new bridging scenario to link the modern with the postmodern.

The old person's fury or delight conveys a message about the integrity of the social contact throughout the life course—and something about the wisdom or folly of the underlying principles. It is with their own lives that encrusted elders offer their critique of the establishment. Their critical equipment includes the distinctive frames, assumptions, and symbolizations that characterize their generations. Their texts are tripartite: (a) the idealized American Way of Life, (b) the personal lives they have brought forward from the past to the present, and (c) the disturbing messages from a once-familiar sociophysical world that has now taken on the aspect of an alien realm. The interpretive task becomes slightly less daunting when personal past and American Way of Life are fused into a single stance from which the text of a postmodernizing society can be evaluated. Both the interpreter and the text are modified through their interaction, although gerontology has not yet learned how to construe elder patterns as discerning commentary. For example, the establishment of legalistic and other symbolic barriers to residence in the Sun Cities serves to protect space from time. More specifically, these measures imply a parallel to our special handling of artistic treasures: we house "masterpieces" within mental and physical structures that are intended to preserve them from the erosion of change. But the elders are their own masterpieces, representing a way of life that is threatened by the dissolving acid of postmodern time. It is good old time— good old purposeful, productive time—that runs its reliable and comprehensible course within the fortress communities. No wonder they must exert themselves so strenuously to preserve a haven for good time, a clockwork universe. Outside, time has taken on the aspect of chaos. Like a desert storm, this alien time swirls in a blind, mindless rage.

And so these most sincere of critics express their misgivings and their resolve with their lives as well as their words. The world they reject is not the oppressive, class-riven materialism conceived by the Marxists. These people, after all, are the modest winners, those who could cope and who survived to participate in the benefits. What they reject is a world that no longer seems interest in work, decency, loyalty, and other familiar virtues. Such a world would hardly know what to do with the legacy that fortressed elders might othewise have offered them. It is as if they are saying, "The dark ages are upon us—are we the only ones who have noticed? Ah well, we will take it upon ourselves to preserve a decent human way of life. We can preserve only so much of it and only for so long. Too bad you don't appreciate us now. Who and what will you have when we're gone?"

Do we need, then, a gerontology that is more informed by critical theory? Yes, of course. But is it sufficient to cultivate critical theory as provided by sideline academics? Perhaps not. To avoid "the separation of warm emotion and cool intelligence" (Dewey, 1922, p. 258), we might address the critical theory implicit in the thoughts, actions, and dreams of the aged men and women among us.

NOTES

[1] Names of informants and other private individuals are pseudonymous.
[2] Data from the Arizona State University Survey Research Center were made available by Bruce Merrill, Director.

REFERENCES

Arendt, H. (1971). *The life of the mind.* New York: Harcourt Brace Jovanovich.
Dewey, J. (1922). *Human nature and conduct.* New York: Modern Library.
Douglas, M. (1966). *Purity and danger.* Baltimore: Penguin Books.
Habermas, J. (1991). *The philosophical discourse of modernity.* (Trans. F. G. Lawrence). Cambridge, MA: M.I.T. Press. (Original work published 1985)
Kastenbaum, R. (1980–1981). Habituation as a model of aging. *International Journal of Aging and Human Development, 12,* 159–170.
Kastenbaum, R. (1984). When aging begins. *Research on Aging, 6,* 105–117.

Kastenbaum, R. (1991). Racism and the older voter? Arizona's rejection of a paid holiday to honor Martin Luther King. *International Journal of Aging and Human Development, 32,* 199–209.

Meerloo, J. A. M. (1954). *The two faces of man.* New York: International Universities Press.

Norris-Baker, C., & Scheidt, R. (1989). Habituation theory and environment-aging research: Ennui to joie de vivre? *International Journal of Aging and Human Development, 29,* 241–257.

Reich, J. W., & Zautra, A. J. (1991). Analyzing the trait of routinization in older adults. *International Journal of Aging and Human Development, 32,* 161–180.

Arrested Aging: The Power of the Past to Make Us Aged and Old

Laurence B. McCullough

INTRODUCTION: PHILOSOPHY'S CONTRIBUTION TO CRITICAL GERONTOLOGY

This chapter aims to contribute to the development of critical gerontology from the disciplinary perspective of philosophy. Moody ("Overview," this volume) identifies a variety of senses in which the phrase "critical gerontology" can usefully be understood. A central theme of his discussion is that critical gerontology should identify possibilities of utopian, emancipatory change in the lives of the elderly. This

The author gratefully acknowledges the criticism of and suggestions about an earlier version of this chapter by W. Andrew Achenbaum, Thomas R. Cole, Carole Haber, and Nancy Wilson.

constitutes an ambitious agenda. Moreover, the ethical justification for such an agenda has yet to be established. Any such justification must address and rein in the inherent paternalism in such an agenda, a paternalism that cannot be escaped when one treats freedom as a value rather than as a side constraint (Engelhardt, 1986).

This chapter adopts a more modest agenda, one that is in keeping with the traditional role of the humanities, philosophy in particular, as critical disciplines. Moody and Cole (1986) succinctly characterize this traditional role of the humanities as follows: "Apparently, deeper reflection on meaning and aging is called for in the very methods and assumptions that the specialized disciplines of aging use to illuminate the last stage of life" (p. 248). The main assumptions to which this chapter is critically directed concern successful and unsuccessful aging.

Philosophy's critical role can usefully be directed to other disciplines, in this case the disciplines of gerontology. In undertaking this role, philosophy tests other disciplines against intellectual criteria, such as clarity of concepts and language, consistency and coherence of analysis and argument, and applicability of analysis and argument, as well as their adequacy.

The last concerns the comprehensiveness of the accounts of aging offered by the disciplines of gerontology. In particular, adequacy concerns whether the views, theories, or proposals of the disciplines of gerontology identify and take account of the full range of the possibilities for aging in our species. My thesis in this chapter is that the disciplines of gerontology fail to identify and take account of one possibility for human aging: the possibility that time, the past in particular, has the power to arrest some lives, to bring them to a stop, without death occurring. I call this arrested aging. When this profound arrest occurs, the past obliges an individual—morally, aesthetically, and perhaps in other ways, too—to become aged, old, in a way that present, predominant, and taken-for-granted gerontological theories implicitly deny. In that denial is found the inadequacy of those theories, theories implicit in some of the chapters in this volume (Fahey & Holstein, chap. 12; Ovrebo & Minkler, chap. 15).

AN IMMEDIATE REJOINDER
AND RESPONSE TO IT

Some may want to reply immediately that the possibility I have just described is already well known in gerontological literature. I have, the rejoinder goes, simply called unsuccessful aging by another name and therefore have nothing new to say. Nor is an interest in time, the rejoinder continues, new to gerontology. I reply by considering first successful and unsuccessful aging and then gerontological concepts of time.

Successful and Unsuccessful Aging

Rowe and Kahn (1987) define successful aging as follows: "people who demonstrate little or no loss in a constellation of physiologic functions would be regarded as more broadly successful in physiologic terms." Usual aging comprises individuals who display "typical nonpathologic age-linked losses" (p. 144). Others (Butt & Beiser, 1987; Ryff, 1989) employ a similar concept, applied now to the maintenance of psychological function or its loss. Ryff (1989) seems to define successful aging as a state of "positive psychological functioning in . . . later life" (p. 195), whereas Butt and Beiser (1987) provide empirical data about the content of such functioning: "an increased chance of experiencing contentment and satisfaction" (p. 94).

Unsuccessful aging presumably involves the pathological or abnormal loss of physiological or psychological functioning. Such loss is regarded in the gerontological literature as preventable and potentially reversible. For example, Rowe and Kahn (1987) explicitly propose strategies to prevent and treat such an outcome. Butt and Beiser (1987) implicitly subscribe to this view when they conclude that "future studies must address the strengths and competencies that people develop over a lifetime and which they use to transform what might be a final phase of decline and renunciation into one of the integrity and integration" (p. 94). The emancipatory agenda identified by Moody ("Overview," this volume) also subscribes implicitly to this view. Elsewhere, Moody (1986) explicitly takes this view when he writes: "we may suggest that a successful resolution of the old age life review signifies that: (1) my life is intelligible; (2) my life has a purpose; (3) my hopes and desires ultimately can be satisfied" (pp. 25–26).

The possibility for human aging that I shall describe and evaluate here involves an irrevocable loss of the ability to respond to time and thus constitutes a state or condition of permanent metaphysical arrest. Such a state or condition lies beyond unsuccessful aging in territory as yet uncharted in the gerontological literature. Ironically, that state can be marked by contentment and satisfaction, as we shall see.

Time

The dimensions of time involved in this state or condition of arrested aging are also uncharted in the gerontological literature. This is not to say that time does not constitute an important, recognized, conceptual category in the gerontological literature. To the contrary, as Achenbaum (1992) has convincingly demonstrated, time has figured predominantly in the thinking and work of gerontologists from the very invention of the field. Achenbaum distinguishes two main conceptualizations of time in the gerontological literature: physical and subjective time. The first stands outside human experience, but the latter must be understood precisely as experienced. The former is an objective concept of time, and there is a concern to measure both (Achenbaum, 1992).

In an interesting paper Hendricks and Hendricks (1976) advance some criticisms of "objective" time, that is, measures of time that are outside the experience or perspective of individuals and therefore thought to be independent of idiosyncrasy. They seek an alternative to this objective notion of time as "the abstract and impersonal framework that surrounds all personal time and humanity" (p. 27), a view they attribute to Durkheim. This view is remarkably Leibnizian, in that time is not thought to be a property of individuals but a concept by which change in individuals is measured. That change is orderly and sequential and so lends itself naturally to quantification. For Leibniz, I think, time therefore makes no difference. Remarkably, it seems too that changes makes no difference. Leibniz's basic substances, the monads, are ferociously active, endlessly generating perceptions, but not aging one whit. One can hold such a view of time only by persistently and radically ignoring human experience.

It comes as no surprise, therefore, that Hendricks and Hendricks (1976) resist this objective concept of time in favor of a more subjective, individually oriented concept. They put the point this way: "Due to its interdisciplinary parentage, gerontology is ready to consider new descriptions of time. To do so, we must explore the possibility of returning the control of temporal construction to the actor in our analysis of his experiences" (pp. 47–48).

This view of time leads Hendricks and Hendricks (1976) to a redefinition of issues in gerontology. Their formulations of these issues resonate with the language of human possibility and freedom, which, they believe, would be better understood if we abandoned objective concepts of time. For example, they write: "The individual could establish the legitimacy of different measures of time, emphasizing those that allow him greatest freedom of choice" (p. 48). Notice that the concern here is with subjective *measures* of time, a not surprising emphasis given the concern of Hendricks and Hendricks with a *concept* of time that can be employed in scientific investigations. They believe that this new concept of time, more subjectively oriented as it is, makes it possible to investigate questions of meaning: "When time is seen as a process, continually becoming, a man is free to attribute a variety of meanings to his temporal existence" (p. 49). Perhaps so, but this is still an abstract freedom, the freedom of concepts disconnected from the realities that they supposedly conceptualize.

Without realizing it, Hendricks and Hendricks (1976) commit themselves to a Leibnizian, antimetaphysical understanding of time. In doing so, they fail to see that time has power, including implacable power, before which some human beings can sometimes become powerless. Even their abstract freedom to attribute a "variety of meanings" to their existence can be taken from them, as their past arrests their present and eliminates all but one meaning, a meaning within which there are morally and aesthetically no longer any possibilities for novelty and thus perhaps for any humanly significant existence.

As a counterpoint to time as a concept of measure—whether that concept counts as an objective or subjective measure makes no difference—I want in this chapter to take seriously time as a reality. In doing so, I develop a suggestion by Strumpf (1987), who recognizes the importance of distinguishing metaphysical time from physical time. "Metaphysical or subjective time is an internal time of the individual or . . . a sensation immediately experienced within ourselves" (p. 202). Not quite, for in this sense metaphysical time is simply subjective time (Achenbaum, 1992) under another name.

Metaphysical time is a reality, not simply a sensation. It is experienced, to be sure. As a metaphysical reality, however, time's principal dimension is power, not the capacity to be measured. As noted above, measuring time objectifies it, including the measurement of subjective time, the "sensation" of time's pasage. Metaphysical time probably cannot be measured. Indeed, to ask after its measurement is to misunderstand it fundamentally. This dimension to time lies beyond concepts of time found in the gerontological literature.

My response to the rejoinder, then, is that there is a possibility for aging, arrested aging, that has yet to be identified and evaluated in gerontology. This can be undertaken only in terms of the metaphysical sense of time, which is properly the province of philosophy.

ARRESTED AGING:
A NARRATIVE DESCRIPTION

The possibility for human aging that I have termed arrested aging is powerfully illustrated in the novels of Kazuo Ishiguro (1986, 1989, 1990). The characters whose lives figure as the subject matter of these novels do not, I believe, exist only in them. They live among us.

I propose, therefore, to begin my account of arrested aging on the basis of Ishiguro's novels. The interpretation of novels occurs, of course, against a contended background (see Weiland, chap. 5, this volume). My approach is decidedly old-fashioned in that it assumes an author and an author's voice, contra the deconstructionists. Once Ishiguro's characters have been described, I shall undertake an analysis of them on the basis of a new and striking philosophical treatise on the metaphysics of time (Lieb, 1991).

Ishiguro's first novel, *A Pale View of Hills* (1990), does not directly address aging, although one of its main characters, a Japanese woman now living in the English countryside, has a grown daughter. The narrative begins with a visit to this twice-widowed woman, Etsuko, who seems to be in her 60s, by her daughter Niki. Etsuko's other daughter, Keiko, had earlier committed suicide. This seems to be Niki's first visit since her half-sister's death. Niki's visit prompts Etsuko to journey back in time to Japan and to think through—not for the first time but probably for the first time deeply—her friendship of a sort with a woman, Sachiko, and Sachiko's daughter Mariko, who lived in a ramshackle cottage by a river in Nagasaki in the months and years immediately after the close of World War II. At that time, Etsuko was married, pregnant with her first daughter, and living comfortably, though not lavishly; whereas Sachiko lived at the economic edge, pinning her hopes on an American who had promised to marry her and take her to the United States. Mariko seems a distant, independent child, estranged from her mother, who doesn't seem really to understand her—in a way apparently meant to foreshadow Etsuko's relationship to her own daughters. Perhaps that estrangement contributed to the suicide of Etsuko's daughter Keiko; the reader is left to surmise.

Ishiguro's main literary device is recollection, and his novels, beginning with *A Pale View of Hills*, explore recollection and the power of the past that is confronted in recollection. Etsuko, for example, recollects her daughter's suicide indirectly, by way of and in the form of a lengthy reflection—it runs the length of the book—on her relationship to Sachiko and Mariko, culminating in an incident in which Mariko ran away from her mother after her mother attempted to drown Mariko's cats in preparation for leaving for America.

Ishiguro's use of reflection is subtle, for his characters recollect only partially, with interruptions as they are called back to the present. These interruptions permit his characters to underestimate the power of recollection. For example, Ishiguro (1990) has Etsuko say, at a point well into the novel: "Memory, I realize, can be an unreliable thing; often it is heavily colored by the circumstances in which one remembers, and no doubt this applies to certain of the recollections I have gathered here" (p. 156).

Etsuko's memory is at times hazy, then suddenly in focus, much like the view from her apartment onto the pale hills across Nagasaki harbor. At it turns out for Etsuko, memory is relentless, though not fierce, also like the view onto the hills. She remembers Mariko's running away at the end of the story, just as Niki is preparing to return to London. Etsuko's last stated memory is of Mariko running alongside the river toward the cottage where she lived with her mother. But does Mariko throw herself in the river, in anger and despondency over her drowned cats? This reader, at least, asked himself that question. Ishiguro (1990) doesn't answer, returning us instead to the inside of Etsuko's home on a gray, rainy day in which this exchange between Etsuko and Niki takes place:

> "I suppose, Niki, you don't have any plans yet to be married?"
> "What do I want to get married for?"
> "I was just asking."
> "Why should I get married? What's the point of that?"
> "You plan to just go on—living in London, do you?"
> "Well, why should I get married? That's so stupid, Mother." She rolled up the calendar and packed it away. "So many women just get brainwashed. They think all there is to life is getting married and having a load of kids." I continued to watch her. Then I said: "But in the end, Niki, there isn't very much else." (pp. 179–180)

Etsuko, it seems, plans "to just go on"—two husbands dead, one daughter dead, and one leaving from a visit that was cold inside and out—no "load of kids" if "load" means number but a "load" of kids if one means memory, in a book of memories. There isn't much else, for the past is in control. Here is Etsuko as the book draws to its close:

> I would like to have seen her to the railway station—it is only a few minutes' walk—but the idea seemed to embarrass her. She left shortly

after lunch with an oddly self-conscious air, as if she were leaving without my approval. The afternoon had turned grey and windy, and I stood in the doorway as she walked down to the end of the drive. She was dressed in the same tight-fitting clothes she had arrived in, and her suitcase made her drag her step a little. When she reached the gate, Niki glanced back and seemed surprised to find me still standing at the door. I smiled and waved to her. (Ishiguro, 1990, p. 183)

We all instantly recognize this image—the freeze-frame or photograph or painting, arrested forever in time past. Etsuko's life seems over, nothing left to do, no novelty. Sachiko, Mariko, and Keiko people her past, and the past is what awaits Etsuko when she turns from that door. Unlike Nagasaki, which rebuilt on the ruins of its past, Etsuko has nowhere to go, it seems. She won't commit suicide herself; she will go on living but only in the direction set by a past that seems to allow no escape. The book is so elegant and gentle in its writing that this seems only sad, no more. Etsuko herself, though, seems content, perhaps too satisfied.

Not so for *An Artist of the Floating World* (Ishiguro, 1986), despite Ishiguro's elegant writing. This story concerns Masuji Ono, who, we learn from his recollections, was an artist—a propaganda artist, really, and famous in his day—for imperial Japan in the years before and during World War II. Unlike Etsuko in *A Pale View of Hills*, who finds herself recollecting almost naturally, Ono is a reluctant recaller of his past. Indeed, as he does so, he is often unsure of the accuracy of what he remembers, and his first attempts at remembering events are self-serving as a rule. His avoidance behavior is as exquisite as his paintings must have been.

More to the point, he is obliged to undertake his recollections by othes. These include children of the man who used to own his home, a home that man may have lost to Ono not altogether voluntarily. Crucially, Ono is obliged to remember by his older daughter, who reminds him of the failed attempts to arrange marriages for her younger sister. The prospective in-laws, the reader learns, do not want to be associated in the new Japan with so prominent a figure among those who brought the ruinous war on their country.

As the story unfolds, Ono confronts not only his political past but also his ruthlessness in pursuing the politics of art and the politics of war in imperial Japan. At one point, he passes a broken-down man in the street, whom he only vaguely recalls at first but then must come to remember as an artist, formerly a friend, whom he black-balled. Slowly, inexorably, he is revealed to the reader and to himself— though he scuttles away from the truth as a matter of deeply imprinted instinct—as someone caught up in the past, made definite only by a "floating world" of elegant pictures, the rituals of art, his lionization by his students in his favorite tavern, and his sophisticated lust for prominence and power.

Meanwhile, Ono lives in the new Japan (apparently Nagasaki), with its new outlook and a younger generation eager to throw off the past of which Ono was a part—indeed, to repudiate that past. Ono is thus excluded from the present by his rootedness in the past. His life now exists only as he recalls it; recollection is the whole of his life.

His figure seems to me to sag at the end of the novel with the weight of time, thinly and unsuccessfully disguised by Ono's false good wishes. He is a broken-down old man, too. He returns to the tavern, the Migi-Hidari, of his recollections; but it is now gone, its place taken by the glass-fronted modern buildings of the Japan that has left him behind. The images that Ishiguro (1986) weaves into these closing paragraphs exclude Ono, who only looks on and bids his farewell.

Where the Migi-Hidari once stood is now a front yard for a group of offices set back from the road. Some of the senior employees leave their cars in this yard, but it is for the most part a clear space of tarmac with a few young trees planted at various points. At the front of this yard, facing the road, there is a bench of the sort one may find in a park. For whose benefit it has been placed there, I do not know, for I have never seen any of these busy people ever stopping to relax on it. But it is my fancy that the bench occupies a spot very close to where our old table in the Migi-Hidari would have been situated, and I have taken at times to sitting on it. It may well not be a public bench, but then it is close to the pavement, and no one has ever objected to my sitting there. Yesterday morning, with the sun shining pleasantly, I sat down on it again and remained there for a while, observing the activity around me.

It must have been approaching the lunch hour by then, for across the road I could see groups of employees in their bright white shirtsleeves emerging from the glass-fronted building where Mrs. Kawakami's used to be. And as I watched, I was struck by how full of optimism and enthusiasm these young people were. At one point, two young men leaving the building stopped to talk with a third man who was on his way in. They stood on the doorsteps of that glass-fronted building, laughing together in the sunshine. One young man, whose face I could see most clearly, was laughing in a particularly cheerful manner, with something of the open innocence of a child. Then with a quick gesture, the three colleagues parted and went their ways.

I smiled to myself as I watched these young office workers from my bench. Of course, at times, when I remember those brightly-lit bars and all those people gathered beneath the lamps, laughing a little more boisterously perhaps than those young men yesterday, but with much the same good-heartedness, I feel a certain nostalgia for the past and the district as it used to be. But to see how our city has been rebuilt, how things have recovered so rapidly over these years, fills me with genuine gladness. Our nation, it seems, whatever mistakes it may have made in the past, has now another chance to make a better go of things. One can only wish these young people well. (Ishiguro, 1986, pp. 205–206)*

Ono stops to relax, of course. He also stops altogether but does not die. And his farewell condescends; it is almost acid, but "these young people" neither notice nor respond to an old man lost in, because captured by, his memories. Still, there is a contentment to this old man, sitting satisfied in the place of his old glories.

Ishiguro's latest novel, *The Remains of the Day* (1989), continues his exploration of the power of recollection and of the past. The central figure is a butler, Stevens, who works in what was once one of the "great houses" of England. It is not so great now, Stevens implies, because its owner—his new employer—is an American. This fact is difficult for Stevens to accept, inasmuch as it lowers his standing in his own eyes, eyes very much trained to see himself and others in terms of the past, when Darlington Hall was in its glory under its true occupant, Lord Darlington.

These recollections gradually come to light as Stevens motors about the countryside on his very first holiday ever, it seems. He takes this holiday as a result of near insistence by his new employer. He also has a letter from the former housekeeper of Darlington Hall. Leaving the Hall and rereading the letter oblige him to remember his past.

His chosen destination for his motor holiday, which takes five days, is a village where the former housekeeper of Darlington Hall resides. We learn, as various bits and pieces of the past intrude themselves on Stevens's memory, that he treated this woman badly, more than once—badly by the standards of civility that reigned, or were thought by him to reign, in the Darlington Hall of glorious accomplishment and refinement. Stevens is in thrall to the idea of household staff as "professional"—or failing to be professional—and sees himself as the consummate professional, even when his own memories confront him with his failure to live by those standards.

The pain of these memories prompts the more systematic recollection of Lord Darlington, who held many high-level meetings in Darlington Hall during the 1930s in failed attempts to prevent war in

Europe. It turns out, the reader comes inexorably to appreciate, that Lord Darlington was a master appeaser, a dupe of the Germans, a charge made publicly against Lord Darlington that Stevens rejects but cannot refute as he motors along. How can the high-standing "professional" butler have worked for a dupe, a traitor to his country and proper anti-Semite, and not have seen the truth for what it was? Stevens has no answer, except for repeated claims to the importance of his own role in keeping the household running smoothly during those momentous times, including his firing a maid at Lord Darlington's request because she was Jewish. The professional of his dreams thus gets the process right, even if the substance is morally abhorrent.

Again, a repugnant past—certainly by the present's lights and even by the lights of Britain in the 1930s, Stevens must at some level sense—looms out of the dimness of first memories and the clarity of sustained recollection and arrests the main character. He just doesn't fit in the present anymore; his patterns of thought and behavior are those of another time and really not up to the present standard of civility in crucial respects. Yet contentedly, he returns to Darlington Hall, to join its many other relics.

Etsuko stands quietly in a door as her past sucks her in. Ono bids farewell to "these young people" from a bench that may have been where his beloved table stood in his beloved tavern—beloved because there he was everything but here and now an old man passed by unrecognized. By contrast, Stevens seems at first more daring. As the story closes, he tells us that he will take up bantering, an American custom he has observed and come to appreciate—he thinks—in the new master of Darlington Hall, one Mr. Farraday. Stevens, with his few old suits and many old ways is no Python.

> It occurs to me, furthermore, that bantering is hardly an unreasonable duty for an employer to expect a professional to perform. I have of course devoted much time to developing my bantering skills, but it is possible I have never approached the task with the commitment I might have done. Perhaps, then, when I return to Darlington Hall tomorrow—Mr. Farraday will not himself be back for a further week—I will begin practicing with renewed effort. I should hope, then, that by the time of my employer's return, I shall be in a position to pleasantly surprise him. (Ishiguro, 1989, p. 245)

It won't, of course, work; it can't. Stevens cannot banter any more than the random Brit or unacculturated Yankee can successfully tell an Aggie joke. Stevens should know; he's already tried his hand at bantering a couple of times, each time failing and earning odd, awkward responses from Farraday.

Farraday is the new Britain of the 1950s, the time immediately after the war in which the story is set. Brittania no longer rules the waves and barely rules itself. America is now the colossus, and commoners—mere businessmen, not statesmen, and Americans no less—are buying up manor houses, stripping them of most of their "professional" employees and making do with thinner ranks. This reader senses that Farraday kept Stevens on out of kindness to an old man and nostalgia for things that can never exist again. He is a fixture of Darlington Hall, among the other decorations and detritus of its glorious past.

Stevens is thus wholly past, out of time, or at least out of the present, even though we can find him in it. Stevens has no weight, no effect, except to stir old pain in himself—very much so in himself—and others, especially the former housekeeper, Miss Kenton of the grand days, now the married Mrs. Benn, who rebukes him for his past cruelties when they finally meet.

Stevens is aged by his past, a past that makes him old. If he does really try banter again, he will just be a silly old fool. Ono, at least, didn't make that mistake; he just stepped aside and sat down quietly. Etsuko waves from the door and returns, I suppose, to her domesticity, unspeaking. All three, to my mind, are ancient, with no vitality, no effect, no presence, only persistence. Not "older" or "young old" or "old old," just plain old.

ARRESTED AGING:
A PHILOSOPHICAL ANALYSIS

Ishiguro's (1986, 1989, 1990) characters surely display subjective, experienced time. But time, the past particularly, is for them more than a sensation of passage, of an accrued past or of imminent death. Time is a reality possessing power, and so time is indeed metaphysical.

The metaphysics of time is one of the most daunting of all topics in philosophy. In a new work on the subject, Lieb (1991) provides an account of the metaphysics of time in terms of which a philosophical analysis of arrested aging can be successfully undertaken.

Lieb (1991) as I noted earlier, opposes antimetaphysical accounts of time, accounts that, interestingly, have some currency in recent gerontology if the work of the Hendrickses is any evidence. Lieb, by treating time as something real, has a great deal to say about time "as a process, continually becoming" (Hendricks & Hendricks, 1976, p. 49). Lieb explicitly rejects the view of time as a measure of change, from whatever perspective. As a consequence, Lieb's work provides us powerful insights into what it means to take time seriously as a powerful reality.

> In this essay I claim that time is a fundamental reality. Time is not derived from anything else and its reality is most evident in the continuous passing in everything that moves, changes, lasts, or even remains the same. The claim, however, is not simply that individuals move and last but that the passing which occurs in individuals is time itself. Time is a part of things that are in time, and its passing inside them continually provokes them to act. (Lieb, 1991, p. 4)*

As any good philosopher should, Lieb identifies the basic presuppositions of his thought: "The two intuitions from which this essay starts are that each present moment is new and that there must always be new present moments; the world must go on" (p. 8). Finally, Lieb claims that individuals do not exist only in the present but in time: "individuals, even while they are present, are also in the future and the past; they have their being in the three parts of time" (p. 11).

I want first to set out in some detail how Lieb (1991) understands time, the past in particular. I then want to claim that some individuals—Etsuko, Ono, and Stevens among them—cease to be present, in Lieb's sense of there being anything new in their lives, but do not die. Instead, they persist but have become wholly past. Such people are, in a crucial sense that gerontology seems not to have appreciated, aged, plain old, in a way that no niceties of locution can or should disguise. That is, although it is a commonplace dictum of gerontology that variation is true of the elderly, as is the case for all biological life forms, it is also the case that one possible and not so pleasant variation on aging, arrested aging, has not been given the consideration it deserves.

Lieb (1991) shares with Leibniz the notion that what individuals are is what they do; they act. For Leibniz, time was not a real property of individuals, however, only an abstract concept by which the action of individuals could be measured (e.g., by the sciences). Lieb does not make time a property of individuals; it is for him a reality with which individuals must interact to sustain themselves as individuals.

In the present, individuals interact with time and also with other individuals. This dual interaction is essential for individuation to take place, the making of oneself distinct and different from other individuals. Time, according to Lieb, possesses a Lockean power to oblige us to act, and in the present we act against other individuals as a way to preserve our selves, our identities as different from each other, as distinctive in our outlook, style, and makeup. If we do not act, we lose our identity in the present, so there are moral and aesthetic dimensions to the Lockean power of time to oblige us to act. It is as if, were one to fail to act and become singular in the present, one would fail morally and aesthetically. One's life would not be worth living, and it would be ugly.

Lieb (1991) is not altogether clear on this dimension of time, but it provides the impetus, I believe, for his holding that individuals must always act; they cannot not act without ceasing to exist—again, just like Leibniz's monads.

> Time's passage threatens to make individuals entirely past. Their basic action is to remove this jeopardy, though they act in other ways as well. Time, in turn, issues into presence and passes because of a jeopardy that individuals make for it. These two jeopardies occur together. Neither time nor singular individuals ever become still and safe from each other's intrusion. As individuals individualize a portion of their future being, they provoke to passage the time that is tissued with their future being. This passage is a threat to the persistence of individuals, and because it is, as individuals act and extend themselves, they unsettle time again. There is an endless willfulness in individuals; in time, or in its passage, there is a dumb necessity. Both time and individuals act to remove the jeopardies they make for one another, only to introduce them once again. (Lieb, 1991, pp. 45–46)

There may be a fundamental necessity for time to interact with some individuals and for some individuals to interact with others so that the world does not cease to exist. But this does not exclude the possibility—which, as near as I can tell, Lieb would want to deny—that some individuals can cease to act, can cease to be present, and thus experience a profound sort of moral and aesthetic failure because it is a metaphysical failure. This is what happens to Ishiguro's characters, at least on my reading of the three novels.

An individual acts and makes what Lieb (1991) calls its singularity, its distinction or difference from other, contemporaneous individuals against which it contends. As an individual acts, it also becomes past; it comes to have a definiteness that results, I think, from the history of its making itself in contention with time and other individuals.

The past is a part of time. It consists of individuals and time, as the present and the future also do so, but the way that individuals and time are together as the past differs from the ways they form the other parts of time. In the present, for example, individuals and time contend with each other. Individuals try to hold time inside themselves while time passes to avoid being divided by them. In the past, by contrast, time dominates individuals. As time becomes past it transforms the individuals in which it was present, depriving them of their singularity and making them part of the fabric of a vast, stilled time which is as real and full as the present and is effective too. (Lieb, 1991, p. 89)

As individuals act in the present, the only place they *can* act, they create "relative or relational characters" (Lieb, 1991, p. 112), which can exist only in the present. Time becomes past in an individual when those momentary relational properties cease to exist. The result is the definiteness of an individual, a definiteness without relational properties. Thus, there is one past of which all of us are a part, and that one past is the template to which we must respond as we generate new relational properties and preserve our singularity. Each individual is thus "apprenticed to itself" (Lieb, 1991, p. 97) in that its past is a condition on everything that will happen next.

The past thus also possesses a Lockean power, and we have "intimations in our experience that the past is real" (Lieb, 1991, p. 101), in virtue of the effect of that power. Ishiguro's (1986, 1989, 1990) books begin with such intimations and, for good reason, the reader discovers, his main characters resist those intimations. His characters are uncertain of their memories, usually. As they erect their resistance to recollection, the past responds and becomes more effective in the present, as a result of the actions and words of others that oblige, eventually, his main characters to respond. Ishiguro's individuals, as a consequence, become progressively more definite as his stories unfold and so less singular, less vital. Indeed, by the end of the book Etsuko, Ono, and Stevens are fully defined indeed and cease altogether to act against other individuals. They all at once and finally lose their singularity for themselves and for the reader and are only definite in that each is now devoid of the possibility of novelty. They are not simply apprenticed to the past but now are captive of or even enslaved to it.

Lieb (1991), very much in the tradition of American philosophical pragmatism, is an optimist on this score when he writes that the "idea that the past is real will lead us to a fuller interpretation of some experience, and that will be a change in experience itself—for the better we suppose" (p. 102). Not so for Ishiguro's characters. Things may be better for Niki but not for Etsuko, for the "young people" but not for Ono, for Farraday but not for Stevens. In many places, Lieb says that the past is "implacable" in the sense that it must be taken into account. He would deny, I think, what I take Ishiguro to affirm: that the past can wholly consume an individual, robbing him or her of the power to act against other individuals and leaving him or her with only the meager, lifeless power to persist.

As wholly past, persisting in the present, and without a future, Ishiguro's characters confront a harrowing reality: they are plain old or aged, and that state of existence means that they are now without the possibility of novelty that a future affords because they have no bridge from the past to the future in that they have no present. The past, for Lieb (1991), provides "what they [individuals] must form themselves on" (p. 165) and "conditions what individuals do" (p. 165), to be sure, but does so in Ishiguro's novels with a ferocious implacability. Etsuko, Ono, and Stevens lose their "relative characters" and seem, as a consequence, to blend into their surroundings: Etsuko into her house in the country, Ono into the private bench lost in the bustle of rebuilt Nagasaki, and Stevens into the gray eminence of Darlington Hall. Yet none dies.

Winkler (1990) spies something similar in the series of self-portraits that Käthe Kollwitz painted over a period of many years. Winkler's characterization of Kollwitz's last self-portrait provides an apt visual metaphor for Ishiguro's characters: "In her last self-portrait, her face will turn away. She no longer needs the mirror to teach her her features. She has become a form as monumental as one of her sculptures—and hardly an individual at all" (Winkler, 1990, p. 43).

Lieb (1991) claims that there is one past and that in some way each of us is responsible for his or her past. As a consequence of there being one past, each of us is to some extent responsible for *the* past, morally and aesthetically responsible, if I read Lieb correctly. On Lieb's optimistic view that no individual could ever become wholly past, the taking up of moral and aesthetic responsibility for one's own past and *the* past should not be overly burdensome. After all, one can act anew and so undo harms, undertake to make amends, and, if nothing else can be done, apologize and accept responsibility.

Consider Ono. He must take responsibility for the ruin brought on his country by its imperial ambition, an ambition that he helped to define and inculcate in his countrymen. This is the past that Ono resists recollecting, remarking throughout his story that he is telling things "as I recall" them. Others speak and act, morally obliging him (to them and to the reader) to recollect the past as it was, both in imperial Japan and in the effects of his association with that evil for his own daughter and for destroyed friendships. As the past looms up in his story, it does indeed become effective. It is more than a condition on Ono's present; it becomes his present. He must then face the unrelenting burden of moral and aesthetic (he was, after all, an artist) responsibility for that horrible past. The burden ages him, finishes him off, and so arrests him, I think, but it does not kill him. So too for Stevens, mired in the past of his traitorous, anti-Semitic, still glorious master, and for Etsuko trapped by the dead Keiko. That is, as some individuals in their lives interacted with them, to distinguish themselves from them—Niki with Etsuko, his daughter with Ono, and Mrs. Benn and Farraday with Stevens—Etsuko, Ono, and Stevens were morally and aesthetically obliged to become wholly past. As such, they no longer act against other individuals; they do not act at all. They thus lose their present and their future but not their ability to persist. They have no presence either, as the image of Ono at the end of his story illustrates, for example.

Let me try to put Ishiguro and Lieb—more exactly, my readings of them—together. To act in the present and to become past, as Lieb (1991) describes these defining human endeavors, is to age. Lieb thinks that this must always be the case for "the world" (i.e., the collection of individuals) and, apparently, for each individual. On this view, each of us gets older or becomes elderly by virtue of having an ever-enlarging past that conditions our present and to which we apprentice ourselves. Successful aging would seem, then, to involve the passage from being an apprentice to the past to becoming master of the past. Such mastery would, I propose, involve acknowledging one's moral and aesthetic responsibility for the past—in one's personal life, family life, community, nation, and planet—and living out that responsibility in a way that commands respect for a self-consciously moral and aesthetic life.

Philosophical analysis thus enriches the concept of successful aging in gerontology. To the physiological (Rowe & Kahn, 1987) and psychological (Butt & Beiser, 1987; Ryff, 1989) dimensions of successful aging, philosophy adds metaphysical, moral, and aesthetic dimensions. Metaphysically, successful aging occurs when aging individuals continually contend against time, thereby sustaining themselves as individuals. This, indeed, is just what aging means in metaphysical terms. Such individuals can undertake moral and aesthetic accountability and so accrue, as past, the rich sort of coherence that concerns Cohler (chap. 6, this volume). Successfully aging individuals, as present, however, must be incomplete and so at risk for fragmentation. Ideal aging in metaphysical terms thus holds in tension coherence and incompleteness.

Unsuccessful aging is the experience of abnormal and reversible factors that impede sustained metaphysical activity and the moral and aesthetic responsibility and life that such activity makes possible. The value of the latter constitutes, precisely, the justification for the obligation to prevent and address unsuccessful aging that Rowe and Kahn (1987) presume but do not articulate or justify.

I think that Ishiguro (1986, 1989, 1990) is important to gerontology because he shows us a third possibility: arrested aging. Ishiguro shares with Lieb (1991) the view that to age is to come to terms with one's past and *the* past of which one's past is partly constituent. Etsuko perhaps less so, but Ono and Stevens surely fully display devastation in aging, not unlike what happened to Nagasaki and to England in World War II. The atomic bomb made the old Nagasaki wholly past by quite literally removing it from the face of the earth, and the war made the glory days of Darlington Hall wholly past by creating a new economic and political reality. Neither could be a condition for the present or future of Etsuko, Ono, or Stevens. Subsequent possibilities thus get eliminated for Ishiguro's characters. Only their past is present, and so they have no present, in Lieb's—correct—terms. They have no chance for novelty, and so they—and Ishiguro's novels—come to a full stop.

There remains only for Ishiguro to stop writing each novel and for his characters to die. But neither lethal disease nor other life-taking events befall those characters, and because none can act and none possesses novelty, none can enact that most radical, powerful, and final of novelties, suicide. Etsuko, Ono, and Stevens are arrested by *the* past—the period leading up to and following World War II for all three of them. Each resists this fact, each tries in vain to push that past out of his or her life, but each fails and therefore fails to sustain his or her present. The moral and aesthetic burden of the/their past overwhelms them by obliterating both the present and the future. When one's past becomes the whole of one's being, the present is consumed and, along with it, the possibility for novelty that is one's future. One is no longer singular, only definite, with no possibility for avoiding becoming crushed by moral and aesthetic responsibility. Other individuals cease to interact with one except to push one into the past. One shrinks, one becomes broken down, one is old, aged—plain old. One's aging is irrevocably arrested in the past. There can be no present and so, too, no future.

What should we think of those who display arrested aging and perhaps experience something of the sensation that they are out of time? For Lieb, such a state of affairs metaphysically could not occur. If it could, he would, I think, have us conclude that such lives were aesthetically ugly and morally repugnant—a "stern" psychological thesis and a "harsh" ontological thesis (I. C. Lieb, personal communication, 1991). Ishiguro's characters strike this reader as devastated. It would seem to follow, then, that arrested aging is to be disvalued and avoided, a calamitous—but as yet unacknowledged in the gerontologic literature—possibility for aging. This possibility lies beyond unsuccessful aging, given the apparent irreversibility of arrested aging.

And yet Ishiguro's characters themselves seem not, in their own eyes, to be devastated. Each is content, perhaps even satisfied. Each is psychologically entirely coherent and whole, complete. The life of each will go on, quietly. None seems to disvalue her or his life. If respect for autonomy means anything as an ethical principle and if moral pluralism regarding the possibilities for human aging should guide us, as I think they should, then we cannot reliably reach the conclusion that arrested aging ought always to be disvalued. To conclude otherwise risks paternalism.

Ironically, this paternalism seems attractive, for it would be directed to the very metaphysical, moral, and aesthetic conditions for vital, fulfilled human aging. Paternalism here would thus constitute profound engagement with another's humanity, not simply a brute intrusion into his or her autonomy. Antipaternalism, by contrast, would have us stand back and pass the arrested aging by, just as the passersby on Etsuko's lane do, as the crowds pass by Ono, and as guests to the modern Darlington Hall pass by Stevens. Civility—perhaps masking horror in the face of what seems calamity—is requisite, for it restrains harsh judgment. Unfortunately, civility restrains as well as a deeply engaged paternalism, one based on metaphysical optimism.

IMPLICATIONS FOR GERONTOLOGICAL PRACTICE AND POLICY

I want to close with a brief consideration of the implications of the concept of arrested aging for gerontological practice and policy. The two can, I think, be addressed together.

Practice and policy aimed at emancipation of the elderly (Moody, "Overview," this volume; Ovrebo & Minkler, chap. 15) are suspect when applied to the arrested aging. If I am correct, those aging cannot be set free because they are arrested in time, and, if Ishiguro is correct, they may not want to be free. Then too, freedom for the arrested aging is morally perilous because of the potentially crushing moral and aesthetic burden it would bring with it. Practice and policy based on a call to moral agency (Fahey & Holstein, chap. 12, this volume) assume the presence of what arrested aging makes forever absent. Practice and policy aimed at fostering coherence as the antidote to disvalued fragmentation (Cohler, chap. 6) may, ironically, help to produce arrested aging as an outcome because full coherence and the absence of fragmentation are defining features of arrested aging.

Two things seem to follow and also seem worth further study. First, the ethically justified response in practice and policy to arrested aging would seem, at most, to be a civil, detached solicitude. Second, the most powerful preventive posture in practice and policy toward arrested aging may well be to value incompleteness and the threat of fragmentation as the defining characteristics of successful aging in its metaphysical, moral, and aesthetic dimensions.

REFERENCES

Achenbaum, W. (1992). "Time is the messenger of the gods": A gerontologic metaphor. In J. E. Birren & G. M. Kenyon (Eds.), *Metaphors of aging in science and the humanities* (pp. 83–101). New York: Springer Publishing Co.

Butt, D. S., & Beiser, M. (1987). Successful Aging: A theme for international psychology. *Psychology and Aging, 2,* 87–94.

Engelhardt, H. T., Jr. (1986). *The foundations of bioethics.* New York: Oxford University Press.

Hendricks, C. D., & Hendricks, J. (1976). Concepts of time and temporal construction among the aged, with implications for research. In J. F. Gubrium (Ed.), *Time, roles, and self in old age* (pp. 13–49). New York: Humana Press.

Ishiguro, K. (1986). *An artist of the floating world.* New York: Vintage International.

Ishiguro, K. (1989). *The remains of the day.* New York: Alfred A. Knopf.

Ishiguro, K. (1990). *A pale view of hills.* New York: Vintage International.

Lieb, I. C. (1991). *Past, present, and future: A philosophical essay about time.* Urbana and Chicago, IL: University of Illinois Press.

Moody, H. R. (1986). The meaning of life and the meaning of old age. In T. R. Cole & S. Gadow (Eds.), *What does it mean to grow old? Reflections from the humanities* (pp. 11–40). Durham, NC: Duke University Press.

Moody, H. R., & Cole, T. R. (1986). Aging and meaning: A bibliographical essay. In T. R. Cole & S. Gadow (Eds.), *What does it mean to grow old? Reflections from the humanities* (pp. 247–253). Durham, NC: Duke University Press.

Rowe, J. W., & Kahn, R. L. (1987). Human aging: Usual and successful. *Science, 237,* 143–149.

Ryff, C. D. (1989). In the eye of the beholder: Views of psychological well-being among middle-aged and older adults. *Psychology and Aging, 4,* 195–210.

Strumpf, N. E. (1987). Probing the temporal world of the elderly. *International Journal of Nursing Studies, 24,* 201–214.

Winkler, M. G. (1990, Fall). Walking to the stars: Kathe Kollwitz and the artist's pilgrimage. *Generations,* pp. 39–44.

10

Scenes From
Primary Care:
A Drama in Two Acts

William F. Monroe in collaboration with
Thomas R. Cole

Editor's Note: Several years ago, I served as a consultant on an ethically complicated decision: a 90-year-old woman, with severe Alzheimer's disease, was strapped to her bed to prevent her from pulling out the feeding tube that kept her alive. She was not brain dead, permanently comatose, or imminently dying, but her reality as a living, experiencing person was difficult to perceive. The more I learned, the clearer it became that the "case" could not be adequately portrayed in the traditional genre of bioethics. I shared the material I had accumulated with Bill Monroe, then a Rockefeller Fellow at the Institute for the Medical Humanities in Galveston, and asked him to help re-create it in a literary form. The result was *Primary Care*, a play that has been performed for nursing, gerontological, and health professionals in Chicago and Houston. *Primary Care* was performed at Galveston's Strand Street Theatre in January 1991, as part of the conference on Critical Gerontology. Following are the play's major scenes and interpretive *Afterthoughts* by Ronald Carson.

TOM COLE

THE CHARACTERS

Eliot Marcher
Nicknamed "Stony," he is a big, ruddy, physical man and chief resident at Jeff Davis. His dominating personality and his sarcastic humor almost conceal a boyish vulnerability and hide the disillusionment he has suffered in his medical education. His eyes, mannerisms, and aggressive interactions reveal his need to dominate and control people and situations. He is known as a peerless and uncanny diagnostician and prognosticator of diseases. He wears a Mickey Mouse lapel pin on his "cape," a long white lab coat frayed and split up the back seam. Beneath the lab coat he wears ostrich-skin cowboy boots and jeans with a thick leather belt. His brass belt buckle depicts a physician on horseback; the caption reads "Medicine in Texas."

Gale Cordell
A registered nurse, African-American. Usually works the day shift; BSN degree; divorced, no children; early 30s.

Sybil Dean Riegel
A woman, blind, with advanced Alzheimer's disease; widowed and childless; in her 90s.

Patsy Winstone
A nurse, Anglo-Hispanic, working her way through medical school, currently in her third year. BSN degree; single; late 20s.

Marsha LeMarque
Attending physician, faculty member, Internal Medicine, at Jeff Davis, a major teaching hospital. Competent, well-respected, efficient; somewhat strenuously self-fashioned; MD degree; unmarried; in her 40s.

G. Wynn Brooks
A nurse's aid at Jeff Davis, African-American. Usually works the night shift; a "right-to-life" advocate; widowed, with five living children; uneducated; in her 50s.

Margie Dunne   Mrs. Riegel's niece; lives and works in Beaumont; married, with grown children in Austin and San Antonio; early 60s.

ACT I

Scene 1: March 15, noon. Mrs. Riegel's room.

A side view of an elderly female patient with a nasogastric tube is projected onto the back of the stage area. A translucent curtain surrounds an occupied hospital bed. The lights come up gradually. First just the patient's head is intensely lit with a spotlight. Then the spot suffuses to surround her bed. Then the room is lit normally. As the light becomes normal, voices and steps can be heard coming from the hallway outside the patient's room. There is a horsing around, some overly loud conversation mixed with flirting and innuendo. First to come into Mrs. Riegel's room, backing in, is Eliot "Stony" Marcher, MD, chief staff resident at Jefferson Davis, a public teaching hospital somewhere along the Texas Gulf Coast. Behind him, entering convulsed with exaggerated laughter, is Gale Cordell, a registered nurse.

STONY: "Dr. Doom."

GALE: "Dr. Doom"?

STONY: Why not?

GALE: You're crazy, Stony Marcher.

STONY: It's a good name for the fabled "King of the Geriatrics."

GALE: Maybe so, but nobody else would be fool enough to say it to his face. Maybe that's why he kicked.

STONY: It was time. The old aristocrat held back progress as long as he could.

GALE: You're lucky he didn't go to the Resident Evaluation Committee.

STONY: Kings don't "go" to committees. Anyway, what were the Shitflows gonna do, shorten my hem?

GALE: They might want to shorten *something*.

STONY: Mentor Marsha wouldn't let 'em.

GALE: Dr. LeMarque doesn't run things around here.

STONY: Maybe now she will.

(Patsy Winstone, a female med student employed as an RN, comes into the room.)

GALE: Uh-oh. *(She starts out of the room.)*

STONY: It's OK, Gale. Patsy's another card-carrying member of the working class. She's on our side.

GALE: I got things to do anyway. *(She goes.)*

PATSY: I *was* on your side. But I'm beginning to think this whole thing was a big mistake. (*Pause as she glances at Mrs. Riegel.*) This lady is *still* eating through a tube, and nothing has been decided.

STONY: Welcome to the limbo of lost hope. We like to call it "Geriatrics."

PATSY: I don't care what you call it—I just want to be able to present this for clerkship credit.

STONY: Patsy, Patsy, you're gonna make it. Just follow me, do what I do.

PATSY: And what will that get me?

STONY: Would you settle for national renown as a diagnostician?

PATSY: I'd settle for a usable case for my ethics presentation.

STONY: You don't have to impress the psychobabs. You've got it and they don't.

PATSY: Sure I do.

STONY: Nope. You've got it and they don't.

PATSY: It?

STONY: The Right Stuff. I'm going to see to it that you're the best female clinician in the wholly undistinguished and entirely forgettable history of Jefferson Davis.

PATSY: Give it a rest, Stony.

STONY: "Watch me, Tess. Learn from me."

PATSY: That's what you said five weeks ago.

STONY: I know, and the status is still quo. But patience, my dear . . .

PATSY: But I don't have the time.

STONY: Just a little longer. We've gotta keep up the charade. In-and-out, will-she-won't-she . . .

PATSY: The write-up is due next week.

STONY: That's cool. The case conference is this afternoon.

PATSY: You're kidding. You are kidding, right?

STONY: I sense med student anxiety.

PATSY: With LeMarque? Today? Why didn't you call me?

STONY: Cause I'm still dating Kathleen.

PATSY: Dammit, Stony, you know what I mean.

STONY: Look, Patsy, I didn't know until yesterday. Since we're kind of in a hurry to, uh, terminate this case, I decided a blitzkrieg might be more effective.

PATSY: You mean while what's-her-name—the aide—is on leave?

STONY: The dreaded Wynn Brooks. Yeah. You're starting to catch on to the Marcher Method.

PATSY: But what about my preparation? I don't have time to go through all this. (*Picks up and gestures to the chart.*) Is it true what they say about LeMarque? You're her fair-haired boy, aren't you?

STONY: Heh, I'm everybody's fair-haired boy. Anyway, if we play our cards right, we'll get this thing over with and everybody will be a winner.

PATSY: Just tell me what to do and what to say.

STONY: Compliance. That's what I like in my patients . . .

PATSY: And your women. Yeah, I know. Let's get on with it. We have to meet LeMarque in less than an hour.

STONY: OK, here's the drill. First we put the NG tube in and feed her. Then we'll need Gale. (*Picks up and pushes the nurse call button.*)

PATSY: Why was it taken out?

STONY: She pulled it out. She's pulled it out maybe 80 times since I've been on this rotation. Every time they call me to come over and put it back in. But no more. This dead tree has been watered for the last time. Time to tend to the living.

GALE (*walking into the room, bored, tired, automatic*): May I help you? (*Sees Dr. Marcher with the button still in his hand.*) Oh. I wondered who could be pushing her button. I was on my way to lunch.

STONY (*with mock remonstrance*): Now, Gale, you know that you are here to serve and protect. She pull the tube out again this morning?

GALE: No. We took it out.

STONY: You took it out?

GALE: Yeah, so they could take some pictures.

PATSY: Pictures? You're kidding. Why would they want pictures at this point?

STONY: It's just a, you know, "precaution." Two doctors talk to each other, they want a new set of pictures, an update. See how things are changin'?

PATSY: Seems like a waste.

GALE: Seems like a lot of trouble.

STONY: Don't be testy, ladies. Those of us on the front lines gotta help radiology justify that research budget.

PATSY: What's the deal with these restraints? That wasn't part of the data we were given.

GALE: We just started with them. She kept pulling out the tube.

STONY: Terrific. I've been wondering why I haven't gotten any 3AM calls from the Geriatric wing.

GALE: Now we keep her in restraints even when the tube is out. It's easier for everybody.

STONY: Nice touch, Gale. Have you thought about a career in gerontology?

(*At this point, Stony and Gale force the NG tube into Mrs. Riegel's stomach. Mrs. Riegel struggles at first, but Stony calms her by getting her to "sing" "The Old Rugged Cross." She seems startled, betrayed by her own cooperation with the one asking her to sing. They step back from the bed.*)

STONY: OK, hang some formula, and I'll go talk to Mith Martha.

PATSY: You going to try to charm her with your rude and obnoxious ways?

STONY: You mean my manliness and rugged good looks. Nah, my macho charm's no good on her. But I got some other tricks up my sleeve. (*Looks at Mrs. Riegel.*) It won't be long now, Mrs. Riegel. (*He takes a spiral book on medical therapies out of his white coat pocket and reads over a page.*) As I estimate your caloric and mineral requirements, it shouldn't take more than . . . about a week, at the outside. Maybe less without *agua.* (*Looks up at Mrs. Riegel and putting the spiral book on her bedside table.*) I think you and Dr. Grangerford will make a fine, old-fashioned, high-toned antebellum couple.

PATSY: Don't we need a primary caregiver?

STONY: Nurse's Aide Level II G. Wynn Brooks, aka "St. Bernadette," thinks case conferences are bogus from the get-go. She doesn't trust D's.

PATSY: What are D's?

STONY: MDs, PhDs, any kind of D's. If she came, it would make things a lot harder. She'd start her "Live, live!" exhortations, and we'd never get anything decided.

PATSY: Well, where is she?

GALE: GW? She called in. She says, "I be sittin' for a lady for a couple of days."

PATSY: Baby-sitting?

GALE: No, some old fogey in her church. That's what they do when "somebody be about to pass."

STONY: I thought her son was in jail.

GALE: He probably is—Ezra, her youngest.

PATSY: What did he do?

GALE: He got messed up in some kinda gang killin'.

PATSY: Really?

STONY: Probably. Anyway, it doesn't matter why she's off, just so she stays gone long enough for us to get this thing decided.

PATSY: So who's going to be there?

(*Stony looks at Gale. Then Patsy looks at Gale.*)

GALE: I gotta take time outta *my* lunch break? No way.

STONY: Come on, Gale, it's worth it if we can get this one OTD.

GALE: You don't need a nurse—I never had to go before. Wynn just went to stir up trouble.

STONY: Yeah, and because of her, somebody decided that we have to have a primary caregiver present at every one of these. Very democratic and egalitarian. There's so many bleeding hearts around here, it's a wonder we're not all HIV-positive.

GALE: Look, I gotta go over to the cafeteria and get a salad. And then I gotta come back over here and hang her bag, and then . . .

STONY: No problem. Take your time. Just be there at two to say it's the right thing to do. (*Gale leaves the room; he calls after her.*) Hey! I owe you one.

PATSY (*after a pause as she looks over the chart*): Say Stony, Keith told me that your grandmother had Alzheimer's.

STONY: That's right. (*He looks around for his medical therapy spiral book, getting agitated, not looking Patsy in the eye.*) So do you have a problem with that?

PATSY: Well, I just wondered if Dr. LeMarque knew about your, uh, you know, personal experience.

STONY: You mean having to leave Yale for San Antonio State?

PATSY: Why are you getting mad at me?

STONY: If you had to live at home with Mom and Dad and share a room with drug-head brother Dave, you'd know why.

PATSY: Sorry I brought it up.

STONY: No sweat. (*Picks up the chart.*)

PATSY (*after a pause*): So, Dr. Marcher, what's this I hear about your heroics in the pediatric ICU?

STONY: Where'd you hear about that?

PATSY: Everybody's talking about how you came in and saved that little baby in the hot dog stand.

STONY: I think they were waiting for it to cook down a little before they added the mustard.

PATSY: Was it dehydrating?

STONY: They had a scalp line in, but the baby was crying so hard the IV was backed up. They didn't flush it out, and it clotted off.

PATSY: I heard she was seizing by the time you got there.

STONY: Yeah, and the dumbasses couldn't figure out why. One guy goes, "Uh, duh, why is that, uh, baby arching its back?"

PATSY: So you did a cut-down and saved the day. (*In a mock southern dialect*), "My hero."

STONY: Comes with the territory, ma'am.

(*There is an electronic tone from Stony's beeper.*)

PATSY: "Calling Dick Tracy." Are you wanted for another act of derring-do?

STONY: Probably. (*He takes out his voice-transmitting beeper.*) What is it?

SQUAWKY VOICE: Dr. Marcher, we're having trouble with an IV in the neonates.

STONY: Jesus wept, isn't there anybody over there who can handle a needle? All right, I'm on my way. (*Puts away the device.*) Let's go by there before we see LeMarque.

PATSY: It won't make us late?

STONY: (*offhandedly*): No, it'll take maybe 30 seconds. I can show you what a bunch of Bozos I've got working under me over there. Come on—it'll make you feel better to see how pathetic these scutmonkies are.

(*They walk out of the room together.*)

Scene 2: One hour later. Dr. LeMarque's office.

Dr. Marsha LeMarque is at her desk dictating Mrs. Riegel's case. While she tries to organize her thoughts, she becomes progressively more nervous, eventually succumbing to the craving for a cigarette. She keeps a few hidden in her desk for the inevitable emergencies, which seem to arise 6–10 times each day. She smokes with a water filter designed to reduce the tar intake. She enjoys a few puffs during her conversation with her college friend but hurriedly pulls open a drawer, stubs out the cigarette in an ashtray concealed in the desk, and brings out an aerosol can of generic hospital air freshener, which she sprays wildly around the room, when she hears a knock at the door. In one motion she returns the can to the drawer, slams it shut, and waves the deodorizer mist away from her face before telling Stony and Patsy to come in.

LEMARQUE: Come in.

STONY: Excuse me, Dr. LeMarque, is now a bad time?

LEMARQUE: No, no, Stony, uh, Patsy. Now is fine. (*Strides around to the front of her desk.*) We've got to get over to the conference room anyway, don't we?

STONY: No, not really. One of the primary caregivers can't come, and I told Gale, who has the 7–3 shift, that we would meet in your office . . . if that's OK, of course.

LEMARQUE: Sure, sure. That's fine. Should we wait for her?

STONY: We probably ought to get started. She was, uh, going to feed Mrs. Riegel when I left.

LEMARQUE: *Feed* her?

STONY: You know, with the NG tube.

LEMARQUE: Oh yes, of course. I was just dictating the report. Why don't you present the case, Dr. Marcher, and we'll take it from there.

STONY: Sure. I just came from seeing the patient. Let's see. (*Adopts a deadpan, scientific tone of voice.*) Mrs. Sybil Dean Riegel, a 90-year-old white female, was brought by ambulance to the Jeff Davis ER three years ago. She was disoriented times three and had no ID. It was determined that the patient had fallen and fractured her right hip. An operation was performed and was successful. Three weeks postop the patient was transferred to extended care, where she remains today. For the last three years she has been fed through an NG tube. (*At this point, Gale comes into the room. Dr. LeMarque indicates that she should sit down. Dr. Marcher continues his report. Gale sits down somewhat nervously and is visibly ill-at-ease with the "doctor talk" through-*

out the presentation of the case.) She verbalizes the desire to have the tube removed and has repeatedly removed the tube herself. Her personal physician passed away in December without communicating his decision about the tube. However, a do-not-resuscitate order has finally been placed on the patient's chart, and the patient continues the classic downward curve characteristic of AD.

LEMARQUE: Thank you, Dr. Marcher. Uh, Ms. Winstone, what other information do we have on her current status?

PATSY: BP, 112/60; P72, R18, T98; white blood count, 9700, hemoglobin, 12.4; hematocrit, 37; adequate platelets. Weight, 110; height, 5'2". Chest x-ray and EKG are both unremarkable.

LEMARQUE: What about nutrition?

PATSY: 1300–1500 calories per day of Osmolite with additional free water, supplemented by multiple vitamins, zinc, and iron. Patient's weight has fluctuated, initially gaining, then stable, recently losing, now stable again.

LEMARQUE: Physical findings?

PATSY: Her physical exam is unremarkable, lungs are clear, no heart murmur, no tender abdomen, no palpable masses, negative rectal exam, warm dry skin with no breakdown, although she does have abrasions.

LEMARQUE: What about her extremities?

PATSY: Her extremities . . . have good pulses and no edema. There is marked muscle wasting and slight flexion contractures of both knees and elbows.

LEMARQUE: And the hip.

PATSY: A Dawson-Moore hip prosthesis placed three years ago.

LEMARQUE: Neurologically?

PATSY: Neurological exam is incomplete due to extreme dementia, inability to follow commands, blindness, and global confusion . . . otherwise unremarkable.

LEMARQUE: Fine, Ms. Winstone. Very good. Dr. Marcher, anything else?

STONY: Patient incontinent of urine and stool.

LEMARQUE: Family situation?

STONY: Widowed, childless, impoverished.

LEMARQUE: Good. Thank you both for a thorough presentation. Now, Gale, I, uh, appreciate your coming over for this conference. I'm sorry that the night nurse couldn't be here.

GALE: She had something come up. Personal business.

LEMARQUE: Well, I'm sure you have talked to her and can represent the nurses' point of view.

GALE: Sure. That's what I'm here for.

LEMARQUE: Good. Are you aware that new hospital policy requires that a primary caregiver be present during ethics case conferences?

GALE: That's what Dr. Marcher told me about an hour ago.

LEMARQUE: Well, we appreciate your participating, Gale, especially on such short notice. Now, uh, do you have anything to add to Dr. Marcher's presentation?

GALE: Not really. He said all there is to say. She wants the tube out. That's about it.

LEMARQUE: You are sure of that?

GALE (*defensively*): What do you mean?

LEMARQUE: Well, how do you know she wants the tube out?

GALE: She says, "Out, out," all the time and sings hymns about how she wants to go be with Jesus.

LEMARQUE: I see. Does she pull the tube out herself?

GALE: It's like Dr. Marcher says, she pulls it out all the time, whenever she gets the chance.

LEMARQUE: The chance?

STONY: Yeah, they've recently started using restraints.

LEMARQUE: Oh really? Why, uh, why weren't they used before? (*Stony shrugs.*) Gale?

GALE: Well, Dr. Grangerford, he wouldn't stand to have any of his patients in restraints. But since he died . . . Dr. Marcher says we're supposed to keep the patient from hurting himself. And now . . .

LEMARQUE: Yes?

GALE: Well, I just mean that something is supposed to be decided.

LEMARQUE: And what do you think we should decide, Gale?

GALE (*looking at Stony*): Well, if you're asking me, I'd have to say that we ought to just let her go. Nothing's changed since I came to work here two years ago.

LEMARQUE: What is your opinion of the restraints?

GALE: I just don't think that it's right to keep her tied down so we can fill her up with baby formula every 8 hours.

LEMARQUE: And what about the nurse's aide, uh (*checks her chart*), G. Wynn Brooks? What does she believe?

(*Stony's beeper goes off.*)

STONY: That's for you, Gale. I told them to beep me over here when they needed you back on the floor. If that's OK, Dr. LeMarque. I think I can fill you in on the rest of the medical facts.

LEMARQUE: Yes, that's fine. Thank you so much for taking time out of your busy day to visit with us, Gale. You have been most helpful.

GALE: All right. (*She gets up to go out.*)

STONY: Good-bye, Gale. (*He stands up and closes the door behind Gale. He closes it a bit rudely, a bit too hard.*)

LEMARQUE: Anything the matter, Dr. Marcher?

STONY: Oh, it's nothing. Let's see. Where were we?

LEMARQUE (*changing to a more conversational tone*): No, really. What's happened, Stony?

STONY: Nothing. Nothing's happened—that's just it. (*He gets more frustrated.*) We're going nowhere with this case. I mean, this is pure . . . (*He pauses.*) It's just so frustrating to have to tell the nursing staff that nothing's been decided.

LEMARQUE: Well, it *is* frustrating. We all feel the same way. It's been a difficult one. What are your feelings about the case, Patsy?

PATSY: Well, the first thing I thought was "How did you end up getting an Alzheimer's patient with an NG tube?" It's like your worst nightmare.

LEMARQUE: It has been, believe me. But when Dr. Grangerford died just before Christmas, I guess I was susceptible because of the season. Anyway, I just took them.

PATSY: How many?

LEMARQUE: Four, counting that black man who died in March.

STONY: All AD's.

LEMARQUE: Yes.

PATSY: Wow. Didn't you feel imposed on?

LEMARQUE: Yes, as a matter of fact. We just don't have the resources at Jeff Davis. I remember picking up the chart and thinking, uh-oh, an Alzheimer's patient with an NG tube.

STONY: Well, when was it evaluated? (*Pause.*) It has been evaluated, hasn't it?

LEMARQUE: I'm not really certain it has. Dr. Grangerford wasn't there for us to ask questions. I just keep thinking, what if she was my mother? Or what if I'm in that situation someday? It's pitiful to have someone, especially a woman, tied down like that.

PATSY: Doctor, uh, our instructor said that restraints are pretty routine in geriatric care. It's not supposed to be that unusual.

LEMARQUE: I know, I know. (*She stares blankly.*)

STONY (*taking a quick glance at Patsy*): Well, of course, it's not my place to make the decision. But maybe we could remove the restraints—wouldn't that be consistent with policy?

LEMARQUE: Sure, we could do that. But then she'd pull the tube out.

STONY: Maybe that's the answer anyway. I mean, some kind of effort needs to be made to . . . to wean her off the tube.

LEMARQUE: Yes, but Stony, it's been two years—almost three now. She's forgotten how to eat, how to swallow.

STONY: People get it back. And even if she doesn't eat again—maybe that's her choice to make.

LEMARQUE: But we don't know what Mrs. Riegel's wishes would be, so you can't . . .

STONY: Don't you think there's a natural course of events that would just proceed naturally if we didn't intervene.

PATSY: One of the aides wanted to try a baby bottle, but I don't know.

LEMARQUE: Yes, the night nurse. She left a note on my machine. She didn't sound particularly bright.

STONY: It's Mrs. Brooks. She's not bright—in any sense of the word. She's infamous among the residents.

LEMARQUE: Is she incompetent?

STONY: Not really, not in the usual sense, anyway. It's just that she's got her own notions about patient care. It's like she's untamed. You tell her to do something, she'll just stall around or disappear—unless *she* thinks its a good idea.

LEMARQUE: Is she uncooperative?

STONY: Worse. She's "noncompliant." Tenacious, too. We're lucky she didn't show up.

LEMARQUE: Why don't I know this Mrs. Brooks?

STONY: She's around. Kind of a fat black lady? Lets out her breath like she's being strangled.

LEMARQUE: I can't place her.

STONY: Remember the hassle last year with Mr. Moody's heirs? She was the cause of that whole thing.

LEMARQUE: So that was her.

PATSY: Isn't she supposed to have some kind of special relationship with the patient?

STONY: She thinks she has a special relationship with every patient. That's the problem. Everybody's in her family, like she's related to the whole damn world. She's not on the team. That's why she's always coming up with something out of left field. Like that baby bottle idea.

LEMARQUE: Technically, a bottle could be a possibility.

STONY: You've gotta be kidding. A bottle is no better than a tube.

LEMARQUE: Well, you're probably right. In any case, it's already been tried.

STONY: And it didn't work, right?

LEMARQUE: Right. She wouldn't take the nipple.

STONY: Would you, if you were her?

LEMARQUE: Probably not. It would just seem too demeaning.

STONY: Exactly. It's like a total reversion to infancy.

LEMARQUE: And dependency. I mean, speaking as a physician and as a woman, I wouldn't want it. What about you, Patsy?

PATSY: Do you mean, would I want a nurse's aide feeding me from a nipple?

LEMARQUE: Yes, it seems to me that that's the question. Here's this woman, this elderly woman who's surely had a family and dignity. And now they want to take away your independence and autonomy, too.

PATSY: I agree. I wouldn't want to go on in that way.

STONY: So we're all agreed that Mrs. Brooks is out to lunch: no baby bottle. We had a primary caregiver here for the conference, one with a lot more sense. I don't think we need to worry about some plan cooked up by a nurse's aide.

PATSY: But what's the family member going to say?

LEMARQUE: That I don't know. She seemed really confused and indecisive over the phone.

STONY: I bet we can get permission. She'll probably go along with our decision.

PATSY: I guess there was no Living Will.

LEMARQUE: No.

PATSY: Maybe she has a durable power of attorney?

LEMARQUE: I don't think so, but maybe something can be worked out. I'm supposed to meet with the niece this evening. She's driving in from Beaumont after she gets off work.

STONY: What are you going to tell her?

LEMARQUE: I don't know . . . I'm going to drop in on Mrs. Riegel before she gets here. Maybe I'll learn something. (*Pause.*) Thank you, Dr. Marcher, Ms. Winstone. I will give you my decision tomorrow.

Scene 3: 10 minutes later. The Residents' Lounge.

Stony and Patsy join three young resident physicians, Doug, Jenn, and Keith, who are seated in the sterile chairs characteristic of vending machine snack bars. They are in their late 20s or early 30s. Doug, a fourth-year resident, is married, but Jenn and Keith are still single. Stony walks in, buys a root beer for himself and a Diet-Pepsi for Patsy. They exchange the rough banter characteristic of the resident subculture of a large urban teaching hospital, each speaker seemingly less sympathetic toward patients and more cynical than his predecessor.

STONY: You guys don't mind if I bring Patsy in for a second, do you? It looks like we're finally going get Mrs. Riegel OTD. Patsy Winstone, meet the God Squad.

KEITH: Hi.

PATSY: "The God Squad"?

DOUG: Yeah. We just *play* doctor.

KEITH: So what's the story on the Riegel case?

STONY: "Waiting for Godot."

JENN: Riegel? Is that the AD with the tube?

STONY: You got it. (*To Patsy*): You did OK in there, Patsy. What are you drinking, babe?

PATSY: Just a Coke would be fine.

STONY (*Greek accent*): "No Coke, just Pepsi."

PATSY (*accepting a Diet Pepsi; she is in the presence of her superiors*): Thanks.

KEITH: How'd you end up with her?

STONY: I don't know. I've been thinking, it must be fate or a tragic flaw.

DOUG: I thought she was supposed to be your ethics case.

JENN: "Ethics case"? Is this something new?

DOUG: Yeah. You know, the death and dying stuff the psychobabble people cooked up for the third-years.

KEITH: So what did you tell "The Market"?

STONY: I told her that we ought to untie the old lady and let her pull the tube out.

JENN: Then what?

STONY: Then we offer her an Egg McMuffin and call the morgue.

(*The group laughs.*)

JENN: I love it when you talk dirty.

KEITH: He's right, though. I mean, that superannuated babe has been circling the drain for—how long's it been?

DOUG: Three years. I had her when I was a first-year under Grangerford.

JENN: What was the deal with him?

DOUG: Nothing—just maintenance. He was too busy maintaining his upright demeanor and refining his senility to help her along.

KEITH: Why'd they tube her in the first place?

DOUG: I don't know. Some nurse said that she came from the ER that way. Something about finding her back over on Dowling with a dachshund. The dreaded "sundown syndrome"—she got agitated and wandered off.

STONY: Yeah, she took her dog out on a leash and then fell and broke her hip. No ID when she came in. Disoriented, incontinent—but the doggie did his doo-doo in the right place.

DOUG: Oh yeah, now I remember. She was lost and nobody knew who she was, but they traced the dog's rabies tags, and the vet gave them her name and address.

JENN: No family.

DOUG: A husband, but he was non compos, too.

STONY: Not anymore. Now he's dead.

DOUG: Cancer?

STONY: No. Hung himself last December. Right after Grangerford did the tuna.

PATSY: What's this "tuna" stuff?

STONY: Have you ever been deep-sea fishing?

PATSY: Not really.

STONY: Well, if you catch a tuna, they flip and flop around and gasp for breath and generally make a big mess of your boat. That's what happened to Mr. Riegel.

KEITH: Yeah, but at least he was post-tuna by the time they got him to the ER.

STONY: That's why suicide is such a blessing.

JENN: Yeah, when you're on call, successful suicides are the only thing to look forward to. At Christmas time we always get a few extra Yule Logs for the fire.

STONY (*puckering*): Say, do you kiss Ted with that same mouth?

JENN: In your dreams, Dr. Marcher.

(*They all laugh.*)

Scene 4: Early evening, same day. Mrs. Reigel's room.

(*Night nurse's aide, Mrs. Wynn Brooks, comes into Mrs. Riegel's room humming "Amazing Grace."*)

MRS. BROOKS: Mrs. Riegel? Mrs. Sybil Dean Riegel? How are you doing tonight, Sybil Dean? (*Pauses.*)

(*Mrs. Riegel groans and starts to talk inarticulately: "Wah, wah, wah . . . wah, wah, wah."*)

MRS. BROOKS: Fine, thank you. Can you squeeze my hand, Sybil Dean? (*Pause.*) Good. That's real good. Not too hard now. I got to bathe you after while. I know that Gale didn't give you a bath. I swear, I don't know what would happen to you if I wasn't here. You never would get your mouth cleaned up and your back warshed. (*Goes to the table and opens a glycerine swab.*) I know you don't like this, but we got to keep your lips moist and your gums clean, don't we? (*Swabs her mouth while Mrs. Riegel shakes her head gently from side to side.*) I swear, you're just as bad as that little grandbaby of mine. She be bobbin' and dodgin' around just like you. (*Throws the swab away.*) You feel like singin' tonight? How 'bout "Were You There?" No, that's too glum. I feel good tonight; my Ezra done got out of jail. They said he didn't have nothin' to do with that mess. Let's sing "Amazing Grace." Here we go now. (*She begins to hum. Mrs. Riegel begins to hum with her.*) . . . "that saved a wretch like me. I once was lost but now I'm found, was blind but now I see." All right. That sho makes me feel better. How 'bout you? (*Mrs. Riegel gets a bit agitated and tries to say, "Out, out . . . out, out." Mrs. Brooks gets a cloudy look but forces herself to be cheerful.*) I know you want that old tube out, Sybil Dean, 'specially this time of day, but we can't let you do that just yet. Now you set still 'till I can get back here with your supper. (*She goes out of the room humming "Amazing Grace."*)

(*Dr. LeMarque enters Mrs. Riegel's room shortly after Mrs. Brooks goes out. Mrs. Riegel becomes anxious and mumbles, "Out, out" or "ow, wow, wow" when Dr. LeMarque tries to interact with her.*)

LEMARQUE: Mrs. Riegel? My name is Dr. LeMarque. How are you feeling tonight?

MRS. RIEGEL: Wah, wah, wah. Wah, wah, wah.

LEMARQUE: How does that old tube feel? Is it hurting the inside of your nose? (*Moves the tube around to get a better look into Mrs. Riegel's nostrils.*)

MRS. RIEGEL: Out, out . . . out, out.

LEMARQUE (*patting her arms, restrained at the wrist, then leaning over the bed to hear better*): There there, Mrs. Riegel. Uh . . . were you trying to say something?

MRS. RIEGEL: Wah, wah, wah . . . out, out.

LEMARQUE: There, there, it's OK. You want out? Out of the bed? That's fine. I'll call a nurse, just a minute.

(*Mrs. Riegel becomes more agitated, reaches for the nasogastric tube, knocking a pen out of Dr. LeMarque's hand.*)

LEMARQUE (*groping nervously through the bedclothes and sheets for the pen.*): Oh, yes. The tube. You don't like it, do you?

MRS. RIEGEL (*louder now and more emphatically*): Out, out. . . .

LEMARQUE: (*finding the pen, steps away from the bed; now with a new sense of having made a decision*): All right, Mrs. Riegel. It's going to be all right. Maybe we should let you . . . make the decision for yourself. (*Her beeper goes off loudly. She jumps and then shuts it off.*) I'm sorry, Mrs. Riegel, I've got to be going now. But I will come see you a little later with your niece. She is anxious to see you again. So you just rest there and we'll be back just a little later.

(*She goes out. Mrs. Brooks comes in shortly after Dr. LeMarque leaves.*)

MRS. BROOKS: Well, now. That wasn't too long to wait, now was it? Here's your supper and your dessert. (*She hangs a container of formula.*) One of these days I'm going to try a bottle on you. I bet you could learn to like that if you would give it a chance. We could eat and sing all night long—have us a Easter party. We just got to find a way to get a piece of ham and some black-eyed peas through a nipple. (*She laughs and hums a new song.*)

Scene 5: Later that evening. Mrs. Riegel's room.

Marsha Lemarque, Mrs. Dunne (Mrs. Riegel's niece), Mrs. Riegel. Photographs projected on the back wall during Mrs. Dunne's recollection of Mrs. Riegel's past (as Mrs. Dunne hands old photos to Dr. LeMarque). Dr. LeMarque and Mrs. Dunne walk up to the door of Mrs. Riegel's room. Dr. LeMarque turns, half blocking the door.

LEMARQUE: Now, Mrs. Dunne, this is not going to be easy. Your aunt has been through a lot, and she may not know you. Are you sure you're all right?

MRS. DUNNE: Yes, Doctor.

LEMARQUE: Let's go in, then. (*They walk into the room.*)

MRS. DUNNE: Aunt Meem? Aunt Meem? It's Margie. Margie Dunne. Doctor, is she all right? She's so white, so old-looking . . .

LEMARQUE: It's OK, Mrs. Dunne. Your aunt seems to be resting comfortably.

MRS. DUNNE: But that tube, Doctor, going into her nose like that. How can she rest with that tube?

(*Mrs. Riegel starts to stir and tries to pull the tube out. Mrs. Dunne notices the wrist restraints.*)

MRS. DUNNE: She's tied down!

MRS. RIEGEL: Owww . . . Owww . . .

MRS. DUNNE: What's she saying, Doctor? What's the matter?

LEMARQUE: I think she's saying "Out, out." It's the tube.

MRS. DUNNE: Aunt Meem? Aunt Meem? It's Margie. Your niece, Margie Dunne. Don't you remember me, Aunt Meem? Look at her eyes, doctor: she's not showing anything.

LEMARQUE: I thought you knew . . . your aunt lost her sight about three years ago.

MRS. DUNNE: You mean, completely . . . ?

LEMARQUE: Yes, I'm afraid so—it was glaucoma, according to Dr. Granger-ford's notes.

MRS. RIEGEL: Oww . . . Woww . . . Oww. (*Reaches for the tube again.*)

MRS. DUNNE: She's just tied there—like an animal.

LEMARQUE: Mrs. Dunne, I know this must be a shock for you. But we had to see her. We had to see her so that you would know exactly what her condition is.

MRS. DUNNE: I thought I could do this, Doctor, but . . . I didn't know that she'd be . . . I didn't know about the plastic tube and all.

LEMARQUE: Please, come sit down, Mrs. Dunne. The NG tube was put in about three years ago.

MRS. DUNNE: Three years? To be . . . to have . . . a tube . . . like that.

LEMARQUE: That's why we need to discuss our options.

MRS. DUNNE: Our options?

LEMARQUE: Yes, we need to reach some kind of decision about your aunt's care.

MRS. DUNNE: Oh. (*Looks over at her aunt.*) I see.

LEMARQUE: Dr. Grangerford—he didn't really indicate how to proceed.

MRS. DUNNE: Oh yes, Dr. Grangerford. He called me once. He seemed like such a nice man—and a fine doctor.

LEMARQUE: Yes. But unfortunately he didn't indicate what he wanted to do.

DUNNE: Oh, I'm sure Dr. Grangerford would have, well, done everything possible.

LEMARQUE: I'm sure he did, Mrs. Dunne. But you see, when I agreed to take your aunt, I thought there was something we could do for her. But now . . .

MRS. DUNNE: She's not getting any better, is she?

LEMARQUE: No. (*Pause.*) You see, these patients can't speak for themselves. Your aunt can't say what she would have wanted. And without some guidance, some idea . . . (*Pause.*) Mrs. Dunne, did you ever have any conversation with your aunt about life support, a Living Will, anything like that?

MRS. DUNNE: No, I don't think so. Do you mean, would she want to be kept alive like this?

LEMARQUE: You see, she keeps pulling out her tube, as if she doesn't want to be fed.

MRS. DUNNE: Maybe she doesn't like the way it feels in her nose.

LEMARQUE: Well, there was a problem with the first tube. We had some breakdown. But without a tube . . . well, sufficient caloric intake would be difficult to maintain. Signs of malnutrition and/or dehydration would eventually develop, and then, without the institution of extraordinary procedures, some opportunistic infection . . .

MRS. DUNNE: She'd die?

LEMARQUE: Well, yes.

MRS. DUNNE: She'd starve herself to death?

LEMARQUE (*pausing while Mrs. Dunne looks over at her aunt*): You see, we were hoping that you could help, since you *are* the only living relative.

MRS. DUNNE: But I'm not the one—I'm not the legal guardian.

LEMARQUE: Well, the trust officer at the bank . . .

MRS. DUNNE: That's right. Miss Pilot handles all the legal matters.

LEMARQUE: Mrs. Dunne, you don't understand. Our protocol calls for the inclusion of a family member. Miss Pilot has made it clear that she cannot make medical decisions. It's not her place.

MRS. DUNNE: But why do I have to make the decision? It's not my place, either. We've just tried to stay out of it, completely. Uncle Bob was alive . . . and then, when we came over for the funeral, my husband said we had our own lives to lead, and not to get involved.

LEMARQUE: I understand, and I am really sorry this is falling on you. On either one of us. (*Pause.*) Do you have any idea what your *aunt* would have wanted?

MRS. DUNNE: Well, I mean, I've only seen Aunt Meem maybe three or four times in the last fifteen years. She came to my mother's funeral, and we used to send Christmas cards and all, but we just never got over here to see them.

LEMARQUE: I know this must seem sudden, but we really do need to make a decision. The tube's been in much too long.

MRS. DUNNE (*looking over at her aunt again*): I don't know. With the restraints and all—it's just such a horrible way to end your life.

LEMARQUE: Would you want to try an operation?

MRS. DUNNE: An operation? You mean more surgery?

LEMARQUE: Yes. We could try what we call a gastrointestinal tube.

MRS. DUNNE: Isn't that a gastro . . . tube?

LEMARQUE: No, this would be a tube going directly through the stomach wall.

MRS. DUNNE: Oh no, doctor. No more surgery. She wouldn't want that, I'm sure of it.

LEMARQUE: Well, Dr. Grangerford tried a nipple with formula once, but she wouldn't take the bottle, according to the chart.

MRS. DUNNE: You never knew my aunt, Doctor, but she was a very special kind of person—very aware of her appearance and all. She wouldn't want to be treated like a baby—to be fed like a helpless infant.

LEMARQUE: See, this is the kind of information that we need to help make an appropriate decision. What else can you tell me about her?

MRS. DUNNE: Well—wait a minute. I grabbed some old pictures before I left for work this morning.

(*She gets some photographs out of her purse. During the succeeding dialogue family snapshots of Mrs. Riegel and her family are projected on a back wall. While Mrs. Dunne is fumbling in her purse, Patsy comes up, looks over at Mrs. Riegel, and then hesitantly knocks on the open door.*)

PATSY: Dr. LeMarque?

LEMARQUE: Patsy. Still at work?

PATSY: I guess I should have asked you earlier. But I was wondering if I could sit in on the . . . conference.

LEMARQUE: Well, that would be up to Mrs. Dunne. Mrs. Dunne, this is Patsy Winstone. She's one of our best junior medical students.

MRS. DUNNE: Hello, doctor. I'm very glad to meet you.

PATSY: Hello, Mrs. Dunne.

MRS. DUNNE: Have you been taking care of Aunt Meem?

PATSY: Well, not exactly. But I have been studying your aunt's case for an ethics clerkship. I've looked in on her several times.

MRS. DUNNE: Well, it would be a great help to me . . . I just don't know what to do.

LEMARQUE: That's what this conference is for, Mrs. Dunne. Patsy, Mrs. Dunne was just about to provide the family background.

MRS. DUNNE: Yes, I brought these pictures. I thought maybe they might be helpful for you all. You've all been so nice. Taking an interest in Aunt Meem, and all.

(*Here, and as she recalls the memories of her aunt, she seems to be more or less in a reverie. The lights go down to indicate a change of mood and to make the slides more visible.*)

MRS. DUNNE: You see, Aunt Meem was the youngest—it was a big Catholic family. My mamma and daddy went back to live at the old home, where she was still staying with my grandmother. You know, in that day and time there were big houses, and families would live together. Aunt Meem was 17 when I was born. (*Shows picture*). She bobbed her hair then. It was the first and only time, but she always had to be in fashion; that's what mamma always said. I remember she wore earbobs, she called them. She used to let me try on her things.

PATSY: Was she married then?

MRS. DUNNE: No, not then, not till much later. Aunt Meem had to run the boardinghouse for my grandmother after she got too old. It was right over on Fannin. It used to be such a nice big house, with losts of people around— that's how I remember it. I guess they tore it down for some reason. There's one of those boxy-looking savings and loans there now. I drove by it on the way over here. Had to go by the street numbers; everything looked so different.

PATSY (*looking at photograph*): Is that her husband?

MRS. DUNNE: Yes, that's Uncle Bob. He was one of the boarders in the house before my grandmother died. He was from Canada, a real fine carpenter. He was always building things for me when I was a little girl—you know, doll-houses and little churches and things. And Aunt Meem—she just doted on me while I was growing up. She was like a mother to me . . . until we moved away.

LEMARQUE: What about religion? Did your aunt have strong religious beliefs?

MRS. DUNNE: Well, my husband and I don't get to church much anymore, but I just remember how beautiful Aunt Meem used to look when she would dress up and take us to Mass.

(*Patsy puts down the note pad, gets up, and goes over to Mrs. Riegel. She starts attending to her, being a nurse, checking her vital signs, reviewing the chart, making her comfortable. She continues to listen and pay attention to the conversation.*)

MRS. DUNNE: But she was always taking me places with her and Uncle Bob. We'd go down to the ferris wheel they used to have and on—they had what they called the Derby—and we'd ride on that. And there was fabulous ice cream places. We would go and get Dardenella—I think it had a little brandy in it. And Grandma Partlow used to make blackberry wine and made the most wonderful fruitcakes and the best fish chowder and coconut cake you ever tasted. And they had lovely furniture, lovely old velvet furniture, a lot of cherry wood. You can't even buy furniture like that now.

PATSY: My grandmother had some of that velvet furniture. I used to like to sit in one of her side chairs and just listen to everybody talk.

MRS. DUNNE: They had some furniture so ornate that they gave a bedroom suite (pronounced "suit"), a big armoire (pronounced "armor") with carved legs and all, to the Bishop's Mansion on Broadway.

LEMARQUE: Let's get back to your aunt's religious views. Did she go to church a lot?

MRS. DUNNE: Oh yes, she never missed. And when I would go down there to visit her before I got married, which was quite a few years ago—I've been married 48, going on 49 years—we would go to Mass and then go down to the seawall and ride a bicycle.

PATSY: I've got some pictures of my grandparents riding bicycles on the seawall.

MRS. DUNNE: Aunt Meem, Uncle Bob, and I, we'd rent bicycles from someplace down there on the boulevard, and then we'd just go to all sorts of different places and then have a big fish dinner. But then, like I say, we all began to live our different lives and so forth, and we didn't get back. . .

LEMARQUE: So the last time you saw her was after your mother died?

MRS. DUNNE: Yes. And then there were those other times when we were on the way to my son's house in San Antonio, and we would stop in. It was sort of depressing and kind of sad when I'd go, and we didn't really have communication. She would run off—she was always wanting to go home, she said. She would get her little dog—she loved her dog, she loved animals—and just start out. She'd say, "Come on, Cleo, time for us to be gettin' home." And then she'd start saying good-bye to *us*, like she was going to leave. I think she wanted to go back to the old home place.

PATSY: My grandparents moved out of their house, too. I still miss going over there on Sundays.

LEMARQUE: So you were aware that your aunt was confused about her whereabouts?

MRS. DUNNE: Yes. Oh yes. After my mother died and Aunt Meem started to wander, Uncle Bob found an apartment that was easier on him. He liked to putter around the old place, but he'd be up in the attic, or somewheres, and then he'd just come out and she'd be gone.

LEMARQUE: You know that he . . . that his death was ruled a suicide.

MRS. DUNNE: Yes. Miss Pilot told us. The money was running out.

LEMARQUE: And his own prognosis was not good. He had an inoperable neoplasm.

MRS. DUNNE: Well, I'm sure she didn't know. She couldn't have. God does work in strange ways.

LEMARQUE: What were your aunt's beliefs about life and death?

MRS. DUNNE: Well, as I say, she was a dyed-in-the-wool Catholic, and she believed in the Lord, and all, and I know she believed that her soul was secure. She even used to have little—I remember now—altar guild parties. Aunt Meem just did everything for that church, especially the parochial school. She was a volunteer teacher and helped with all the bake sales and everything. I think it was because she didn't have children of her own.

LEMARQUE: But Mrs. Dunne, did she ever talk to you about getting old, dying, that sort of thing?

MRS. DUNNE: Well . . .

LEMARQUE: What she would have wanted in a situation like this?

MRS. DUNNE: I don't think . . . If she could have had her own will, she wouldn't want to extend it. The more I think about it and talk about it, she just loved life so much, she wouldn't have wanted to suffer like this.

LEMARQUE: Did she ever say anything explicit about her illness?

MRS. DUNNE: I don't think she was aware of anything after she started to slip. I just never talked to her about getting old and, you know, the Oldheimer's. I think the last time she didn't even know us. That's when my husband said there was nothing more that we could do for her.

LEMARQUE: Can you tell me what— You said that you're fairly sure that she never would have wanted to be resuscitated or kept alive artificially.

MRS. DUNNE: Well, she always liked to dress up, and if she wasn't able to do things physically for herself, I think that would have been a great hurt to her.

LEMARQUE: So she was an independent person. That was important to her?

MRS. DUNNE: Oh yes, yes indeed. Very independent and full of life. I'm sure she wouldn't want the tube. I think she would rather go on in peace.

PATSY: But she's stable. She's still healthy. She's not dying.

LEMARQUE (to Patsy): But intake has not been ordinary or natural. The purpose of this conference . . . (now to Mrs. Dunne) what we need to decide . . . is what a woman like your aunt would want: whether she would want the tube removed.

MRS. DUNNE: Well, if you take it out, I don't know how the hunger pains would be. Would she suffer a great deal?

LEMARQUE: No. We could make sure that she was comfortable.

MRS. DUNNE: You mean, you could give her something to alleviate that. Like a B_{12} shot or something.

LEMARQUE: Don't worry, Mrs. Dunne. We have many pharmaceutical choices. She would not be in pain.

MRS. DUNNE: Well. I feel she would be relieved if she could go in peace. That's probably why she's not eating.

PATSY: Can you be sure, Mrs. Dunne?

MRS. DUNNE: Yes. She was my aunt. I am sure.

LEMARQUE: You think that would have been her preference? To die with dignity?

MRS. DUNNE: Yes, that's right. To go in peace. She just loved life and loved people, and if she knew she was tied up in a bed like that, it would have been a sad feeling to her. (*Turning directly to Dr. LeMarque*): You're the professional, Doctor. You know the situation. There's no hope of life ever being regained as normal, right?

LEMARQUE: That's right. The Alzheimer's is irreversible.

MRS. DUNNE: Well, then, Doctor, let's do it, let's let her go. She was such a gracious person. She wouldn't want to keep on this way.

ACT II

Scene 1: The next morning. Mrs. Riegel's room.

Mrs. Riegel is agitated and moaning. Patsy Winstone is standing over the bed observing the patient. Dr. Marcher comes in behind her with a spring in his step and gives the sides of Patsy's waist a squeeze with both hands. Patsy has changed her mind about the case. Stony and Patsy argue about the ethics conference decision. Patsy leaves; Stony releases Mrs. Riegel from the restraints. Dr. LeMarque arrives, assesses the situation, departs. The lights go down, with Stony and Gale huddled over Mrs. Riegel on either side of her bed. Gale is trying absentmindedly to feed her, but she is paying attention to Stony, and the food is getting on Mrs. Riegel's chin and chest. He continues talking about the plans for the next weeks—a "feeding" regimen and drugs and sedatives to give during Mrs. Riegel's anticipated decline.

Scene 2: One week later. Dr. LeMarque's office.

A week has passed. Marsha LeMarque takes a phone call from Gale: Mrs. Riegel still has strong vital signs. Stony strides in, openly listening in on the conversation. He is angry that Mrs. Brooks has been sneaking onto the floor to care for Mrs. Riegel, "turning the geriatric wing into a nursery." Dr. LeMarque agrees to reprimand the nurse's aide.

LEMARQUE: I'll go over there this evening and get this thing cleared up.

STONY: Good, because Mrs. Brooks's interference is taking its toll on everybody on the service. The sooner it's resolved, the better. If it were me, she'd be looking for another job. (*He starts to leave.*)

LEMARQUE: Uh, Stony. Before you go. Do, uh, you think this changes anything at all—I mean, this different feeding regimen.

STONY: You mean about our decision?

LEMARQUE: Well, yes.

STONY: How can it? We followed all the accepted procedures and reached a determination after an Ethics Case Conference. All parties were heard from, even the family. It was a joint decision agreed to by everyone—everyone except one nurse's aide who doesn't even have a high school diploma. She's not even remotely qualified to make a medical decision of this magnitude. (*Starts to leave again.*)

LEMARQUE: Yes, I know, but . . . she must be doing something right.

STONY: I beg to differ, Dr. LeMarque. She's doing everything wrong.

LEMARQUE: But she is able to feed her. She seems to be the only one who can. She's keeping Mrs. Riegel alive.

STONY: No. You mean, Mrs Riegel is trying to die, and Wynn Brooks won't let her.

LEMARQUE: Are we sure, right now, that Mrs. Riegel wants her life to come to an end?

STONY: What life? Mrs. Riegel has no life—her life already has come to an end. Read the literature on these cases. She's terminal. She may be biologically tenacious, but she's still dead, anyway you look at it.

LEMARQUE: Well, she's not really terminal.

STONY: But she's totally incapable of human interaction. You've seen her. She's begging to die.

LEMARQUE: You have a reputation as a diagnostician. Should we classify her as one of the "living dead"?

STONY: "Living dead," "nearly dead," "newly dead," whatever. The point is, she's dead, or might as well be.

LEMARQUE: So you're saying we should let her die or—make sure she dies. I'm not sure that I'm comfortable with that.

STONY: I'm just saying that we developed a policy, a course of action, and established procedures—and we shouldn't lose our nerve just because some uppity aide with a GED has made things more complicated.

LEMARQUE: More complicated. Yes indeed, it does seem more complicated now.

STONY: Not really. If we keep her alive, we're just wasting staff time and resources.

LEMARQUE: But our first obligation is to the patient.

STONY: Excuse me, Dr. LeMarque, but in a case like this, that's nothing more than a platitude. We ought to be spending our time with people we've at least got a chance to cure.

LEMARQUE: But Stony, don't you have *any* doubts?

STONY: Nope. I mean, either you trust and abide by your procedures or you don't.

LEMARQUE: Yes . . .

STONY: She's free-lancing. If it was a resident, he'd probably be reprimanded, thrown off the service, maybe prosecuted.

LEMARQUE: OK, I think I see . . .

STONY: She's enforcing her own will on the patient.

LEMARQUE: So you think she's being paternalistic?

STONY: Sure. I mean, look at the ethics course in med school. The first thing we learn is about the evils of physician paternalism and the importance of patient autonomy. What Mrs. Brooks is doing is pure paternalism—it goes against the wishes of the family, the physician, the other caregivers, and the patient herself. She's the one who kept saying, "Out, out." And she's the one who took the tube out in the first place.

LEMARQUE (*staring quietly, contemplating something, then rousing herself back to the present situation*): You've taken a special interest in this case from the beginning, haven't you?

STONY: I suppose so.

LEMARQUE: Any special reason?

STONY: Well, yes, as a matter of fact. My grandmother had Alzheimer's.

LEMARQUE: Oh no. I didn't know that. Was it difficult for your family?

STONY: You bet it was. The whole thing basically killed my grandfather. He just closed himself off from everybody.

LEMARQUE: Was he taking care of her?

STONY: Yeah, as best he could. Until Gramma got sick, he used to take me out. We'd go fishing on his farm or ride horses down to the bottoms or maybe just fix some fences or shell some corn. But all that stopped.

LEMARQUE: He wasn't able to cope.

STONY: Oh, he coped OK. He coped by stopping everything else. You might say he "coped out." And his big trust fund. That was just like Gramma, too, disappearing little by little. So I watched that disease take all three. And when it was over, nothing was left. No grandmother, no grandfather, no money. Ten years of total hell, and then it was over and they were gone. He sold the farm and everything else of value—stocks, CDs, even an old baseball card collection that belonged to my father. The college fund for me and my brother was depleted, and I had to transfer to San Antonio State. It's a miracle that any med school would have me.

LEMARQUE: What happened to your grandfather?

STONY: Died about six weeks after Gramma. When he was able to look up from his nursing, he saw that there was nothing left for him to live for either. That's the reason I told the admissions committee that I wanted to be a doctor, not a nurse. I didn't want to be a caretaker for the dying. I wanted to make people well.

LEMARQUE: Is that why you wanted pediatrics?

STONY: Yeah, either peeds or surgery. I hate death and I hate losing. That's why I'm good at what I do. I can't stand the ambiguity of internal medicine, and family practice—gimme a break. At least you can make most of the *kids* get better. They're young—there's some kind of hope. They've got another fifty years of productive life ahead of them. I mean, what's an AD got? Ten, maybe fifteen years of progressive hell—and they put everybody else through hell, too. No thank you. You can have your geriatrics. I mean, look at it: you can't restore health, you can't restore function; if you save a life, what are you saving it for? You can't even give them education or counseling 'cause they can't understand what you're saying.

LEMARQUE: Yes, but you can relieve symptoms and suffering. You can avoid harm.

STONY: But what happens when the symptom is AD dementia, when the suffering is just being kept alive? Go ahead, Dr. LeMarque. You want to relieve symptoms, you want to avoid harm? Then let her go. She's ready. Let her die.

Scene 3: That night. Mrs. Riegel's room.

Dr. LeMarque walks into Mrs. Riegel's room. She checks the patient's vital signs. She looks around and in drawers for some evidence of the "crime." Then she finds a chair and moves it into an unlit part of the room, behind a curtain that can be drawn around Mrs. Riegel's bed; from that vantage point she can observe the scene. After a short while Mrs. Brooks comes in.

MRS. BROOKS: Well, how are you doing this evening, Miss Sybil Dean? I'm doing fine, thank you, but that youngest boy of mine has been giving me fits again. But I'm going to raise that boy right if it's the last thing I do. You know, the world has changed since you and me was growing up. You right about that. It sure has changed. (*She goes about the room, tidying up, never seeing Dr. LeMarque.*) Come on, let's get you up in this chair. They think you going to die, but you not going to die 'long as I'm taking care of you. (*Mrs. Riegel shuffles to a chair near the bed with Mrs. Brooks's help.*) Now, let's see how strong you are. Squeeze my hand. No, I mean squeeze it hard. That's right, that's right. Oh my Lordy, you got a powerful grip. Now how about your heart? Let's see how its doing. (*She takes Mrs. Riegel's pulse and listens to her breathing by putting her head up against Mrs. Riegel's chest. Mrs. Riegel's left arm comes up to lightly embrace her head.*) That's right, you go ahead and give me a hug, and I'll give you one, too. Are you ready for your supper? I bet you got some appetite tonight, probably thirsty, too. Well, I got something for you, just like always. I'm here to take care of you, Miss Sybil. You know *that* now. (*She goes to her purse and takes out three half-finished infant bottles of formula. She wipes off the nipple of one and brings it over to Mrs. Riegel.*) I know, I know. Don't take it too fast, now. You know it makes you get sick if you takes it too fast. (*Mrs. Riegel starts to take the formula.*) There now, I told you it was going to be all right. (*Pause.*) It's like I was saying yesterday, we just got to make do the best way we can. And if you don't feel like eating from a spoon, I don't mind feeding you out of a bottle. (*Hums a quiet song and attends to Mrs. Riegel, combing her hair and showing her affection. Eventually, Mrs. Riegel finishes the first bottle.*) I believe you're still hungry, aren't you? Well, let me get you some dessert. But you know it's going to taste 'bout like the main cou'se. (*Mrs. Brooks turns to the formula and the bottles, carefully putting the used bottle back in her purse wrapped in tissue. When she turns back, Dr. LeMarque has come into the light and is assuming a confrontational stance. Mrs. Brooks is taken aback.*) Whoa! Lordy, Doctor, you 'bout scared me to death.

LEMARQUE: Yes, Mrs. Brooks, I suppose I would be frightened too if I had been doing what you have been up to.

MRS. BROOKS: You scared me. I didn't say I was frightened.

LEMARQUE: Aren't you ashamed of yourself? If we weren't so shorthanded in the nursing department, I would have you fired even as we speak.

MRS. BROOKS: You do what you gotta do, Doctor. But I ain't frightened and I ain't ashamed.

LEMARQUE: Didn't Dr. Marcher speak to you about this?

MRS. BROOKS: He come around here, try to scare me.

LEMARQUE: What did he do?

MRS. BROOKS: He do the po-lice in different voices.

LEMARQUE: The police? What do you mean?

MRS. BROOKS: He say one thing, then somethin' else. Talkin' 'bout how bad this is and what's gonna happen. Tryin' to make me ashamed.

LEMARQUE: Well, you should be ashamed. Sneaking away from your floor, ignoring the orders moving you.

MRS. BROOKS: Yes ma'am, they give me those transfers to 4LP. But I got my own orders and my own chart, and they says to feed Miss Sybil. You see, I got some friends in the neonates. The ICU. Those poor little babies don't never take all their supper, and so they gives me what's left over. Miss Sybil, she likes it real good. And they just be throwing it out over there anyway.

LEMARQUE: Do you realize that that formula is not sterile?

MRS. BROOKS: Course I know it's not sterile. But the food I eat ain't sterile. And Miss Sybil, she don't seem to mind.

LEMARQUE: What gives you the right to come in here and countermand a physician's orders? You are in violation of this hospital's code of ethics. Don't you care about other people's rights?

MRS. BROOKS: Rights? This ain't about rights, Doctor, this is between me and Miss Sybil. Where I come from, the Disciples, they got rights, and they put you off the sidewalk. The Blackstone Rangers, they got rights, and they knock you down. I don't care nothing about "rights."

LEMARQUE: Look, Mrs. Brooks, I respect your position on this matter. I can tell you, this was not an easy decision to make. We contacted the family, the legal guardian, anyone and everyone who was appropriate.

MRS. BROOKS: You didn't call me. I woulda told you 'bout Miz Sybil.

LEMARQUE: I beg your pardon, Mrs. Brooks, but you were contacted. You just didn't show up when we scheduled the case conference.

MRS. BROOKS: You doctors just waited till you knew I couldn't come so I wouldn't raise no fuss. I know how such things are done.

LEMARQUE: I can assure you, Mrs. Brooks, no such attempt was made to exclude you from what was a very difficult, very painful process. But the point is, a decision was made, steps were taken, and you have refused to keep up your obligation as an employee. You are being paid to do your job as assigned, and your job is not on this floor.

MRS. BROOKS: I'm not doing no job when I take care of Miss Sybil. She's my friend, and that's why I take care of her. I'd do the same thing for any of my friends, and she'd do the same for me if she could. Ain't that right, Miss Sybil? Yes sir, we take care of each other, don't we?

LEMARQUE: Have you thought about how you would feel if you were in Mrs. Riegel's position? Wouldn't you want to be allowed to die with dignity? (*She gestures to take in the entire room*). Look at this—it's so . . . pitiful. No one would want to go on in such a humiliating state. This lady's life is over. Why won't you let her go in peace?

MRS. BROOKS: Cause she ain't gone yet, Doctor. She ain't gone for me. She waitin' on the good Lord to call her home, and he knows when the time is ripe. I loves her, and I know she loves me, don't you Miss Sybil? And I'm going to take care of her till she dies.

LEMARQUE: What makes you think that she even knows who you are?

MRS. BROOKS: Oh, she knows me, all right.

LEMARQUE: You might as well be a robot.

MRS. BROOKS: No, Doctor, you wrong about that. Plum wrong. Miss Sybil takes the food I gives her to eat, and nobody else can feed her without her choking and gaggin. Miss Sybil know I'm her friend. Then, after she eat, sometimes we talk and sing.

LEMARQUE: You sing?

MRS. BROOKS: Ain't nothin' wrong with singin'.

LEMARQUE: No, of course not. But you don't really think . . . I mean, she's not really listening.

MRS. BROOKS: No, she ain't listening. She singin'. We sing together, don't we, Miss Sybil? Sometimes we sing spirituals, but sometimes Miss Sybil, she likes them old-timey songs.

LEMARQUE: I'm sorry, Mrs. Brooks, but I simply cannot acccept your interpretation of this situation. You are obviously letting your personal values affect your professional judgment.

MRS. BROOKS: Come on now, Miss Sybil, let's show this doctor what all you can sing. (*Tries several songs, "Just a Closer Walk with Thee," "Amazing Grace," "Were You There?" without success.*)

LEMARQUE: Look, Mrs. Brooks, I'm not going to write you up, and you will not be reprimanded. But you must abide by the collective consensus and the approved policies and procedures, or you will be terminated. (*Pause, waiting for a response that does not come.*) Don't you think this poor woman should be allowed to die naturally? (*Pause.*) Don't you think she deserves a death with dignity? (*Pause.*) I just don't think it's right for us to continue to keep her alive merely for our own benefit or comfort, or to satisfy our personal value judgments.

(*Mrs. Riegel starts to get agitated.*)

MRS. BROOKS: Don't you talk that way in front of Miss Sybil, Doctor. You'll get her all upset. Come on now, honey, I know what you doing—you waiting for me to do your favorite. OK, but you got to help, cause I don't know all the words. Here we go now: "Daisy, Daisy, give me your answer do, / I'm half crazy, all for the love of you." (*Mrs. Riegel begins to pick up the tune after the first "Daisy." She gamely finishes the second line of the song.*) That's all I know of that song. I never heard that one, but Miss Sybil, she taught it to me.

LEMARQUE (*taken in by the spectacle*): Mrs. Riegel taught *you* that song?

MRS. BROOKS: She sho' did. She sings some more, somethin' 'bout ridin' "a bicycle built for two," but I haven't been able to figure out the rest. I'm working on it, though, ain't I, Sybil Dean?

LEMARQUE: What else can she sing?

MRS. BROOKS: Well, she like school and church songs, mainly. She like "Row, row, row your boat."

LEMARQUE (*moved*): Would you ask her to sing that one for me, please? Would you, Mrs. Brooks?

MRS. BROOKS: I sure will. Come on, now, Sybil Dean, let's you and me do "Row, row, row your boat" our special way. You ready? Here we go: "Row, row, row your boat, / Gently down the stream, / Merrily, merrily, merrily, merrily, / Life is but a dream."

(*Mrs. Riegel begins to nod her head in time to the beat, then to groan with the music. Then she and Mrs. Brooks sing together. Dr. LeMarque, dumbstruck, hesitates for a minute and then joins in the song. The lights go down; the round is completed. In the darkness the audience hears Dr. LeMarque say, as the last singer of the song, "Merrily, merrily, merrily, merrily, / Life is but a dream."*

Scene 4: A fortnight later. Mrs. Riegel's room.

Stony Marcher is conducting mock "rounds" for Patsy and the three residents. It has been clear for several days that Mrs. Riegel is near death. The group enters Mrs. Riegel's room to guess the "ETT," the Estimated Time to Tuna. Patsy is a somewhat reluctant member of the group and hangs back a bit. She looks at Mrs. Riegel while the others guess how much longer the patient will survive. Coming closer, Patsy announces that Mrs. Riegel has already died. Stony, caught off-guard and humiliated, is left alone in the room with his patient.

STONY (*looking down at her*): Well, Mrs. Riegel, you've finally evened it up, haven't you? Final score: Eliot Marcher, still brilliant if somewhat tarnished physician, 1. Sybil Dean Riegel, gracious lady, 1. A tie—or should we say, a dead heat. Pa-dum-pum. Well, all I can say is "Shantih Shantih Shantih." (*A tone sounds. Stony takes out his stethoscope and begins to listen. The tone sounds again, this time followed by a squawky voice: "Dr. Marcher, you're needed for an emergency in Pediatric Intensive Care." He takes the beeper out of his belt. Stony takes one last look at Mrs. Riegel and perhaps comes to see her as a person for the first time.*) Sorry, Sybil Dean, gotta run. I, uh . . . let's get together, OK? We'll do lunch. (*Into the beeper*): I'm on my way.

(*He leaves. As he does so, the light in the room begins to dim, but Mrs. Riegel's bed is still illuminated. Mrs. Brooks comes in and begins to pull a curtain around the bed. The curtain is sheer and translucent. Perhaps Mrs. Brooks pauses to take one last look at her friend. Perhaps she takes Mrs. Riegel's hand in hers or says very softly, "Goodbye, Miss Sybil." Then she finishes pulling the curtain around the bed and leaves. Now the larger spot fades, leaving only the smaller spot on Mrs. Riegel's head and shoulders. This light, rather than fading, becomes more intense, and Mrs. Riegel can be seen clearly through the closed sheer curtains. She remains visible until the house lights come up, signaling the end of the play.*)

11

Free to Die: Afterthoughts on *Primary Care*

Ronald A. Carson

'Tis grace hath bro't me safe thus far
And grace will lead me home.

Sybil Dean Partlow Riegel enters the lives of those entrusted with her care not by choice but by accident. In her 88th year, poor, living alone, and afflicted with Alzheimer's disease, Mrs. Riegel takes her dog for a walk, falls, fractures her hip, and is brought to a public hospital emergency room, disoriented and without identification. Following successful surgery to place a hip prosthesis, Mrs. Riegel is transferred to an extended care unit of the hospital, where she is fed through a nasogastric tube. She resists the tube feeding by saying she wants the tube out and by repeatedly removing it herself. Her condition worsens over the ensuing 3 years as a consequence of

Alzheimer's disease. When the director of the geriatric service dies unexpectedly, Dr. Marsha LeMarque assumes responsibility for Mrs. Riegel's care, along with Elliot Marcher, MD, a physician-in-training who reports to Dr. LeMarque. As the action begins, Dr. Marcher discovers that the geriatric nurses have recently placed Mrs. Riegel in wrist restraints.

In Dr. Marcher's opinion, Mrs. Riegel is among the living dead, by which he means "biologically tenacious" but "totally incapable of human interaction." There is no room for hopeless cases in Marcher's heroic view of medicine—"I hate death and I hate losing. . . . I can't stand ambiguity"—so he concocts a subterfuge to hasten Mrs. Riegel's death, the rigging of an ethics case conference called by Dr. LeMarque to clarify Mrs. Riegel's status. For this he needs accomplices. He enlists Patsy Winstone, a medical student employed as a cardiac nurse, who signs on because she needs a case to work up for clerkship credit. Ms. Winstone is not without misgivings about the charade that Dr. Marcher has devised. "This lady is still eating through a tube and nothing has been decided," she tells him.

Upon assuming responsibility for Mrs. Riegel's care, Marsha LeMarque discovers that there is no treatment plan and that, although Mrs. Riegel's physical condition is well documented, her wishes regarding the direction of her care are unknown. Dr. LeMarque therefore convenes an ethics case conference and invites Mrs. Riegel's niece, the patient's nearest relative, to visit and shed light on the situation. Dr. LeMarque is drawn into the case in ways that further frustrate her. Mrs. Riegel reminds her of her own mother and evokes fear of dependence and feelings of pity. "It just seems such a horrible way to end your life." Nonetheless, she has the good grace to drop in on Mrs. Riegel to see if she might "learn something," and she does.

Mrs. Riegel's niece, Margie Dunne, who has not seen much of her aunt in the past 15 years, barely recognizes her—"so white, so old-looking." Dr. LeMarque explains that nothing more can be done for Mrs. Riegel and that a decision is needed about how to proceed. "Do you have any idea what your aunt would have wanted?" Should they continue with the nasogastric tube or surgically insert a gastrointestinal tube or stop tube feeding? Mrs. Dunne deflects the questions and responds personally, passing family photos to Dr. LeMarque and to Ms. Winstone, who has joined them. Her memory prompted by the freeze-frame fragments, Margie Dunne recollects the past, thereby remembering Aunt Meem—youngest child in a big family, dutiful daughter, devoted granddaughter, "like a mother" to Margie in her youth, "a dyed-in-the-wool Catholic," an active volunteer, and "very independent and full of life." "She believed that her soul was secure. . . . She was such a gracious person."

The drama of this central scene in which Mrs. Riegel's identity is reconstructed drives toward a perplexing ending. The play's action leads us to expect that once the doctors and nurses see Sybil Dean Partlow Riegel in this confused mind and tethered body, their best selves will be called forth, and they will care for her. But is that what transpires? Mrs. Dunne's reminiscences lead Dr. LeMarque to the conclusion that Mrs. Riegel should no longer be force-fed but only offered liquids by mouth and relieved of distress. Is this "primary care"? Perhaps.

Much turns on the interpretation of Mrs. Riegel's barely articulate "out, out." Is it life she means, the candle, the poor player strutting and fretting his life upon the stage before being heard from no more? No, it is the tube she wants out, and more deeply it is the prison of her condition and her situation from which she desires release. Locked in (*geriegelt!*) as she is by her disease and by the wrist straps, Mrs. Riegel is as restrained from dying as from living. There is no escape until she is attended and nourished, held and nursed by aide Wynn Brooks, humming "Amazing Grace" and showing her affection.

Mrs. Brooks takes Mrs. Riegel's now unbound wrist in her hand and presses her head to Mrs. Riegel's chest—feeling the pulse, hearing the breathing—"I'm here to take care of you, Miss Sybil"—whereupon Mrs. Riegel's arm lightly embraces Mrs. Wynn Brooks, as if to signal her sense that once again her soul is secure. Now it will be all right to die. Ivan Illych and Gerasim come to mind, the servant holding his master's pained body, enabling him to die.

In the end it is Wynn Brooks who frees Mrs. Riegel from the need to cling to life. For her, Mrs. Riegel has care coming not because of who she is as a person but because she is a child of God. Perhaps the meaning of this simple truth for those to whom it is unavailable is the lesson learned by Patsy Winstone. Recognition of Mrs. Riegel as a person with a life story gave her presence and stature (Mrs. *Regal*) and recalled Ms. Winstone to her vocation of attentiveness and receptivity. She came to realize that Mrs. Riegel "still had something to give." Such an aptitude for grace requires a response of the sort Wynn Brooks provided: primary care—generous, heart-felt, hands-on care.

PART III
Political Gerontology/ Ideology Critique

12

Toward a Philosophy of the Third Age

Charles J. Fahey and Martha Holstein

Human ingenuity has assured that most people in developed countries will live longer, more certain lives, with less pain, in a social
environment congenial to personal freedom, relationships, culture,
recreation, and leisure than at any other moment in history. But there
is another face to this triumphant "democratization" of longevity. As
the 20th century draws to a close, this last stage of life—a period that
we are calling the third age—has largely been emptied of cultural and
social meaning. Our task in this chapter is to suggest some new ways
of thinking about an old life stage in a new historical epoch. We hope
to ponder and give substance to the prophetic words of Carl Jung,
that we would not "grow to be seventy or eighty years old if this
longevity had no meaning for the species. The afternoon of human
life must also have a significance of its own and cannot be merely a
pitiful appendage to life's morning" (Campbell, 1979, p. 17).

Authors listed in alphabetical order.

Special thanks are due the San Francisco chapter of OWL, the Older Women's League,
for careful readings and thoughtful comments.

241

The place to begin, we believe, is with a civic conversation that draws people of all ages into a dialogue about personal meaning and communal responsibilities, the foundation for policy choices, personal decisions, and community action. In the end, we hope that even if the vision we propose falls short, it will invite people of all ages to consider how we might achieve a society that continually seeks to develop the capacities of all of its members and to provide them with the opportunities for exercising these capacities (White, 1961). And finally, we hope that it kindles interest in Rabbi Abraham Heschel's (1961) reminder of 30 years ago, that "old [men] need a vision, not only recreation; old [men] need a dream, not only a memory."

BACKGROUND

The division of life into stages, which are often richly described, has deep historical and psychological roots (see Cole, 1992; Erikson, Erikson, & Kivnik 1986). However, the post-Enlightenment emphasis on individualism, value-free scientific reasoning, and practical management of health and welfare has made it particularly difficult for our society to consider a compelling cultural vision for the third age. As a result, traditional gerontological research, informed by this individualistic, rational approach to understanding, though contributing enormously to the health and welfare of older people, has not probed normative and existential questions. Questions about meaning, if asked at all, have focused on the individual quest.

Such probing requires that we ask different questions than our dominant research methodologies, particularly in the social sciences, permit. It calls for deductive thinking in addition to inductive analysis. It means we must concentrate on the value questions that are most often relegated to the historically devalued private sphere. It means that we look for answers in literature or philosophy or history or theology, as well as in sociology or psychology.

It also means seeing older people in a new way. Our awareness of the old primarily as recipients of services misses much: it tells us nothing about the "fierce energy" that burns within (Maxwell, 1968). It does not explain how it feels to have a lively mind in a senescent body. It does not tell us that "old age gives a chance to find out what a human being is, how we could be worthy of being human" (Myerhoff, 1980, p. 198). It ignores the "amused eyes of those serviced with dentures, lenses, tiny loudspeakers, sticks and hip-pins; when the flesh has become absurd and cannot be taken seriously" (Blythe, 1979). It forgets that old age can be a time to enlarge one's sense of personal and communal history, to forge ties in the intergenerational tapestry, to gain perspective in self-knowledge about one's own relation to aging and the end of life.

WHAT IS THE THIRD AGE?

It has become a truism to say that old age may be defined in multiple ways. At whatever point it begins—often gradually and unremarked, noted by others before ourselves and frequently denied—we would still suggest that most people at some point in their lives—perhaps their late 60s or early 70s and beyond—share some significant characteristics that define them as entering their third age. Because we view the third age dynamically, as a period in which we change as we journey through it, and because we believe that there are emancipatory possibilities contained even in decline and death, we prefer not to divide life's last stage into a third and a fourth age as some commentators have recommended. Instead, we will honor the third age's heterogeneity and its contradictions, its dichotomies between strength and frailty, because these are intrinsic to the human condition.

Even though life stages are increasingly fluid—a grandmother at 38 and a first-time mother at 42; a law school entrant at 60 and a corporate vice president at 29—chronological age provides a starting point for thinking about the third age. In the third age, we are inexorably closer to death than at other times in our life. The knowledge of our own finitude, if acknowledged, makes the third age a time of vivid tension between the needs of the self and others. Florida Scott Maxwell (1968) reminds us to hoard whatever energy remains but not to burden others with one's pain. Yet even when lives become narrowed because of disabilities, we hear voices like Alice Bell's, a very old, very sick, very poor woman in Pat Barker's (1983) novel, *Union Street*. Almost completely homebound and dependent upon others, she insists that, despite her helplessness, she has a role: to be like a mother to the younger women on the street and, to the older women, a friend they can trust to keep their confidences.

For many, the third age is also a time for coming to terms with who one has been and who one will be, however short the time remaining. Central to this coming to terms is the narrative construction of a life story, marked by dominant themes and expressive of continuity (Kaufman, 1986). Reflecting from the vantage point of her 82 years, Lois Swift, a community leader in San Francisco's deteriorating Tenderloin district, organizes her themes around acceptance of all kinds of people and gratitude to her parents, to the training she has received from the Tenderloin Senior Organizing Project, to HUD for low-income housing, to each new day (Holstein, 1991).

But it is also a time when there are few socially expected roles. At every other stage of human life, until the last one, even our culturally diverse society has forged socially sanctioned roles and norms to guide behavior. Implicitly, these expectations affirm the social value of that life stage. At younger ages, a rough correspondence exists between individual survival needs and society's needs for continuity. But for people in their third age, by any standards a long period of time, society has few sanctioned cultural norms or expectations. Cast into the retirement role, which, in a work-oriented society, is often to be relegated to being a nonperson, the older person may be likened to an actor or actress playing an extemporaneous role without the audience's support and with equally uncertain fellow players. And unlike the integration that awaited them in adolescence, retirees often remain isolated and hidden, their collective experiences and wisdom generally undesired and unreachable by others. Alice Bell's son is emblematic of what many people see in an older person, particularly one with a disability. He saw not her contributions as she defines them but rather a wretchedly dependent old woman who drains others but gives nothing.

The third age is also a time when the cumulative effects of gender, race, and socioeconomic variables, as played out in a strong market economy, are profoundly experienced. Constraining her choices and restricting her freedom, these variables establish the boundaries of Lois Swift's freedom. Her old age and that of others like her is made infinitely more difficult because of conditions she did not and cannot control, some caused by chance and others by her particular social location in this moment of history. The bedrock on which she constructs her old age is socially and politically molded and historically situated.

There are other, more general, markers of the third age. At some time, most older people will face both physical decline and loss. More frequent bouts of acute illness, an enhanced likelihood of chronic disease, and the need for assistance from others before the ultimacy of death are probabilities. Family life is also shifting; older people will be part of three-, four-, and five-generation families. They will participate in new family constructs and new ways of patterning intimate relationships.

Freedom may be the most quixotic gift of the third age. Despite losses and economic and other constraints, many older people are potentially freer than ever before to exercise moral agency and to make choices about their lives. No longer essential to the reproductive or the productive system, the two anchors of our social structure, they are particularly well situated to cultivate new qualities; yet instead of this freedom becoming a personal and social asset, it often stimulates negative public appraisals and personal uncertainties. Nurturing and honoring the gifts this freedom bestows and encouraging its use to forge lasting social ties with others—essential elements in the nourishment of civil society—rests with both society and older people.

The third age, then, is defined by practical and noticeable changes in family and health status, occurring for different people at different times; it is a period in which the time remaining is distinctly shorter than the time past. It is also delineated by political and economic decisions that influence labor market participation and structural lags that often hinder social integration. Nonetheless, though they may lack positive norms, social expectations, or even social approbation, many older men and women defy the social constructions, adapt to disability, and flourish despite lives that appear, on the outside, as impoverished. The words of the Catholic poet Paul Claudel, written at 80, capture this well: "No eyes left, no ears, no teeth, no legs, no wind! And when all is said and done, how astonishingly well one does without them!" (cited in Cowley, 1980, p. 17).

A PHILOSOPHY FOR THE THIRD AGE

At 80, the literary critic Malcolm Cowley (1980, p. 30) observed that "old people would like to have a clearly defined place and function in American life," and Ronald Blythe (1979, p. 22) after conducting hundreds of interviews with older people suggested that "with full-span lives the norm, people may need to learn how to be aged as they once learned to be adult." Simone de Beauvoir (1973) reinforces the urgency of the old pursuing ends that give our existence meaning by insisting on the importance of devotion to individuals, to groups, or to causes, to social, political, intellectual, or creative work. "One's life has value so long as one attributes value to the life of others, by means of love, friendship, indignation, compassion" (p. 803). To these comments, we would add that neither the individual nor society can afford to let these years evaporate through inertia, inattention, or despair. If longevity means something for the the human species, then these purposes must be discerned, discussed, and supported by each of our social institutions. The demands for the continuity of the human family urge us to understand how older people can continue contributing to society. And our efforts to formulate effective policies and services further require that we examine the values that do and ought to support our efforts.

So far, our vision has been limited. Even the recent struggle to resist ageism by celebrating only age's positive features obscures much. It misses the laughter, the shaping of life to conform to its new, more limited parameters; it cannot see the way older people live with disability and suffering and often experience transcendence in spite of the pain. It denies decline and praises old age—as long as it remains like middle age; when illness or weariness sets in, then goals become simpler: staying out of a nursing home, not full participation in whatever life remains (Cohen, 1988). The old remain isolated from the "core institutions, processes, and values of modern society which has little use for their obsolete skills, morals, or closeness to death" (Cole, 1984). If society thus finds little to honor in accumulated wisdom and leaves even less space for the old to bear witness to what they have learned from their life experiences, then the social meaning of longevity has little or no relevance.

The recent emphasis on a productive aging society (see Moody, 1989; Pifer, 1986) continues to present a partial and exclusionary vision. Even when generously defined, that is, severed from economic metaphors, it separates the "productive" from the "nonproductive" and by implication further marginalizes and negates those whom the "gatekeepers of ideas" (Epstein, 1988) deem nonproductive.

A number of the unique features that mark old age, however, also suggest its potentialities. We will primarily build upon three of these: the experience of disability and the inexorable trajectory toward death; the gift of freedom and the potential for exercising moral agency; and the communities of memory, the vigorous displays of mutual support, and the practical wisdom that long experience can cultivate.

The specifics of the vision that we will propose rest on a complex foundation. Whereas most developmental research until recently ignored old age, new research on adult development grounds our belief that the third age is replete with opportunities for continued growth and development and therefore with the potential for contributions (see Erikson et al., 1986); and research in norm formation and role development encourages us to believe that large numbers of older people can forge enormous—and beneficial—shifts in the social structure (Riley, 1985). The humanities, particularly literature, and our experiences with older people thinking and talking about their lives also provide striking examples of the rich possibilities inherent in old age. In our thinking, however, we are mindful of the lessons political and moral economy teach. They tutor us about the boundary conditions in which adaptation and change occur and describe the differential experience of old age at least in part as a function of larger social, economic, and political forces.

In the questions we ask and the answers we propose, we will move beyond descriptive potentialities and risk prescriptive ideas for people to consider and discuss. Although other, earlier work (e.g., Gutmann, 1989; Pifer, 1986; Riley, 1985) informs our vision of how older people can participate in a willing society, our specific suggestions emerge from and are enmeshed in our subjective experiences and our philosophical and political biases. Because these filter what we see and what we propose, we wish to note them. The communal traditions in philosophy and their expression in our respective religions—Roman Catholic and Jewish—influence us deeply. With these traditions come normative values that evoke communal responsibility and active citizenship as the backdrop for personal freedom and downplay atomistic individualism and the social contract as the central features of our personal and collective lives. Hence, in suggesting the content of our vision, we will turn to the confluence of our personal experiences, notions of the good society based on theories of the common good, feminist morality and its emphasis on context and relationships, and specific religious teachings that both precede and transcend the post-Reformation focus on economic self-interest.

Borrowing from Socrates, "what I enjoy most is talking to men who are really old. It seems right to inquire of them, as if they have traversed a long journey which we perhaps will have to traverse, to ask what the journey is like, rough and difficult or easygoing and smooth" (Plato, 1956, p. 126), we look to the old as our teachers. Contrary to the view that old age has nothing to teach an advanced technological society, we affirm that people in their third age can be our guides through one of the most poignant but potentially ennobling periods of human life. Because our secular society has few models for either dependency or death, people in their third age can help us to understand that death is not bereft of meaning. The examples of Socrates and the Stoics are useful reminders of how death can be transformed into a virtue, a somewhat different approach from our current death-defying technological approach to prolonging life. The vision we speak to affirms that finitude is a central human experience from which we all can learn. We can ask the old to minister to us: to bear witness that the fullness of life is possible even as death approaches (Harrison, 1985) and demonstrate that it is in caring and being cared for that many of the most profound human interactions occur.

Laurie Shields, the co-founder of the Older Women's League (OWL), died slowly and painfully, but she never stopped being mother, friend, and mentor. Neither her humor nor her directness ever failed her, and sitting with her became a loving community of memory, as conversation wove together into a consistent narrative the long-ago trips to Ireland, reflections about her late husband and wondering if she would meet him in some unknown afterlife, and current concerns such as her fervent wish to live long enough to vote against George Bush. Laurie's gift to younger women was about friendship and about closure. Her way of dying reinforces the strength of community, on a personal level, an often unnoticed contribution that people in their third age can offer.

A vision for the third age will celebrate voices such as Lois Swift's or Alice Bell's or Laurie Shields's. Their life narratives can tell stories that attest to the excellence of practices. They can also construct communities of memory that ground history in the lived experiences of the ordinary men and women whose stories are generally hidden from our more traditional historic accounts.

But this emphasis on community can transcend the personal. From an OWL member, who reminds us that "we know work needs to be done but we are often isolated so we become role models for each other rather than for all of society" (1991, personal communication) to the feisty, fighting, proud old people that Barbara Myerhoff (1980) describes so vividly in *Number Our Days*, we can see how older people are sources of strength and support for one another despite profound social neglect. As these individuals find great satisfaction with others of their own age, they can model for us a cooperative, relationship-oriented moral philosophy, based less on the individual decisions of "rational calculators" than on sustaining community, demonstrating that in daily life we need skills of communicating, initiating, persuading, and responding, a process of shared and open reasoning, not private calculating (Jordan, 1989). An evolving feminist moral theory can provide some guidance. It stresses the value of relationships, (Gilligan, 1982) and suggests that our ability to be human is inextricably linked to others, conditioned and affected by relationships in our public and private lives. By suggesting that community is the basic context for enabling people to contribute their gifts, it urges us to attend to how people can live together. A vision can put forth this ideal for consideration in contradistinction to earlier periods in life, when community and the maintenance of civic society are often relegated to a supporting part in the press of economic and family activities. For at least two reasons, the third age is an ideal time for this struggle to occur: in this age, life assumes its richest moments in relationships, and women, the dominant group among the old, do not easily conform to the social contract myth, that the individual is essentially solitary, bound to others only through self-interested free choice. Anthropologist Victor Turner (1969) reminds us that "at certain life crises, such as . . . the attainment of elderhood and death . . .

the passage from one structural status to another may be accompanied by a strong sentiment for 'humankindness,' a sense of the generic social bond between all members of society" (p. 116).

But instead of encouraging this ideal, the limited view of the liberal state, the moral economy of the life course, and our society's inability to give meaning to frailty or finitude have exiled the old, privatized their significant life events, and rendered the passage beyond liminality, from marginalization to centrality, particularly difficult. A substantive philosophy for the third age will mark this passage, encourage a view of retirement so that it symbolizes entry as well as exit, and celebrate relationships.

Such a vision, resting conceptually on community, also has a larger social significance. At this time, American society urgently needs the wisdom that many of its oldest members can offer. An explicit philosophy for the third age can help shape public expectations and attitudes and encourage older people to offer both "stereoscopic social criticism" (Stout, 1988) and a longer historical view to a society that is in deep trouble, unable or unwilling to engage in conversations, if not actions, that confront social decay, fragmentation, and managed civic life. This may be the first generation of children growing up in America who expect that government will distort the truth and that honesty can be trumped by any number of often undefined or vague national interests. Older people's accumulated wisdom about the meaning of life, death, and suffering, their opportunity to reflect, to exercise the virtue of patience, and to consider today's decisions and values in historical perspective can permit them to play the vitally needed role of "moral entrepreneur," drawing our attention to new needs while encouraging others to act together in new ways (Jordan, 1989, p. 170).

A recent, simple example suggest the possibilities. At a rancor-filled community meeting about a shelter for homeless families, a small older woman rose to speak. She attested to her 40 years in the neighborhood and described the changes in its ethnic composition and the richness that resulted. She welcomed the homeless shelter. An older man, the child of Russian immigrant parents, also speaking for the shelter, reminded his neighbors that he and his children have done well in America, but he wondered what his parents looked like when they stepped off the boat and if they too would have been hissed out of the neighborhood. These neighbors are symbolic of the ability of the old to provide a history, a context, to remind us of the ebb and flow of change and of our moral obligations. Providing this context can be one form of moral leadership that the gift of longevity can bestow. However, that context needs to be expanded so that older people honor their continuity with the young or with generations unborn by supporting that which directly benefits children, such as school bonds.

One special, community purpose for longevity, then, may be that it allows one group—potentially freer than any other group from those things that oppress us, things like dehumanizing work or consumerism or the expectancies of others—to view the whole of society, to become the instruments of change. They can facilitate movement beyond the aggregate of private decisions or pluralistic politics, transcending "gridlock," the physical analogue of disregarding the whole. Given appropriate settings and respect, they can refocus attention on what must be done to reestablish a concern for community and the common good. They can ask what features of our society hold out the hope of transformation from within. As vanguards to help transform society, they can pose questions, test answers, foster a morality or relationships (see Gilligan, 1982), and help to redefine individualism so that it honors people in their diversity but does not degenerate into selfish concern for the self and obsessive accumulation. This role means searching for social consensus or, at a minimum, a common ground and understanding when and why these forms of agreement disintegrate. In this struggle a companion struggle can occur: an examination of the limits of liberty and a question of when it is appropriate for "collective opinion" to hold sway against claims of private moral autonomy (Caplan & Callahan, 1981). This effort, made possible by the freedom not available to younger people, who are often consumed by institutions, money, and achievement, may be uniquely possible for people in their third age.

With whatever assistance is necessary and in whatever forums emerge, older people can start public conversations, the first step in reconceptualizing the politics of the common good (Lasch, 1988). This call for conversation does not insist that a common view of the common good must be reached but rather that discourse is essential if common moral understandings and a common language—essential for establishing community—be developed. Such common moral understandings do not mean unanimity of beliefs; instead, they signify a willingness to go on talking, to reach workable compromises even when total unanimity is impossible. For example, this kind of conversation can question the goals of a consumer-directed, youth-oriented society that drives older people into consumption and into the denial of decline. By becoming aware of the threats to cooperative activity that a focus on money and power impose, the old can help to emancipate us from the "vicious cycle inherent in modern consumer culture" (Delattre, 1988, p. 62). Goods can possess, destroy, and overwhelm us. Hence, the importance of reversing inertia that drives us to the mindless accumulation of possessions. From the long view that only the old can possess, they can teach us that one more hit of a credit card in the machine will not solve the problems of being human and, as important, that the price we pay for our consumerism is ecologically destructive and politically destabilizing.

In this, the most utopian part of our vision, we see the old pushing us to the limits of our common humanity. As a reminder of the vulnerability to disease and death that all living beings share and the fragility of humans and our planet, they can help develop communal values that hold politics accountable for achieving humane and just social practices. Through neighborhood associations, in combination with communities of faith and other model communities and associations yet to be evolved, the old can help struggle with formulating a futuristic blend of the virtue of community without its oppressiveness. To borrow from the women's movement, old age may offer us that moment when communal ties are honored but not oppressive, when a cohesive sense of community is experienced, where ethical "ought's" are rationally derived and a plurality of life-styles encouraged (see Farganis, 1986).

But the entire responsibility cannot rest with the old. A reflective, morally vigorous old age depends on certain economic and cultural assumptions. Social change is also essential. We must assure that every person will have sufficiency for decency in the third age, as in prior ages. If we are to expect the old to be the exemplars of altruism and "other-regardingness," then we, as a society, must set the terms that make this role possible by reaffirming social expectations at all ages. True liberation and the creation of real choice means modifying what can be chosen as ethically acceptable actions. Individuals make choices, but institutional patterns shape choices and make one choice more likely than another (Epstein, 1988). Society will be responsible for making genuine choices possible so that older people can test the vision we propose. In a very practical way, facilitating the old's active commitment to public leadership can begin to heal social structures: work, families, churches, synagogues, political parties, unions. People in their third age, who have already made innumerable adjustments to internal and external shifts that shaped their long lives, can provide models for the rest of society. In particular, women, with their practiced flexibility resulting from their varied life roles, may play an important role in modeling how adjustments and changes can occur (Riley, 1985).

At the same time, in a narrower sense, while taking a leadership role in insisting on a moral vision, older people may be able to challenge the sharp and at times venomous attack on the burdens the "nonproductive" old impose on society. This increasingly hostile view can corrode the bonds of intergenerational solidarity, undermine social regard, wound self-respect, and harm us all. The prevailing "rational calculator" model, reinforced by a deficit-reduction mentality, has practical ramifications in communities across this country when the declining middle class protect their gains at the expense of those just below them on the social and economic scale.

Finally, returning to the old, the availability of moral agency and moral freedom carries a great responsibility. The old cannot be immune from criticism for using their moral freedom to select a vapid life. By excluding them from moral approbation, we divorce them from the human community. To take the old seriously as moral beings, we must be prepared to approve and reprove their behavior (May, 1986). But we must also understand the underpinnings for the contemporary spoken choices of many older people. To do so, the moral economy framework is particularly powerful (see Minkler & Cole, 1991). In wrestling with questions of moral obligation, we heard a 75-year-old retired psychologist say, "I've paid my dues; no one is going to tell me what to do" (1991, personal communication). But, like others, her actions were vigorously involved.

In sum, an explicit vision for the third age is a starting place for an exploration of the personal, social, and species significance of old age. It can do a number of things. It can suggest ways for us to learn from the old, thereby encouraging them to teach themselves and then us the many ways dependency, decline, and death are experienced and made meaningful. It can indicate how communities of memory that transcend the closed world of the senior center or the retirement housing complex may emerge as the thread that weaves past, present, and future into an integral pattern. It can alert society that it has yet to evolve forms, values, and structures that respond to a new social reality, for example, that the nuclear family may no longer adequately serve as the source of love and support for its oldest members. A vision can guide an individual's passage from liminality to reintegration. And it can open leadership places in politics and social life now tacitly denied to the old. But this vision, because of its many value assumptions, must hold in exquisite tension a benchmark versus a coercive standard. The specific vision for the third age that we have proposed straddles the line between a value-based vision of what the good life can and should be and the operating assumptions of the liberal state, which emphasizes free enactment of different notions of this good life. It is our hope that people will choose, with appropriate social support, to be actively engaged.

That foundational struggle challenges us to ask how we can accord older people authentic respect and freedom to choose while also insisting on responsibility and commitment. And can we ask this explicitly of the old while we emphasize the rights of noninterference, although selectively bestowed on those whose economic resources give them the freedom to choose, for all others? In advocating for such a role, we are not suggesting that it replace alternative personal ends. As with other major responsibilities, it should allow people to live by their own designs while serving as an important organizing principle, as a job or a family might be for a younger person. This tension between a vigorous expression of freedom and the imposition of preferences is critical and should lead to ongoing conversation about ways to balance individual freedom and social connectedness (Stout, 1988). Hence, our suggestions should be interpreted as a provisional telos, respectful of individual dignity and choice but insistent on attention to and active leadership on behalf of the common good. By proposing and testing this value-based, normative conception, we provide explicit standards that we hope will become deep-seated preferences.

PROCESSES: THE THIRD AGE AS REFLECTIVE WISDOM

To give volition to the philosophy of the third age, we need rituals to mark it, places for establishing connectedness, and a process and a content for dialogue. We also need a societal shift to counteract the decade-plus emphasis on the self, a shift that would stimulate recognition that we are and ought to be interdependent at all ages. The following are beginning suggestions for translating the content of a vision into practice.

Through the media, voices like Alice Bell's must be heard, overcoming the silent message of the walker or the wheelchair. The writings of the old, powerful expressions of heroism and defeat, anguish and triumph, frivolity and gravity, must become part of the public image of old age. Not only the triumphant late bloomers or the aged Picasso but ordinary people thinking about the narrative conclusion for their life story need to become part of the public domain. How else can we learn what the old have to teach if we do not find ways to listen to them? Media images of old age tend to show either the vigorous, the charming, or the neglected, but there is another image, one that attests to the kind of dying that Laurie Shields exemplified.

Because we emphasized the need for public conversation, faith communities can provide societal vehicles for older people to be reflective about the issues of late life and to be our teachers. They can also structure ways to consider the "big" issues: war and peace, the economy, and meaning beyond work and consumption. Instead of bingo for the old, they can create real dialogue and a true sense of community. The German Evangelical Akademies offer a model for this form of civic conversation; the American Bishops' statement on the economy, a possible starting place.

But before they can do that, churches and synagogues must examine themselves to see if they are reinforcing the very tendencies that exclude the old from community. Do they recognize the human community for what it is—people often alone, not living in traditional nuclear families? Do they see that people need opportunities to talk about what matters?

Other forms of localism, where individual voices are not silenced, might be tested. As an experiment, people living their third age might strive to design something intermediate between community and society, and as their life space narrows—for health and other reasons—that necessity can become a virtue as the old help restore the advantages of the smaller group, the association, in a society largely based on bureaucratic anonymity, to achieve common ends (Lasch, 1988).

A simple but remarkable example of this form of association exists in San Francisco's Tenderloin district, an area dominated by drug deals, prostitution, and crime. But with the assistance of the Tenderloin Senior Organizing Project (TSOP), individuals like Lois Swift work in the single-room hotels and also as part of a newly formed Leader's Group to confront problems. To date, they have succeeded in moving bus stops, controlling the hours of building construction, and forcing HUD to reconsider conversion of old Section 8 housing. Associations such as TSOP demonstrate, in part, the suggestion of Jeffrey Stout (1988) that politics foster a public life in which members find *some part* of their identity as citizens of a republic directed to the *common* good. The bridge between local action and larger-scale social change must then be addressed.

On a larger scale, there is the possibility of adding to the political work of the aging organizations. Without destroying what is, can the old age movement become a social movement that actively seeks revisions in the social order? Can the old age organizations, government, and professionals—our starting place—play a role in defining a new belief system that incorporates the essential care components but also talks about the essence of being old in its personal and societal manifestations?

CONCLUSION

Significant advances in medical care and in health and social services have extended both the life span and the quality of life for many older people. Yet old age remains a life stage largely devoid of social expectations. It is a life stage set adrift, often devalued both in terms of personal respect and increasingly in terms of a challenge to public expenditures directed at the old. The explicit search for and defining of a meaningful content for this life stage—on the personal, societal, and species level—can be an important step in guiding individual aging, grounding public and private institutional and policy responses, and penetrating the resistant ageism that harms people of all ages.

REFERENCES

Barker, P. (1983). *Union Street*. New York: Ballantine Books.

Beauvoir, S. de. (1973). *Coming of age*. New York: Warner Paperbacks.

Blythe, R. (1979). *The view in winter: Reflections on old age*. New York: Harcourt Brace Jovanovich.

Campbell, J. (Ed.). (1979). *The portable Jung* (pp. 127–146). New York: Penguin Books.

Caplan, A., & Callahan, D. (1981). *Ethics in hard times*. New York: Plenum Press.

Cohen, E. (1988). The elderly mystique. *Gerontologist, 28*(Suppl), 24–31.

Cole, T. (1984, November). *Thoughts on old age and the welfare state: Political economy, history, and health policy*. Paper presented at the 37th Annual Scientific Meeting of the Gerontological Society of America, San Antonio, TX.

Cole, T. (1991). *The journey of life*. New York: Cambridge University Press.

Cowley, M. (1980). *The view from eighty*. New York: Viking.

Delattre, R. (1988). The culture of procurement: Reflections on addiction and the dynamics of American culture. In C. Reynolds & R. Norman (Eds.), *Community in America: The challenge of habits of the heart* (pp. 56–66). Berkeley: University of California Press.

Epstein, C. F. (1988). *Deceptive distinctions: Sex, gender, and the social order*. New Haven, CT: Yale University Press.

Erikson, E., Erikson, J. & Kivnik, H. (1986). *Vital involvement in old age*. New York: W. W. Norton.

Farganis, S. (1986). *Social reconstruction of the feminine character.* Totowa, NJ: Rowman and Littlefield.

Gilligan, C. (1982). *In a different voice.* Cambridge, MA: Harvard University Press.

Gutmann, D. (1989). *Reclaimed powers: Toward a new psychology of men and women in later life.* New York: Basic Books.

Harrison, B. (1985). *Making the connections: Essays in feminist social ethics.* (Ed. C. Robb). Boston: Beacon Press.

Heschel, A. (1961). *To grow old in wisdom.* Paper presented at the 1961 White House Conference on Aging, Washington, DC.

Hochschild, A. (1973). *The unexpected community: Portrait of an old age subculture.* Berkeley, University of California Press.

Holstein, M. (1991). Not old, only older—Lois Swift: Aging well in San Francisco's Tenderloin. *Generations, 15,* 1.

Jordan, B. (1989). *The common good: Citizenship, morality, and self-interest.* Oxford: Basil Blackwell.

Kaufman, S. (1986). *The ageless self.* New York: Simon and Schuster.

Lasch, C. (1988). The communitarian critique of liberalism. In C. Reynolds & R. Norman (Eds.), *Community in America: The challenge of habits of the heart* (pp. 173–184). Berkeley: University of California Press.

Maxwell, F. S. (1968). *The measure of my days.* New York: Penguin Books.

May, W. (1986). The virtues and vices of the elderly. In T. Cole & S. Gadow (Eds.), *What does it mean to grow old: Reflections from the humanities* (pp. 41–61). Durham, NC: Duke University Press.

Minkler, M. & Cole, T. (1991). Political and moral economy: Not such strange bedfellows. In M. Minkler & C. Estes (Eds.), *Critical perspectives in gerontology.* Amityville, NY: Baywood.

Moody, H. R. (1988). *Abundance of Life.* New York: Columbia University Press.

Myerhoff, B. (1988). *Number our days.* New York: Touchstone, Simon and Schuster.

Older Women's League, Chapter Seminar, San Francisco chapter. (1991).

Pifer, A. & Branle, L. (1986). The public policy response. In *Our aging society* (pp. 391–413). New York: W. W. Norton.

Plato. (1956). The republic. In E. Warmington & P. Rouse (Eds.), *Great dialogues of Plato* (pp. 118–342). New York: New American Library.

Riley, M. W. (1985). Women, men, and the lengthening life course. In A. Rossi (Ed.), *Gender and the life course* (pp. 333–347). New York: Aldine Press.

Stout, J. (1988). Liberal society and the languages of morals. In C. Reynolds & R. Norman (Eds.), *Community in America: The challenge of habits of the heart.* Berkeley: University of California Press.

Turner, V. (1969). *The ritual process: Structure and anti-structure.* Chicago: Aldine.

White, W. (1961). *Beyond conformity.* New York: Free Press of Glencoe.

13

Definitional Ceremonies: Depoliticizing and Reenchanting the Culture of Aging

Marc Kaminsky

To address to their children and their better off fellow Jews the overt statement, "You are treating us badly" would embarrass and alienate them. By making their self-definition and protest indirect and ceremonial, the old people arouse guilt without having to state openly the humiliating facts of their condition. Their self-esteem is built upon their conception of themselves as independent, even supporters of others. The statement of

Barbara Myerhoff's major ethnographic essays on "the culture of aging and Yiddishkeit" are collected in *Remembered Lives: The Work of Ritual, Storytelling and Growing*

need in any form, especially to those they
need most, is unthinkable. And the very point
of the ritual is that it need not be thought.
Fortunately, in ritual, fictions can be presented which disguise truth, save face, and
convince all concerned that everything is in
order. For rituals allow people to maneuver,
fight on their own terms, choose the times,
places, conditions and shapes of their assertions, as Burke says of proverbs. Such ma-
neuvering may result in action, encounter or
change, or may end in poetry.
—Barbara Myerhoff, "We Don't Wrap
Herring in a Printed Page: Fusion,
Fictions and Continuity in Secular Ritual"

1.

The ethnographic essays that Barbara Myerhoff (1935–1985) wrote
after the early 1970s are concerned with forms of creativity in the
everyday life of elderly East Europen Jews. These include *collective
acts of imagination* such as secular ritual, mural making, and demonstrations in which elderly Yiddish-speaking immigrants melded the
street-theater techniques of New Left protest with signs of their days
on the picket lines in the "era of Great Strikes" (1909 until the war
years) on the Lower East Side. In *Number Our Days*, which is widely
regarded as a classic study of the culture of aging, Myerhoff (1980a)
also presents profoundly moving and memorable portraits of *individual acts of imagination*, focusing on the (oral) storytelling and
(written) autobiographical narratives of Jacob, the president emeri-
tus and moral leader of the community that she studies, and of
Shmuel the Tailor, a wise, tragic, skeptical outsider whom she takes
as her mentor and key informant. These men are representatives of a
social type that modern Yiddish culture produced in abundance: the
"worker intellectuals" whom Howe celebrates in *World of Our Fathers*. And both, it is crucial to note here, owe their formation as
intellectuals to the Jewish Labor Bund. This dimension of their cultural history remains outside the boundary of "data" that is rendered

Older (1992), a volume that I edited under the auspice of the Myerhoff Center at the
YIVO Institute for Jewish Research. Work on this chapter was likewise supported by
the Center's Research and Publication Program. I would like to offer my thanks and
gratitude to Dr. Maury P. Leibovitz, president of the Center; Polly Howells and Diane
Demeter, co-chairs of the Center's Committee on Research and Publication Projects;
and the Lucius N. Littauer Foundation. I also gratefully acknowledge that the preparation of this work for publication was made possible by a grant from the Memorial
Foundation for Jewish Culture.

significant by being treated as material for interpretation in Myer-hoff's accounts. In the ethnographic essays, the popular socialism that saturated Yiddish immigrant culture is never even mentioned, a remarkable and problematic omission. And yet the erasure is not complete: traces of the actual social process that have shaped these immigrant lives, and that is evident in their forms of creativity, appear in the category of cultural resistance that Myerhoff proposes. Myer-hoff showed that these Yiddish-speaking old people, like members of other marginalized groups, create "definitional ceremonies" when they face "a crisis of invisibility." Here, art making and other forms of creative activity become a means of opposing ageism, neglect, and segregation by the dominant society.

The concept of definitional ceremonies is important and warrants inquiry on a number of grounds. First, it occupies a unique position in Myerhoff's work. Her contribution took the form of a *narrative* description of culture; what distinguishes her narratives is that the "structure of feeling" (Williams, 1961) of the culture is given powerful articulation. Her concept of definitional ceremonies is *the sole theoretical description of culture* that she formulated. Second, it is an important move in anthropological theory, in its effort to get beyond the schematic, bipolar thinking that marks social thought in the United States on the question of the relationship between "the individual and society." In the concept of definitional ceremonies, Myer-hoff offers a genuinely integrative, interdisciplinary concept that links life-history work and ritual theory. Third, it takes creativity as its object of study. This is a quality and process that is exalted in American culture and honored by being made the object of kitsch attention and mystification; that is, social science has usually deemed it an insufficiently serious research topic. Fourth, in and through this concept, Myerhoff is able to represent and analyze the oppositional character of these "elders'" cultural productions, even as she occludes its social and cultural sources. Nothing they do is construed in terms of politics; everything they do is subtracted from the realm of politics and credited to the account of spirituality, of an existential self-affirmation. Here, too, "complex seeing" (Brecht's phrase) is crucial. The problem remains to see the intersection of the sphere of the spirit and of politics and to move toward an adequate account of this difficult terrain of culture, where resistance movements of subaltern peoples often take shape. This is a problem of urgent general significance: witness the role of the Catholic church in revolutionary struggles in Latin America and in the Polish Solidarity movement, the role of the black churches in the civil rights movement in the United States, the forms of spiritual resistance that Gandhi developed in the struggle to decolonize India. These are familiar instances. The culture of Jewish socialism must be viewed in the larger context of modern emancipatory movements, in which politics and religion have been inseparable dimensions of a whole social process. But it must be returned to its particular history—to the religious, cultural, and politically radical mass movements within Jewish life that formed it—and its own changing forms must be recognized. The conflation of Moses and Marx, in the late 19th and early 20th centuries, by the members of the cohort that Myerhoff studied, meant not only a radical secularization of the culture of rabbinic Judaism; it also meant a spiritualization of politics. This formula, while too schematic, suggests the complexity and difficulty of this area of study.

With one crucial exception, as noted above, Myerhoff's contribution centered on narrating and interpreting "the made-upness of culture," not on constructing theory.[1] The far-fetchedness, even awkwardness of that phrase, is characteristic of Myerhoff's stylization of ethnographic thought and experience: she intensifies, she draws attention to, she renders distinct and memorable the discourse she takes from others, and in the act of infiltrating it with added meanings, she makes it her own. The made-upness of culture displays the labor, the difficulty, of bricolage—of all hyphenating acts and events; it shows the strain of assemblage, the artificiality of the "graduation-siyum" and "birthday-memorial" created by elderly Jewish Americans, trying to hold together the divided world through which they have moved. Myerhoff takes up her observer's post on the hyphen, bridging alien languages, connecting explicitly what the elders fuse behind the curtain of collective symbols.

The delicately textured descriptions of collective life that are the ethnographer's primary task come to us strongly accented: Myerhoff stamps key words and phrases with her own intonation. Among the essential Myerhoffian phrases, "definitional ceremonies" occupies a position of unique importance: this is not so much an application of theory as an extension of theory. Here, she thinks beyond the already formulated terms of interpretive anthropology, and this attests to the pressure put upon her by the range of her observations and concerns. Crystallizing an as-yet-unformulated experience into a new idea, she was responding to the lived incompleteness of existing theory while responding to the "flow of expressive behaviors" that constitute, as Geertz (1973) says, the "social discourse" whose meanings can be discovered only in and through a dialogue across cultural and conceptual boundaries (p. 18).

This new idea, then, is the product of the dialogue that Myerhoff is carrying on between Victor Turner (1986) and a number of wise old men and women, including Shmuel and Hannah, who have scathing and funny things to say about this foolishness of making up culture.

In the concept of definitional ceremonies, Myerhoff takes us into the heart of her project as an anthropologist; she defines her intention and draws together in a complex figure of thought her key words and the theories and experiences that depend upon them. Here, in "Life Not Death in Venice" (Myerhoff, 1986), is the crucial formulation:

> Definitional ceremonies are likely to develop within a group when there is a crisis of invisibility and disdain by a more powerful outside society. ... Definitional ceremonies deal with the problems of invisibility and marginality; they are strategies that provide opportunities for being seen and in one's own terms, garnering witnesses to one's worth, vitality, and being. Thus, it was the custom for Center members to display and dramatize themselves in many forms, informal and formal, planned and spontaneously: by storytelling, creating difficulties, making scenes; by positioning themselves to be noticed, recorded, listened to, and photographed.
>
> Definitional ceremonies were the elders' most regular and formal patterns of display. ... At first these events seemed to resemble what Turner described as social dramas. ... As with Turner's social dramas, the ends of these affairs were always marked by the enunciation of the participant's collective symbols, reiterating their common membership and deepest shared commitments. That the ceremonies changed nothing was signal, and is what distinguished them from social dramas. (pp. 266–268)

In this passage, Myerhoff wants to distinguish definitional ceremonies from social dramas on political grounds. Like poetry, definitional ceremonies make nothing happen, whereas social dramas settle social disputes and realign social relationships. Social dramas are political processes and have political outcomes; definitional ceremonies may have political beginnings—they are caused "by a more powerful outside society" that subordinates and ignores the old people—but have no political consequence. They function as existential offerings, heightenings of being.

The grounds of the distinction between Turner's (1986) idea and hers lie, in fact, elsewhere. Myerhoff has worked up and transformed *both* Turner's idea of social process ("social dramas") and his idea of individual process ("liminality"). Ritual, for Turner, in its collective dimension concerns social conflict; as an individual process, Turner values it "as a framework that engenders creativity in individuals"

(Moore & Myerhoff, 1977, p. 8). Hence, his espousal of "communitas groups," which Myerhoff sought to embody as a social practice in her workshops on "ritual, storytelling and self-creation." The attempt to live through these ideas testifies to a desire for wholeness of being—for joining theory and practice, the professor's intellectual life and the active social meanings she professed through the doing—that the texts likewise evidence: through the tone of moral seriousness, and through interpretations that make linkages among separated realms of thought and action.

The whole integrative pull of Myerhoff's thought is registered in her fondness for the word "intertwining." Where the old women knit and embroider, she intertwines and amplifies. The dynamic, surprising, relation-oriented, concrete character of her thinking is embodied by a verb that refers to traditional women's work. What distinguishes definitional ceremonies is that, in this concept, Myerhoff intertwines a collective idea and an individual idea. Turner (1986), in his reception of the term, stresses one side of the equation. This gloss turns upon an ambiguity in the use of "definitional": what is at stake is both the group's definition of itself as a collectivity and its members' definition of their individual identities. Turner separates the necessary interrelation that Myerhoff's texts insist on, as they develop the term in both its individual and collective senses. Here, then, is the patrilineal account that Turner (1986) gives of the term's conception:

> George Simmel, Lewis Coser, Max Gluckman and others have pointed out how conflict, if brought under gradual control, stopping short of massacre and war, may actually enhance a group's "consciousness of kind." Conflict forces the antagonists to diagnose its source, and in so doing to become aware of the principles that bond them beyond and above the issues that temporarily divided them. . . . These considerations, I think, led Barbara Myerhoff to distinguish "definitional ceremonies" from "social dramas," which she conceived as a kind of collective "autobiography," a means by which a group creates its identity by telling itself a story about itself, in the course of which it brings to life "its Definite and Determinate Identity" (to cite William Blake). Here, . . . meaning is engendered by marrying present problems to a rich ethnic past, which is then infused into the "doings and undergoings" (Dewey's phrase) of the local community. (p. 40)

This emphasis, which "collective autobiographies" condenses in a marvelous phrase, is everywhere supported by Myerhoff's readings of specific cases. Yet it erases the whole emphasis on the self and late-life identity work that Myerhoff makes through a series of connecting terms, particularly her discussions of reminiscence, life review, life history, and storytelling. These are performed definitional ceremonies that explicitly refer to individual identity, and they are equally prevalent in her writing.

Evidently, the concept admits of both uses, and one aspect of its usefulness to Myerhoff lies precisely in its ambiguity. It can cover a range of interpretative moves and finesse the large question it raises: in what ways are "the individual" and "the social" interrelated? This question, as we have seen, points to enormously important and interesting contradictions that her work embodies, worries over, struggles against and, at times, with. It is a struggle she at once disguises and reveals—and sometimes revels in. That she uses a conceptual term in the way that rituals make use of symbols—as refuge for a paradox, as a strategy for having it both ways without having to own or reconcile the differences—indicates to me that she was "working" the term deliberately, and is evidence of her rhetorical power in constructing her argument and manipulating the reader's attention whither she wished it to go. What must be affirmed here is the ethnographic and conceptual terrain she constitutes as a unified field of work through this conceptual assemblage.

The idea of definitional ceremonies is one of the strong moves Myerhoff made to join together the life-history method and the work on ritual, and to give it legitimacy as a subject of anthropological inquiry. The most powerful and dynamic aspect of the idea is that it regards life history and ritual as mutually formative. This dialectical construction of the object of study moves beyond all the bipolar oppositions that normally mark thinking on the individual-social issue, including Myerhoff's: it is a move of creative social thought, not a settled achievement. The issue is, necessarily, the subject of a confusing debate, given its ideological character. In the past decade, there has been a well-articulated critique of interpretive (or symbolic) anthropology from a "political economy perspective," and this has been met by a corresponding attempt to incorporate key elements of Marxist social thought within a liberal position (Marcus & Fischer, 1986). Bruner (1986), in repudiating dualism and idealism, and in grounding anthropology in history, reflects the course of this debate:

> The anthropology of experience rejects all such binaries as static-dynamic, system-process, continuity-change, ethnography-history, because these oppositions postulate a fixed and timeless world of essences, an imaginary world.... By contrast, the anthropology of experience sees people as active agents in the historical process who construct their own world. Using Myerhoff's phrase, we are "the authors of ourselves." (p. 12)

This phrase, which Geertz (1986) also cites with high approbation as summing up the vision of interpretive anthropology, refers to the elders' definitional ceremonies. Geertz construes the self-authorization to refer to individuals who make themselves "someone to whom, in the famous cry of Willy Loman's wife, attention must be paid" (p. 373). Clearly, Myerhoff's formulation is as laudable (inspirational, quotable) as it is slippery. It accommodates a range of emphases that are grounded, at one polarity, on the Marxist idea of "men making their own history" and, at the other, on the liberal idea of social amelioration through interest-group politics. This is the crucial ideological conflict at stake in Bruner's historical reading of Myerhoff's phrase in terms of social authorship and Geertz's stress on the representative individual hurt by the system.

The extraordinary richness of Myerhoff's idea withstands what I might describe as her own last-minute attempt to bleach it of politics. In the decisive formulation of the term in "Life Not Death in Venice," she disavows the possibility that the elders' definitional ceremonies can make any actual impact on the "outside society." This assertion is immediately contradicted by the case with which she exemplifies the concept. Three pages later, she writes "that the elders succeeded in altering more than their own version of themselves," as a result of their ceremonial protest march. City officials began to implement a previously unenforced ordinance, "providing a four-block section [on the boardwalk] where the old people could walk without fear of traffic. A limited but decisive victory" (Myerhoff, 1986, p. 272). In "Surviving Stories," one of the last essays she wrote, Myerhoff (1988) revises this separation of "the manipulation of one's image" and politics. The attempt to depoliticize an idea saturated with politics is abandoned, and this allows for a more unified working-through of the concept. She comes to explicate definitional ceremonies as a politics of last resort, a social assertion made by a powerless group with no other means of contesting the local powers-that-be through whom they encounter the larger society. Here, definitional ceremonies are viewed as a form of political opposition undertaken by resourceful people with no other access to the mass media or other established channels of power.

An issue of great general importance that Myerhoff engages, within the terms of definitional ceremonies, is the fate of the individual in American society: the lived inner experience of fragmentation. Even as she shares the "humanist" version of American individualism, she feels pulled toward an alternative vision: by her feminism and her profession. This alternative worldview construes society, not as a neutral arena in which individuals compete for money, status, and power, but as a positive domain in which individuals are created through a process that involves nurturance, active mutual responsibility, and negotiation of differences in and through democratic institutions (Williams, 1958). This is the worldview that the "Center folk," as Jews and as socialists, live as the truth of their lives. And this personally lived truth accounts not only for the respect and love they evoke in Myerhoff but for the immense appeal that her account of them has for her readers. Through their lives, she represents—in a safely distanced, miniaturized form—the idea of a good society.

In Myerhoff, then, the dominant individualist orientation is considerably tempered by the ethnographer's perspective that takes identity formation as a social-cultural no less than psychological process. The social conditions that are the immediate context of her writing—a set of conditions that she presents as the "background" against which the elders become visible—include the "factors" that have made identity a crisis throughout the life cycle and have given rise to what Russell Jacoby (1975) has called "the permanent emergency of the individual" (p. 101): to the individual stripped of cross-generational ties, of cultural and religious traditions, of ethnic and historical memory, and of communal structures that support "a sense of selfsameness" (Erikson's phrase) throughout the life cycle. Jacoby's mentor, Christopher Lasch, has called this set of social conditions "the culture of narcissism." And the key themes of this general critique of our common life appear, in Myerhoff's writing, as the corporate negative of which the elders are the individualized positive. These conditions appear as the backgrounded macroforces that cut through the elders' lives and which they overcome through their collective acts of self-creation.

This critique has been made under many terms and from many positions. What I want to do here is point to diverse and professionally important discourses, such as the literatures on "the fall of public man" and "the borderline personality," in order to suggest that the common recognition of a lifelong identity crisis in American society marks out the situation in which Myerhoff's writing is widely received as compelling: valued as information and as inspiration, as counterexample. And for this reason: she poses the struggle for self-definition as a cultural question.

She takes all the common markers of identity—ethnicity, age, social, economic, and professional status—and construes them as eminently malleable materials under a constructive process of self-definition that is a concurrent articulation of culture and individuality. The local community becomes a stage, "an arena for appearing";

the events she analyzes become imaginative media for self-presentation and social polemic. Ritual becomes PR for the dispossessed, who have no access to more expensive and more commodified means of acquiring *Dasein* through self-display. The terms of social life in our culture require us to "get a hearing" and "make our voices heard." Competitive individualism and movements of cultural nationalism by minority groups have "the struggle of self-definition" in common: they are counterparts and reflections of the same general conditions. The former accedes to, the latter resist, historical forces that require the hardening and homogenization of the self and culture. Myerhoff's writing speaks from the heart of this complex crisis, poses its criticism of a society that makes "personal integration" a struggle, and demonstrates—celebrates—the symbolic strategies used by a low-status group to attain some of the rewards that come with successful performances: attention from the "outside society," and the self-esteem that accompanies the attention, is the scarce good the elders get through their ritualized self-definitions.

A second general issue of great importance that is engaged here is the fate of democracy: not as a set of formal institutions and settled procedures but as a lived experience, part of the fabric of everyday life: democracy as a lived practice that has to be continually renewed, in conflict—and struggle. Myerhoff is deeply aware of this issue. In *Number Our Days* (1980a) she records axial crises in which the old people define their definitional ceremonies as democratic practices

> "He livened up the Center, that's true," said Sophie. "But he does not have an open mind. He don't like Communists. Everybody here was a Socialist, a Communist, an anarchist twenty years ago. A Jew is a Jew, this is basic. You see what happened. When he came in here he thought he was a *gantzer macher* and would run the Center. But he was a newcomer. He doesn't understand our democratic process." (p. 134). . . .
>
> "This is a democracy, Jake. We don't give literacy tests. Anybody elected goes on the Board." (p. 174)

Myerhoff's powerful analysis of the conflicts in which these utterances are embedded shows that they are overdetermined: she offers an interdisciplinary description of the elders' quarrelsomeness and their quarrels, interpreting their psychological, cultural, social, and political determinants. She then arranges motives for oppositional behavior on a hierarchy of validity, within which the pursuit of self-interest i n the form of "face" and recognition from the group and the reaffirmation of the group's common bond—"a Jew is a Jew"—displace and dissolve the political motive.

2.

The strength of definitional ceremonies as a concept lies in the mediations it makes: it is an archway through which separated categories communicate with each other and are restored to the common ground of active and interacting relationships. In this capable form, it is a thick, particular version of the general notion of secular ritual, which was developed within the context of Myerhoff's collaboration with Sally Falk Moore (1977). The continuity, at the level of theory, cannot be overstated. On this collaborative work of substantiating a concept of secular ritual, Myerhoff's individual work on definitional ceremonies depends for some of its materials as well as for its method. Many of the "dimensions of explanation" that the co-authors delineate in "Secular Ritual: Forms and Meanings" provide Myerhoff, in her ethnographic essays, with both a paradigm for organizing the narrative and a table of ideas upon which to lay out exegesis. ("A Death in Due Time" [Myerhoff, 1975] and "We Don't Wrap Herring in a Printed Page" [Myerhoff, 1977] are vivid examples of the application of the Myerhoff-Moore exegetical paradigm.) But the work with Moore gave her not only a theoretical model fashioned for her specific use; it also gave her the experience of generating theory, of going beyond existing theory. And in definitional ceremonies she went beyond the work on secular rituals.

In "Secular Ritual," Moore and Myerhoff (1977) are conceptualizing the move from Durkheim's sociology of religion to Geertz's and Turner's interpretive anthropology: the cases they offer of "the secular" belong to the area of political anthropology. Myerhoff and Moore's interdisciplinary discussion, then, mediates among religion, art, and politics. The "unseen" occupies a pivotal place in linking the "sacred" and "secular" realms: it is treated, in their text, as standing in a one-to-one correspondence with "doctrine." Religious rituals make particular "belief systems" appear credible by making them available to the senses as experience; political rituals accomplish the same task on behalf of "ideology." The crucial connection is between "the unseen" and the belief system that authoritarian organizations require as a condition of membership. Here, for Myerhoff's work on definitional ceremonies, is the crucial passage:

> ... not only is doctrinal efficacy a matter of faith, but frequently the anthropologically or politically presumed social and psychological "effects" of ritual necessarily are something more inferred than proved. For example, in Vogt and Abel's chapter [Moore & Myerhoff, 1977, pp. 173–188] we see an analysis that supplies a functional rationale for a no-

choice, one-candidate "election" in Mexico. Staged trials and planned "demonstrations" are a familiar part of the recent history of many nations. Thus there are traditions and ideologies as well as conventions of sociological interpretation which postulate that declared political objectives will be enhanced by a particular ceremonial display, or ritual performance.

All of these are ideologically, though perhaps not sociologically, different in kind from religious rituals. They offer internal explanations of their own efficacy which are distinct in obvious ways from those of religious rituals. The latter are other-worldly in rationale, the former exclusively this-wordly. The religious ritual moves the other world to affect this one. The secular ceremony moves this world and this world only. Hence two quite different explanations of causality underlie the two rituals. *Yet this difference brings out an important similarity between them. They both "show" the unseen.* [Emphasis added.] Religious ritual "shows" the existence of the other world through the display of attempts to move it. Analogously, a secular ceremony "shows" by acting in terms of them the existence of social relationships (the Government, the Party, etc.) or ideas and values which are inherently invisible most of the time. It objectifies them and reifies them. It displays symbols of their existence and by implicit reference postulates and enacts their "reality." Moore shows how newly independent Tanzania tries to give its national government and socialist ideology palpable immediacy through the medium of regular local political meetings. In such a setting questions of doctrinal and operational efficacy are urgent political issues. (Moore & Myerhoff, 1977, pp. 14–15)

Here, religion (with its no longer credible dogmas) and (socialist) politics, abstracted as "the secular," are linked through the concept of "the unseen." This was an *ideal* metaphor for Myerhoff.

In her concurrent work on definitional ceremonies, Myerhoff extended, vitalized, and transformed this writing of "the unseen." First, rechristened "invisibility," the metaphor is the keystone that gave the conceptual arch she constructed its felt stability along with is *Aufhebung.* The term, carried over from the domain of religion, transfers its "aura" onto a sociological category, where it acquires embodiment and social meaning as a general term for the plight of oppressed peoples. Myerhoff embeds "invisibility" in experience; in her use, *"the invisible" no longer refers to an order of ideas but to an order of beings.* So, in "Life Not Death in Venice," invisibility mediates between "hierophany," the showing forth of divine beings, and social oppression. These are the active meanings that appear throughout her writing on secular rituals: the hidden gods appear among ecstatic worshippers or an elated audience at a sacred drama; a socially impotent group appears "solid," worthy of respect, before an atten-tive, and now interested, audience of powerful representatives from the "outside society," including elected officials, TV and print journalists, leaders and executives of religious and social organizations.

In the move from the doctrinally oriented discussion of secular ritual to the life-historical and cultural orientation of her case studies, Myerhoff enriches the idea of secular ritual by materializing the character of what is shown forth, not socialist ideology (as the object of a hidden polemic that assumes that the United States = democracy and socialism = bureaucratic domination) but a living group of old Jewish socialists in all their heterodoxy, earthiness, charm, wisdom, difficulty, quarrelsomeness, manipulativeness, hurt. The crucial move that Myerhoff makes here is to connect religious ritual with an entirely different sociological notion of the "invisible" and, in the conceptual leap that gives her idea its specific character, to make invisibility refer not to a marginalized group in general but specifically to *the individual's identity and the worth of the group.* "Invisibility" is given sociological flesh so that it can live, resurrected, in the sphere of the spirit, as an intellectually credible category of human inwardness. *Identity* and *value* are the terms that Myerhoff the social scientist used in print for the inner things that in her public lectures and talks with colleagues she called, simply, soul.

Capable concepts beautifully demonstrated in moving essays are such finished things, it is hard to imagine that they were once discoveries, a working through by the scientific imagination of the sudden sense of fit, of wholeness, that occurred when two or three conceptual fragments lying around the writer's worktable were put together in a new way. Myerhoff's writing is charged with the radiant and productive atmosphere of the ethnographer's workshop, of intuitions carried through to fully embodied conceptualization and semiotic exegesis. In my reading of her work, "the invisible" is the site of immense intellectual and imaginative energy, the locus of a specific act of conceptualization and, through the developed concept, a source of continuing inspiration: for her and her readers.

I believe, there is no way to prove this, that the complex associations that came together, for Myerhoff, in the concept of definitional ceremonies were joined under the white heat that "the invisible" supplied for her. First, this whole category decisively ratified the existence of secular *rituals*: the contradiction in terms appeared transcended, and a unification of domains was effected by a material aesthetic technology. The means of transmission, not the message, was what the religion and the politics had in common. Second, the "aura" of what is made visible through religious ritual was transferred, as a value, to the quality of being that was made public in definitional ceremonies. A subtle sacralization of psychological and social experience was effected. This could not be directly admitted into Myerhoff's scientific work. But her descriptions of the awe and ecstasy of the Center people, in a state of *communitas*, are, it is evident, personally felt; they are not less "objective" because they are deeply experienced. Third, bringing together two categories that had immense moral authority for her, released in her the only form of faith that she was capable of: the conviction of the creative scientist that the idea she had discovered was both true and (aesthetically, morally) beautiful.

To metaphorically connect divinity with the hidden worth of oppressed people, and to make her writing the site where the valuable showing forth would take place and reach a wide audience—here was an idea that was also a calling; here was a project that permitted her to forge a "path of the heart" without violating her sense of reality; her professional commitments could be kept but charged with her will to vocation; the internal voice of her skepticism and the voice of her will to believe, rather than paralizing productivity, were reshaped in a project on which the contending voices within her could dialogically collaborate.

3.

To summarize and interpret (via Bakhtin [1984] and Raymond Williams) the concept of definitional ceremonies, I want to make the following points.

In this idea, Myerhoff proposes a genre of social discourse that has the following characteristics:

1. Its unity as a concept depends upon a genre-shaping intention, rather than any specific form of cultural performance. The common meaning of various types of storytelling, public rituals and ceremonies, meetings, murals, protest marches, and other enactments and displays is not a content separable from the form of expression. This common meaning resides precisely in the genre-shaping intention that gives all the various kinds of cultural performances their form-and-content unity. The common meaning that is to be discerned across the range of creative expression is made available through common symbols, and these collective symbols are the cultural materials upon which this category, as a unified genre, depends.

2. The genre-shaping intention is to affirm the value of the individual by grounding her personal identity and worth in the culture and social history of the group. In practice, this assertion of value is polemical and oppositional: it is made against the dominant social evaluation, which denies the meaning and value of the group's culture and social history. Hence, the intention is to contest the evaluative and interpretive social discourse of the dominant culture. To do so, this assertion of value must directly or indirectly quote, cite, refer back to the dominant valuations, and directly or indirectly "answer back." In situations where "answering back" is too risky, the cultural performance must both lodge a complaint and persuade the auditors that the protesting word they are actually hearing is an innocuous or even flattering word. The concurrence of the two semantic intentions create what Bakhtin (1984) called double-voiced discourse.

3. The double-voiced social discourse of the actors is created out of an assemblage of common symbols, which are reaccentuated by individuals and the group in its current historical moment. The newly constructed enactment reflects the group's immediate situation and its common history. In the process of cultural creation, the process of the individual is inseparable from the social creations of the group. Common traditions, symbols, and expressions are the cultural materials that are reworked by creative individuals. The power of the creation depends, in part, upon the individual's having authentically lived through the common meanings and thus his capacity to draw upon them as personal experience (Williams, 1961). The communication of the individual's personal experience to the group enables the group's members to experience, simultaneously, their membership in the collective culture and their individual identity (Williams, 1961). The individual's life-review process, which constructs an Eriksonian sense of selfsameness out of personal memories, is simultaneously working up the memories of the group because the individual's memories are inseparable from the language, traditions, culture, and social history of her time and place. The term *personal*, here, means authentically lived and is as much a social as an individual concept. The individual's personal memories, in their content already "intertwined" with the historical experience of the group, can be given form only in and through the language of the group (a culturally bounded linguistic zone, marked off from other "dialects") and its collective symbols. The language of the group and its collective symbols (i.e., the concrete means of storing, transmitting, reshaping, and creating meanings) owe their continued vitality to the creativity of gifted individuals as well as to the creativity of the group,

whose democratic culture and organization facilitates the collaborative making (planning and implementation) of cultural performance and events.

In conceiving of definitional ceremonies and applying the concept to her fieldwork with elderly Jews, Myerhoff saw novel tasks for ritual: she construed "definitional" to refer both to an Eriksonian developmental conflict and to a Turnerian social conflict, and to propose that the same social process—the cultural performance of reworked collective symbols—could offer a creative resolution of both crises. This is a proposal of enormous value. It is a pioneering theoretical move that has very wide practical application: both in ethnographic studies and in cultural work that enhances the sense of identity and self-worth among minority groups, while it builds a sense of a coherent, active community.

Myerhoff's concept of definitional ceremonies, once all the domains of experience it potentially links are reincorporated into the term, transcends the dualism that separates psyche and history, self and politics, the personal and social. Definitional ceremonies provide a self-effacing group with the internally legitimating means and the public techniques of contesting bad conditions and social injury. Myerhoff's ethnographic writings constitute an anthropology of the creative act. This is their value: these texts seek to theorize and describe the social-individual process of persons making the culture that makes them the persons they are.

NOTES

[1] This phrase appears in the "Introduction" to *Secular Ritual* that Myerhoff co-authored with Sally Falk Moore (Moore & Myerhoff, 1977). The academic formality and propriety of this text renders this phrase all the more striking by emphasizing its spoken-speech quality. It is evidently born of utterance and calls attention to its origin in the collaborative dialogue of *speaking* co-authors. Co-produced in scholarly dialogue, this phrase not only presents an idea but also represents (offers a linguistic image of) the process of reaching for it, in a language-stretching effort of formulation. This phrase echoes throughout Myerhoff's writing on ritual, although it is not repreated in precisely its original form. In "We Don't Wrap Herring in a Printed Page," the emphasis on the fictive, precarious character of rituals is carried in Myerhoff's (1977) writing of them as "made-up productions" (p. 199). The significance of this phrase in Myerhoff's work is most fully evidenced in "Telling One's Story" (1980b): "made up" is the key term of this text, and the key idea of definitional ceremonies is developed entirely in and through this key term,

which as verb and adjective saturates the discussion of "made-up ventures" and "making oneself up."

BIBLIOGRAPHY

Aronowitz, S. (1990). *The crisis in historical materialism: Class, politics and culture in Marxist theory* (2nd ed.). Minneapolis: University of Minnesota Press.

Bakhtin, M. M. (1984). *Problems of Dostoyevsky's poetics*. (Ed. and Trans. C. Emerson). Minneapolis: University of Minnesota Press.

Bruner, E. M. (1986). Introduction: Experience and its expressions. In V. W. Turner & E. M. Bruner (Eds.), *The anthropology of experience* (pp. 3–30). Urbana and Chicago: University of Illinois Press.

Geertz, C. (1973). Thick description: Toward an interpretive theory of culture. In *The interpretation of cultures*. New York: Basic Books.

Geertz, C. (1986). Epilogue: Making experience, authoring selves. In V. Turner & E. M. Bruner (Eds.), *The anthropology of experience* (pp. 373–380). Urbana and Chicago: Univerity of Illinois Press.

Gramsci, A. (1988). *An Antonio Gramsci reader: Selected writings, 1916–1935.* (Ed. D. Forgacs). New York: Schocken Books.

Jacoby, R. (1975). *Social amnesia: A critique of contemporary psychology from Adler to Laing.* Boston: Beacon Press.

Kaminsky, M. (1972). *What's inside you it shines out of you.* New York: Horizon Press.

Kaminsky, M. (Ed.). (1984). *The uses of reminiscence.* New York: Haworth Press.

Kaminsky, M. (in press). Myerhoff's "third voice." *Social Text, 33.*

Marcus, G. E., & Fischer, M. M. J. (1986). *Anthropology as cultural critique: An experimental moment in the human sciences.* Chicago and London: University of Chicago Press.

Moore, S. F., & Myerhoff, B. (1977). Introduction: Secular ritual: Forms and meanings. In S. F. Moore & B. Myerhoff (Eds.), *Secular ritual* (pp. 3–24). Assen, The Netherlands: Royal Van Gorcum Press.

Myerhoff, B. (1992). A death in due time: Conviction, order and continuity in ritual drama. In M. Kaminsky (Ed.), *Remembered lives: The work of ritual, storytelling and growing older.* Ann Arbor: University of Michigan Press.

Myerhoff, B. (1977). We don't wrap herring in a printed page: Fusion, fictions, and continuity in secular ritual. In S. F. Moore & B. Myerhoff (Eds.), *Secular ritual* (pp. 199–224). Assen, The Netherlands: Royal Van Gorcum Press.

Myerhoff, B. (1978). A symbol perfected in death: Continuity and ritual in the life and death of an elderly Jew. In B. Myerhoff & A. Simic (Eds.), *Life's career—aging: Cultural variations on growing old* (pp. 163–205). Beverly Hils, CA: Sage Publications.

Myerhoff, B. (1980a). *Number our days.* New York: Simon and Schuster.

Myerhoff, B. (1980b). Telling one's story. *The Center Magazine, 13*(2), 22–40.

Myerhoff, B. (1986). "Life not death in Venice": Its second life. In V. Turner & E. M. Bruner (Eds.), *The anthropology of experience* (pp. 261–286). Urbana and Chicago: University of Illinois Press.

Myerhoff, B. (1988). Surviving stories: Reflections on *Number our days.* In J. Kugelmass (Ed.), *Between two worlds: Ethnographic essays on American Jewry* (pp. 265–294). Ithaca, NY: Cornell University Press.

Myerhoff, B. (1992). *Remembered lives: The work of ritual, storytelling and growing older.* (Ed. M. Kaminsky). Ann Arbor: Michigan University Press.

Schappes, M. U. (1977, September–October). Irving Howe's World of our fathers: A critical analysis. *Jewish Currents.*

Turner, V. (1986). Dewey, Dilthey, and drama. In V. Turner & E. M. Burner (Eds.), *The anthropology of experience* (pp. 33–44). Urbana and Chicago: University of Illinois Press.

Williams, R. (1958). *Culture and society: 1780–1950.* New York: Columbia University Press.

Williams, R. (1961). *The long revolution.* New York: Columbia University Press.

Williams, R. (1986). The uses of cultural theory. *New Left Review, 158,* 19–31.

14

Justice and Mother Love: Toward A Critical Theory of Justice between Old and Young

Nancy S. Jecker

Theories unify only by banishing variety, particularity, and difference. Invariably, they exclude entire realms of human experience by reducing, simplifying, and assimilating. A task of critical theory is to attain a more widely encompassing unity. Its methods should result in opening the knowledge circle to allow others entrance. One invites and makes room for other perspectives by (1) questioning: turning criticism reflexively on oneself and one's traditions, theories, concepts, and methods; (2) enlarging: stretching traditional categories of thought to create an opening for change; and (3) unifying: revealing the extent to which apparently discordant ideas are interconnected.

Understood in this way, critical theory is "revolutionary" in a Kuhnian sense. It evolves from unity toward disparate schools of thought, then reemerges with a new paradigm in which the fetters of tradition are cast away only to be reinvented.

This chapter questions whether currently favored justice theories can support obligations of justice between generations. I argue that the foundations of these theories must be enlarged and suggest what the needed revision might be. The changes proposed call for fundamental shifts of emphasis, away from mutual disinterest toward filial affection and away from voluntary consent toward a conception of responsibilities that bind without consent. Toward the end of the chapter, I locate common ground between my approach and currently favored justice theories by showing how the proposal defended follows from subtle shifts in the more traditional theories.

QUESTIONING

Discussions of justice often start with considerations of rational self-interest and voluntary consent. Most of the major social contract theories of the 17th and 18th centuries start with this. Writing in the 17th century, Hobbes (1980) pictured human nature as impelled by the desire to acquire and hold power, and every man's power he envisioned as hindering the effects of every other man's power. Continually in competition for power and continually under threat of violence and death, people attain to civil society in one of two ways:

> One is by Naturall force; as when a man maketh his children, to submit themselves, and their children to his government, as being able to destroy them if they refuse. . . . The other is when men agree upon themselves, to submit to some Man . . . voluntarily, on confidence to be protected by him against all other. (p. 228)

Hobbes concludes that "the Lawes of nature (as *Justice, Equity, Modesty, Mercy* and (in summe) *doing to others, as wee would be done to,*) of themselves, without the terrour of some Power, to cause them to be observed, are contrary to our naturall Passions." (p. 223)

Although Locke was concerned not to be classed a Hobbist (Clapp, 1967) he shared Hobbes's belief that people originally exist in a state of nature, and remain so "till by their consents they make themselves members of some politic society" (Locke, 1955, p. 13). People agree to forgo the freedoms present in a state of nature only because of the advantages society affords. In a state of nature, persons rightly fear that another "would get me into his power without my consent, would use me as he pleased when he had got me there, and destroy me too, when he had a fancy to it" (pp. 14–15). To avoid this, people agree to transfer their rights to a magistrate.

Locke's contemporary, Robert Filmer (1949), likened the authority of the sovereign to the divinely given right of Adam to rule over Eve, their children, and all of creation. Working outside the social contract tradition, Filmer inspired and challenged that tradition by proposing that the father's authority to rule the family was conferred by divine decree, as was the authority of kings to rule subjects, males to rule females, and elders to rule the young (Filmer, 1949; Laslett, 1967).

Writing in the same social contract tradition as Locke, Hume (1978) described the original principle of human society as

> the natural appetite betwixt the sexes, which unites them together and preserves their union, till a new tye takes place in their concern for their common offspring. This new concern . . . forms a more numerous society; where the parents govern by the advantage of their superior strength and wisdom, and at the same time are restrain'd in the exercise of their authority by that natural affection which they bear their children. (p. 486)

Observing that individuals develop larger affections for persons with whom they stand in special relationships, Hume concluded that natural affection is antithetical to the requirements of an impartial and equal justice for all. On these grounds, Hume inferred that "we have naturally no real or universal motive for observing the laws of equity" and that "the sense of justice and injustice is not deriv'd from nature, but arises artificially" (p. 483). The "artificial" remedy comes when we recognize that our unequal affection is "much better satisfy'd by its restraint, than by its liberty, and that by preserving society, we make much greater advances in . . . acquiring possessions" (p. 492). Thus, although our natural desire is to acquire possessions for ourselves, our family, and our nearest friends, and although this desire is "insatiable, perpetual, universal, and directly destructive of society" (p. 492), the desire itself is fulfilled by restraining itself in order to make life in a society possible.

The idea that principles of justice further our own goals and interests is shared by more recent philosophers of justice as well. Placing himself squarely in the social contract tradition, Gauthier (1987) intends to ground justice on an agreement struck between rational persons who are concerned to maximize their own utility. Gauthier begins with a presumption against moral or other contraints on the pursuit of individual ends and then proceeds to argue that certain moral principles would nonetheless be agreed to as the object of a fully voluntary *ex ante* agreement. Although the premoral stage of this agreement is hypothetical, Gauthier describes parties to the agreement as actual individuals who are aware of their different levels of power and authority, natural abilities, and life goals. Such individuals would accept constraints on maximizing behavior so long as the net advantages of constrained maximizing are greater than those of uncontrained maximizing.

Rawls (1980) also identifies principles of justice as the object of a collective agreement. Parties to this agreement "do not recognize any principles of justice as . . . antecedently given; their aim is simply to select the conception most rational for them, given their circumstances" (p. 564). Rawls imposes upon the choice situation a requirement of impartiality by placing choosers under a veil of ignorance. Parties are ignorant of such things as their natural talents and abilities, their social advantages and disadvantages, and their paticular inclinations and aspirations. Despite their ignorance, parties have sufficient information to rank alternative principles of justice and to make "a rational decision in the ordinary sense'" (Rawls, 1971, p. 143). For example, parties know that whatever their ends and aspiriations may be, the means to achieving them will in general require protecting liberties, widening opportunities, and increasing means for promoting their aims. According to Rawls (1971), the concept of rationality that guides parties' choice of justice principles "must be interpreted . . . in the narrow sense . . . of taking the most effective means to given ends" (p. 14) and of advancing one's system of ends as far as possible. This conception excludes sacrificing personal ends to promote the ends of others and assumes that "parties take no interest in one another's interest" (p. 127) and are "mutually disinterested" (p. 128). Therefore, they "are not willing to have their interests sacrificed to the others" (p. 129).

Common to all social contract approaches is that duties of justice (1) result from voluntary consent, rather than being incumbent upon individuals independent of their agreement; (2) promote individuals' interests, as opposed to requiring altruistic sacrifices; and (3) are instrumentally rational, rather than arising from natural sentiments that constitute a "given" in human experience.

When one turns from the general problem of justice to the problem of justice between generations, several differences are bound to strike one. In the first place, voluntary consent cannot provide a basis for the duties of young to old. Whereas adults can choose whether or not to procreate, and collectively they decide whether or not to continue the species, children can hardly choose to be born, nor can they collectively choose whether their generation will come into existence. Likewise, parents are increasingly able to control the timing and circumstances of reproduction and the gender and health of offspring, and they exercise an enormous influence over the development of their children's personality, character, and goals. By contrast, children are obviously not free to select the parents who will bear them, and they wield relatively less influence over their parents' personality, character, and goals. If, as other have argued, grown children have duties of justice toward their parents (Okin, 1989) and toward members of older generations generally (Jonsen, 1991), then these duties must be founded on premises other than voluntary consent.

The premises of instrumental rationality and self-interest also pose difficulties for duties of justice between young and old because younger persons can gain few advantages by fulfilling duties of justice to older individuals. Although our actions now can influence whether or not younger persons will benefit us in the future, nothing that we do now will affect the benefits that members of older generations have conferred already. In particular, disenfranchising older persons from a share of social resources will not cause those benefits to be taken from us. In addition, although most of the benefits younger persons confer will come in the future, most of what older generations as a group will contribute to those that come after them has been contributed already. For example, most of the contributions older persons as a group are going to make to culture and science have been made. Hence, leaving older persons out of justice considerations does not risk forsaking a pool of benefits we might otherwise receive.

ENLARGING

How might these insights help us to fashion a more encompassing theory of justice, one that can accommodate problems of justice between old and young? Rawls (1971) provides a partial answer to this question in the course of discussing the related problem of justice between nonoverlapping present and future generations. Rawls begins by noting that obligations to generations who live in the future represent a "special" problem and "must be treated in another fashion" (p. 211). Parties concerned solely to advance their own interests have no more reason to take the interests of future generations into account than they have to consider the interests of their elders.

Whereas present persons can make future persons better or worse off, the forward direction to time means that when future persons exist they will not be in a position to benefit or harm their deceased predecessors. If the source of justice is the mutual advantage it confers to disinterested parties, then present generations have no rational basis in justice to sacrifice on behalf of posterity.

In response to this problem, Rawls (1971) argues that any demands justice places on present generations are contingent on the assumption that persons choosing principles of justice *care* about their immediate progeny. In particular, Rawls's motivational assumption specifies that "good will stretches over at least two generations . . . we may think of the parties as heads of families and therefore as having a desire to further the welfare of their nearest descendants" (p. 128). Although the concern of parties is confined to their own children and grandchildren, because parties select principles without knowing the generation to which they belong, this limited concern is expressed as a concern for all future generations.

Consider how the motivational assumption Rawls (1971) introduces might be invoked to support obligations between living generations of young and old. Following Rawls's general approach, the most obvious interpretation is that persons in the original position stand as representatives from the same generation, yet the interests of earlier generations are taken into account because parties *care* about their immediate predecessors, (i.e., their living parents and grandparents) (Jecker, in press b). On this interpretation, parties want to guarantee justice to *specific* older persons for whom they care. Yet the veil of ignorance assures that *all* older persons are looked after because parties do not know who their loved ones are. This interpretation has the advantage of symmetry with Rawls's (1971) own account of intergenerational justice. Whereas Rawls supports justice between present and future generations by assuming that parties belong to the same generation but care about their descendants, the suggested interpretation of justice between young and old generations assumes that parties belong to the same age group but care about their predecessors.

To elaborate this proposal further, we might suppose that parties in the original position are both the parents of a family of procreation and the descendants of a family of origin. Each member of the original position cares about the well-being of both someone in the next generation and someone in the last. Assuming that for anyone in the prior generation there exists someone in the present who cares about that person, persons in different generations will have obligations of justice to each other. On this reading, it is not the fact that generations before us have lived an arbitrary number of years since birth that gives rise to the problem of justice between generations. It is instead the fact that generations before us are our elders, and generations after us are younger relative to us. Rather than drawing an arbitrary line between old and young (e.g., 65) and insisting that we must return to the original position to solve justice issues between these groups, this approach notes a *perennial* conflict between members of different generations within a family. This conflict arises regardless of the year of one's birth and lasts throughout the march of each generation from youth to old age.[1] On this interpretation, it is not membership in a particular age group or birth cohort but one's place in a family lineage that frames the problem of intergenerational justice. This reading is in keeping with the historical and genealogical meaning of "generation," defined as "the offspring of the same parent or parents regarded as a single degree or step in the descent of a person or family from an ancestor" (*Oxford English Dictionary*). This interpretation also matches Rawls's (1971) suggestion that parties in the original position represent "continuing strands" in a family lineage (p. 192).

The justification for introducing a motivational assumption must be that when the veil of ignorance is lifted, parties will discover that they actually do care about their parents and grandparents, as well as their children and grandchildren. On this reading, the principles of intergenerational justice derived from the original position are valid for us, given certain psychological and sociological facts about our society; namely, that we reside in families (though not necessarily traditional families) and that families represent a common locus of intimacy. In our society, many find their closest attachments to other within a family circle (i.e., in relationships to parents, siblings, spouses, or offspring). Indeed, the very meaning of the family has been defined by some in terms of loyalty and affection, as opposed to simple biological relatedness (Gutis, 1989). Admittedly, if people in our society ceased living in families, or if the nature of relationships within the family changed so that bonds of attachments were not commonly formed there, then the argument that includes filial affection would lose its force for us. Yet this limitation is in keeping with the general limitations and assumptions already inherent in Rawls's (1971) account. On the one hand, Rawls admits that "it is impossible to develop a substantive theory of justice founded solely on truths of logic and definition. The analysis of moral concept and the apriori ... is too slender a basis. [Instead,] [m]oral philosophy must be free to use contingent assumptions and general facts as it pleases" (p. 51). The motivational assumption, including the extended version of it that I am proposing, is one example of this phenomenon. On the other hand, Rawls (1985) views his own theory as "a moral conception worked out for a specific kind of subject," namely, "the basic structure of a modern constitutional democracy" (p. 224). He leaves open the larger question of "whether the theory can be extended to a general political conception for different kinds of societies existing under different historical and social conditions" (p. 225). The extended motivational assumption I have introduced also is worked out for a specific kind of society. I refer to a society in which the basic structure of society includes families, and families are the place where caring activities and relationships between generations occur.

UNIFYING

What common ground exists between the proposal I am defending and the social contract theories described in the first section? It is possible to interpret my proposal regarding justice between generations as evolving from subtle shifts in the social contract approach. This interpretation begins by noting that social contract theories conceive of the family in patriarchal terms and then proceed to argue that other duties of justice, such as the duties of citizens to the state, are grounded on this traditional model of the family. Hobbes (1980) for instance, likens the duties of citizens to those of children in the family. He regards children in a family as obligated to submit to the government of their father because of the superior power and protection a father offers. Further, Hobbes conceives of children's obligations to fathers as freely chosen. As one Hobbes commentator puts it, "it is because children freely agree to submit to the authority of parents [i.e., fathers], not because of the fact of birth itself that parents acquire their right of dominance over their children. . . . The obligations of children are not natural, but as artificial and consensual as the obligations of citizens or of subjects" (Blustein, 1980, p. 68). Understood in this way, the underpinning of parental authority is the child's consent to obey parents. Wanting to remain alive, children come to recognize that their parents possess the power to kill or abandon them. This justification of patriarchal authority forms the foundation of Hobbes's (1980) account of political obligation and the duty of citizens to obey sovereigns.

Locke's (1955) conception shares with Hobbes's (1980) the idea that the ethical basis of paternal authority arises artificially, rather than arising from fathers' procreative acts. According to Locke (1955), the father's government is not supported "by any peculiar right of Nature," and "so little power does the bare act of begetting give a man over his issue, [that] if all his care ends there . . . this be all the title he hath to the name and authority of a father" (p. 50). Like Hobbes, Locke is concerned to limit the scope of paternal authority so that children are *born* freemen, rather than slaves. Referring to fathers and sons, Locke writes that

> his power extends not to the lives or goods, which either their own industry or another's bounty has made theirs; not to their liberty neither, when they are once arrived to the enfranchisement of the years of discretion. lThe father's empire then ceases, and he can from thenceforwards no more dispose of the liberty of his son that that of any other man. (p. 51)

Even before children reach the age of maturity, Locke regards their liberty as intact. "Tis one thing," he observes, "to owe honor, respect, gratitude and assistance, another to require an absolute obedience and submission. The honour due to parents, a monarch in his thrown owes his mother, and yet this lessens not his *authority*, nor subjects him to her *government*" (p. 52; emphasis added). Locke's account, like Hobbes's, extrapolates the conditions for a just state by drawing upon the analogy of a just family.

The patriarchal family that Hobbes (1980) and Locke (1955) use as a model for justice broadly construed is carried over in present justice theories. True to this tradition, Rawls (1971) proposes that the foundations of a just society are the principles chosen by heads of families, presumably fathers, in an original position. The fact that Rawls represents parties in the original position as superiors, rather than subordinates (i.e., mothers and children), within a family eventually infects the entire conception of justice that emerges. Like Hobbes and Locke before him, Rawls identifies the central problem of justice to be deciding on a just transfer of "primary goods," defined as income, wealth, power, and authority. Thus, the very problem of justice, as the social contract tradition conceives it, is a problem faced by breadwinners, traditionally males, who own and distribute material property and wealth within both family and state.

My approach establishes obligations between generations by retaining a filial model, but shifting its emphasis from free choice and self-interest to filial affection. In so doing, it comes much closer to embodying the perspectives of mothers and children, who traditionally occupy a subordinate status within the family. The central problem of justice between generations in my account is not to transfer property from fathers to sons but to clarify the responsibilities of

those who care for the younger generation (i.e., mothers) and those
who care for the older generation (i.e., adult children, particularly
adult daughters). Thus, my emphasis is the duty incumbent on those
who stand in caring relationships. For most of Western history, it has
been mothers who dispensed love and caregiving to children because
it is mothers who have been assigned the responsibilities of nurturing
and caring for children as a regular and substantial part of their work
in life. (For a detailed and incisive account of mother love, see Ruddick, 1990). The duties of mothers and daughters have been assigned
mostly by default, not voluntary choice. In addition, it is love and
affection that often impel mother's discernment and fulfillment of
filial duties. Relegated to a subordinate role in the family (as well as
the state), mothers have hardly been in a position to decide what their
duties will be or to bargain with men to maximize their share of
primary goods. Thus, the duties between generations my account
envisions are not freely chosen, instrumentally rational, or self-serving. They arise instead from our natural sentiments and reflect our
capacity to sacrifice our own interests to promote others' ends. (For
more on specific duties between old and young, see Jecker, 1989.)

Inklings of the approach I am advocating can be detected in the
writings of traditional social contract theorists. In the course of discussing the right of succession, for example, Hobbes (1980) relates
that it is filial affection that determines the transfer of power from
one sovereign to the next. A monarch's will, according to Hobbes, is
"that a Child of his own . . . be preferred before any other; because
men are presumed to be more enclined to advance their own children. . . . When his own Issue faileth, rather a Brother than a stranger;
and so still the neerer in bloud, rather than the more remote, because
it is alwayes presumed that the neerer of kin, is the neerer in affection" (p. 250).

Locke (1955) also penned passages on the relevance of beneficence
and filial affection to the broader problem of justice. Referring to the
authority and responsibility of parents, Locke submits that "though
the power of commanding and chastising them go along with it, yet
God hath woven into the principles of human nature such a tender-
ness for their offspring that there is little fear that parents should use
their power with too much rigour" (p. 53).

Perhaps the most notable discussion of filial affection, however, is
Hume's (1978). Hume made much of the fact that people harbor a
natural affection toward their immediate circle of family and acquaintances, yet, in the same breath, he discounted the possibility
that this natural sentiment could provide the underpinnings for justice. Justice, Hume reckoned, could not possibly spring from such

partial love but instead would require an impartial sympathy for all humankind. Because there is "no such passion in human minds, as the love of mankind, merely as such, independent of personal qualities or services, or relation to oneself" (p. 481), Hume concluded that an artificial source for justice must be found. Hume goes on to identify the utility or advantage produced by accepting and following rules of justice and equity.

Building on Hume's (1978) *initial* insight, my proposal shows how to support principles of justice from a foundation of limited affection. By placing partial and limited affection under certain restrictions, such as a veil of ignorance, we ensure that duties of justice extend to all members of a generation, rather than being confined to kin relationships. Rather than deriving justice from universal love, this approach broadens the scope of partial filial affections. It demonstrates that special affections and personal relationships can be rendered compatible with broader requirements of impartial justice (see Jecker, in press a).

Not surprisingly, the approach defended her garners support from recent feminist scholarship. First, feminists have raised doubts about the starting point of voluntary consent assumed by justice theories. Baier (1986), for example, argues that voluntary consent theories are gender-and class-driven. Whereas men traditionally have enjoyed freedom of choice about the relationships they form and leave,

> the important relationships . . . which structured women's lives for most of the known history of our species, relations to spouse, children, fellow workers, were not entered into by free choice. . . . Contract is a device for traders, entrepreneurs, and capitalists, not for children, servants, indentured wives, and slaves. They were the traded, not the traders, and any participation they had in the promising game was mere play. (p. 247)

Zaretsky (1982) extends this point when she notes that primary ties of dependence, nurturing, and mutual help are inevitable for all members of society, even in a society like ours, organized around individualism and independence.

Second, recent feminists have faulted modern moral theories for neglecting the moral orientation of benevolence and personal relationships. Gilligan (1982), for example, argues that care for particular individuals in the context of close personal relationships is underrepresented in currently favored justice theories. This orientation, she believes, dominates in the thinking of most women. The result is that current justice theories evaluate women's justice reasoning as underdeveloped and "compromised in its refusal of blind impartiality" (p. 18). Whereas Gilligan develops an alternative ethic, which she

dubs "an ethic of care," to convey the moral universe that she believes dominates the moral thinking of most women, the Rawlsian
approach I have defended takes Gilligan's concern in the *opposite*
direction. I try to show that attending to caring relationships is quite
possible *under the rubric of justice* and begin to fill out the areas of
justice where this attention is both possible and necessary.

Finally, recent feminists have challenged the premise of instrumental rationality that underlies much social contract theory. Along these
lines, Gibson (1977) has argued that the value neutrality assigned to
rationality in these approaches renders it too weak to carry the moral
weight placed upon it. Examining Rawls's theory, in particular, she
charges that instrumental rationality provides no basis for criticizing
a society whose institutions systematically promote and whose
members acquire and act upon final ends and goals that are objec-
tionable. According to Gibson, "No questions [can] arise about the
sources of people's desires or about whether pursuit of the chosen
ends is really in their interests" (p. 197). For this reason, the account
of justice parties choose may reflect and further morally repugnant
aims. Thus, Rawls's and other procedures for choosing principles of
morality or justice are, at least in principle, compatible with an unequal or exploitative society.

Others feminists, such as Lloyd (1989) and Jaggar (1989), make the
broader point that *no* account of reason can provide a complete
normative method or ideal. This is because the "man of reason"
inevitably lacks the human emotion, insight, and experience by which
a robust moral life is lived. Such a life receives direction from "outlaw
emotions," emotions that Western philosophy has traditionally excluded from the knowledge circle.

Modeling justice on a revised filial model rings true for still more
basic reasons. If we understand justice in terms of self-interest, voluntary consent, and instrumental rationality, this puts us at a loss to
explain why justice is owed to those who are *most* in need of justice.
The vulnerable and dependent members of our family and our society, including the frail elderly and young children, surely fall outside the scope of justice, because their contributions to the public
good are not likely to measure up. Nor will excluding the weakest
individuals threaten those who are more powerful. Troubled himself
by this possibility, Hume (1965) invariably dismisses it:

> Were there a species of creatures intermingled with men, which, though
> rational, were possessed of such inferior strength, both of body and
> mind, that they were incapable of all resistance, and could never, upon

the highest provocation, make us feel the effects of their resentment; the necessary consequence, I think, is that we should be bound by the laws of gentle usage to these creatures, but should not properly speaking lie under any restraint of justice with regard to them. (p. 41)[2]

As Western history sorrowfully attests, excluding such "creatures" from our conception of justice can have but one result: to make a travesty of justice. Furthermore, it is foolish to forget that *all* of us undergo fraily and dependence as much, or more, than we enjoy vigor and independence. In both youth and old age, human creatures need and grope for others' support. We spend our lives evolving from an initial to a final stage of dependence; any autonomy or independence we accomplish are a fleeting, not a lasting, glory.

NOTES

[1] My use of "generation" differs from Norman Daniels's (1988) use of this term. Whereas Daniels restricts the term *generation* to nonproximate future or past persons, I use this term to refer to proximate or overlapping generations, as well as nonproximate and nonoverlapping generations.

[2] See Hume (1965). More recently, other philosophers working in the social contract tradition have drawn similar conclusions. Gauthier (1987), for example, argues that rational individuals would refuse to accept constraints on their maximizing behavior for the purpose of transferring but not increasing, benefits. Nor would rational persons consent to moral duties without reciprocity from others. Gauthier thus acknowledges that his theory "denies any place to rational constraints, and so to morality, outside the context of mutual benefit" (p. 16). Before an agreement on morals goes through, each party must find initially acceptable what others bring to the bargaining table.

REFERENCES

Baier, A. (1986). Trust and antitrust. *Ethics, 96,* 231–261.

Blustein, J. (1980). *Parents and children: The ethics of the family.* New York: Oxford University Press.

Clapp, J. G. (1967). John Locke. In P. Edwards (Ed.), *The encyclopedia of philosophy,* Vol. 4 (pp. 487–503). New York: Macmillan.

Daniels, N. (1988). *Am I my parents' keeper: An essay on justice between the young and old.* New York: Oxford University Press.

Filmer, R. (1949). Patriarcha. In P. Laslett (Ed.), *Patriarcha and the other political works of Sir Robert Filmer.* New York: Oxford University Press.

Gauthier, D. (1987). *Morals by agreement.* New York: Oxford University Press.

Gibson, M. (1977). Rationality. *Philosophy and Public Affairs, 6,* 192–225.

Gilligan, C. (1982). *In a different voice: Psychological theory and women's development.* Cambridge, MA: Harvard University Press.

Gutis, P. S. (1989, July 7). Court widens family definition to gay couples living together. *New York Times,* pp. 1, 12.

Hobbes, T. (1980). Leviathan. In C. B. Macpherson (Ed.), *Hobbes: Leviathan.* New York: Penguin Books.

Hume, D. (1965). An enquiry concerning the principles of morals. In A. MacIntyre (Ed.), *Hume's ethical writings* (pp. 23–156). Notre Dame, IN: University of Notre Dame Press.

Hume, D. (1978). A treatise of human nature. In L. A. Selby-Bigge (Ed.), *A treatise of human nature* (2nd ed.) New York: Oxford University Press.

Jaggar, A. (1989). Love and knowledge: Emotion in feminist epistemology. In A. Garry & M. Pearsall (Eds.), *Women, knowledge and reality* (pp. 129–156). Winchester, MA: Unwin Hyman.

Jecker, N. S. (1989). Are filial duties unfounded? *American Philosophical Quarterly, 26,* 73–80.

Jecker, N. S. (in press a). Impartiality and special relations. In D. Meyers, C. Murphy, & K. Kipinis (Eds.), *Kindred matters: Rethinking the philosophy of the family.* Ithaca, NY: Cornell University Press.

Jecker, N. S. (in press b). Intergenerational justice and the family. *Journal of Value Inquiry.*

Jonsen, A. R. (1991). Resentment and the rights of the elderly. In N. S. Jecker (Ed.), *Aging and ethics.* New York: Humana Press.

Laslett, P. (1967). Filmer, Robert. In P. Edwards (Ed.), *The encyclopedia of philosophy,* Vol. 3 (pp. 212–203). New York: Macmillan.

Lloyd, G. (1989). The man of reason. In A. Garry & M. Pearsall (Eds.), *Women, knowledge and reality* (pp. 111–128). Winchester, MA: Unwin Hyman.

Locke, J. (1955). Of civil government, second treatise. In R. Kirk (Ed.), *John Locke: Of civil government* (pp. 1–205). Chicago: Henry Regnery.

Okin, S. M. (1989). *Justice, gender and the family.* New York: Basic Books.

Rawls, J. (1971). *A theory of justice.* Cambridge, MA: Harvard University Press.

Rawls, J. (1980). Kantian constructivism in moral theory. *Journal of Philosophy, 77,* 515–572.

Rawls, J. (1985). Justice as fairness: Political not metaphysical. *Philosophy and Public Affairs, 14,* 223–251.

Ruddick, S. (1990). *Maternal thinking.* Boston: Beacon Press.

Zaretsky, E. (1982). The place of the family in the origins of the welfare state. In B. Thorne & M. Yalom (Eds.), *Rethinking the family* (pp. 188–224). New York: Longman.

15

The Lives of Older Women: Perspectives from Political Economy and the Humanities

Beverly Ovrebo and Meredith Minkler

Critical gerontology may be seen as evolving along two paths simultaneously—paths that sometimes intersect and move in common directions but that have tended to remain distinct. The first path views critical gerontology as embracing a broad framework of political economy of aging and considers how political, socioeconomic, and related factors interact to shape and determine the experience of growing old. Critical gerontology in this sense is deeply concerned with the intersection of gender and aging and views gender (along with race and class) as a pivotal variable influencing the trajectory of growing old by predetermining an individual's location in the social

289

order (Estes, 1991). Although often implicit, concerns with social justice lie at the basis of such political economy perspectives.

The second path views critical gerontology as an important alternative to the ever more technical and "instrumental" orientation of academic gerontology (Moody, 1988). Within the latter dominant orientation, as Moody notes, "the problems of later life are treated with scientific and managerial efficiency, but with no grasp of their larger political or existential significance. The life world of the last stage of life is progressively drained of meaning" (p. 82).

Critical gerontology in the sense developed by Moody (1988) and by Cole and others (Cole & Gadow, 1986; Cole, Van Tassel, & Kastenbaum, 1991) is particularly focused on these larger questions of meaning. Viewed within this framework, the role of gender is critical both in terms of its political significance and in terms of the existential questions it helps to illuminate. The former concerns with the political import of gender represent a place where the two paths in critical gerontology intersect; the latter, more existential focus, represents a point of divergence.

In this chapter, we will attempt to travel both pathways toward the end of viewing in broader relief women's experience of aging and growing old in contemporary American society. A political economy perspective thus will emphasize the structural constraints within which aging takes place. An existential and humanistic perspective will be used to explore how older women create meaning in an unjust world in spite of the enormity of these structural constraints.

It is customary to view such topics as women and aging within either a social science paradigm or a more existential and humanistic framework, but the narrow vision born of such isolated approaches severely limits our understanding of the richness and complexity of the human condition. Further, such distinctions reinforce what Weiland (chap. 5, this volume) describes as the "rift in gerontology . . . reflecting the tired, but still true two-cultures debate (science v. humanities)." We therefore have chosen to follow the less popular tradition exemplified by Simone de Beauvoir (1970), for whom subjects such as old age and the condition of women are explored with careful attention to both "objective data" and "subjective experiences." Neither strictly a Marxist nor a "pure" exitentialist, de Beauvoir's refreshing ability to straddle both worlds in works such as *The Second Sex* (1972) and *The Coming of Age* (1970) has vastly contributed to our understanding of the intersections between the political economy and meaning dimensions of aging and womanhood.

Beauvoir (1970) saw social stratification in Western societies as based on a utilitarian ethos, wherein humans are valued contingently, in terms of their worth as producers and consumers. In contrast, a social justice perspective presupposes the valuation of humans unconditionally, what Frankl (1990) terms a person's "dignity" and Kant (1789), the view of human beings as "sacred ends." The quest for meaning, for a life with purpose, begins with experiencing one's dignity as a human being. How is aging with dignity achieved in a society that values people in terms of their conditional and instrumental value? And how do those who are systematically and structurally devalued because of their gender, age, class, race, and/or sexual identify find and make meaning in their old age?

This chapter builds on the idea of an "empowering" or "liberating" gerontology, as put forth by Moody (1988). We will focus on how old women construct meaning by analyzing works about older women, written by women. In particular, we will focus on the struggle for meaning in old age as it is experienced by some old women who are poor, lesbian, and/or black. How do women age well in a society that devalues them as women and old people, especially those women who have confronted a lifetime of oppression and marginalization based on their social class, race, and/or sexual identity? And what are the structural barriers that constrain such women's choices and sharply circumscribe the territory for which they construct maps of meaning?

We will begin by creating a political economy context for analysis and then will explore some interpretations of the "meaning dimension" of old age as it is experienced by women who are poor, lesbian, and/or African American. We will then briefly compare and contrast what these interpretations suggest may be the spiritual crisis involved in aging for each group of women and the heroic archetypes each group has constructed. We conclude with a comparative analysis of the life crises and possibilities experienced by each of the three groups, as well as the resolution of these crises, as they are suggested in the novels and characters we have examined.

PERSPECTIVES FROM POLITICAL ECONOMY

Simone de Beauvoir (1970) once declared that aging is a class struggle. Like race and gender, social class is a primary stratifier and hence a primary filter through which to see and understand differential life chances. In Dowd's (1980) words: "the individual's experience of growing old and the nature of age relations vary so significantly by social class that there is a need for unified analysis in which both age *and* class are considered" (pp. 21–22).

Estes (1991) has echoed these sentiments, arguing that "analyses of class and age must be concerned with understanding how individual elders, given their unique biographies and historical moment, are made differentially dependent according to their preretirement class, gender, and racial/ethnic status" (pp. 25–26). Viewed from this perspective, women who are working class or poor, black or lesbian, may be seen as doubly or triply devalued in old age. This devaluation is reflected in part in their high rates of economic vulnerability. Women as a whole thus make up 63% of the elderly population but close to three fourths of the elderly poor (Davis, 1986).

Single older women are at particularly high risk for poverty, with 90% of all elderly poor women being either widowed, divorced, separated, or never married (O'Rand, 1986). Black women are especially vulnerable in this regard, chiefly because of their very high rates of widowhood. Fully 30% of black women are widowed before they reach age 65, for example (compared to 16% of white women), and close to three quarters are widowed by age 75 (Grambs, 1989). Not surprising, older black single women constitute the poorest group in American society (Grambs, 1989). It is far more difficult to accurately assess the economic situation of older lesbians, in part because of their "invisible" status: Not only do the majority of our social institutions render gays and lesbians invisible, but as Catalano points out, older members of these groups "have learned to make use of anonymity and deception as survival techniques (Catalano, Valentine, & Greever, 1981, p. 50).

Because gays and lesbians occupy an inferior legal status that makes even the longest-term relationships invisible in the eyes of the law, data are unavailable on the number of older lesbians who are living with partners. We do know, however, that a significant number of elderly lesbians live alone and that their status as single women puts them at risk for economic hardship. Indeed, well over half of all single older women living alone are "economically vulnerable," living either below or within just 200% of the poverty line (Villers Foundation, 1987).

Older black, lesbian, and/or working-class women who are in the labor force suffer the adverse effects of gender on their economic chances, effects that operate over the life span but whose impact is particularly pronounced in old age. The continued occupational segregation of women in the low-paying, peripheral sector of the labor market, the "in and out" pattern of their work participation due to child and parent care responsibilities, pay and pension inequities, and high divorce rates thus result in women's entering old age at a significant economic disadvantage. For many of these women, heavy dependence on Social Security and/or Supplemental Security Income (SSI) as the main or only source of income reflects and reinforces a lifetime of economic vulnerability: fully a third of older single women who receive Social Security, for example, rely on it for more than 90% of their income (WEAL, 1985). Programs like Social Security and SSI lack what Margolis (1990) has termed a "compassion index" and as such reinforce and reproduce inequalities in income on the basis of race, social class, and gender. Black and working-class women in the labor force thus earn less money on which retirement benefits are calculated and are also more likely to have to retire early for health reasons than are white women and/or women of higher social classes.

Older black women's disproportionate representation in domestic service and other jobs not covered by Social Security put them at an additional disadvantage. And older women who are unmarried (including most older lesbians and African-American women) are further disadvantaged by the structuring of Social Security and SSI in ways that favor married persons over singles. SSI, for example, which sets a minimum (albeit an inadequate) income floor for low-income elders, sets its maximum benefit at 90% of the poverty line for married couples but lowers it to just 76% of the poverty line for single persons. The legislation thus contains a de facto gender, race, and sexual orientation bias that disadvantages the majority of older women who qualify for assistance.

Although we have focused primarily on women's differential experience of aging on the basis of income, other critical differences by race, class, and sexual identify are also worthy of attention. The powerful role of race and class in influencing health status, for example, has been widely documented and is consistently recognized throughout the life course (Estes & Rundall, in press). Among elderly women as well as men, health problems are twice as prevalent in the poor as in middle- and upper-class groups (NCHS, 1984), and an inverse relationship between socioeconomic status and activity limitations also has been noted. Differences in health status between single and married persons are also well documented and suggest that older lesbians may be at elevated risk. Older women living alone thus have significantly higher rates of activity limitation due to chronic illness than their married counterparts (NCHS, 1984) and have up to 10 times the latter's rate of institutionalization (Commonwealth Fund, 1988). Although strong networks may, of course, help single lesbian elders retain their functional independence and avoid institutionalization, the invisibility of this population has prevented adequate data collection that would allow us to gauge accurately the proportions who are in fact immersed in strong supportive networks.

Differences in health status on the basis of race are also note-worthy, with white women at birth having almost a 5½-year life expectancy advantage over African-American women (NCHS, 1990). Significant racial differences in chronic conditions and activity lim-itations also are apparent by race, with elderly black women suffering poorer health and greater disability in old age than do white women of the same age (NCHS, 1988). Findings like the above have led researchers to propose a "double jeopardy" hypothesis of minority aging which suggests that the disadvantaged position of older blacks in areas such as health and income reflects the combined effects of racism and ageism (Dowd & Bengtson, 1978). By extension, older black women occupy a triple-jeopardy status, with both gender and age compounding the burdens imposed by race.

The concept of multiple jeopardy is a useful one in understanding the compound disadvantages suffered not only by older black women but, as we have seen, by elderly poor women and older lesbians as well. Members of all three groups thus suffer the com-bined effects of ageism and sexism, effects that for some merely compound what is already experienced as significant devaluation on the basis of race, class, or sexual identity.

Multiple jeopardy goes well beyond such traditionally examined dimensions as health and income. The area of caregiving, for exam-ple, lends itself to a multiple-jeopardy analysis. It is now well estab-lished that families, principally women family members, provide 80% to 90% of the care given to the elderly in noninstitutional settings (Stone, Cafferta, & Sangl, 1987). Yet the nature of the caregiving experience may differ significantly by race, class, and sexual identity. Archibold (1983) thus has observed that while the resources available to middle- and upper-class women allow them most frequently to assume the role of care *manager* for elderly parents or spouses, working-class and poor women are more frequently required to be hands-on, direct care*givers*, whose own health may be compromised by this more demanding form of caregiving. As predominantly single women with correspondingly limited economic resources, older les-bians may be similarly more likely to serve as hands-on caregivers to partners and elderly parents. Because the majority of older lesbians have no daughters, they further are likely to lack the kinds of respite and other assistance from a next generation of women that many heterosexual women caregivers are able to call upon.

The caregiver role is also particularly important to consider from the vantage point of older African-American women, for in addition to their not insignificant direct caregiver role with respect to elderly family members, older black women play a vital role as caregivers to infants and young children in the extended family (Grambs, 1989; Staples, 1976). The past decade has seen a doubling of the number of grandchildren being raised by their grandparents, for example, and this trend has been particularly pronounced in black families (U. S. Bureau of the Census, 1991). Factors such as the rise in teenage pregnancy and the crack cocaine epidemic, moreover, have meant that many grandmothers who took on this caregiving role in their 30s or 40s are continuing to raise grandchildren—and not infrequently, great-grandchildren—into their late 60s or 70s (Minkler & Roe, 1991). As we shall see later, such cross-generational caregiving contributes to the older black grandmother's position of status and importance in black families. Yet the stresses involved in this extensive caregiving role may take a significant toll on her physical and emotional health.

Whereas older black women, working class women, and lesbians appear to suffer substantial caregiver burden, their situation as potential recipients of caregiving may be a vulnerable one. As predominantly single women, many of whom lack partners or daughters, lesbian women may be at particular risk in this regard. Moreover, recent changes in Medicare reimbursement policies that have had the effect of encouraging physicians to send patients home "quicker and sicker" have especially hurt older women living alone, for whom premature discharge may mean inadequate opportunities for recovery and hence health complications, nursing home admission, and/or a return to the hospital (Shaughnessy & Kramer, 1990).

The whole area of institutionalization represents another domain in which older lesbians and black and working-class women can be seen to occupy multiple-jeopardy status. Working-class and poor women are heavily devalued by a nursing home industry that openly discriminates against prospective patients who are low-income and hence financed by the government's Medicaid program (Wallace, 1990). Many nursing homes further manage to discharge residents once they do become Medicaid-eligible, thus freeing their beds for higher-income private-pay patients (Hawes & Phillips, 1986).

For older black women, nursing home discrimination on the basis of income may be compounded by direct racial discrimination. Studies in New York (Sullivan, 1984) and St. Louis (Wallace, 1990) thus have revealed substantial discrimination on the basis of race, with hospital discharge planners not infrequently steering black residents away from "white" nursing homes even when the latter are located in ethnic minority neighborhoods. For older lesbians in need of nursing home care, discrimination on the basis of social class and sometimes race may be compounded by another factor, which gives the whole topic of institutionalization a particular poignancy. For those older lesbians who have "come out" earlier in life, often at tremendous personal cost, there is an ultimate and often humiliating irony in being forced to end one's life in an institution where sexlessness is assumed and a strict taboo placed upon sexual expression of any form, let alone an identity based on sexual preference.

Older women who are working-class, poor, lesbian, or African-American, in short, come into their old age with significant disadvantages born of a system that differentially values and devalues individuals on the basis of gender, race, class, and sexual orientation. A lifetime of occupational segregation and economic vulnerability combines, for many of these women, with class- and gender-based inequities in Social Security and other health and social programs for the old to further reinforce their devalued position in late life. For those in need of nursing home placement, institutionalization may represent the final devaluation, with admission denied on the basis of class or color or, for older lesbians, accompanied by a stinging denial of one's most basic core identity.

Yet older lesbians and black and working-class women also come to late life having survived decades of oppression and/or stigmatization and often have evolved special strengths and capacities that may help them meet the challenges of old age. Older black women and lesbians, for example, have both had to come to terms with a stigmatized identity early in life and may therefore be in a better position than are heterosexuals to confront the new stigma of old age (Berger & Kelly, 1986). Older lesbians may also possess unique strengths born of their refusal to adhere to rigid sex role stereotypes. Consequently, they may be more flexible in assuming varied roles in late life than are heterosexual elders, who are more frequently wedded to traditional notions of "appropriate" male or female behavior (Berger & Kelly, 1986; MacLeod, 1989).

The special strengths of the older African-American woman have been widely documented, as has the pivotal place she occupies in the life of the family and the community (Grambs, 1989; Staples, 1976). The role of religion, the effective use of a broad and versatile support system, and positive self-images are among the factors that researchers have noted in trying to capture and understand the forces behind the strength of older black women. Such forces and factors, moreover, are believed to help explain why older black women, despite high rates of poverty and disability, are the *least* likely of any older age/sex group to take their own lives (Gibson, 1986). They further may help explain the "mortality crossover" that occurs around ages 80 to 85, at which point older blacks have a longer life expectancy that do older whites (NCHS, 1989). As Gibson (1986) notes,

> The unusual strengths of very old Black women are well known. Elderly Black women have been a wellspring of support and nurturance over time. The rapid growth of this group, coupled with the growing tendency of Black families to be without men, may mean that a modal Black family of the future ... will be composed of several generations of women. (p. 195)

Within this modal family, the grandmother's historic role of care-giver across generations appears, as noted earlier, to be taking on even greater importance. The older black woman today indeed in "both a beneficiary and a victim of Black tradition" (Grambs, 1989, p. 212), providing the glue that holds families together, holding a position that reflects leadership and strength, yet also suffering pain and loss, particularly as epidemics of drugs, AIDS, and homicide mean that she may outlive some of her children.

We have begun this look at the lives of three groups of older women by venturing down the political economy pathway in critical gerontology—a path that has helped us appreciate the structural constraints faced by women who are not only old and female, but also black, lesbian, working-class, or poor. We have seen the com-pounded devaluation such multiple-jeopardy status may impose; yet we have noted too that for many of these women, earlier oppression and inequalities have given rise to special strengths and abilities as they enter late life.

A political economy of older women takes as its data the objective reality of women's lives, the world as it is, "set over against us" (Frye, 1964, p. 31). Novels, on the other hand, start with the world we *want* to live in. In the words of Northrop Frye (1964): "The world you want to live in is a human world, not an objective one; it is not an environ-ment, but a home; it's not the world you see, but the world you would build out of what you see" (p. 19). Novels draw on the realm of the imagination. Through myth and metaphor, novelists speak of life's possibilities, constructing maps of meaning out of the stuff of ordinary life. To understand how older women are able to make meaning and find dignity in their old age, we will move from the political economy pathway in critical gerontology to walk the more humanistic and existential path that encourages us to hear the words and feel the joys, pains, conflicts, and triumphs of women themselves.

PERSPECTIVES FROM THE HUMANITIES

We will now turn to literature, examining the interior struggles of older women against structures of oppression. We have taken as our data novels by women novelists about older women. Our analysis is informed by the work of Northrop Frye (1964), who viewed literary criticism as seeking in part to connect art to its mythic and symbolic roots.

First we will explore the existential crisis that may confront working-class women as they age, drawing on the work of Doris Lessing (1983) and Simone de Beauvoir (1970). Next we will look at lesbian elders, as informed by the writings of Barbara MacDonald (1983), May Sarton (1973), and Elsa Gidlow (1986). Finally, we will consider the struggles of old black women, taking as our data a novel by Toni Morrison (1987) and a critical essay on Morrison's work by Holloway and Demetrakopoulos (1986). The novels we explore are not offered as definitive works on older women—in the past few decades, a rich and varied literature by women and about women has emerged and continues to emerge. Our analysis of these novels is presented instead as one possible interpretation.

A Good Neighbor

Doris Lessing's (1983) *Diary of a Good Neighbour* deals with class pain and social alienation, telling the story of how two women cross the divides of class and age to become friends. Maudie, a 90-year-old cockney woman, is the quintessential female industrial worker—poor all of her life, marginally employed in low-skilled factory work, the survivor of a lonely, abusive marriage. She is dying poor and alone in a cold-water shack in a London slum neighborhood. She is one of the last survivors of the age of industrialization. She has outlived her friends and her social world. Janna is the quintessential modern successful woman—stylish, economically comfortable, independent, busy, intensely private. Her home is her sanctuary. She is the kind of woman who has "made it," a feminist role model for the postindustrial age.

Each woman is bitterly lonely. Each suffers an alienation she cannot name. Janna helps Maudie die, and Maudie helps Janna live. Defying all reason or explanation, these two women from different classes and ages become each other's good neighbor. Through the support of a friend, Maudie dies with her dignity intact. In traveling with Maudie down the bitter road to death, Janna discovers her humanity and her life possibilities.

In befriending Maudie, Janna confronts her own aging and discovers her humanity, unleashing a capacity to care that is foreign to her. Her old life is shattered. She is no longer in control, yet she is empowered. She is liberated from the Modern Professional Woman's life, a kind of perfection that is, in the words of Sylvia Plath, a "cold womb." She becomes a novelist, fictionalizing Maudie's life so that even Maudie would have approved. In imagining Maudie's story, a vital truth is told.

Through friendship with Janna, Maudie experiences her unconditional worth as a human being. Her dignity is reclaimed. The death she suffers is horribly painful. It is not a dying she would choose. "Dreadful. Dreadful," she mutters. Yet in the same breath she tells Janna, "This is the best time of my life." Lessing has spared us none of the hard no's of death and dying. She has not romanticized the inevitable, tragic end.

The Diary of a Good Neighbour provides an intimate portrait of the class-based pain of aging that Beauvoir (1970) so richly described. The anguish humans suffer in searching for meaning within a utilitarian ethos is derived from the conditional valuation of human life. It is the pain of retirement, when one has exited from a productive role as a worker. It is the pain of aged strangers who have outlived social worlds that no longer have instrumental value. It is the pain of people in the prime of their careers, who are haunted by the question "Is this all there is?"

A Chosen Life

In *Look Me in the Eye*, Barbara MacDonald (1983), a lesbian elder, makes the point that lesbians generally discover at an early age that they are lesbians. In discovering this, and *choosing* this, they "move out of that safe harbor of social acceptability" (p. 2). A dominant theme for many lesbians of all ages is isolation and estrangement. It is a lifelong estrangement, experienced most profoundly in old age, when one is invisible both to lesbians and to one's age cohort.

Look Me in the Eye refers to the invisibility MacDonald experienced within the lesbian/feminist community. She felt unseen, viewed as mentally inferior as she physically weakens. She felt patronized, spoken "about" not "to." Being an old woman took on the quality of a "master status." To other lesbians/feminists, she was no longer a lesbian. She had become an old woman.

MacDonald (1983) presents May Sarton's (1973) novel, *As We Are Now*, as a map of meaning for old lesbians. In this novel, Sarton names the no's of old age, death, and malignant ageism, offering a redemptive fable in which the old lesbian who is her protagonist reclaims her life and her wholeness. Sarton's protagonist, Caro, is a very old lesbian living in a nursing home. She survives systematic neglect and mistreatment by hanging onto the values she has had all of her life—reading, writing, and listening to music. Caro starts a journal, and her first entry begins: "I am not mad, only old. I make this statement to give me courage. To give you an idea of what I mean by courage, suffice it to say that it has taken two weeks for me to obtain this notebook and pen" (p. 95).

Caro takes a lover, a poor country woman who works at the nursing home. Sarton shows how love transcends society's taboos against sex that is cross-class, intergenerational, and/or between members of the same sex. In taking a lover, Caro is labeled a pervert by her caretakers. The humiliation and mistreatment she is subjected to escalate. Caro triumphs by consciously choosing to take her own life, by burning down the nursing home while she is inside.

MacDonald (1983) identifies the power of old women as "when she sees that the challenge is not how to live—the challenge is how to die" (p. 99). This is the source of power: when one is not afraid to die, only then is one not afraid to live. "Such a woman won't do what she is told, she will only do what is important for her own life direction" (p. 100). The old woman chooses life by "holding death in her hands" (p. 100).

In her epilogue, MacDonald, three years older, writes about what it means to live with the daily weakening of her strength. She has cancer and is rapidly going blind. She writes that her body has two jobs: "to make sure that I live, and to make sure that I die" (p. 114). She transforms loss by turning her sight to an inner world. Nearly sightless, she finds safe harbor in the core of her being, a place that is restorative, inviolate, more of her own making.

A second map of meaning for lesbians as they age is offered by the lesbian poet Elsa Gidlow (1986) in her autobiography, *Elsa: I Come with My Songs*. Elsa was born poor in Toronto, Canada, and lived poor all of her life. Poetry was the core of her being. She viewed her life mission as the bearing of gifts to the world:

> I come with my songs;/I come singing./If indeed you
> have wrongs/I come to undo them.
> Make ready your terrible beauty./I come with my songs.
> (from *Elsa: I Come with My Songs*, Gidlow, 1986)

Gidlow (1986) was profoundly influenced by her mother and by her understanding of her mother's life. Her mother gave her courage and the gift of songs. It was a bleak working-class existence, yet it birthed the poet: "She endured so much with courage, she transcended pain and sorrow that would have crushed so many—and *could sing*. She did indeed bloom in beauty. What more could be said of any life?" (p. 339). Gidlow was old herself when her mother died, yet her mother's death shocked her deeply. It forced a reevaluation of her life. She came to view her life as a process of continually being born: "We call our forebears ancestors, but in a sense our childhood being is our nearest ancestor. . . . If we are alive and growing, we are continuously giving birth to ourselves" (p. 1).

Gidlow made a garden. She extended her circle of friends so wide that she founded a community. It was a diverse community, where each contributed in practical skills, point of view, and life experience. Gidlow called her community "the chosen place." She discovered the pleasure of conversation, deeming it a kind of lovemaking, for, as she wrote, love crosses all boundaries and shapes itself. As she entered her 80s, she weakened and suffered physical pain. But as she wrote: "Bodies can be crushed. The spirit has the power to resist" (p. 406).

Gidlow (1986) believed in a nurturing, unquenchable spirit, a "creative consciousness out of which all life emerges." In this spirit, she found and continually gave birth to herself. This spirit *was* herself. As she wrote: "Pride of spirit will not permit me to acquiesce to victimhood" (p. 407). Hers was not an easy life. She faced all that lesbians may confront—rejection, ostracism, lost love, torment. She suffered class pain: patchwork schooling, lifelong poverty, often joblessness. She confronted the hard no's of old age and death. Yet one does not have the image of Gidlow holding "death in her hand." Life flowed through and out of her. Old age was not a distinctive stage of her life. It was all part of the same vital process. There were no victims.

She came with her songs. She undid terrible wrongs. Her life was filled with terrible beauty. She *could sing*. What more could be said of any life?

Black Grandmothers

Toni Morrison's (1987) work is filled with the "presence of ancestral figures as a sort of timeless people whose relationships to the (other) characters are benevolent, instructive and protective" (Holloway & Demetrakopoulos, 1986, p. 15). One such ancestral Morrison figure is the character Baby Suggs, in the novel *Beloved* (1987). Baby Suggs is the matriarch of a clan broken by slavery and the race hatred of the postbellum era. She is the center of her family, and when her children leave—the sons "run off" and her daughter-in-law jailed for killing her infant daughter—Baby Suggs gives up.

She takes to her bed to finish her final task—dying. Lying under an old quilt, Baby Suggs sees only colors. She meditates on one color at a time—orange, then blue, then pink. During a lifetime spent on the hard business of surviving, she had no left-over energy to notice anything more than the black and white of life. Before she dies, she wants to notice the colors.

Even in death, her spirit permeates the novel and the lives of her clan. The job of protecting the family falls to her daughter-in-law, Sethe. Sethe draws her one surviving child close to her, and they live isolated in Baby Suggs's house, in self-imposed exile from the community of freed slaves who are their only community. In vain, Sethe endeavors to do what Baby Suggs would have done—to keep her child from the past that was still waiting for her.

Baby Suggs embodies the mythical and magical qualities of old black women. She is a reigning deity. Her role was to preserve the clan spiritually and physically. Through songs and stories, she protected and passed on the history and future of the black people. The crisis that broke Baby Suggs was the killing of her grandchild by her daughter-in-law. She did not judge because she understood too well that it was a murder motivated by love. Sethe acted out of mercy and necessity—white men had already condemned the child to die. Yet the murder broke the natural order: that the old should precede the young in death, that mothers must protect their babies. The murder was proof of Baby Suggs's powerlessness to preserve the natural order in the face of race hatred.

Holloway and Demetrakopoulos (1986) write that old black women are the keepers of the clan, which is extended through the responsibility to nurture and care for all who happen to come under their roof. Old black women are archetypal mothers, guardians of the family, black heritage, and the African spirit. Holloway and Demetrakopoulos locate the revered status of old black women within the African worldview, whose main goal is "survival of the tribe" and presupposes a "oneness with nature." It is marked contrast to the Eurocentric worldview, which presupposes the primacy of the individual. The African worldview rests against a background of respect and reverence.

In addition, the reverence for the old is explained by other qualities of black culture: the preservation of an oral tradition, the link to ancestors and to traditional culture, and the distribution within the clan of meaningful work at all ages (Beauvoir, 1970). Black culture, carried on by old black women through stories and songs, innoculates the young against assimilation to white cultural values and protects them from the ravages of racism, displacement, and colonization.

MAPS OF MEANING

For women who are working-class, lesbian, and/or black, the journey through old age is often filled with hardship. A political economy perspective reveals the structural inequities old women confront. Literary analysis takes us inside women's spiritual struggles, where we witness their heroic efforts to age well. In this section, we will enlarge on themes touched on in the previous section, focusing on the maps of meaning (see Table 15.1) women pursue in their struggles for meaning and purpose in old age.

In the novels we have chosen to examine, aging is experienced as a process of "outliving." For the working-class old women portrayed, it meant outliving a social world and a social role. Retired, they were no longer viewed as having a productive role in society. Factory workers such as Lessing's Maudie are the last survivors of the great age of industrialization. They are, in the words of Dowd (1984), "aged strangers." Having outlived their social worlds, they have become immigrants in time. Everything is strange to them, but *they* are the ones viewed as out of place (Dowd, 1984).

TABLE 15.1 Maps of Meaning: Spiritual Crises for Old Women According to Class, Gender (Sexual Identity), and Race

	Aging as "outliving"	Spiritual crisis	Resolution	Heroic archetype
Class	Outliving one's era and one's productive role	What is my worth?	Experiencing one's unconditional worth	A good neighbor
Gender	Outliving one's friends and lover(s)	Who am I?	Holding death in one's hand; experiencing deep core of being	A chosen life
Race	Outliving one's progeny	How do I survive?	Preserving clan through song and story; being carrier of a culture	Black grandmother

Lesbian elders often outlive their lovers and their closest friends, the only people to whom they are out, who know them as they truly are. Having "come out" and formed their significant social relationships before the emergence of a visible gay community, they are "aged strangers" to post-Stonewall lesbians.[1] Isolated from other old lesbians, each woman silently suffers the anguish of being "the world's oldest living lesbian."

For old black women, aging all too frequently brings the anguish of outliving one's progeny. Old and young die out of order. Black women who attain old age are survivors, yet the survival is bittersweet. It makes of them witnesses to a tragedy—the death and destruction of black youth and adults.

For old working-class and/or lesbian women in the novels we chose to explore, "outliving" provokes an existential crisis. For working-class elders, old age erodes dignity. Outliving causes them to question their worth as human beings. Is their value only conditional? If they are no longer productive workers, are they useless? What is the value of a working-class woman when she no longer works?

For lesbians, old age provokes an identity crisis—who am I if I am no longer a lesbian? For women whose identity is grounded in the love of other women, whose core being is affirmed through sexuality and romantic relationships, outliving lovers and intimate friends has the power to crack the foundations of the self.

As they grow old, black women continue to confront the crisis of a lifetime: how to survive in the face of overwhelming odds. Old age presents an added crisis: how to preserve the family from the past that is still waiting for them.

For all three groups of women, old age may provoke a spiritual crisis. For those who are working class and/or lesbian, the crisis is likely to be existential in nature—who am I, and what am I worth? Existential anguish is in this sense the product of a Eurocentric worldview, where the individual is often the focus and measure of all things. In an Afrocentric worldview, the clan is the focus of survival and the measure of worth (Holloway & Demetrapokolous, 1986). Old black women thus may suffer the spiritual crisis of an entire people— what is the meaning of life when the old outlive the young? When the past, once suffered, still awaits?

The resolution of the spiritual crises of old age requires great courage. These acts of heroism are seldom observed or noted, except in novels and other works of art. This is one reason that fiction and biography are so important to a culture. Stories tell us important truths about ourselves. They describe life as it is and as it could be.

The resolution of the working-class existential crisis may lie in experiencing one's unconditional worth as a human being. A heroic archetype in this sense might well be the "good neighbor," a person who loves without reason or condition, a friend who salutes one's dignity, a traveler-companion along the hard road to diminishment and death.

For lesbians, the resolution of the existential crises of aging may be found in the process of "coming in." It complements the "coming out" process of lesbian adulthood. The existential question for lesbians is "who am I?" It is never fully resolved. In adult life it is answered by affirming a life choice to love women. But aging has the power to shake the foundations of lesbian identity. Old age brings with it the loss of life partners, negation of sexuality, estrangement from age and gender cohorts, the cessation of new intimacies. In old age, the familiar question "Who am I?" resurfaces. "Coming in" requires a second affirmation of the self. The lesbian quest for meaning may lie in facing the hard no's of existence and discovering the deep core of one's being. The lesbian quest for meaning calls out for the creation of "a chosen life." A heroic archetype for old lesbians might be the artist, whose greatest creation is her own life.

The resolution of the spiritual crisis for black women may reside in becoming a grandmother. Old black women become "magical in their wisdom . . . magical because of their will to survive, because of their embodiment of the mythology and wisdom of Africa" (Holloway & Demetrakopolous, 1986, p. 14). Through stories and songs, black grandmothers heal and instruct their clans; they protect the history and future of the black people; they pass on the wisdom and legacy of an oral tradition. The black grandmother is a heroic archetype, the highest status a woman can attain in the black community. In taking up this vestigial role, black women may become *Mother Africa* incarnate.

CONCLUSION

The heroic archetypes we have presented are, in the words of Holloway and Demetrakopolous (1986), "feminist icons." The good neighbor, the artist, the black grandmother—all three may be seen as embodiments of empowered and empowering womanhood. They are symbols of hope, metaphoric possibilities of all that old age could be. As the poet Deanna Mason has said, "feminism is concerned with the care of the *human* condition" (personal communication, December

16, 1990). The maps of meaning outlined in this chapter speak to the experience of certain groups of women, but they also suggest deeply human struggles.

Literature is a powerful arena for examining the interior struggles of women as they age. We have offered a methodology for integrating perspectives from political economy and the humanities to examine meaning and justice issues in old age. A just and meaningful old age is not easily attained. For women whose aging is made harder by structures of oppression, aging well is a heroic challenge. A political economy perspective provides important indices of the hardships and inequities old women confront. Literature provides interior portraits of women's struggles against the "dominant X" of ordinary life (Stevens, 1955). Together the two paths or perspectives offer the potential for a far richer understanding of the lives of older women than either can provide independently.

NOTES

[1] "Stonewall" refers to the June 1969 riot in a New York gay bar, which marked the beginning of the gay rights era.

REFERENCES

Archibold, P. G. (1983). The impact of parent-caring on women. *Family Relations, 32,* 39–45.

Arendell, T., & Estes, C. L. (1991). Older women in the post-Reagan era. In M. Minker & C. L. Estes (Eds.), *Critical perspectives on aging* (pp. 209–226). NY: Baywood.

Beauvoir, S. de. (1970). *The coming of age.* Paris: Editions Gallimard.

Berger, R. A., & Kelly, J. J. (1986, April). Working with homosexuals of the older population. *Journal of Contemporary Social Work,* pp. 203–210.

Catalano, D. J., Valentine, W. E., & Greever, L. (1981). Social services for aging gay men. *Catalyst, 3,* 47–60.

Cole, T. C., & Gadow, S. (Eds.). (1986). *What does it mean to grow old? Reflections from the humanities.* Durham, NC: Duke University Press.

Cole, T. R., Van Tassel, D. D. & Kastenbaum, R. (Eds.). (1992). *Handbook of aging and the humanities.* New York: Springer Publishing Co.

Commonwealth Fund Commission on Elderly People Living Alone. (1988). *Aging alone.* Baltimore: The Commonwealth Fund.

Davis, K. (1986). Aging and the health care system. *Daedalus, 115,* 227–246.

Dowd, J. J. (1980). *Stratification among the aged.* Monterey, CA: Brooks/Cole.

Dowd, J. J. (1984). Mental illness and the aged stranger. In C. Estes &

M. Minkler, (Eds.), *Readings in the political economy of aging* (pp. 94–116). Farmingdale, NY: Baywood.

Dowd, J. J., & Bengston, V. (1978). Aging in minority: An examination of the double jeopardy hypothesis. *Journal of Gerontology, 33,* 427–436.

Estes, C. L. (1991). The new political economy of aging: Introduction and critique. In M. Minker & C. L. Estes (Eds.), *Critical perspectives on aging: The political and moral economy of growing old* (pp. 19–36). Farmingdale, NY: Baywood.

Estes, C. L., & Rundall, T. G. (in press). Social characteristics, social structure and health in the aging population. In M. Ory & R. Abeles (Eds.), *Aging, health and behavior.* Beverly Hills, CA: Sage.

Frankl, V. (1990, Fall). Facing the transitoriness of human existence. *Generations,* 7–10.

Frye, N. (1964). *The educated imagination.* Bloomington: Indiana University Press.

Gibson, R. C. (1986). Outlook for the black family. In A. Pifer & L. Bronte (Eds.), *Our aging society* (pp. 181–197). New York: W. W. Norton.

Gidlow, E. (1986). *Elsa: I come with my songs.* San Francisco: Booklegger Press & Druid Heights Books.

Grambs, J. D. (1989). *Women over forty: Visions and realities.* New York: Springer Publishing Co.

Hawes, C. & Phillips, C. D. (1986). The changing structure of the nursing home industry and the impact of ownership on quality cost and access. In B. H. Gray, (Ed.), *For profit enterprise in health care* (pp. 492–541). Washington DC: National Academy Press.

Holloway, K. F. C., & Demetrakopoulos, S. (1986). Remembering our foremothers: Older black women, politics of age, politics of survival as embodied in the novels of Toni Morrison. In M. J. Bell (Ed.), *Women as elders: The feminist politics of aging.* New York: Harrington Park Press.

Kant, I. (1789). *Foundations of the metaphysics of morals.* (Translation by R. P. Wolff, 1969.) New York: Bobbs-Merrill.

Lessing, D. (1983). *The diary of a good neighbour/Jane Somers.* New York: A. A. Knopf.

MacDonald, B., with Rich, C. (1983). *Look me in the eye: Old women, aging and ageism.* San Francisco: Spinsters Ink.

Manton, K. G., (1983). Differential life expectancy: Possible explanations during the later ages. In R. C. Manuel (Ed.), *Minority aging* (pp. 63–74). Westport, CT: Greenwood Press.

Margolis, R. J. (1990). *Risking old age in America.* San Francisco: Westview Press.

McLeod, B. (1989, March). *Gay men and lesbians: Issues in aging.* Paper presented at the 35th Annual Meeting of the American Society on Aging, Washington, D.C.

Minkler, M., & Roe, K. M. (1991). Grandmother caregivers for infants and young children in the crack cocaine epidemic. Unpublished preliminary findings.

Moody, H. R. (1988). *Abundance of life: Human development policies for an aging society.* New York: Columbia University Press.

Morrison, T. (1987). *Beloved.* New York: New American Library.

National Center for Health Statistics. (NCHS) (1984). *National health interview survey, supplement on aging* (DHHS Pub. NO. [PHS] 87-1323). Washington, DC: U.S. Government Printing Office.

National Center for Health Statistics. (NCHS) (1988). *Health: United States, 1987* (DHHS Pub. No. [PHS] 88-1232). Washington, DC: U.S. Government Printing Office.

National Center for Health Statistics. (NCHS) (1990). *Vital statistics of the U.S., 1987* (vol. 2, sect. 6) Washington, DC: Public Health Service. 1989.

O'Rand, A. M. (1986). Women. In E. Palmore (Ed.), *Handbook of the aged in the United States* (pp. 125–142). Westport, CT: Greenwood Press.

Sarton, M. (1973). *As we are now.* New York: W. W. Norton.

Shaughnessy, P. N., & Kramer, A. M. (1990). The increased needs of patients in nursing homes and patients receiving home health care. *New England Journal of Medicine, 322,* 21–27.

Staples, R. (1976). The black American family. In C. H. Mindel & R. W. Habenstein (Eds.), *Ethnic families in America* (pp. 221–247). New York: Elsevier.

Stevens, W. (1955). The motive for metaphor. In W. Stevens (Ed.), *The collected poems of Wallace Stevens* (p. 288). New York: Alfred A Knopf.

Stone, R., Cafferata, G. L., & Sangl, J. (1987). Caregivers of the frail elderly: A national profile. *Gerontologist, 27,* 616–626.

Sullivan, R. (1984, January 28). Study reports bias in nursing homes. *New York Times.*

U.S. Bureau of the Census. (1991). *Current population reports: Marital status and living arrangements: March, 1990.* Series P-20, #450. Washington, DC: U.S. Government Printing Office.

Villers Foundation. (1987). *On the other side of Easy Street: Myths and facts about the economics of old age.* Washington DC: Author.

Wallace, St. P. (1990). Race versus class in the health care of the African American elderly. *Social Problems, 37,* 101–119.

Women's Equity Action League (WEAL). (1985). WEAL facts: Letter to the editor. In *Equity for women.* Washington, D.C.: WEAL.

Acknowledgments

The editors gratefully acknowledge permission to reprint from the following previously published works.

Overview. Lines from "The Circus Animals' Desertion" are reprinted with permission of Macmillan Publishing Company from *The Poems of W.B. Yeats: A New Edition*, edited by Richard J. Finneran. Copyright © 1940 by Georgie Yeats, renewed 1968 by Bertha Georgie Yeats, Michael Butler Yeats, and Anne Yeats.

Chapter 5. Passages from Wallace Stegner's *Crossing to Safety* appear with the permission of his publisher, Random House, Inc., New York. Copyright © 1987 by Wallace Stegner.

Chapter 5. Lines from *The Poetry of Robert Frost*, edited by Edward Connery Latham. Copyright 1942 by Robert Frost. © 1969 by Holt, Rinehart & Winston. © 1970 by Lesley Frost Ballantine. Reprinted by permission of Henry Holt and Company, Inc.

Chapter 9. Passages from Kazuo Ishiguro's *A Pale View of the Hills*, *An Artist of the Floating World*, and *The Remains of the Day* appear with the permission of the author, Mr. Ishiguro's United Kingdom publisher, Faber and Faber, and his United States publisher, Alfred Knopf. © Copyright Kazuo Ishiguro.

Chapter 9. Passages from Irwin C. Lieb's *Past, Present and Future: A Philosophical Essay About Time* appear with permission of the University of Illinois Press.

Chapter 14. Lines from "I Come With My Songs" by Elsa Gidlow reprinted by permission of Celeste West, Booklegger Publishing, 555 29th Street, San Francisco, CA 94131.

Index

Index

NOTES

NOTES